FROM THE ROOF OF AFRICA

FROM THE ROOF OF AFRICA

✕✕✕✕

C. W. NICOL

ALFRED A. KNOPF   New York   1972

THIS IS A BORZOI BOOK
PUBLISHED BY ALFRED A. KNOPF, INC.

Copyright © 1971 by C. W. Nicol

ISBN: 0394-41459-4
Library of Congress Catalog Card Number: 72-154917
Manufactured in the United States of America

FIRST EDITION

To Sonako,

    to eagles,

        and to faraway peoples

Bright sun over the High Simien

And on the plateau, in the long grass, wind

Slides softly,

Down into the bouldered valley,

Brushes scattered thickets of Giant Heather

And sighs

Over cliffs, where raven cries

Or circling hawks, might hang, it seems, for ever

With a far-below world

      down, down, down

          to streams like lace by tiny tukals

            in handkerchief barley fields.

On the top, coloured rocks, where water chatters

And lobelias, tall and sentinel-still against hill rims,

Long leaves, rustling and whispering.

And I, scribbling letters,

Think of home and long-ago peoples,

Watching eagles

      slowly wheeling.

Contents

A Note on the Illustrations

There are two sections of illustrations
within the text: one of four pages in full color,
which falls between pages 114 and 115; the other of sixteen pages,
falling between 242 and 243.

FROM THE ROOF OF AFRICA

BUREAUCRATS
AND TRIBESMEN

I shuffled my feet, flexed fingers, and fiddled with an old Canadian bus ticket, which I had found in one pocket. Other people waited, or argued with the dark-suited officials, gesticulating and thrusting papers through the barricade of glass-fronted desks. This was the eighth visit, in less than two weeks, that I had paid to the offices of the Immigration Department of the Imperial Ethiopian Government. Next to me, staring impassively, holding my passport and a sheaf of documents, sat Ato Tadessa of the Wildlife Conservation Department.

Tadessa got up and again went over to the desk. We had been waiting nearly two hours. He spoke to a man behind the glass, who spoke to another, who called a third. Then they called me over. With a look of utter boredom, the man behind the glass flipped open my passport.

"Are you Canadian or British?"

Taking a deep breath, I explained once more. I was born in Wales of British parents. I have a British passport. I came to Ethiopia from Canada after working for the Canadian Government. Just before coming, I acquired Canadian citizenship but did not have time to change the passport. I jabbed at some writing in the back of the passport. "A person having some connexion with a Commonwealth or a foreign country . . . may be a national of that country, in addition to being a national of the United Kingdom."

"But we were told you were Canadian."

"Well, I never bloody well told you anything, and what the hell difference does it make? This is my passport, this is my contract with your government, and this is the telegram telling me to come without a visa—and that would have been unnecessary if your blasted embassies took the trouble to answer letters! Your government brought me over to work and I damn well want to start work!"

The Ethiopian glared at me. "You have a tourist visa. It cannot be changed."

I exploded, and said rude things about the Ethiopian Embassy in Washington, the Immigration Department, and the Imperial Ethiopian Government in general. Ato Tadessa talked fast in Amharic, ignoring me. He and the official seemed to be arguing. Suddenly the official tossed my passport, pages fluttering, across the room to another man. I stormed out, with Tadessa hurrying after me.

I flagged down the first taxi that clattered along and offered the driver a dollar to take me to the British Embassy. After a brief discussion with the other two passengers, the driver agreed and I got in.

The rickety Fiat bumped and farted through busy streets, the driver chattering with the other passengers and unconcerned about the dozens of pedestrians who seemed intent on killing themselves under his wheels. The horn blew almost continuously through crowds of walking people and strings of donkeys laden with firewood and hay, as the taxi jostled and dodged in the busy traffic of Addis Ababa.

The British Consul kept me waiting less than a minute. I described my visa troubles. As there was no Ethiopian Embassy in Canada, I had arrived, on the instructions of the Wildlife Conservation Department, without a visa. At the airport, the authorities stamped my passport with a tourist visa, which supposedly cannot be changed in the country. And, of course, it is illegal to work with a tourist visa. Would the Consul request the Ethiopian Government to send me back to Canada? The Consul, a big, bearded, and assured figure, nodded and smiled.

"Don't worry about it. Try once more tomorrow, and tell your office people that you can't break the law by working with a tourist visa and that they should immediately arrange your papers or give you your ticket back to Canada. And tell them that you have consulted your Consulate and that the matter will be handled by them if this nonsense goes any further."

Bureaucrats and tribesmen

I thanked the Consul, shook hands, and promised to keep him informed.

A purple dusk; and over the tin roofs of Addis Ababa, a blue haze of eucalyptus smoke. The air sharp with the scents of hot spices as women crouched in front of open doors, cooking evening meals, tending pots of spicy sauces on charcoal braziers, fanning the coals with woven grass fans, calling shrill, cheerful greetings to returning neighbors. With city-busy traffic hurrying, and all taxis filled, I strode along the darkening streets, glancing into the open-doored bars at the dark-skinned harlots, their eyes brown and deep, features fine and delicate, figures like goddesses. Above, the tall, swaying ranks of eucalyptus trees, the bubbling whistle of kites, and on one side of the road a man urinating into the gutter. Once on the piazza, street boys with trays of junk blocked my way here and there, or tagged along for a while, with their chewing gum and condoms, socks, shirts, and Ethiopian pictures, carved wooden stools and simple pottery, rugs of woven wool and the skins of colobus monkeys. Down the hill I strode, past the stone lion and the big round bank to the Ras Hotel.

Major Gizaw was in the office the next morning. I told him about the visa and said that if my papers were not pushed through soon, the department would have to pay for my ticket back to Canada. He said very little to me, but phoned the director of the Immigration Department. There was a vociferous exchange in Amharic, alternating between tones of anger and extreme politeness. The Major put the telephone down and smiled. I should go over right now, and it would all be settled by the afternoon. We exchanged courtesies and I left.

Major Gizaw, the director and general manager of the Wildlife Conservation Department, was a slightly built and extremely handsome ex-air force officer who had previously been one of the most notorious poachers in the Empire. As his family was close to the Emperor, and as his hunting seemed a good qualification for the job of conserving the country's fast-dwindling wildlife resources, he was elected to the job by the Emperor himself. Though ever gentle in

5

speech and manner, and always courteous, the Major varied between periods of furious, energetic cooperativeness and total lack of understanding of whatever issues were at hand. My contract with the department was for three years, and my job was to develop a new national park in the Simien Mountains, the high, cliff-rimmed plateau of the northwest. In the beginning, the Major thought I was too young for the job, and his manner reflected this attitude. Within ten days of arriving in the country I handed in my resignation because of a dispute with the Major over what I considered essential medical supplies for the Simien. John Blower, the senior game warden, was the man who had recruited me. He watched with a wry grin as I pounded out the resignation, and assured me that he and the other game wardens frequently threatened to leave. It was at times, he said, the only way to push things along.

The resignation obviously shocked Major Gizaw. John Blower was called into his office. Why had Mr. Nicol become so unreasonable? Ato Balcha, the portly, worried little second-in-command, shook his head and clucked. John nodded.

"You must understand," he told them, "that Mr. Hay, Mr. Brown, and myself have all worked in Africa before, but Mr. Nicol worked in Canada, and things are not the same there. He doesn't understand the way things work in Africa and is very impatient to get on with the job and get all the things he needs. You will just have to cooperate with him or he will certainly leave."

The resignation was not accepted, and I got the medical supplies.

Those first days in Ethiopia were ones of extreme loneliness. My wife and two children had gone to her home in Japan, intending to join me when I had built a house in the mountains. At night, tired by the thin atmosphere, and frustrated by trying to get equipment and papers, I sat in black depression, searching my socks, pants, and bed for fleas, and wondering how to break the contract and escape back to Canada. Outside, the night was loud with the barking of dogs, the roars of caged lions at Sidist Kilo, and sometimes the whoop of a hyena.

As I was obviously reaching the end of my tolerance, and wasting time in Addis Ababa, John Blower decided that I should go for a week's study visit to the Awash National Park. There I might see what could be achieved by a determined warden despite the hindrances of bureaucracy and the Ethiopian system. As I bounced about in the front seat of a truck going to the Awash Park headquarters I was excited by the animals that crossed the road or sped off into the brush. Baboons, warthogs, waterbuck, gazelles, lesser kudu, many fowl, all animals that I was seeing for the first time in the wild. Around the headquarters was a complex of roads, staff quarters, offices, garage, store, oil tanks, and wells. As the truck was being unloaded, Peter Hay, the game warden, came to check if all he had ordered had arrived, and to greet me. We shook hands and he showed me where the guards had pitched a large tent for me on the banks of the Awash River. He left me alone that night, and I was glad of it. There are few better ways to sort out your feelings and thoughts than to potter about a campfire, with nobody to worry or distract you, yet with enough to do to keep your mind from wandering too far.

As I brewed tea over a wood fire in front of the tent, surrounded by the sounds and colors of an African night, an old excitement gripped me and my mind's focus moved into perspective. The Addis Ababa depression lifted. Here were new things to sense and to know. I tended the fire, and gazed, smelled, listened. Black ants marched in long, determined lines past the tent, and in the swift, muddy river, a swirl of water, a snort, night noises along the riverbank, distant thunder of the falls. A baboon screeched, and a flight of ibis flew low over the water. New sensations and old memories, shadows dancing on tent canvas, the delicious taste of food eaten by a campfire, the sad happiness of longing for my wife and the wondering over loves, old and lost. All this, and the warmth of the night.

In the morning Peter Hay showed me the park files. As I skimmed through them, reading the reports, letters, plans proposed and never acknowledged, requests for equipment and staff disciplinary procedures, I wondered how he had been able to do anything at all. Although it had already become obvious to me that the Addis Ababa head office was not very good, the files indicated that it was absolutely useless, either entirely stupid, apathetic, or ignorant. I had seen the way it operated. I had asked for equipment to come to Awash, referring to a list written out for me by Peter Hay, only to have Major Gizaw refuse me nearly all of it on the grounds that "they have it all in Awash," which they didn't.

"One day," Peter said, "I sent in a request for nails. We were doing a lot of building. Major Gizaw came over the radio and asked what I wanted nails for. So I said, 'Well, Major, I suffer from the altitude when I come to Addis, and the doctor says I need iron in my blood, so I eat the bloody things.'"

We laughed about this and other anecdotes. There seemed to be no end to the stories. Outside the office, game guards waited until the radio schedule finished so that they could bring their problems and complaints to Peter. The Omo game warden, George Brown, came on first. Reception was good, and it was early. He asked if the legislation drawn up to declare the boundaries of the Awash National Park had been signed. It hadn't, but Peter said that he understood that the draft was completed and was now with the Minister of Pen. George Brown's voice, with its crisp, cynical British accent, came over clearly.

"The Minister of Pen?"

"Roger on that. There seems to be some slight delay over the signing. They've had it a couple of months now."

"Ibex three to Ibex two. Well, the trouble is," said the voice on the radio, "the Minister of Pen is having a quarrel with the Minister of Ink, because the Minister of Ink stole the Minister of Pen's rubber. Over." Ethiopians in the office grinned, and tried not to laugh with us. It was not generally accepted to say things about the government, especially over the radio.

⬖⬗⬖⬗⬖

The main problem for the park, and the reason for the warden's frustration over the lack of legislation, was the vast damage caused by the great herds of cattle and camels which grazed the land down to dust, leaving lush grassland bare desert scrub in the course of a few weeks. The herds were owned by the fierce, proud Danakil and Karaiyu nomads, who roamed at will through the park area, and all their other grazing grounds, as they have done for generations. The warden and his men were having constant trouble with them, and only effective legislation, backed by a powerful force of police, and softened by fair compensation, could possibly hope to save the land, the wildlife, and the park. At this time (1967), Ethiopia was the last African country south of the Sahara to establish national parks, which, for a country holding pretensions to the leadership of Africa, was in some ways an embarrassment.

On my first day out in the park, driving with Peter, one of his game guards, and a local policeman, we came across one herd of over a thousand camels. Peter stopped the Land Rover. We got out with our weapons. The Ethiopians carried old bolt-action .303 rifles; mine was a light, semi-automatic carbine of Second World War vintage. It was hot, the light harsh, dark pools of shadow cast by the acacia trees. Tribesmen appeared over the brow of the hill, whooping and ululating, their cries bringing more of them down from the slopes of Fantale, the sleeping volcano to the right of us. The four of us, two British and two Ethiopians, walked up the hill toward them.

To me, it was an unreal world, too much like a movie setting. Peter looked across and grinned.

"How many rounds do you have in that thing?"

"Don't know. Fifteen or twenty maybe?" It was his gun anyway, or at least he had borrowed it from someone.

"Well, if we have to start shooting, don't miss with any of them, will you?"

Christ. Sweat ran down the back of my bush shirt. We went farther up the hill, until we faced, above us, some forty tribesmen, strung out in a half-moon line, some crouched behind trees and rocks, all with rifles cocked and pointed at us. The policeman was shouting at them, and a group of the younger nomads began leaping up and down, shrieking and brandishing their long, curved knives, sometimes thrusting them into the earth.

I glanced sideways at my companions. It didn't seem to bother them, least of all Peter. The policeman was yelling up at the tribesmen, telling them that this was a national park, that the government had given orders that they should move out and stay out. The tribesmen shouted back: Go away or we will kill you! This is our land. The leaping, knife-brandishing dance of the young men became more and more frenzied. Other men tried to outflank us, ducking down, crawling through the long, dry grass. The Danakil warriors are supposed to present their brides with the testicles of an enemy before marriage. Mine felt distinctly uncomfortable. I shifted the carbine on my shoulder, wishing for extra magazines. A young man charged down the hill, pointing his rifle at me, screaming. I jacked the first round into the breach, swinging the carbine up to aim at his head. An older tribesman sprang after the youth, hitting him from behind so that the youth sprawled forward. I eased on the safety catch. Peter looked over at me.

"They know what will happen to them if any harm comes to us." I slung the carbine over my shoulder again. The thought did not comfort me.

"Stop." The game guard held up his hand. "The policeman says that if we go any closer they really will kill us." We were thirty yards from the ranks of tribesmen. Their fuzzy hair was sticking several inches out from their heads, and long, curved knives were slung in front of their loins. Lean, naked chests, crossed with bandoliers. One of them lay over to my extreme right, his rifle resting on a rock and pointing at me. Should the shooting start, I would dive for that clump of brush and take him first. Peter had six rounds, the guard fifteen, and the policemen ten. This, against forty tribesmen, most of them crouched in good firing positions. The policeman was still shouting at them. And I was wondering at that time just why the hell I should be here, walking about with a loaded gun, in a country not my own, indulging in armed confrontations with a lot of nomads hiding behind rocks.

At a signal, the tribesmen moved out of sight over the brow of the hill. We followed slowly. They moved away from us, down the hill, driving their great mass of complaining camels, shrouded in a pall of dust.

We went back to the Land Rover and continued the patrol, running into one other, smaller group of nomads. Their reaction was similar. They sat down behind a natural wall of rock and aimed their rifles at us. There was nothing we could do. Peter said that he was sure that we could fight off and defeat one of these bands, leaving several dead, but after that, the whole park would have to be evacuated quickly, as the entire tribe would be down on us. What was needed was to force the government to treat these people fairly for a change. They had seen nothing but empty promises and had been pushed from pillar to post. They would be pushed no more.

We drove back to park headquarters. Carefully, I took the round out of the breech and unloaded the carbine.

The next day, at the new sugar estate of Metahara, a young English-speaking police lieutenant assured me that tribesmen never, never pointed their guns at foreigners. Major Gizaw flew down in the department's Cessna a couple of days later. He too seemed unimpressed by my adventures. I told him, with feeling, that nobody had ever pointed a gun at me before, and that I didn't like it. Neither had I realized, though I told no one, how easy it would be in such a situation to make the decision to kill a man, even a man for whom one felt no animosity.

※※※※

Time passed in Addis Ababa from frustration to frustration, but after a month and a bit my assistant Ermias and I were ready to leave.

Ermias was a slim, soft-spoken, handsome Amhara. He had completed his third year at Alemeyu College of Agriculture and Animal Husbandry, and was now assigned to our department for a year of compulsory national service. All university and college students had to do this before their final year. Ermias was a rare young man. He actually wanted to go into the field, and he liked manual work, even though he was the son of a government official. Like most Ethiopian students, his English was superb, and we could talk with ease about anything. After only a short time, we bantered and joked like old friends.

We were assigned a Toyota pickup and a driver named Abegas. We loaded and fueled up the night before, and started out from Addis Ababa early in the morning. That day the road was lined with flags and soldiers, and all the schoolchildren were marching in honor of the state visit of Kenyatta. Banners were strung across the road, "Welcome to Our Great Friend."

Children waved to us as we drove out. It was a long ride, and somewhere along the way, I got dysentery.

※※※※

The ancient capital of Gondar, cradled by hills and watered by two swift-flowing rivers, is dotted with stone castles and churches.

The oldest castle, built by King Fasilidas, is supposed to date back to around 1635. It is a city with a great tradition of literature, religion, and intrigue. Gondar is a curious place. During the brief Italian occupation, the Fascists sought to make it their capital, and many fine buildings were erected, wide streets laid, and pines and cedars planted among what before was ruins and thatched, mud-walled hovels, and what is now a sea of tin roofs and eucalyptus. Today, with the Ethiopians in custody, the fine buildings, both old and new, have fallen into disrepair. Broken windows are left unrepaired, and rain drips onto the marble floors of the enormous post office, provincial government headquarters, and the bank. Off the main streets run rock-strewn alleys, dusty in the dry season, muddy in the rains, bordered by ramshackle, mud-walled houses and foul with flies and the stink of animal and human dung. Here and there, isolated from the rest, are fine houses for important officials, for foreign doctors and overseas aid workers from various countries.

The Arab quarter is busy, with open-fronted shops. It is perhaps slightly cleaner than most of the rest of the town. There is an open market, and from the surrounding hills and the plains which slope down toward Lake Tana, the peasants trek in with their donkeys to sell sheep, chickens, eggs, grain, honey, and a few vegetables. On the piazza, the main street, there is a cinema, a pharmacy, a jeweler, and a goldsmith, Arab shops which sell clothes and other odds and ends, a photographer or two with dozens of fiercely posed portraits of Ethiopians in uniform or with guns, and a couple of general stores which sell imported foods at fantastic prices. At one end of the piazza are the somber ramparts of Fasilidas' castle, with a parade square in front of it and a couple of gas stations just along the way, and at the other end is the great frontage of the post office. Going up the road, opposite from the market and the Arab quarter, are rows and rows of bars which are open from late in the morning until deep into the night. At night a cacophony of raucous music, Ethiopian and American, blares out into the street, while groups of the richer men and students wander from bar to bar, drinking, joking, sometimes fighting, dancing with the harlots, many of whom are strikingly beautiful. Those with less money might sit in dingy talla houses, with horns of talla, the local beer, or long-necked flasks of sweet, honey-brewed tedj; here the harlots are less well dressed, but often just as beautiful.

Bureaucrats and tribesmen

Overlooking Fasilidas' castle is the Iteghie Menen Hotel, a good, Italian-built place with wide gardens full of flowers and brilliantly blossomed shrubs and trees, and a tall, thatched veranda in the back of the dining room, with a view of the castle through a trellis thick with bougainvillaea in which nest and perch a variety of small birds. I had to spend a few days in Gondar, to get my supplies and to offer letters of introduction to the Governor General of Begemdir Province, under whose ultimate jurisdiction (after that of the Emperor, who of course controls everything in the country) came the district of Simien. As it was the best hotel at that time, I chose to stay at the Iteghie. Ermias, whose salary was less, stayed at the Lumumba Hotel on the piazza. Soon after we arrived, Ermias came down with malaria, probably contracted in Awash. This kept us in Gondar a few more days. Then came the enforced holiday of the anniversary of the Emperor's coronation, when cannons boomed and drums beat, and the tannoy, a system of loudspeakers suspended on poles, on the piazza relayed a horrendous, crackling din of patriotic music and speeches.

By the time we went north to Debarek it was Sunday. It was one hundred and ten kilometers distant, the road climbing just outside Gondar to nine thousand feet. We arrived around noon. Debarek, the capital of the Simien district and the departure point from the main road for the ride into the mountains, was the dirtiest, ugliest town I had ever seen. Wherever we stopped, men and children gathered around to stare. Not the open, smiling stare of the Canadian Eskimos, or the curious, though relatively discreet looks of Japanese country people. I was well accustomed to these, and didn't mind. But this was a dark, seemingly hostile stare, with men draped in shammas or gabis, thick toga-like cotton robes, pushing in as close as six feet to peer from face to face as we talked or asked questions. Debarek was crowded, with many people on mules or horses, and others strutting about with their rifles and bandoliers, arrogant as fighting cocks, their once-white gabis gray with dirt, their bodies and clothes stinking with rancid butter and stale sweat. Ermias and I escaped to a cold, dirty bar where we drank tea. Wind from the hills swept through windows from which the glass had long since gone. Pictures of the Virgin, of Adam and Eve and the serpent, and of Haile Selassie in various poses and uniforms were all about the cracked walls. Ermias, his gentle, handsome face creased with a frown, was shaking his head.

"No, you should not feel upset when they stare. They do not mean harm. You see, they are only wondering why you came."

There was a commotion outside. A crowd moved down through the wide market square; a throng of men close behind a heavily built man cloaked with a black cape and astride a fine mule. They went across the road and moved toward the police station. Fifteen or more of the men behind the mounted figure carried long rifles, mostly old weapons of Italian and Austrian make, though one man, in the fore, carried a modern FN automatic rifle, his narrow chest swathed with belts of ammunition. The rest of the men, armed with hardwood sticks, trotted behind those with rifles. Nearly all were barefoot.

"The Governor has returned from the church. We may go and see him now." Ermias picked up my briefcase.

"What does he want all those guns around him for when he goes to church?" I asked.

"It is the custom, you see," said Ermias as we followed the crowd. "And the Governor is a powerful man, he must have enemies."

An armed guard, in shamma and tight jodhpurs, showed us into the Governor's house. It was not really much of a place, though larger than the other houses in Debarek. Typical of most Ethiopian roadside dwellings, the house was rectangular and built of eucalyptus and mud, with a tin roof dotted with lines of light, pointed nail holes and blackened with soot. Windows were holes, no glass, closed with shutters made of wood and tin. We stepped into the main room. Four or five armed men stood at the door. All around the whitewashed walls men sat on low benches, rifles or sticks between their knees. The Governor, fiercely handsome, with fine Amhara features, white hair, broad shoulders, and an arrogant glare, sat in a large chair in one corner, facing the rest of the room. A servant stood by him, and no person turned his back to him. We shook hands and exchanged greetings, and were ushered to chairs on the left side of the Governor. A boy brought in a small round table and another brought a bottle of clear araki and three small glasses. I looked around the room. Despite the lack of fine furnishings, there was a sense of dignity about the place. Fresh grasses had been cut and strewn about the hard-packed dirt floor. At the Governor's feet was a thick, handwoven wool rug. Heavy-breasted serving women crouched over in one corner, pouring talla for the men. They poured us alcohol and we drank, the men watching my face. Ermias stood up and with a bow, both arms extended, he handed the Governor my letter of introduction from the Wildlife Conservation Department and an order from the Governor General's office to provide me with a police escort for my first trip into the Simien Mountains.

The Governor's authority extended over the whole of the Simien, to the great loop of the Takazze River which bordered on Tigre Province. He held the title of Dejasmatch—"Leader of the Outside" —gained during the Italian campaign. It was a title which carried great prestige, perhaps equivalent to lord or baron, though it was not hereditary. Only the Emperor could grant such titles. In the old days, these were the officers who formed the inner guard and camped around the king's tent.

The Governor, Dejasmatch Araya, read the letters and put them on the table. No one smiled. Turning to us, the Governor spoke. Ermias translated. "I cannot help you. I do not want you or anybody from the Wildlife Department here. I will not give you police and I do not see why you should come here. We protect the Walia ourselves. We do not need you. I hold no personal grudge against you, and I am sorry that you left your country to come here. But I will never help the Wildlife Department. It has hired thieves, liars, and poachers to be its soldiers in my district. They will get no help from me, and you should go back to your country."

He gave an order and a thin, sly-faced fellow in a turban and ragged Western clothes entered and bowed.

"This man, Ineyu, will arrange your mules and guides." The Governor spoke to Ineyu, who bowed again and left. We would get guides, but no police.

"What is all this about the Simien guards, Ermias?"

"I don't know, but perhaps he wants his own relatives and followers to get jobs as game guards. He says he won't help the department. We work for the department. You see what it is like with these people. They are not educated. Do not argue with him."

I drained my glass of raw liquor and stood up. The Governor spoke again.

"He says he is sorry for you," said Ermias. "He does not have a grudge against you, only against the department." I raised my eyebrows. And thus I was to carry, without police escort, the salaries of twenty men for several months into the mountains, where it was said there were many shifta, outlaw bandits. We shook hands and left.

There had been an American game warden before me. He had resigned after a couple of months. I was beginning to see why.

Ermias and I walked back to the bar. We wanted to buy some bread, canned fish, and red wine, get the hell out of Debarek, and eat lunch somewhere along the road. There was nothing else to do here. Our equipment was unloaded and stored at Ineyu's little house by the market square. Beggars and children gathered like flies around the Toyota. I emptied my pockets of small change, and Ermias and driver Abegas shooed the others away. We went over to the bar, followed by a horde of scruffy, barefooted, noisy children, chanting at me in mock Italian: *"Babone commastare . . . feranji, feranji,* give me centime . . ."

We took our food and drove out of the Debarek, halfway down the incredible winding road that clings to the massive cliff faces of Wolkefit Pass. Gelada baboons bounded down the slopes and across the road as the car whined its way down and around the hairpin bends under the roadside canopy of eucalyptus trees that had been planted by the Italians. Here and there waterfalls splashed by the road, and springs trickled out and down over the rocks. Below us were patchwork fields of barley and rape, and here and there on this sea of rolling hills were dark green huddles of remnant forests, many of them hiding a church, or a mosque, or a graveyard. Standing off the main line of cliffs, rampart pinnacles and spires, old volcano cores and massive flat-topped ambas* reached for the clouds, and towered almost to the height of the high, lost-world plateau rims of the Simien. Shifting curtains of rain hung in the distance. Above and below us, predator birds were circling and seeking. Many people had died to build this road. We stopped the car, got out, and stood in wonder at the enormity of the achievement.

"This," said Ermias, "is one thing the Italians did that we should always be grateful for."

---

* *Amba* is an Ethiopian word which means mountain. Westerners have come to use the word to denote the massive, sheer-walled, flat-topped mountains that are common in parts of the country.

Yes, if you can remember it among all the other bitter memories, I thought. The memorial, inscribed with the names of the Italians who died building the road, had been torn down by the patriots.

As we ate lunch, the Governor's Land Rover came past us, bristling with the rifles and shotguns of his bodyguards. He waved as he passed.

Below, in a patch of forest, we could hear the gruff cry of a colobus monkey, and all about the hills and rocky cliffs, the bleat of goats and the high yells of shepherd boys.

The High Simien looked so distant, so sheer and vast and majestic. Something akin to fear, self-doubt perhaps, clutched at my stomach.

Ermias and I refused to stay in Debarek overnight. We drove back to Gondar, to cold beer, good food, and clean beds. We would leave at dawn, returning to Debarek to begin the long mule trek into the High Simien.

SIMIEN,
THE ROOF OF AFRICA

Our equipment lay scattered in untidy heaps of boxes and bundles around the market square. Ineyu's men yelled and squabbled over what should go where, and how it should be loaded, and who should fetch what, and who should tie and who should hold the animals. One evil, red-haired, swaybacked bastard of a mule, loaded with two of my boxes, kicked at the handler and rolled on the ground, all four legs flailing the air with savage abandon. The boxes splintered and cracked, and the handler hauled off and beat the seemingly insensitive animal with his stick. Ineyu ran over, cursing, seized the mule by its lower lip and kicked it in the ribs until it got up. Boxes and saddlery hung lopsided. At Ineyu's orders, three men hustled to remove the stuff. The mule rolled its eyes. Ineyu sprang onto its back, thumping the animal's ribs with his booted heels, galloping around the marketplace, scattering peasants and children. After he leaped off, still cursing the mule, it stood quietly to be loaded again.

Three game guards reported for duty, one of them with a hammer-action .410 shotgun and the other two with rifles. They helped with the loading and threw stones to chase away the crowds of giggling children. At last, two hours late, the string of twelve pack animals and our two riding mules moved off from the market square and out through groves of eucalyptus onto the crisscrossed trails to the Simien.

Ermias, leaning on the high wooden pommel of the saddle, with his broad-brimmed hat, chukka boots, and .38 pistol, looked like a hero from a Western. I was exhilarated, and rode easily, even though it had been ten years since I had been on a horse for more than ten minutes or so. I'd never ridden a mule before, and found the gait very easy and enjoyable. The mule picked its way over the boulder-choked paths without a stumble. We rode through hills green and golden with barley, and through meadows loud with the squawking of wattled ibis. In untidy patches of bare earth and nettles, round thatched houses huddled together in small, scattered groups, and on hilltops near Debarek there were churches surrounded by groves of cedar, hagenia, acacia, and olive.

As people passed our caravan on the trail, the men exchanged loud greetings, sometimes stopping to embrace relatives or friends in the ritual way of the Simien people. One, the supposed inferior, would stoop to kiss the superior's knee, at which the superior would catch his chin in one hand, raising his face to kiss both cheeks, whereupon the kisses were returned. A long recitation of greetings followed, inquiries as to the welfare of relatives, children, parents, cattle. By the time all this was finished, the man would have to run to catch up with the rest of the caravan. As Ermias and I passed, those people walking would bare their heads and bow to us; others, riding horses or mules, dismounted to let us go by, while Ermias exchanged greetings, urging them, no, no, stay on your animal.

Countless times we had to stop to readjust the pack loads. The Simien people would not listen to me when I told them to balance the packs and sling them on either side of the animals. The saddlery was terrible, and the weight always rested too high, abrading the spine and causing hideous saddle sores. The muleteers beat the animals for any reason, lashing out with their thick sticks, kicking and thumping the poor beasts. I had seen how Eskimos treated their sled dogs, and thought it harsh, but the Eskimos are gentle compared with the Ethiopians. Yet the animals were tough and hardy, and would jog along just as jauntily after a beating. Mules especially liked to dash forward, loads bouncing, to get ahead of the muleteers and grab a few mouthfuls of barley from the crop patches along the way before the men caught up and chased them off.

We forded three shallow streams with high-cut banks which indicated the extent of the flash floods of the rainy season. After the third stream, we climbed steep, eroded pathways until we stood on the spine of a long, hog-backed ridge, some nine thousand eight hundred feet above sea level. The eucalyptus groves and tin roofs of

Debarek seemed deceptively close, for by now we had been traveling almost two hours. In the distance, toward Gondar, the solitary conical hill of Wokun, and to the northeast, the hills of Simien, each hill hiding in its belly the immense river-knifed gorges that converged on the mighty loop of the Takazze River, which runs down to the Sudan and adds its waters to the Nile. Castles of cumulus loomed by the line of the escarpment edge, piling up against the high walls, spilling over in swirling banks of mist on the plateau moorlands. By four P.M. we had reached the path cut into the side of the Sankabar ridge. It was narrow and rocky, slopes and cliffs above and below. The men went warily, scanning to the left and to the right, above and below, rifles held at the ready. This was a notorious place for ambush. Eight months before, two shifta had been shot to death here. They had been robbing villagers on their way home from market, when a vigilante band saw them, crept through the groves of giant heather, and opened fire on the robbers from a few yards. Now our guards were nervous. Ermias said that they had been involved in the killing, and feared revenge from the relatives of the dead bandits. No police came here. Remembering Awash, I loaded my .30.06 sporting rifle, slipped the safety catch on and rested it in front of me, against the pommel of the saddle. But no human disturbed the peace of the place, only the gelada baboons, scrambling and tumbling across the path and down the slopes as we neared them, the big males stopping, once in safety, to grimace at us. Their shrill yells and questioning grunts echoed. I doffed my hat to them, saying that I hoped for a long and amicable relationship, and for joint cooperation in upholding the aims and principles of wildlife conservation. Ermias laughed, and we kicked our animals into a canter.

We came out onto the summit of the ridge, among grassy meadows surrounded by forests of giant heather. Cliffs dropped incredibly to the left. Looking over them and down from them was like looking from an aircraft. It was a cloud-top world, the rest of the earth distant and far below. Tiny houses, threads of rivers, and the horizon so far away that it was impossible to define. And thus we looked down on the hills, hill after hill as far as could be seen. At Sankabar, the escarpment itself falls three or four thousand feet. Springs fed small streams which trickled out of the groves of dark green trees and splashed over the edges, making somber wet patches, bordered by lush vegetation and brilliant mosses, on the cliff faces. I found a spring, dismounted and drank. I wanted to camp here for the night, but the men assured me that it was just a little farther to Geech, so we went on.

It got dark. My mule stumbled and grunted. I was saddle sore, cramped and soaked by fine, cold rain. We stumbled through the dark and the rain for two and a half hours. At last I reached the Geech camp site. It was at eleven thousand eight hundred feet. Two tents had been set up, with a camp bed in each, but six of our pack animals were missing, left behind somewhere along the trail; one of them, I was told, had a broken leg. All our food, sleeping bags, pots, pans, lamps, and stoves were somewhere between Geech and San-kabar, and with all the gear was Ermias. I dismounted and began to unsaddle the mule. A guard ran out and took the animal from me, another led me into a tiny, low-walled stone hut in which all the men huddled around a fire. I sat with them for a while, taking coffee with no sugar from a rusty tin can, eyes streaming from the smoke, for there was no chimney. Finishing the coffee, I went out into the cold air. I did a few exercises in an effort to get warm, but I was too tired and stiff for it to be effective. Damn and blast the fucking mules and the fucking muleteers. I went into one of the tents and curled up on a camp cot. The tent, badly pitched, was drafty and flapped. No mattress, no sleeping bag, no food. Dark and damp and cold. I curled up in a tight little ball, but it was impossible to sleep. Fantasies of warmth and food, and of slow, warm, lazy sex flitted through my mind. My God, this was a barbaric place! Only three months before I had been in the Canadian Arctic. It had never been as bad as this. Eskimos did not lose vital equipment, or at least, very rarely. Nor did they squabble and screech at each other all day. And after a long, cold trip there were always steaming mugs of sweet tea and a billy of hot food. Boiled seal ribs . . . great, jam-covered hunks of bannock . . . maybe some dried fruit, boiled up and mixed with oatmeal and powdered cream. Warmth of a sleeping bag, warmth of a good tent, or the muffled dome of an igloo, all yellow inside with the lamplight; warmth of a full belly . . . warm thighs, warm arms, warm breasts against my chest . . . time spinning off . . . Ethiopia, Canada, Japan, home . . .

Ermias staggered in at eleven P.M., shivering with cold and faint with exhaustion. One of the men had gone back to find him. He came swaddled in a blanket, bringing with him our sleeping bags. Numb with cold, we rolled them out. What a joy to sleep!

Morning came with the bite of frost. I got up and looked around. It was a good camp site, though a bit exposed. A clear stream ran close, through a small valley thick with stands of giant heather which led down to the Djinn Barr Valley and a big stream which we had crossed in the dark last night. The first warden, the American who quit after a few months, had built two low stone huts. It was in one of these that the men had slept last night. The huts were four meters in diameter, and round, roofed with thatch over a frame of poles. They had no windows, and the doors were so low one had to stoop over double to get in. The interior of the hut that the American had lived in was dark and cold, and everything stored inside it was covered with mold. Park equipment, what little there was, was piled up inside this hut. For the most part, the stores checked out with the American's inventory, but a few things were missing; a couple of axes, half a dozen sickles, a big cross-cut saw. The whole lot had been left in the charge of the chief game guard, Nadu Worota. I made a note to ask him about the missing gear, but later forgot about it. The park files, letters, and other documents were packed away in a wooden box. I pulled them all out and took them to my tent to read over.

Those files depressed me . . . letters requesting money and equipment . . . no money in the bank for the park or for the warden's salary . . . reports of armed bandits on the Sankabar trail. Men asking for rifles. For bullets. For uniforms. For blankets. Game counts . . . a few Walia ibex, klipspringers in twos and threes, a few duiker and bushbuck, colobus monkeys. Guard training programs and progress reports. Hmm. Something had to be done about teaching them to keep their rifles clean. Were any of them good shots? Perhaps I could teach them some unarmed combat, train up a team as Major Gizaw suggested, and demonstrate to His Majesty. But this damned money business . . . and the road. These would have to be priority considerations . . . and where the hell were we going to get some earth-moving machines?

Game guards straggled into camp for their pay. They wore dirty, ill-fitting British surplus uniforms, or parts of uniforms, with gabis or shammas wound around over their uniforms. Some wore boots, but no socks, and the boots were scuffed and cracked. Their rifles were filthy around the bolts and trigger mechanisms, and the rifle bores were so clogged with dirt that only a faint glimmer of light could be seen through the barrels. Ermias set up office and we paid the men their back pay, signing and countersigning numerous complicated forms. Those who were unable to write gave their forefinger prints. On receiving their pay they sat around, slowly counting and recounting the money.

Chief Guard Nadu came into camp. I had heard a lot about him. John Blower, senior warden, had said that he "seemed a decent enough chap, a bit of a dandy though." He had told of feasts in Nadu's house, of talla and good coffee. In Gondar, in Debarek, everybody knew Nadu, or Agafari Nadu, as he preferred to be called. Ethiopians are big on titles. They would sell their soul for one. Dejasmatch; Kenyasmatch Fitawrary, Grazmatch. Nadu's title, "agafari," came from the time when he served the former Governor General, General Naga, as his usher. Every important man in Ethiopia has a man who stands outside his office or whatever, whose job is to usher in visitors and petitioners. Especially for the petitioners the "agafari" is a man of consequence. Without pleasing him and winning him over, there is little hope of seeing the big man himself. Generally, with unimportant men, peasants, poor people, the agafari is overbearing, pompous, officious, or condescending. With important visitors he is generally effusive, bobbing and bowing and polite in the extreme. In fairness, as I later found out, the job of an official of importance in Ethiopia would be impossible if there were not someone at the door to sort through the scores of petitioners who wait from morn till dusk to try to put their case to him.

Anyway, Nadu had been an agafari for the former Governor General, and although I didn't consider this nearly as important as being chief game guard of a national park, Nadu did, and he preferred to be called "agafari." It wasn't much of a title, but a title it was. He was a youngish man, perhaps in his early forties, with a youthful, unlined face, fine, handsome features, and slight tinges of gray in his tight, curly black hair. He wore no uniform, and his rifle was carried for him by his own body servant, who stood behind him. Nadu carried an old .45-caliber service revolver and a dagger. In the six months which had elapsed between the American's leaving —followed shortly by his Ethiopian assistant—and my arrival, everything had been left in Nadu's charge. Ermias called him into my

23

tent, and over coffee we discussed the situation. I asked many questions. Had the men been assigned regular patrols? Nadu nodded, yes, of course, yes, regular patrols. Was there any poaching of Walia? Oh, no, the people would never kill Walia. Did you send patrols to the lowlands, to the base of the escarpment? Oh, yes, of course, yes. Nadu answered all our questions with assurance. All seemed to be well. We related the local Governor's accusations against our men. Was there any truth in them? He denied everything. Dejasmatch Araya is jealous, he said, and wished only to replace the game guards with his own relatives and followers. However he, Nadu, had been commanded by His Majesty himself to protect the Walia. His rifle and binoculars were given to him by His Majesty, as well as a large prize of money with which he, Nadu, had built a fine stone church in Amba Ras. Ermias explained. Nadu had caught some Walia ibex and handed them over to General Naga, who presented them to the Emperor. Many people liked to please His Majesty in this way, for he loves animals, said Ermias. I asked if Nadu had caught the animals himself. He said he had. I was most impressed. This was indeed a very useful man to have as a chief guard. He was obviously a man who commanded great respect among the local people. He was a chief, a balambat, and he knew the Walia. I asked Nadu again if he was sure that the Dejasmatch's accusations were false. He emphatically denied them all; why, the Dejasmatch sends his followers out with rifles to shoot bushbuck and klipspringer for his table!

"What? Is that true, Ermias?"

"I don't know. It is quite likely."

I said they would have to be arrested if ever we caught them at it. Ermias translated this and Nadu stared at me. Ermias explained that we couldn't touch the Governor's people, he would make trouble for us.

"God damn it," I thumped the box on which I was sitting, "if they're poaching they're breaking the law, and I'm not afraid of anybody in this country except the Old Man himself!" Ermias and Nadu both shook their heads. It was not possible. Well, we would see.

"And," said Nadu, "even though I presented him with a fine fat ox on his first arrival to be governor of our country, he is yet against me."

Simien, the roof of Africa

We drank our coffee and nodded sagely to each other. I felt myself on the verge of a political struggle with the Dejasmatch. It exhilarated me.

Nadu's body servant dragged a sheep to the tent. Nadu presented
it to us and made a speech about my arrival. We thanked him, and
the sheep was dragged off to get its throat cut. I told Nadu, through
Ermias, that he should continue to arrange the guard patrols until I
could become familiar with the country. Reports of poaching were
to be submitted to me.

The next morning Ermias and I walked up to the escarpment
edge in the hope of seeing Walia ibex. In the high moorland leading
up to the Geech escarpment, above the giant heather groves, the
grass rats were chirping everywhere. It seemed to me that there
were two species, one smaller than the other. They stood by their
burrows in the coarse grass, rather like ground squirrels, giving their
shrill, birdlike warning cries and ducking down at the last possible
moment as we passed. Flocks of birds, choughs and chats, were
feeding on the high, rolling moor, and now and then a lanner falcon
passed low over the ground, almost touching the grass, seeking to
bowl over any unwary rat. At the cliff edge we saw another big herd
of gelada baboons, but no Walia. On our way back to camp, Nadu
and another guard galloped up. Nadu said we should never go
about alone, in case the mist came over and we were lost. I pulled
out the small compass I always carried in little-known country, but
Nadu didn't know what it was.

In the afternoon we followed the small stream running by the
camp, down the length of its tumbling waterfalls and still, cold
pools, to where it joined the Djinn Barr stream. We were looking for
sand to mix with cement. We found none. Nothing but coarse
gravel. We were told that sand was only available in the lowlands,
two days' journey away. I offered a reward to any man who could
find deposits closer to camp, but felt pessimistic; the basaltic rocks
didn't seem to make anything but coarse gravel or soft sludge. I sat
for a while down by the Djinn Barr stream, watching the caddis larvae, thinking about how to go about introducing trout, thinking
about a dam upstream to make pools large enough to attract water-
fowl. Coming down, we had startled a black duck in one of the
small pools. The bird was very nervous. Apart from that we saw
only one little duiker. The seeming lack of animals in the forest

bothered me. Cattle were numerous, and many trees had been cut. Obviously there was too much human disturbance. In a walk of a few hours in the Canadian bush, even if you didn't see animals you could find signs. Here there were none. No tracks, no droppings. I climbed back up the long slope to camp, dizzy and gasping for breath, head pounding and legs heavy. It was almost twelve thousand feet above sea level. The scarcity of wildlife in the forest depressed me, for I had expected more.

My jobs, in order of priority, were: first, the protection of the Walia and of its habitat; second, the establishment of temporary headquarters and a gate camp on Sankabar ridge; third, a road from Debarek, probably up to Sankabar. With a road to Sankabar, and an office, stores, stable, and quarters, we could then haul in bulky items such as sand, cement, timber, a cement mixer, a generator, and so forth with ease. It would be much quicker and easier to pack in goods the twelve or so kilometers from Sankabar to the center of the park than to drag them all the way from Debarek.

According to the reports of the American, Nadu was a capable and trustworthy man. Nadu was supposed to be organizing the anti-poaching patrols of the ragtag game guards. He had given the right answers to all my questions. Fine. Then I could get on with establishing a base at Sankabar and building the road.

I gave orders that we should be ready to go down to Sankabar in the morning. We would look the place over for permanent water and a good building site. Ermias and I rode two small park mules. Three game guards came along with a pack mule loaded with two light tents and a grub box. We were all armed. Halfway down to Sankabar, at the grassy meadow overlooking the awesome abyss below Geech, we met Nadu and a dozen of his followers. Four of them carried rifles, the others sticks. We exchanged the greetings of a sunny morning. He sat like a lord on his big golden horse, bandoliers crossed about his chest and a pistol at his waist, white cotton gabi looped over his shoulders, and a scarf tied in a turban about his head. The guards ran and bowed to him.

"Let us go!"

Those men lounging about on the grass, staring at me, leaped to their feet at Nadu's command. He led the way, while we jogged along behind on our mules, the others running at our stirrups and our rear, shouting and laughing, singing the wild Ethiopian songs of heroic exploits. Fine dust from the precipitous pathway rose in a cloud, settling on the leaves of shrubs and flowering dog-rose. Peasants, coming down from Sankabar and Michibi with their cattle, bared their heads and stood aside to let us pass. Several shouted after us.

"They ask us when we will build the road," said Ermias.

"Soon, soon," I said.

We stopped on Sankabar ridge, near where the boundary of the park should be demarcated. A constriction in the ridge commanded the main approach into the Simien. It used to be a checkpoint in the old days. The Italians certainly would not have dared to come in here, for in this place a few riflemen could hold off a hundred. Nadu pointed out some house sites. He preferred high knolls. Good for defense, but poor for getting water. The ridge was rowdy with gelada baboons, some two hundred of them, screaming warnings or grunting reassurances to each other as we approached along the path. Here, the stands of giant heather were old and largely untouched. With bent, lichen-festooned limbs they shaded the pathways of the northern approach, and made a quiet green shelter for klipspringers. Flowers and shrubs of a hundred species blossomed everywhere, with here and there the heavy fragrance of new-blooming jasmine, sweet and somehow unexpected. To the south side lay the deep, gouged valley of the Khabar River, sometimes called Serecaca, thickly forested, steep-sided. On the other side of the ridge the escarpment fell three or four thousand feet. Its top was bordered by giant heather. Here and there the heather forests were broken by grassy glades and stands of yellow flowering trees of giant Saint-John's-wort. I was enchanted by the place. I walked by the cliffs, watching lammergeyers, griffon vultures, falcons, and eagles soaring above and below me. Here I chose the site for my house, and imagined living here with my wife and children.

A grassy ledge at the edge of the escarpment sheltered our camp. It was quiet. We faced the vast curve of an enormous cliff face. An old volcanic plug stood off from it. Away, away, the horizon lost itself in a haze of rolling hills. Guard Turu came back from a village a few kilometers away, bringing with him four sheep and their owner, a thin, barefooted peasant, proud in his tattered British Army greatcoat. The three guards and the peasant argued and gesticulated about the price of the sheep, eventually bargaining the price down to six dollars (Ethiopian). It was a good animal, young and fat, with a big, juicy fat tail. Joking and chattering, the guards slaughtered and butchered it, and built a great fire from the plentiful dead wood lying around. Dusk gathered among the stars and stretched out the shadows of the lowland hills. Far-off lines of dogtoothed ridges stood out and then slid into darkness.

We sat about the fire, roasting mutton on the coals, dipping it in salt and red pepper paste. The guards were relishing this rare treat. Guards Turu and Ambaw, both in their thirties, said very little. Turu was short and quite muscular. Ambaw was slightly built, with a high-pitched voice and quick movements. The third guard, Mitiku, was in his forties; a soft-spoken man, thin and energetic. Ermias brewed coffee. We filled our big enamel mugs and sat with them cradled in our hands, talking and philosophizing. I passed the kettle and the sugar over to the three guards. They did not drink. Ermias asked why and translated the answer. They were waiting for us to finish so that they could borrow our cups. I was annoyed. I knew that they had all been issued canteens and cups. What had they done with them? Ermias asked and they all said that cups had not been issued. But we knew they had and we told them so. Were they sure? Well, yes, maybe cups were issued, but they had lost them. On further questioning it turned out that they gave them to their wives to carry butter from the market. "That's what we use them for here. We don't use them for water or drinking." What do they do on patrol? In camp? The three guards shrugged and looked from one to another. I finished my coffee, cleaned out the cup, and put it away in the grub box. Ermias, a more kindly soul, passed his around.

It got cool, but not as chilling as in Geech, a thousand or so feet higher. Bats dodged above the campfire's upward spiraling sparks, and in the blackness of the surrounding giant heather, insects sang. The three guards kept their rifles within easy reach, laughing nervously as they told stories about the shifta. And what about those men who hid in the hills when the Italians were here? Were there many in the Simien? Oh, yes. And Dejasmatch Araya? He seemed like an old warlord. The guards laughed. The Dejasmatch is a fox, they said. He fought against the Italians, and then for them, and then, when they were losing, he fought once more against them. But his title? The guards laughed; ah, the Italians gave many such titles, but then, when His Majesty returned with the British, he was wise enough to let these men keep their titles, so they fought for him. They said that sometimes, overlooking the Wolkefit Pass road, old Dejasmatch Araya would boast: "See this road we built? Aiy! We shot lots of people around here."

Mitiku said that he had fought for the Italians too; then they caught him and were going to shoot him in Gondar, but a British major forgave him and he joined the Ethiopians. Oh, the British were good fighters, brave and savage, but the Italians were fine builders and did much for our country, said Mitiku. Ah, yes, if only they had stayed for twenty years we would have roads all over our country, even a road to the Simien. They laughed about the people going down the cliff on ropes, terrified, to set off the dynamite fuses to blast out the road. Aiy, lots of them died. But they built the road quickly. Mitiku became quiet.

"How long will it take our country to develop like England or Italy?" he asked.

The others said nothing. I said I didn't know.

"Maybe a hundred years," he said.

"What do you think, Ermias?"

"I don't know. His Majesty is wise, and has done many things, but our people are not educated, it is not easy, you see."

Mitiku spoke again.

"What did he say?" I asked Ermias.

"He said, 'Please stay with us for many years and help us. Please build the road for us, and all the people will bless you. May God help you and Ato Ermias with your task.' "

"Amen," said the other two guards.

Mitiku got to his feet and made a speech, blessing us for the feast. We acknowledged it, and I felt a bit rotten about the cup. I gazed up at the myriad pointed dome of the sky, marveling at the brightness and clarity of the stars. Below, strings of red lights looped about the hills. They seemed like street lights, but through binoculars I could see that they were fires. The guards said the people were burning off the forest to claim land for farming. Some of the fires were big, and burned close to the escarpment.

I brought the talk back to the road, and to the building of a camp in Sankabar. It was a fine place. They were all enthusiastic. It had water, wood, and Walia. The road could easily be built there.

"They say they have paid taxes for the road," said Ermias.

The men pulled grubby pieces of paper from their tunic pockets. "Oh, yes," they told us, "we have paid taxes for the road, for schools, a hospital. None of them have been built."

"What has happened to the money?" I asked.

"Those government officials have probably kept it. This is a problem in our country. Our officials do not always work just for the country and the people."

One of the guards laughed. "Ah, a governor has eaten the money," he said.

Mitiku said, "But now that His Majesty has sent you to the Simien, the road will be built, and we will get our school and our hospital."

I glanced uncomfortably at Ermias, and said that we would do our best. Ermias nodded, and spoke at length to the men in his fine, educated Amharic. I didn't understand, but the men all nodded toward me, and made sounds of agreement.

❖❖❖❖

I was awakened in the early morning by Mitiku, calling softly at the door of my tent. "Mister! Mister! Walia!"

Scrambling into clothes, I fumbled at the foot of the sleeping bag for binoculars. At the edge of the cliff, Ermias and the other two guards sat watching and whispering. The cliff curved in a sheer wall, broken at the top and bottom by grassy ledges and forested slopes. Here and there, cavelike hollows pitted the rock, and narrow trails, in many places only a few inches wide, ran from ledge to ledge. Mitiku pointed.

The Walia were clear through the binoculars; large, reddish-brown wild goats, the big males with massive, knurled, backsweeping horns. The females were more dainty, their horns quite small. The kids were darker in color. The Walia moved with ease on the cliff, running as if on air up the rock faces. They browsed on the small ledges, choosing carefully, chewing slowly. We counted eleven animals scattered over one cliff face. Of themselves the

Walia did not fill me with awe and wonder as have other wild animals. They are attractive enough, especially the big males, but they are too close to goats to induce that special sense, that strange feeling of recall, way back in the long-ago mists of our innocence, when we feared and sought after beasts of such grace, power, beauty, speed, or mystery that we worshipped their spirits and made masks and totems of them. The fascination of the rare Walia ibex lay not in themselves, but in the fact that they lived and moved with such easy grace on those terrible cliffs, defying and almost ignoring them. The cliffs seemed fit for eagles and soaring birds, but not for walking, hooved animals. My scalp tightened and tingled. I knew it before, but now I felt it. The Walia and the cliffs, the birds, plants, streams, and all living things here were part of a pattern that was unique, a pattern that must be kept and nurtured, and perhaps eventually understood.

After sunrise, we rode on up through the erosion-scarred slopes of Geech village. Dusty, dried-up gullies fanning and spreading like a disease over the hide of the hills. Red and blue-gray scabs of bare volcanic rock or sterile subsoil in great patches all over the slopes. Not even weeds growing on those patches. And here and there were odd small trees which the peasants had overlooked in their destruction, each tree holding in the mesh of its roots a little island of soil and grass, the little islands sometimes six feet above the lower, dead surface. Sad little islands with sad, withered little flowers. The Geech people had tried to grow barley here, hacking down the heather forest, exposing the thin skin of soil to the sun, wind, and rain. As we rode up, fine dust got in our eyes; the animals' hooves dislodged clods of soil which crumbled and rolled in dried bits down the slopes. Geech, with its scattered tukals, or round houses, was a place of dire poverty. The houses were large but haphazardly built, walls made of clumsily piled boulders, into which were set the knurled and bent branches of tree heather, plastered with mud which cracked and fell out. Smoke seeped through walls and roofs, or through the low doors. Roofs were made of a framework of poles, lashed with ropes of grass. Over the poles was thatch. Eaves were scraggly, untidy, so that the houses glowered under a fringe of sticks and grass like beetle-browed delinquents. Around the houses were rough fences of tree branches, enclosing potato patches, and keeping in a few chickens which pecked at will in and out of the houses. Nettles grew in profusion. Village dogs snapped and growled, prancing around our mules until driven off by stones. People ran out, calling greetings, and we rode up onto a rutted trail, across two dribbling stream beds, whose gullies were devoid of trees, and then, to another gully, bordered with shrubs and lobelias, with a stream of clear, cool mountain water. Up then to the grasslands of the park area, with the chirping, scurrying rats and the patient, waiting augur buzzards. Geech, with its spreading erosion and its promise of further poverty, depressed me.

I went to my tent, brewed tea, and began to type out my plan for the development of the Simien. It was rough and far from detailed, but the skeleton of the idea was formed in my mind.

Certainly, the park could not be developed without an access road from Debarek and the main Addis Ababa-to-Asmara road. It was also obvious that the country between Sankabar and Geech presented great difficulties for road builders. It was steep, rocky, laced with run-off streams leading into the deep valley of the Djinn Barr. It didn't seem likely that the Ethiopian Government, despite its promises, could at present afford to build a road through this country.

However, from Debarek to Sankabar the route was tough, but not so bad as the Geech-to-Sankabar run. Sankabar had magnificent scenery, with the escarpment on one side and the great valley of the Khabar stream on the other. Gelada were numerous and amusing, and tame enough to be photographed by the laziest of tourists. The giant heather forests were lush, with flower-dotted meadows that would make good camp sites. Water was good and permanent. On the cliffs there were Walia, quite easy to see, and many kinds of birds, from tawny eagles and lammergeyers to cackling francolin. Therefore, to my way of thinking, Sankabar should be the road head and gate camp of the park. I would build quarters there, a house for myself and my family, and small houses for the guards. There should also be a stable, store, office, and water tanks, and a rest house for visitors.

I typed furiously, in between sips of tea, carried away by visions of a fine mountain national park. Land Rovers of tourists. Smart, tough guards. Colorful guides in national dress, and fine, caparisoned mules, setting off from Sankabar with caravans of adventurous visitors to explore the higher areas of the park. And a powerful little Unimog truck, hauling supplies, rations, cement, a generator, beer for the warden.

First, the road needed to be surveyed. The Imperial Ethiopian Highways Authority could be persuaded to do that. Then we would need blasting equipment, dynamite, a couple of bulldozers and other earth-movers, dump trucks, masons for culverts and bridges, money for fuel, coolies, and so on. The government would have to clear up any squabbles over land. It would take a lot of money. It was November, seven months until the onset of the rains.

Ah, but wouldn't it be great! I could just imagine myself driving up from Gondar to Sankabar in the morning, taking lunch at a pleasant restaurant with an Ethiopian decor, built of stone, with a round design, big picture windows, vivid Ethiopian paintings on the walls, carved wooden chairs, rush mats. Good Ethiopian food, hot wat sauce and fresh injera, wide pancakes made from the grain of the grass called teff, with cold beer or sweet tedj. I could sit there with my after-dinner coffee and brandy, looking out of the window, chatting with visitors who would envy my job and my life, telling tall tales about animals, poachers, and shifta . . . ah, yes . . . and pretty girls and rich, beautiful ladies all being disappointed to discover that I'm married. The visitors could fly into Gondar, spend a little time there looking at castles and churches, drive up to Sankabar, take lunch, see the cliffs and mountains, the birds, the gelada, and maybe Walia, and then drive on back to Gondar by dusk if they wanted to, perhaps on to Axum. The more adventurous could ride or hike into the Geech highlands, stay overnight at tasteful but simple stone rondavels which would be equipped with cooking, heating, and sleeping facilities. They could look after themselves, escape from the noise of motor engines, from the luxuries of well-equipped hotels and lodges, and the annoyances of having too many other people around. As I saw it, the park would offer a choice—facilities endowed by a road to Sankabar, and the peace and purity of the highland . . . walking, riding, friendly night with wine, song, and stories around warm fires in the stone huts.

With this road-head camp established at Sankabar, and tourists and money rolling in, I would then shift up to Geech with my family, and build a fine stone house up there. A three-hour hike or ride would do us all good, and it was not too far to get a sick child down and out to Gondar in an emergency. My plan was simple, cheap, and sensible. This way the Simien Mountain National Park would develop easily over the next five years. Or so I thought.

With my magnificent plans typed and headed, with paragraphs and conclusions, I decided we should go down to Gondar, phone Major Gizaw, and try to get things moving on the road. Apart from this, Ermias had to go to the hospital for a final checkup on his malaria, and we had to get this trouble with Dejasmatch Araya, the district governor, sorted out. I gave orders for the guards and mules to be ready the next day. We would go down via one of the proposed road routes, taking three guards, Mitiku, Turu, and Hussein. It was bitterly cold in the tents at Geech, and we went to sleep early.

I awakened to the sound of two thick-billed ravens as they tussled and clattered over a leg of sheep in the grub box outside my tent. Shivering, I made tea and porridge over the primus while sun stole away the frost carpet.

✕✕✕✕

Ermias and I rode ahead while the guards brought up the rear with the pack mules. The route we took was longer but easier than the regular mule trail. It presented difficulties for a road builder: gullies, streams, steep curves, sharp descents. We would have to get it properly surveyed. The building of the road was feasible though, nothing like the incredible Wolkefit Pass road which climbed the great Simien escarpment itself.

✕✕✕✕

The next morning, at Gondar, after collecting my mail, I phoned Major Gizaw in Addis Ababa. It took almost two hours to get through, with the operator at the desk in the huge, high, Italian-built post office shouting and bellowing into the phone: "Addis Ababa! Hello? Addis Ababa! Hello! Anchi (You, girl)! Addis Ababa!"

. . . Echoes around columns and marble floors. Once I got through, I told Major Gizaw about the district governor's attitude. I said that this was an internal political situation which he, as director of the Wildlife Conservation Department, would have to handle himself. I said I had formulated a plan for the initial stages of development of the park, and would like to talk it over with him. Major Gizaw was ever polite. Certainly he would come, in the Cessna, in a few days' time. I should wait for him on November 16 at Gondar airport. I paid for the call and went out, down the long steps to our Toyota, besieged by beggars and shoeshine boys. We bought building supplies and rations. In the afternoon we went to the Agriculture Ministry's local office. The director there was keeping eight of our rifles, and we needed them for the guards, who were worried about their prestige, and about the shifta. The director wasn't in. Come back tomorrow.

✕✕◈✕✕

The next morning Ermias and I paid a call to the provincial headquarters of the Imperial Highways Authority. The chief of the Imperial Highways Gondar office was bland and very polite. We said we understood that he had been given instructions to give us assistance. He said he couldn't do anything for us unless he had a letter from his head office. We should write a letter to our head office so they would write to his head office which in turn would write to him. We made polite noises and left.

Outside, driver Abegas had confiscated a young duiker with a broken leg from a peasant who had obviously snared it. We took the duiker, its coat disheveled and befouled, to the Agriculture Ministry office. The vet there was a Dr. Wan, a small, compact man with a high, wide forehead and lively eyes. He took the animal very gently and laid it on the bench. He reset and splinted the leg, then gave the animal an injection while the Ethiopian veterinary assistants watched.

"This animal is very delicate, very young," said Dr. Wan. "I think it will die. It has a bad fracture and sickness of the bowels. It also suffers bad shock. Very difficult."

I thanked him and said we only wanted to try, that we didn't ex-

35

pect the animal to live. He told me about treating the Governor General's klipspringers. Dr. Wan was one of a group sent by the government of Taiwan. He was supposed to stay in Ethiopia for three years and set up a veterinary service in the province. The rest of the Chinese team were scattered all over the country. I asked him about a sickness we had seen in the Gelada, causing a large swelling in the animal's side. Dr. Wan had a little trouble with English. It was the stilted, academic speech of a man who has studied much, but has spoken very little with native English speakers. He did not, for example, understand the word "baboon." Then I noticed a Japanese dictionary on his desk. As I had spent two and a half years in Japan and was married to a Japanese girl, my spoken Japanese is reasonable. I asked, in Japanese, if he spoke the language. He looked surprised. Yes, he did. I gave him the Japanese for "baboon" and explained what I had seen. He was delighted to meet someone in Gondar who could speak Japanese, as delighted, indeed, as I was. I invited him to dinner at the Iteghie Hotel so that we could talk at leisure.

Back at the hotel, the husky-voiced manageress, Señora Anna, agreed to let me keep the duiker in my room. I cradled it in my arms and fed it warm milk. It was very weak; its eyes were sad, limpid, soft brown. Three hours later it died. I muttered to myself about the man who had snared it, though knowing that even had he heard and understood the language, he could never understand why I was angry. I felt the unforgettable and oft-repeated grief at the death of a wild creature.

Dr. Wan came in the evening and we got to know one another. Dr. Wan had been a boy during the Japanese occupation of Taiwan. He had been educated by them, and like many Taiwanese, he liked and respected the Japanese. Because of the education he received, judo, kendo, etc., he was very Japanese in his thinking. We found that we shared many interests. After dinner we went out on the town and got a little drunk. When we left the last bar, Dr. Wan insisted on walking back to the hotel with me. He said that everybody in town knew him, and that it was better if he went with me. I suppose I was a little drunk. The night was quiet and cool, the music over. Two police came past in heavy greatcoats, carbines over their shoulders. A bar girl hurried past, shamma over her head.

Once in bed, I lay awake thinking about Dr. Wan. He hadn't seen his wife and children for over two years. His work was hard, and largely without thanks. Every disease of domestic stock was prevalent: anthrax, rabies, rinderpest. He had done experiments under circumstances that were amazing even to me, who knew nothing about veterinary science. Where did he get the guts to stick to it? Two years without his wife and children. I hadn't seen mine for two months, and I felt it keenly. And it was much worse here than in the Arctic. There we traveled, fished, hunted, took samples. We didn't see many women. But here there were so many beautiful women, and they were so easy to have. It made you think about sex, even if you were scared of venereal disease and didn't intend to be unfaithful anyway.

❈❈◈❈❈

We had a couple of days to spend before Major Gizaw flew up, so Ermias, Abegas, and I went back to Debarek to look for a house to rent there. There was not really much looking to do. Only two places had cement floors, and only one place had windows with glass panes. We chose the latter, agreeing to share the rent with a teacher from the Debarek school. If we started work on the road out of Debarek, we would need this place.

We returned to Gondar on November 15. Major Gizaw was due to fly up from Addis Ababa the next day.

We went out to the airport that morning. I checked with the radio room to see if the Major had filed a flight plan. They radioed Addis Ababa, who said they knew nothing about it. We went back into town, guessing that he would come in the afternoon. We drove around, doing odd jobs in town. Around ten in the morning, as we came into the gravel driveway of the Iteghie Hotel we saw Major Gizaw and Dr. Bali, a botanist I'd met in Addis. He had come to Ethiopia in search of the rare Yeheb nut tree. This time, I guessed he came along for the ride. I got out of the car and went over.

"Major Gizaw! I'm glad to see you. We were just going to phone the airport to see if they got your flight plan and estimated time of arrival."

The Major was very angry, and blustered at me. "What do you mean, Nicol? Keeping us waiting out at the airport. You knew I was coming today, I told you so and you agreed to meet me."

I was taken aback, and argued with him. He pulled out a piece of paper and waved it. "Here is my flight plan."

I shrugged. "Well, Addis said you hadn't left."

Over coffee, I told Major Gizaw about the meeting with Dejasmatch Araya, and what Nadu and the others had said about him. I told him that this trouble would have to be cleared up before I could do anything. He said there was nothing to worry about, everything would be settled right away. I told him about my plans for development, a copy of which had already been sent. No trouble, said he. Go ahead with everything. We would go right now to see the Governor General, Colonel Tamurat.

There were always a lot of people waiting to see the Governor General. A fat agafari bowed in deference to Major Gizaw, and showed us through to a waiting room. In the corridor outside, priests sat robed in their black cloaks, with their white turbans, clutching silver hand crosses which the people kissed. We waited for quite a while before Major Gizaw went in. I got bored and leaned by the windowsill, watching little groups of people arguing and gesticulating outside the courthouse. I tried snap-punching flies buzzing around the room, and got one. Then Major Gizaw went in, and I was alone in the waiting room. Tried kicking at the buzzing flies. Gizaw came back.

"It's all settled. The Governor General has spoken to the Dejasmatch over the telephone and we will go around to his house now. He is in Gondar today, which is very lucky for us. I will explain to him, and if he still refuses to cooperate with us, His Excellency will speak to him again. But I am sure that he will cooperate; he knows now that these are the orders of His Imperial Majesty. Come on, Nicol."

Dejasmatch Araya's Gondar house was situated behind Fasilidas' castle. It was an Italian-built house, enclosed by a high stone wall.

Servants announced us, and the Dejasmatch himself came out, all smiles, kissing Gizaw, turning to me, shaking my hand, asking over and over again if I was well. He led us into his house and we sat in the drawing room. The furniture was lined up around the walls. It was battered, shoddy old Italian stuff. Clearly the Dejasmatch didn't place much importance on furniture. There were many photographs on the walls, mostly of the Dejasmatch, posing with this or that person, or glaring out in the typical, fierce, photograph stare of the Ethiopian, and there was one picture of him dressed as a patriot, cradling a rifle and swathed in bandoliers. A servant brought glasses of whiskey. While Dejasmatch was out of the room, Major Gizaw pushed his glass over to me and said I should drink it for him, as he had to fly and didn't want to take any alcohol. Dejasmatch Araya returned and sat by us. Major Gizaw spoke to him at length in Amharic. I understood very little, but gathered that he was going on about the benefits the national park would bring to the Simien, the money the tourists would bring into the country, and the fame which would spread.

Dejasmatch replied in loud, ponderous tones. Major Gizaw translated some of it. He would do anything to help me. At his orders five hundred peasants would start working on the road this month. In two months the road would be finished. I would have no trouble, for the people obeyed his orders. We would work together like brothers. Major Gizaw stood and bowed, making a speech of thanks. He promised that the Wildlife Conservation Department would get earth-moving machinery, dynamite, tools, money for culverts and bridges. Dejasmatch Araya said we should lend him a tent so that he could stay by the road head and supervise the work. He would not eat all day; he would simply chew on a stick. He would not rest until the road was finished. They would take the road through Sankabar and on all the way up through Amba Ras and Derasghie, where the Emperor Theodore was crowned at the church. Major Gizaw told me to make a note to give Dejasmatch a tent. I did so. Dejasmatch Araya said then that he would like some rifles and ammunition, so that he could arm some really good men to protect the Walia—brave, true men whom he would recommend himself. I also made a note of this, trying to suppress a grin.

"But I'm not going to give him any rifles or ammunition, Major

Gizaw. I can't spare them. I don't even have enough for our staff, and even if I had, I wouldn't give him any."

"It doesn't matter. I'll just tell him that we'll give him a rifle when we have a spare one."

"And what's all this about the Simien men being thieves and robbers? Your department hired them, you should find out about it. His accusations are serious."

Dejasmatch went into detail over this one, but Gizaw didn't translate. I decided I should study more Amharic. Gizaw turned to me, his tone confiding. "Nicol, His Excellency has some men we should hire. I've told him that he should consult you about it, as the responsibility is yours. But I think you should try to take some of them. We must cooperate."

It was as Nadu had said. "OK," I replied. "You send me the documents, salaries, extra rifles, ammunition, uniforms, and equipment, and I'll look over the men. If they're good I'll take them on probation. If they're no good, I won't."

Gizaw frowned, sounded impatient. "Of course, of course, it's your responsibility." More discussion with Dejasmatch Araya followed. Many promises. Yes, yes, the Wildlife Conservation Department would provide all machinery and tools, build bridges and culverts, blast rocks. Dejasmatch Araya would order out five hundred men a day, and stay on the job to see that they worked. They were all afraid of him. Before he came, the Simien was a nest of robbers; now they dared not take even a sheep. Bows and profuse thanks. More whiskey? No, thank you, lord, no. What? More whiskey? No, thank you, lord, no . . .

Outside, after more handshaking and bowing, we left him, he reminding us about the promise to give him a tent. As we drove off in the car I turned to Major Gizaw, shaking my head.

"I don't understand. He has completely changed his attitude, or apparent attitude, a complete about-face from the time I met him in Debarek. Do you think he means it this time?"

"Oh yes, now he has taken my advice and the advice of Colonel Tamurat and he knows why you are here."

I was puzzled. The change was too abrupt.

"And should I give him a tent?"

"Yes, I think you must."

"OK. I'll requisition one from headquarters; I can't spare one for him."

We had a late lunch at the Iteghie Hotel. It was past three in the afternoon, and Gizaw said they had to leave. Over the surrounding hills thunderclouds piled, black and purple-silver. Wind in gusts, buffeting the high-flying kites and vultures that always hang over the town.

"It looks bad, Major Gizaw. Do you have to go? Why not stay here until the morning? Then Dr. Bali can see the castles."

Dr. Bali said he didn't mind. Gizaw insisted that they should leave. The weather was nothing, it was clear in the direction which they were going, to Lalibela. They hurried through coffee and left. I said good-bye and went up to my room to write letters. The window was open. I looked out, listening to the slow roll of thunder, watching the circling kites.

A PLANE CRASH

When we were nearly ready to go back, Angelo, the assistant manager, called to me as I was entering the hotel.

"Mr. Nicol, have you been to the hospital?"

I stopped. "Hospital?"

"Didn't you know? Your friends with the plane. They crashed in Addis Zemen. They brought them back to Gondar last night."

I hurried to the emergency ward. A Swiss doctor came out, said he was sorry but they could have absolutely no visitors, no disturbance. I said I just wanted to know how they were, and what I could do to help, that Gizaw was my boss, and Bali my friend. The doctor said that Dr. Bali was regaining consciousness and would be all right, but that Major Gizaw was badly injured about the face and head. His condition was critical, but they thought he would live, although he had lost much blood and was still unconscious.

"You can just look through the door," said the doctor, "but don't try to speak to them."

I followed him. He pushed open a door on which there was a big sign in English and Amharic: "No Visitors." Major Gizaw lay completely still, his head swathed in bandages. Dr. Bali moaned, and the Swiss doctor went to him. I left quietly, took a horse-drawn gari (a little cart with two pneumatic wheels that will sit two people beside the driver) up to town, and telephoned Addis Ababa. After that I went up to see the Governor General, who let me in immediately. I said that Gizaw had important documents with him, as well as personal effects. I wanted to know who had taken them out of the wreck, and who was looking after them. The Governor General

A plane crash

phoned the police. He said he deeply regretted the accident, and that he had already been to the hospital. When I came out, Ermias and Abegas were waiting with the Toyota. I told them, and they said they would go to the hospital right away. I argued, said there was nothing we could do, that the hospital staff were busy enough without having to deal with visitors every five minutes.

"We must go," Ermias repeated. He said it was their duty. I went back to the post office and sent a cable to the department, just in case they hadn't really understood what I told them over the telephone.

We hung around in Gondar for a couple of days, in case we might be needed. People were coming up from Addis Ababa. Major Gizaw's wife flew up in the afternoon. There was a panic at headquarters, and work stopped. Later, I phoned them and told them they had to get money, equipment, and so on for the Simien. There had been a mix-up over our salaries. We needed tents, rifles, money, and many other things immediately. Time was short. With Major Gizaw in the hospital, Ato Balcha would have to take over, but when I spoke to him over the phone he was almost incoherent, and said it would have to wait until Major Gizaw recovered, that he himself had no authority to do this or that. I said that Gizaw could be in the hospital for months, that it couldn't wait. Ato Balcha was adamant. He had received no orders, and he could not do anything without authorization.

There was nothing to do but to fly to Addis and raise hell. Accident or no accident, time could not be wasted.

Various Ethiopians greeted me as I went in the office. Much handshaking. A few guards saluted, others just stared. The office people asked questions about the cold in the Simien, about Gondar, about Ermias' health. The headquarters at that time was in an old Italian-built two-storied house. Ato Balcha's office was on the second floor. I knocked, went in, and found Balcha behind his desk, looking worried. He seemed surprised to see me. The desk top was a mountain range of untidy papers. Balcha stood there, holding my hand. Ethiopians are forever holding hands. He was upset about the accident, it was so terrible for Major Gizaw, but God saved their lives, and that was a blessing. Balcha was a short, portly Galla, round-faced, with very closely cropped hair. His English was excellent, and he also spoke Italian, French, Galla, and of course, Amharic. He disliked responsibility, but he usually had to take it anyway. He had many children, six, I think. I said that now that Gizaw was out of action, he must take over and lead us, that the work must go on, and that by working we could prove to the Major that he could put his trust and faith in us. Balcha stuttered and seemed almost scared. He asked me to sit down, and called the office boy to bring me coffee.

Then I sat and waited for half an hour while Ato Balcha argued with the licensing officer and the accountant. Telephone calls and people with papers interrupted him throughout. He didn't seem to be getting anywhere.

Finally I stood up. "Look, Ato Balcha, I have flown down from Gondar to see you. There is a lot to do. Could you talk to me now, or give me a definite appointment later on this morning?"

"Oh, Mr. Nicol, sir, I am always ready to talk with you. You are working for the Simien, and it is our duty to help you, yes, in every way. We must do everything to help you."

Someone went on arguing in Amharic. I smiled, and started to go out. Balcha called me back, got angry with the others, told them to go out, to come back later, later.

"First of all, Ato Balcha," I said, "you are making me nervous. Please relax, be happy."

He sat down, complained about the unreliability of everybody in the office. I nodded and made sympathy noises, pulling out my plan for development of the park, as well as typed notes on the meeting and the agreements with Dejasmatch Araya. I told him it was imperative that we get bulldozers, money, and surveyors for the road, and that we had to start now. He stared at me, wide-eyed, and started telling me about the limits of his authority, that he couldn't do this, or that, or sign anything. I said that if he didn't, the development of the Simien Mountain National Park would be delayed another year, and that if the department wasn't going to do what I advised, and what we had discussed with Major Gizaw, the Governor General, and Dejasmatch Araya, then I might as well quit and stop wasting everybody's time and money. He got upset.

"But we didn't know anything about this road! We were advised by foreign experts to make a national park in the Simien, and we are trying to do it, but they didn't say anything about a road."

I looked at him in amazement. "How are we to develop a national park forty kilometers into the hills unless we have an access road to bring things in? How can we build? Or get tourists into the place?"

And anyway, I knew for damn sure that the original recommendations to establish a park in the Simien included the building of a Land Rover track from Debarek. Balcha obviously had not even read these. He insisted he could do nothing without Gizaw, it would have to wait. I went out and stormed in John Blower's office, cursing about Balcha, the department, and Ethiopians in general. John was annoyed too, but not surprised. He put down what he was doing and reached for some notepaper. John said that the road had always been a priority project, and it had been stated as such in all the reports by Leslie Brown, the wildlife expert with UNESCO, the one who first really recognized the danger of extinction of the Walia and the possibilities of a park in the Simien. John, who had been several times to the Simien on study visits, had also written a memo to Balcha about it.

⬕⬔⬕⬔⬕

While I was in the capital, Ermias returned to the Simien and established a camp in Sankabar, very near the site that I had chosen for my house. He was out on patrol one day with two guards when they heard shots. Two men were firing at something on the cliff. Walia maybe, or perhaps klipspringers. Ermias and the guards caught the men. They were tax collectors, arrogant, swaggering rifle carriers, working for Dejasmatch Araya. On seeing the uniforms and weapons of the guards, they became scared. One claimed that they had only been shooting at gelada. Ermias told them that he'd have to arrest them, as the gelada were protected. "No, no, we were just sighting our rifles on that mark on the cliff," said the other tax collector. Ermias scanned the cliff with binoculars. He could see no dead, fallen animal, and no scavenger birds circled there. Whatever they had been shooting at had escaped. They said they were on government business, that they shouldn't be disturbed. He could do nothing but let the men go, with a warning.

⬕⬔⬕⬔⬕

That night, after dinner with some friends at a Chinese restaurant in Addis Ababa, we came upon a man waving a big monkey-skin

45

rug at us. He was a Gurage tribesman. At least twenty gentle black and white colobus monkeys had died to make that rug. He had three or four other rugs over his arm. I told my friends to go on up to the Ras Hotel and wait for me in the bar. I showed the man my game warden's identification card. He smiled foolishly, backing away. I shouted at him and caught his elbow. He jerked his arm away and swore at me. Taking his arm and wrist, I spun into a hammerlock. He tried to struggle and kick me, but the hold was too painful. I marched him around the corner and up the road, past the front of the Ras Hotel and the coffee bar by the Imperial Theater. He howled all the way, and people stared. Street boys ganged up and followed behind. I thought I might have a fight on my hands, and hoped they didn't use knives. A policeman stood on duty at the traffic circle by the big stone lion. I stopped, and with my free hand, showed him the identification card, which said, in English and Amharic, that the bearer of the card should be given every assistance in the execution of his duty. It said I had the right of arrest, seizure, and inspection of licenses. The policeman took the card and stared at it for a long time. I knew that the police had been ordered to arrest people selling these rugs, and the man I caught was still hanging onto his wares. I told the policeman, in my poor Amharic, that he should take this man to the station. He glared at me, asking, "Where did you get this paper?" and "Who are you?" He wouldn't take the man, and started talking to me rapidly; I couldn't understand, but it sounded tough.

"Here, give it to me, you stupid son of a pig!" I snatched the card from him and shoved it in my pocket. We were surrounded by street boys and other people now. The man I had caught was wailing his woes to the sympathetic crowd. He was Ethiopian and I a *"feranji."* He tried to struggle, and I clamped onto him till he stopped. I would have gladly broken the bastard's arm. I found myself wondering, should I take him to the station myself? But how? I couldn't drag him about like this, or the crowd would start stoning me. Oh well. I let the man go and shoved him against the policeman. The policeman started toward me, his hand going to his gun. My hand coiled back and I crouched, looking him in the eye, madder than hell, not giving a damn. He was very close. He'd catch a good one before he ever got his gun out. He stared at me, and his hand came away. I relaxed, gathered a gob of spittle, and spat on his boots. I smiled at him, turned, and pushed through the crowd, heading toward the Ras bar for a drink. My friends asked what happened. I said nothing. But I was trembling with the after-reaction of my bad temper.

※※※※

The next morning, in the office, I complained about the incident to both Balcha and Zaudu, the licensing officer. They laughed, and teased me about it.

"Ah, Mr. Nicol, you will get beaten! They will fight you!" I told them to file a complaint against the police for failure to execute their duty. But they would do nothing. I said that we must arrange patrols through the town.

"But we do that. Lieutenant Berhanu does it with some game guards with the Volkswagen bus."

"Yes, but if I go with them, dressed as a tourist, and wander around, then we'll get more people. Those people probably know your vehicles and run. With me, we can catch them."

Neither Balcha nor Zaudu seemed interested. I spoke to the game guard lieutenant, but he was very vague, and I got the idea that he didn't want me to interfere. The records showed a ludicrously low rate of arrest and prosecution, a tiny fraction of what a good game department should expect to get. However, when I spoke to the game guards themselves in the yard, they were very enthusiastic, laughing, saying how many dealers they would catch. Tadessa, the fellow who had helped me with my visa, told me that what I wanted to do was dangerous, that the dealers would beat me up. I said I liked a good fight, and that anyway, it was our duty to do something. He said that some of the guards had been beaten up by skin dealers in the market, and the police then arrested the guards and put them in jail for several days.

"What?" I couldn't believe it. "Didn't the department do anything about it? What about Bekele?" He was the so-called legal officer. "Didn't he help them?"

Tadessa shook his head. One of the guards said that the people in

47

the department didn't want to help, and the men looked at each other meaningfully. The guards were all around us. Tadessa shook his head.

"It is dangerous, they can beat you with sticks." He picked up an axe handle leaning against the wall of an outhouse. "Like this." He swung the stick, not meaning to hit me. I sidestepped, blocked, caught his wrist, and feinted a chop to the back of his neck. The guards laughed and were impressed. Tadessa told them I had been trained in Japan, and some of the guards, who had served in the Imperial Bodyguard in the Korean campaign said that the Japanese were very strong. One of them took the stick. He said he had been two years in the commando, that the Imperial Bodyguard training was much better, and that I held the stick incorrectly. I grinned, took the axe handle and swung it slowly overhead. He stayed where he was, caught it with both hands, and tried to throw me in a back throw. He couldn't. I said that this was a good move for a very short club, but a bit dangerous if the club was long, like this one. I showed him how the stick could come out of my hands and clout him over the head if the block on my arm was strong and made me let go, and I said that if he made even a slight mistake, the stick could break his arm. To prove my point, I brought the axe handle down fast and hard, like a two-handed sword, stopping it just as it rapped his forearm, raised to block. The other guards nodded. They could see what I was trying to show them. They started to try it themselves.

The ex-commando, if indeed he was that, was annoyed. He took the axe handle, said that what I was showing them was only good if I did it slowly, and that he, with this club, could get me anytime he wanted. I told him to try it. The others stepped back, watching. He came in fast, taking me by surprise, swinging not at my head, but strong and viciously at my legs. I jumped, dodging the stick, and drove him against the outhouse wall, feinting blows to his nose, throat, groin, and stomach, and disarming him. The others laughed and the ex-commando grinned. Office workers, watching out of the windows, said I should teach everybody. The guards came around, yes, yes, I should go with them and catch lots of Gurage skin traders.

In truth, I had been a little bit shocked, for he very nearly got me. I was out of training, overconfident. If it had been a real fight I could easily have gone down.

Ato Balcha reacted to John Blower's note by saying that he hadn't really said that it was a new idea to build the road, and then he wrote some letters, one of them to the Imperial Highways Department. I said a survey should be done immediately, and I think that's what he wrote, though of course, the letter was in Amharic and I couldn't understand any of it. I got my salary fixed up, but the office staff said they couldn't do anything about the game guards' back pay. They were missing their salaries for last June, before I came. A game guard relative of Gizaw's wife had been sent up from Addis Ababa with the money, but had never delivered it. He was called into the office, and when asked about it he answered in a surly, superior manner that he had signed for the money and he should deliver it himself. As it was now late November, five months later, I thought it suspicious, but office staff assured me that the money would be sent through the bank in Gondar. My daily log was full of little jottings like that.

With John Blower's help I got tents, raincapes, uniforms, boots, water bottles, packsacks, and bandoliers for the Simien guards. Ato Balcha promised to bring it all up by Land Rover in a few days, as he was coming to Gondar to visit Major Gizaw.

Major Gizaw had regained consciousness and would live, but he was still weak and needed blood. General Seyoum, the big, bullet-headed police chief, marched a squad of volunteers from the police barracks to the hospital to donate blood for Gizaw. I went to give blood too, but I was the wrong type. By now, both Dr. Bali and Major Gizaw could sit up in bed. Dr. Bali looked fine, but Gizaw's face was badly smashed up. His fine, handsome, almost delicate features were gone, and he looked like a boxer. I guessed that he would have to have plastic surgery, but he was extremely lucky to be alive, and he knew it. If they hadn't hit a tree they would have flown into the side of a hill. The first thing that Gizaw did when he came to was to ask about the passengers, Dr. Bali, and one of Gizaw's relatives, who had come along for the ride. Although there was still a "No Visitors" sign on the door, the doctor had said I could go in, that I might as well ignore the damn sign, since all the Ethiopians did. There were people all around the bed. Gizaw asked about the way things were going in the Simien, and I said he shouldn't worry about the work, that it was all right. I felt embarrassed about staying against the doctor's wishes, so I left, just as Ermias and Abegas went into the room. For them, it was the second visit that day. They stood there, bowing and smiling and asking Gizaw over and over how he felt.

I wanted to go back to the Simien, but we had to wait until the Land Rover came with the tents and equipment. By the time it arrived, there were a hell of a lot of people just hanging around in Gondar; Ato Balcha, Ato Bekele, Fasil, two drivers from the department, a friend of Gizaw's, Ermias, myself, and Gizaw's wife. Just hanging around, going down to the hospital, waiting about in corridors or in the ward, bothering everybody. I thought it utterly stupid. His wife surely should be there, but not all the others, especially as it was clear he shouldn't have any visitors. I knew the doctors were getting upset, and I stayed away, and told his wife why I stayed away. In the end, the major himself got a little upset and told them to go back.

There was a telegram from the Emperor, and I think it was he who saw that a brain specialist flew up from Addis Ababa. Everybody went about with long faces, saying what a wonderful man Major Gizaw was, and what a good worker, and how brave, and tutting and sighing, shaking heads, even weeping. I became impatient. Flying into a tree didn't make him a martyr; it was an accident, through his own error, and he damn near killed two other people, besides writing off the department's plane. I was sick of them all. I ordered Ermias back to the Simien, and waited a couple more days, fuming and stamping, for some money to arrive at the bank. Abegas and I took all the gear, including eight rifles and a hundred and eighty-two rounds of ammunition for the guards, and drove it up to Debarek, where it was packed in by that old rascal Ineyu. I kept the rifles with me.

Once I'd collected the money, I stayed in Debarek, and sent Abegas back to Gondar, taking with him a hundred dollars for fuel, for which he signed a receipt, and which he was told very clearly was for fuel only. I thought Abegas would be useful to Major Gizaw's wife who would need transport while she was in Gondar.

The night was cold in Debarek. There were a few fleas and the odd bedbug in the bed, and pigeons clattered and cooed on the tin roof. At dawn the three game guards came with mules.

We set off through Debarek, with rifles and bandoliers over our shoulders like hill bandits. It was the day before market day in Debarek, and many people were coming out of the hills with their grain, chickens, eggs, and sheep. The guards were stopping continually to kiss and greet friends and relatives, losing the pack mules which trotted off to steal barley, or to roll on the ground. I became impatient and went on ahead. My mule, Abebich, moved quickly over the rough ground, and soon I had climbed the high hill onto the great ridge overlooking Debarek and its environs. There was no sign of the rest of the caravan, so I went on. Dark clouds and mist were rolling in over the hills, and it began to drizzle. Soon the fog was thick, and I couldn't really remember the path. I dismounted. Some shepherd boys were watching me. I called to them and waved, but they ran away as I approached, hiding behind bushes, stopping to watch. I went after them, walking. They ran again. I couldn't catch up with them.

A hamlet of round houses nestled in a hollow. Rain dripped off my hat and into my boots, and my hands were blotched red with cold. My pack and poncho were with the other mules. Damn fool. I led the mule down among the houses and called out. The people were hiding inside, and I called for a long time before one old woman peeped out.

"What is it?" she asked.

"I am the Walia guardian," I answered, in my bad Amharic. "Sankabar . . . this road? That road?" I pointed.

Other people came out of the low-walled thatched houses, two grown men, several women and girls, a few children. Their dress, and the silver crosses around the women's necks, told me they were Christians. They gabbled at me, asking about my guards. I pointed back toward Debarek.

"Four mules, four men, later," I said. Again I asked about the road to Sankabar. The old woman pointed to the sky, to my wet clothes. It was raining quite hard, and the fog was growing thicker. Thunder rolled. The wind was turbulent, tumbling clouds over the slopes, for we were close to the great faces of the escarpment. The people invited me into one of the houses belonging to a young weaver and his wife. A loom, simply made of wood and cord, was set in a shallow hole in the earthen floor of the house. Sheepskins were laid at the edge of the hole, and the weaver sat on them, his legs in the hole, working the loom, weaving white cotton gabis. I sat in the dark house, watching him work, smoke from the central fire stinging my eyes, and it was as if my world became lost to me in the dark and the smoke and the sounds; unreal and distant, and I felt out of place, an invisible intruder from another time, for this young man, and his house and loom, and his young wife in her long, dirty gown, her hair braided and buttered, and the yells of boys herding goats into the rough, nettle-filled compound, and the roll of thunder in ancient hills, all these belonged to a time far removed from my age and my people.

A small boy came into the house and told me that Abebich was grazing. The young man stopped weaving and came to sit across the fire from me, gazing into my face. His wife broke twigs and arranged them on the ashes, blowing the coals until flame danced and crackled, illuminating, the low, smoke-tarred poles of the roof. The fireplace was a circle of round stones. There was no chimney, no window, and the door, low and uneven, was closed by a roughly tied frame of tree heather branches. Children gathered in the doorway, staring and giggling at me. The young man pointed to the rifle; he seemed nervous about it. I'd taken the magazine out when I came into the village, but he was still nervous. I slipped the bolt out and put it in my pocket, passing the rifle over to him. He wanted me to give it to him; I shook my head, said it belonged to the government. A girl of about fourteen ducked in through the door. She smiled at me and chattered brightly to the young wife. The old woman came in, and we all sat around the fire. The wife took a flat pan of beaten iron and laid it on the fire. She poured a little water onto it, wiped it around with her hand, and tipped the water off. Then a handful of coffee beans, and more water, washing off the beans and tipping away the water again. A little more water was poured on, and the beans stirred around with a twig as the water boiled, sizzled, and evaporated on the hot pan. Once the water had boiled off, the coffee beans roasted with a superb smell. With this done, she put the roasted beans into a small wooden mortar and pulverized them with an iron pestle, some kind of a bar from a machine. Thud, thud, thud as she pounded, crouching, heavy breasts moving under the loose cotton gown. The younger girl laid out a few coffee cups, small, with no handles, rather like Japanese sake cups. She swilled them out, using her hand, tipping the water onto the floor. Water was boiling in a kettle. The grounds were tipped in and the coffee made. It was bitter and strong. The woman passed the cups around, filling them as soon as they were emptied. The coffee is made three times with the same grounds, and to be well mannered, you must partake of each brew.

A child brought a hatful of small chicken eggs. I paid for them, and the old woman boiled them for me. There was coarse barley bread too, and in my pocket I had a big bar of milk chocolate. I offered pieces of it to the young man and the women. It wasn't a fast day, a Wednesday or Friday, when they could take no animal products, but they refused nonetheless.

"Milk, sugar, stuff like coffee, very good, eat," I said, taking a piece myself. They refused, a look of ill-disguised disgust on their faces. I gave a bit to the boy who brought the eggs. He took it, sniffed it, and threw it on the floor. Surprised, and maybe a little offended, I ate the rest myself.

Night came, and the mist bound tighter and tighter about the hunchbacked houses and the dark, weird, ghostly trees that knelt and bowed about the hillsides. The game guards had surely taken a different path. The old women said I should sleep the night and I resigned myself to it, partly, I suppose, for the experience. I had no sleeping bag with me, but I surely couldn't find the path now. A heifer came to the door and pushed its head inside. The young man gave it salt, and it stood there, snuffling and crunching. The girl kept saying, "Salt, salt," and making eating motions, rolling her eyes, grinning at me. I smiled back. The old woman laughed and said I should take the girl with me to Sankabar, to be my wife.

"I have a wife," I said. "She will come in five, six months."

"Long time, long time," said the old woman, and the girl stared and smiled. I shook my head and smiled back.

Her fingers were fast and busy, spinning cotton with a hand bobbin into thread for her brother's loom. The cotton came from the borders of the Sudan, by donkey caravan. The Simien weavers made it into thick, warm gabis to sell in the markets, at Debarek, Zarema, Adi Arkai, or the hill markets in the mountains. Old trails scarred the Simien, old and deep, for the people had moved thus over the hills since Bible times, and little was changed.

An older man came in, father of the weaver. He had been plowing. He was tall, his head shaven, teeth all brown and snaggled. He greeted me, and we sat by the fire, talking about the people we knew, about Nadu, so good, brave, strong, and Nadu's brother—and Guard Mitiku, and Guard Ambaw, and Dejasmatch Araya, who was a *"tillick sou,"* a big man. He called for talla, and the wife brought it to us in horn cups, tipping a little into her palm and sipping it first before handing it to us. It was the thick barley beer of the Simien, looking more like liquid mud than anything else. He messed about with my rifle, and asked me to give him one, and to make him a Walia soldier, for he was a good man, and knew all the Walia, and I was his lord. If he had a rifle, no man would come here without his knowing.

It was very dark now. Opaque and wet, the mist flashed blue-white and silver with the lightning. We were swallowed in the guts of the thundercloud, and the growl and roar of it were almost continuous. Yellow light from the fire flickered over the faces around me. It was a night for ghosts, for the dead to rise from the tree-hidden graveyard on the hill, and for the evil prowling of hyena men. Tired and cold, I let my mind weave fantasies about time, and only my clothes and my rifle were of the twentieth century. The mud on the walls was cracked, and much of it fallen, and wind gusted in, scattering ashes and smoke.

In the Simien, the people go to sleep early, for there is no light but the flickering fire, and the mountain air grows bitter cold at night. Injera and wat, filling, hot, spicy, and rich in proteins, are the national food of the Amhara people, and I had thought that this is what they usually ate, but in the Simien, the peasants very rarely had such fine food, only on special feast days. It was a diet for the rich, for the big men. These people ate a meager supper of talla and roasted barley and the eggs which I had bought. They had lots of eggs, but they kept them to sell in the market. Everybody left except me, the young man, and his wife. I put the wooden saddle at the head of the sheepskin by the dying fire, curled up in a ball and tried to sleep. My host nudged me, pointing to a high cot, woven out of branches, covered with skins of sheep and goat. I shook my head, no, no, I couldn't take his bed. He insisted and I gave in, taking off my boots to climb onto the cot. He gave me an old, threadbare gabi, filthy dirty. It was bitter cold, and damp from the mist. The cot was lumpy, and over a foot too short, and it was high, right against the sloping roof, so that my eyes smarted and watered with the smoke. The young man lay with his wife on a cowhide on the rough dirt floor, sleeping in their clothes as they always did. The uncomfortable cot irritated me, and I was cold and bothered by the smoke, the drafts through the walls, the damp, and the smell of the dirty gabi, the animal skins, my own clothes. Trying to concentrate, I put strength in my belly, trying to force my body to generate warmth. And then, my God, the fleas! They were all over me, crawling, biting, biting. I scratched, wriggled, tossed, turned. Fleas, all the damned night, cold, and the fleas.

With relief, at first light I climbed down from the bed, went out shivering, and climbed up the hill to wash my face in a small, icy-cold stream. My whole body ached and itched, and I scratched my groin with a fury, shuddering at the thought of it. How the hell could people live that way! Those people live worse than animals, I thought, and felt shame, for they had treated me with kindness, and generosity, and they had little to give. I jumped about to get warm, did breathing exercises, chopped the edges of my hands against the trunk of a small tree. But for all their generosity, certainly that would be the last night I slept in a peasant's house. The cold one could do something about, and the smells, and the smoke, and the dirt were nothing, but the fleas, God! From now on, I'd be damned sure to travel equipped with poncho, sleeping bag, billy, and food.

I caught and saddled Abebich. The young man said he would guide me to Sankabar for two dollars. It was expensive, but I agreed, even though I was sure of the way now in the early morning light. He took his stick, and a new gabi, and we went through the woods of giant heather, all clean and fresh in the cold air, dew clinging like diamonds to the maidenhair lichens and the close-cropped grass. He stopped after a kilometer and asked for the money. I gave him a dollar, saying he would get the rest when we got to Sankabar. He started whining, making those disgusting begging motions with hands and fingers, and this disappointed me, for I had been a guest in his house, and felt that he should have trusted me.

Halfway there we heard voices and the thin note of a bugle. It was Ermias and a search party of guards, out looking for me. They said they had searched in the night, and I felt sorry, for I had been careless; I never thought that anybody would worry over me, for I had been on many expeditions in the Arctic, and traveled alone. Ermias feared that the mule had kicked me, and that I was lying on the way, injured. He thanked the young man, telling him he was a Christian, and a good Ethiopian. I gave him the second dollar, and apologized to Ermias, but I felt pleased at his initiative and concern. Ermias was a good man.

The camp he had set up at Sankabar was a good one, neat and orderly, with my tent and his set on a knoll with fantastic views all around. We sat in Ermias' tent and he brewed a big potful of coffee; we drank large enamel mugs of it, strong and sweet, creamy with canned milk. Ermias made spiced omelets and brought out a bowl of a strongly spiced hard cake or biscuit, made from barley flour and butter. Ermias said this was the richest, most concentrated food they had, and this was what their warriors used to carry with them to battle. It was good. The sun rose high and warmed the camp.

I boiled up some hot water and stripped outside the tents. I counted over a hundred dead fleas in my undershirt, killed by my scratching throughout the night. The seams of all my clothes were thick with them. It is hard to kill a flea, so I don't like to think of how many got away. I found many fat, disgusting white lice. My whole body was peppered with bites, as if I had caught a pox. Underclothes and shirt I boiled outside in a bucket, and the rest I soaked in insecticide and scrubbed. I took a pair of scissors and cut off all my pubic hair and much of the hair off my head, and I washed with hot water, soap, and disinfectant. When I had finished washing and dusting myself down, it looked as if I had just finished raping a flour sack. I sat on the grass, hooting with laughter at the thought. I used a whole spray bomb on the inside of the tent and the grass around it. Then I changed into clean clothes. It felt good. Ermias was shocked when I told him about the fleas, but he must have known.

A few guards reported for their back pay. We dealt with them, assigned a couple of anti-poaching patrols, and in the afternoon labored at breaking out stones for the buildings in Sankabar.

THE GUARDIAN
OF THE WALIA

The game guards were still sitting in a semicircle by the fire outside their tents. They were swaddled and hunched in their gabis like old women. I came up the slope, all sweaty and dusty, stripped down to shorts and heavy boots, hands all stiff from jabbing and yanking on the six-foot crowbar, from swinging the heavy sledgehammer, and from carrying slabs of rock from the bluff, from which I had broken them, to the building site above. I laid the tools by my tent, wiped myself off with a wet cloth, and brewed tea. It was late afternoon. The guards had sat around the fire all day, from the time I started work in the morning, through lunch break, and half the afternoon. I was curious. How long would they stay like that? I sat on the camp bed, sipping tea, trying to figure them out. They were so different from any other people I had known or worked with. If I gave a direct order—do this, do that—they did it quickly enough, and when I passed by them carrying water, they jumped up to take it from me. Ermias had told them that while he was away they were to help me with the work. Yet they had let me work alone for two days. Out of sight, out of mind. Of course I could, and should, have ordered them to work, but I wanted to see what they would do without direct orders.

Ermias and Nadu were out of camp, gone to buy mules for the park. I was breaking and carrying field stones for the foundations of my house. The rock was tough, volcanic basalt. Coolies from Geech were supposed to come to work for me, but they had not yet arrived. The fierce mountain sun had burned my back, arms, legs, neck, and face, but I felt fit, muscles slightly sore from the work.

The altitude here was around ten thousand eight hundred feet, and I had a little difficulty with my wind, but that was improving. I liked to work with my body, and could not understand the Simien guards. They had all been farmers before the government had employed them as game guards, and farmers are usually hard-working men. I finished the tea, picked up the tools, and went back to work, leaving the guards still sitting around their fire. Tomorrow was a holy day, the feast of some saint or other, and they certainly wouldn't do anything then.

As it happened, the next day the sunburn on the backs of my legs was so bad I could hardly walk. The guards invited me to drink talla with them. Game Guard Techale had been giving an impassioned speech to the other men. Techale was a Christian Amhara from Shoa Province, in the south. The department sent him to Simien on probation, for he had been kicked out of the other parks for causing trouble. He was not a big man, but thin and wiry like so many highland Ethiopians. He was about thirty years old. Techale was subject to strange, morose fits, erupting in violence. His temper was terrible, but the other side of his character was honest, generous, and loyal to those whom he respected. He was a good soldier, with ribbons from the Congo campaign, where he had fought with the UN forces. He spoke a little English, and with that, and my pitiful Amharic, he tried to explain what he had been talking about.

"Sir. Awash, Omo, lots of money, allowances, new uniforms. Simien, nothing. Awash, beds, blanket, lamp, good house, can bring wife. Simien much cold, only tents, no good money, no blankets. Nothing. Office people, no good, no good."

I listened to him, and understood that the guards in the other parks were receiving a special field allowance, but the Simien men were not. This was certainly unfair. Techale said that Major Gizaw refused the allowances for Simien. The conditions here for the men were at least as tough, if not tougher than conditions in the other parks. Techale said the men were entitled to blankets, heavy overcoats, beds, mattresses, lamps, a fuel supply. He was probably right. What little money and equipment I had received to date was a tiny fraction of what the Simien project was supposed to get, and what equipment I had gotten for the men had only been obtained through a lot of argument in Addis Ababa. I made notes, and prom-

58

ised them I would try to get them all they were entitled to. I wondered, however, if they would earn it.

The Simien-born men were proud of their new positions. They had good rifles, and uniforms, and a monthly salary, which, though it was very little, was more than they had ever received before. Guard Tedla had been a vigilante leader, and some said he was a shifta. Turu, Berehun, and Mitiku were relatives of Nadu, and although they owned land, it was poor, and gave little return for their labors. Nagur, the youngest of the guards, was from Silky Mountain, two or three days' journey away to the northeast. He understood things better than the others, he could read and write, and had served in Gambella with a Peace Corps volunteer who did game surveys down there. His father was a captain of the vigilantes. Quarrelsome old Kasahun, from Tigre Province, had been kicked out of the other parks too, for fighting and arguing. He must have been over fifty—his hair was white, and his face lined—but he was lean and active, with as much stamina on the march as any of them. Both he and Mitiku spoke some Italian. There were twenty game guards on the roll, but several of them had not reported for duty. There was a lot I wanted to say to the men, but it would have to wait until Ermias got back.

In the evening, I went out alone and sat on the cliff top, watching the Walia grazing on ledges below, and the sailing flight of the big birds.

Later, after Ermias came back with mules he had bought for the park, he translated a lecture I gave to the guards, telling them that they were not children, and we did not wish to have to order them about all day, but if we had to, we would. They looked ashamed, and the next day they began to work.

❈❈❈❈

What with working, cooking, washing up, tidying, writing reports, patrols, and all the other jobs to be done, I felt I should take advice and get a servant. It would be the first time in my life I had ever used a personal servant, and I found it strangely embarrassing. All the guards had their women servants, for they considered it undignified for a man to cook, or carry wood and water. I asked Nadu to find me a reliable man, and in a few days he brought a man to camp. The man he brought looked young, but was in fact several years older than I. He was of medium height, with a fine, intelligent face. He wore the baggiest homemade shorts, a ragged shirt, and a gabi. Nadu said that his man, Abahoy, was like a son to him. He assured me that he was trustworthy. I liked Abahoy from the start, and took him on at a salary of forty dollars a month, just a little more than the guards were getting so that they would not look down on him for being a servant. His duties were to keep my tent clean, wash my clothes, and fetch water and wood. Most of the cooking I could do myself. Abahoy learned quickly. He learned how to light the primus, fill the pressure lamps, take the lid off the pressure cooker. Each time I came in he had hot tea waiting for me. He was quiet and didn't argue or cringe. My clothes were clean, the tent tidy.

On December 5, Nadu invited us to Amba Ras to take part in his harvest feast. We left in the early morning, Ermias, Abahoy, and four guards. The weather was superb, and the sun glinted yellow and gold off the fields of ripe barley. Bishop birds darted among the heavy heads of grain, and the pathways were lined with flowers. Doves whirred in flocks over our heads. The Amba Ras plateau was gentle; it was high, but the fields and meadows rolled almost like the English countryside, except that there were no trees. It was bordered on all sides by deep gorges and the mighty cliffs of the escarpment. At the head of the Amba Ras, the cliff fell sheer for over three thousand feet, and tumbled another two thousand into steep valleys. As we went along, people called out to us, for they knew we were guests of honor at Agafari Nadu's feast.

Guard Mitiku strode beside our mules. As we passed a pile of rubble he pointed to it.

"Felasha," he said. "Our people fought with them and drove them off Amba Ras Mountain."

I asked if there were many wars in the old days.

"By the truth, there were wars when the Islam armies of Gran invaded the land. But they could not conquer Simien."

On asking Ermias about the rubble, he said it had once been a Felasha synagogue. The Christian Amharas of the High Simien had, in their history, fought and defeated the other religions and tribes, but now there was peace, thanks to God and His Majesty.

The guardian of the Walia

When we reached Nadu's home, the guards went forward to bow and kiss him. The harvest was in progress. A line of about a hundred and fifty villagers advanced on the barley, grasping it with the left hand, cutting it with a sickle in the right. They moved slowly up the hill, chanting, a sound that rose and fell with an old rhythm of life and urgency. They sang of their own prowess and strength, and of the generosity and goodness of the great Agafari Nadu. He stood on a rocky mound with me, Ermias, and a fat ex-Imperial Bodyguard captain, who was his brother-in-law. Like ants, lines of people followed the advancing cutters, and hurried to and from the felled barley, tying it in bundles, carrying them on their heads to the stacks. Two forty-five-gallon drums of talla and dozens of drinking horns, some of them made from the horns of Walia were placed up by the stacks. As they felt the need, the people dipped a horn and drank. We drank too, and felt gay in the sun and the golden barley. Ermias and I joined in, Ermias singing and cutting, and I carrying bundles of grain on my head to the stacks. The villagers cheered and laughed, clapping at the sight. It was high here, over eleven thousand five hundred feet, and my chest heaved with the effort. More and more talla was forced upon me until I had to give up, to stretch out on a rock and sleep.

By five o'clock in the evening, an hour before the sun dipped down over the ridge of Sankabar and the distant cone of Wokun hill, the harvest was all cut and stacked. Nadu led the way up to his house and welcomed us in for the great feast. The people followed, chanting and singing. Nadu's house was big, seven or more meters in diameter, with walls of stone. A low earthen bench, covered with skins, ran around the walls. In the center of the house, just away from the pole, was the fire, as in all the other houses I had been in. The roof was thickly thatched, with no chimney, and the door was made of thick, rough-hewn cedar planks. On one side of the house stood high, wide earthen urns, full of grain. Nadu was a rich man. He had barley and teff from land he held in the low, warm valley of the Balagas River, below Amba Ras. He had many sheep and goats, cattle, horses, mules, and many servants and followers. One servant was pure Negro, and they called him "slave."

Women servants brought warmed water to wash our hands, and set grass-woven baskets before us, laden with fresh injera and hot wat sauce. An oxen was slaughtered, and the meat brought in great raw hunks for us to carve off with the curved daggers set out for us. The raw meat was dipped in fiery-hot red-pepper paste and eaten with the injera. I loved it, and decided to worry about tapeworms later. The villagers sat outside, and Nadu's servants and followers brought them meat, injera, and talla. It was a vast noisy throng. Nadu was greatly respected by the people, and they blessed him. The ex-captain said that Nadu held a great feast every year, that any villager short of barley for food had only to ask him, and that all travelers passing through Amba Ras were brought to his house to eat with him. He was their lord, and his father before him had been their lord. It was Nadu who built the new stone church in the village, and it was he who kept law and order there. Nadu's elder brother, who lived in Debarek, was chief of the vigilantes, and they kept the people protected from the shifta, and settled many of the blood disputes which often occurred over the sharing of tribal land.

We feasted and drank until we were utterly satiated. I had eaten raw meat while living with Eskimos, but had forgotten how heavy it lies on the stomach. Nadu kept urging, "Eat, eat more, for the love of Mary, for my sake and happiness, eat, for you have eaten little, only a little, eat, eat." My head spun, sweat broke out all over my body, the roof pressed in closer, closer, and all became diffused with gray. I fainted. Ermias shook me.

"Mr. Nicol! Mr. Nicol!"

I came round, my trousers wet from the horn of talla that had slipped out of my hand. Breath came hard, and the grayness clung to me.

"Excuse me, I'd better go out."

Out of the dark, smoky house into the cool night air. People called out to me, many of them still ate and drank. Was I drunk? I stood on one leg, touching forefingers. Don't think so. My lungs were straining for air. Somebody once warned me: Don't eat too much when you're tired at high altitudes. That's what it was, altitude sickness. I went back into the house and sat on the bench, leaning against the wall.

Coffee was served, with the same ceremony I had observed in the peasant's house I had stayed at. Nadu had a radio, and listened to the news. He was a very advanced man for the Simien. Oryx horns hung on a cupboard against the walls, a souvenir of his stay in Awash Park. He told Ermias and me what great friends he had been with Peter Hay, and how Mr. Hay had said, "You are the only man who can work harder than I." I couldn't imagine Hay saying that.

The ex-captain was boasting. He had served with the UN forces in the Congo, and in fact, Techale had been under him at that time. The others listened in awe as the ex-captain told them stories of the fighting, and of the bravery of the Ethiopian soldiers. They were the bravest, fiercest, and strongest fighters in the world, and every Ethiopian was a hero.

We slept in Amba Ras that night, Ermias and I sharing a cot in an outhouse. There were a few fleas, but I had dusted my sleeping bag with powder before coming, so I slept well enough.

When we left, Nadu and his servants accompanied us as far as the church, carrying our weapons. The guards stopped at the outer walls of the church to kiss the walls and pray. Tall, lonely eucalyptus trees stood by the round church, and erosion gullies spread everywhere on the boulder-strewn slopes.

On the way back, Techale picked a fragrant herb and stuffed pieces of it up his nostrils. He said that it protected people against vampires and wizards, and he delivered this with a dark look. He did not like Nadu.

❈❈❈❈

Eucalyptus poles and logs were needed for the building of my house in Sankabar. The nearest groves were at Michibi, about an hour and a half's ride from our site. Nadu and the ex-captain came down the day after the feast, stopping at my tent for coffee and bread. Together we galloped along the narrow, dusty path cut into the rocky sides of the Khabar Valley. We charged along, a band of horsemen, mule riders, and runners, racing the animals to their utmost, yelling, whooping, jostling for position, hooves pounding, servants and guards running behind, urging the animals to go faster. Nadu and I raced, slashing at overhanging thorn branches with machetes, rifles crashing up and down on our backs. We reached the wide meadow of Michibi, laughing and breathless. The captain said good-bye and welcomed us to drink at his house in Debarek. We thanked him and rode off to see the eucalyptus trees, and to argue about the price.

The largest house was that of a balambat (elder) of Michibi, an old man called Techane. Techane came out of the house to greet Nadu. We said we wanted to buy trees, and surprised the old man, for he had never sold trees before. He led us around the groves by his house. Other people came from nearby houses, and we looked at their trees too. We bargained for thirty big trees and many small ones from the old man, and for lots of twenty or so from some of the others. Some of the people asked ridiculously high prices for the trees, five or six times the price in Debarek, and although we knew they needed money, they would not come down. The bargain was sealed with old man Techane. We promised to come the next day with the money and fell the trees. The old man invited us into his house. It was very big, elliptical, measuring about thirty by twenty feet inside, and with a roof peak at least eighteen feet above the dirt floor. He served us coffee and a basket of roasted barley and peas.

Like everybody else I had talked to, the old man wanted to be a game guard and have one of our rifles. He had an old Italian gun, but it was in poor condition. He told us how he had protected the Walia ever since the Emperor had given his orders that the beast should not be harmed. The guards laughed at him. No, he said, I know about the Walia. Then he told us a legend.

"As everybody knows, the Walia are holy animals . . ." He looked about. The game guards nodded, yes, yes, that is right. "When the saint, Kedus Yared, returned from Jerusalem, bringing with him many holy books, he had the Walia carry these books on their backs, and he said, thereafter, that the Walia were holy, and the church has protected them." The guards nodded, yes, that was true.

"Well, the old people said that the Walia would be almost destroyed, until in the end, foreigners would come to protect the Walia, until again they would thrive, and one day a white man would ride a Walia into the church of St. Michael in Amba Ras."

I was astounded. Was the old man certain there was such a story? If so, it could be used to help us. Ermias questioned him. Yes, he was certain, he had heard the story from his father's father, before the Fascists came. In that case, why did the people shoot and kill so many Walia? They all answered that this happened during the Italian occupation, when people fled and hid in the Simien, and they had many rifles. At that time they shot the Walia for meat. Perhaps they did not know the animals were sacred, perhaps God would forgive them in those times of war. One guard, a Christian, said that it was the work of the Moslems, who did not consider the Walia a sacred animal, but the others argued with him.

On the way back, Ermias and I talked about this legend. These people must have a wealth of folklore and stories; what a pity it was not to really understand them! Below, in the lowlands beneath the great cliffs, forest fires flickered and looped here and there, in red necklaces, around hills as far as I could see.

Abahoy came with Nadu to my tent as I was drinking tea with Ermias. Nadu told us, after a lot of preliminary palaver, that the second batch of trees, the lot by the ruined house behind old man Techane's house in truth belonged to Abahoy.

"Why didn't he come with us today? We could have agreed on the price with him, and not with that other man." Ermias listened as Nadu talked, corrected from time to time in his telling of the story by Abahoy himself.

Then Ermias spoke. "If Abahoy goes to Michibi, Techane's son will kill him. Last year they had a quarrel, and Abahoy stabbed the son and ran away, hiding in the hills. Later, they made an agreement, and now Abahoy must pay five hundred dollars to the man. Techane is his uncle."

"Did he kill the son?"

"No, he wounded him, but seriously. You saw the son today, the skinny one; he was carrying a rifle. His name is Abahoy too."

"OK. I'll pay the money to him. Write out a receipt, please, Ermias."

I counted seventy one-dollar notes and handed them to Abahoy. He signed his name slowly and carefully on the receipt. He began to count the money, but Nadu took it from him, counted ten dollars, gave the ten to Abahoy, and stuck the rest in his pocket. They argued. I was puzzled.

"Agafari was a mediator in this case," explained Ermias.

"What did they quarrel about?"

Ermias translated the question. Abahoy burst into a flood of impassioned eloquence.

"You know, when he gets excited, I can hardly understand him; his Amharic is different from mine," said Ermias. "He says the other man stole his grain and his chickens, and came with a rifle to kill him, but his aunt got the rifle, and then Abahoy got angry and stabbed him in the stomach."

"Well, tell him not to stab anybody around here."

Ermias told him he had to behave here, and both he and Nadu denied strongly that any such thing could ever happen again.

Cutting and trimming the trees was two days' hard work, spaced by lunch breaks in old man Techane's house, drinking talla and eating his roasted barley and beans. He said one day he would kill a sheep for me. Chickens pecked about inside the house. I was sitting on a low-backed stool made of wood and leather. I scooped up a chick, held it up, and stroked it. Guard Berehun said something, and they all looked at me.

"He says you are a very kind man, and you love animals," said Ermias.

"I do," I said to Ermias, "but it wouldn't stop me from popping this little fellow in the pot when he gets bigger."

The old woman looked at me, spoke to Nadu and then to Ermias, who laughed and hung his head.

"They want to know if you do not miss a woman."

"Of course I do, I am a man," I answered.

The old woman spoke again, eyes very serious, and the old man looked intently at me.

"They say that for fifty dollars you can have their daughter, take her to Sankabar with you to be your wife."

I was startled, because they weren't joking. "I have a wife, she is coming in a few months," I said. "She would kill me."

Nadu laughed. "She will never know!" He looked at all the other guards, who were grinning. "Our wives don't know." Ermias laughed as he translated. "These men, you see, have so many wives, he has four, he has three." The guards laughed and joked about it. Mitiku was accused of having six, each in a different village. The women looked on solemnly. I shook my head. I was a coward, I said, and though she was beautiful, I dare not risk it. I looked across at the daughter, who was staring at me. She was extremely pretty, perhaps seventeen or eighteen, with a full, round body and fine, heavy breasts. My God, life was cheap here if that was all their daughter meant to them. There was a baby in the house. Perhaps it was hers, and certainly she had no husband. I found it hard to keep my eyes off her.

"What about you, Ermias?" I asked.

"No, I have a fiancée," he said. But the Simien men thought he was even stranger than I for not taking a woman.

Sonako and I had been married for six years. She had been to Canada with me, lived in Montreal, stayed there alone while I went on three Arctic expeditions, two whaling trips, and three sealing trips for the Canadian Government. She went with me to Nova Scotia while I was working at a whaling station there, and we lived in a little cabin by the sea, with her belly heavy with our first child. Now she was in Tokyo, but when the house was ready she would come to Ethiopia. It worried me. Would she like the country? Could I get the house built in time? And the road? Could she take the isolation and the many annoyances of Ethiopia? I missed her so much, and counted off the months, weeks, days.

The house. With inadequate funds, and no road, it was going to be a big task. Only the stone was local, and that had to be broken out of the hillsides and carried by hand to the site. The timber, cement, sand, tin sheets, nails, windows, thatch, everything had to come in by pack animal or coolie.

The felled, stripped trees at Michibi were split by a carpenter who lived in Debarek. This timber would go to make the walls of the house. In the future, all the other houses I built in the Simien would be of stone, but at this time I had been led to believe that building with eucalyptus would be quicker and cheaper. The split logs were dragged by teams of oxen to the head of the trail to Sankabar. From this point, our coolies had to carry them, a log at a time, to the site. In a day, a man could only carry two logs. I carried some myself, and knew that it was a hell of a job. Nadu had an idea. If I would pay to have a lot of talla made, and set a tent aside, with lots of drinking horns, then he and some of the guards would go to the head of the trail on the day the villagers came back from market. He would entreat each villager to carry one log or roof pole to Sankabar. In return for this, they would get a rest and free talla at our camp. On the day after the Debarek market, two hundred or more people would pass through Sankabar. If Nadu's idea worked, it was brilliant. He assured me it would work, and I gave him ten dollars for the first batch of talla. He said the people would do anything he ordered them to. I insisted that he should not order them, but rather ask them, and to repay them with talla was fair enough.

And sure enough, a week later, the logs began to arrive in a steady dribble with the returning villagers. Few of them refused Nadu. Abahoy and his wife, Mollu, were kept busy, pouring and serving the talla. Nadu said the people were glad that we had chosen to make a camp in Sankabar, and they blessed us, for now they could pass in safety, day or night, whereas before, this place had been notorious for bandits. With a government camp here, the bandits would not return.

Ermias and I marked out the foundation of my house. Like the traditional houses of this area, it would be round, for I wanted it to blend with the country. It would consist of three round houses, linked by short corridors, with a kitchen annex adjoining the central rondavel. The central rondavel would be the living and dining room. It would have a big fireplace and would be six meters in diameter, with one third of the wall, the part backing onto the fireplace, built of stone. The two rondavel wings would be five meters in diameter and would be used as bedrooms and storerooms. The walls, built of logs, would be plastered with a mud wattle, and then again with small stones and cement on the outside to make it weatherproof. The floors would be of cement; the roof a frame of strong poles, over that tin sheets, and over that a grass thatch, for warmth and beauty. To hide the ugliness of the tin inside the house, we would make a latticework of bamboo slats for the ceiling, or we could use the tough, attractive reed mats that the lowland people used on their beds. The house would have many windows, pre-made in Gondar, and outer wooden shutters.

The site of the house was as fine as any I had seen. It would be in a small meadow, sheltered by surrounding trees on protecting hillsides. Each window would command a fantastic view. To the escarpment edge was a mere two hundred yards, but to get to the cliffs, one had to pass natural barriers, woods, tight and close-grown, a series of rocky outcrops, the cracked and eroded faces of an old lava flow, over which a small stream from the spring by the house trilled its way in a series of waterfalls and cold, clear pools. Thus, we would have the superb escarpment views, but would be protected from the horror of having a young child toddle down to the edge and fall off. The sun rose and warmed the hollow at about seven in the morning, and winds that were strong a little higher up could hardly be felt. It was a fine, fine place, and already the giant, orange- and red-bellied lammergeyers cruised in easy flight over the place, looking for scraps, and around our nearby camp the thick-billed ravens contested for scavenging rights in their throaty squawks.

The dysentery which I had contracted on my way up from Addis Ababa began to get worse, and there was blood in my feces. I was getting weak and overtired from the hard labor. Ermias and I went down again to Gondar, partly so that I could get treatment and partly to send off the monthly report, get money (we hoped), and buy building materials. We traveled with Nadu, going by a different route, because, he said, the road was better. It was indeed. To me, it seemed as if there was only one really difficult spot along that route, just outside Debarek, where the road had to surmount a high, steep ridge.

I visited Major Gizaw and Dr. Bali in Gondar where they were re-cuperating. I also had a meal with Dr. Wan, the veterinarian, and drank with him at his house. I went out on the town only a few times, but drank little because of my illness. Dr. Wan was like an older brother, often lecturing me about my temper and my responsi-bilities as a student of the martial arts.

No money had come through the bank, and no word about prog-ress on preparations for the road. Just one registered letter saying I had to collect taxes from the coolies. I sent them a telegram, saying I was a game warden, not a tax collector.

We had to spend a couple of nights in Debarek on our way back. We needed to look around for sand deposits and for bamboo for the ceiling of my house. First though, we went to see Dejasmatch Araya to apologize for the fact that over a month had passed, and still the department had not fulfilled any of its promises about the road. The Dejasmatch was waiting for us in the big dilapidated stone court-house. He said he had ordered the people to start work on the road on December 15, and that five hundred men would have come out on his orders if only we had shown we were sincere by bringing the machinery. I told him how bitterly disappointed I was, and that I was ashamed to be here and not have the work on the road begun. The Dejasmatch said that we representatives of the government must do our work; we were like a machine to be driven, but if the driver did not know the way, or if we did not receive fuel, we could not work. If only there were more men like His Majesty! He was a worker, and a fighter! Ermias said we must follow his example, and I nodded piously.

Guard Chane Endeshaw said there was both sand and bamboo down in Zarema, at the bottom of the Wolkefit Pass, at four thousand feet. We went to investigate. This bamboo was solid and heavy and tremendously strong. But before cutting it, we needed to ask permission from the local sub-district governor, or the locals would give us trouble.

There was sand down there too, but the cost of trucking it up would be astronomical. We would have to search the deep river valleys of the Simien for other deposits.

When we went to cut the bamboo, we took Nadu with us. He said the sub-district governor was a relative of his, and lived in Dib Bahar. We stopped in the village and sent a guard to look for the chief. The main road led through the village, flanked by tall eucalyptus trees and rows of ruined Italian houses. It must have been a nice place when the Italians were here, but it was now a typical, dirty, ramshackle Ethiopian roadside town. No electricity, no running water, people defecating in the streets, flies, beggars, officious police. The governor invited us to a little bar to drink. Nadu asked for permission to cut bamboo, and it was given. We drank araki and talked.

I asked about the many big fires we could see in his district from the High Simien. He said they were made by shepherd boys, roasting heads of grain. I said this was untrue, that the fires were made by the people cutting down the forests and burning them off to clear land for farming. He denied it. Nadu said that they were only grass fires, to burn off the land and kill the rats. I laughed at him. Why, I could see the felled trees with my binoculars, and the fires were big, some of them two or three or even more kilometers, burning in an unbroken line all day and night. Ermias told the governor of Dib Bahar that the forest was protected, and he said he would do his best to tell the people. He then complained that the wild pigs and baboons were destroying the crops, and that we should do something about it. I promised to try, if I could get the ammunition.

"But you must stop your people from killing all the leopards," I added. "Leopards are the natural enemies of the baboons, and they kill them and keep them in check."

This was difficult for Ermias to explain, and he took a long time over it. The governor and Nadu scoffed and argued, saying that leopards do not kill baboons, and that the clearing of forests and destruction of leopards had nothing to do with the increase of the baboon population. Ermias got annoyed, said they could never understand, and it was no good trying to tell them.

That day and the next we cut and trucked two loads of bamboo, then cut them into short lengths and lashed them in bundles to go on the mules.

Back in the Simien, at night, I watched the fires, some right near the bottom of the escarpment. They were everywhere. Surely this would prove itself to be the biggest problem for a game warden here . . . the destruction of the habitat and the inability of the peasants to see what they were doing.

A LONELY CHRISTMAS

Nadu was complaining about some of the guards. They did not obey orders. They stayed in their villages, working their farms while other guards did their share of duty. They ignored the letters Nadu sent to them by runner, telling them to report to the new game warden. Some of them had deserted the camp at Geech, after staying only a couple of days. Some of them threatened the peasants with their rifles and took presents of eggs, chickens, and talla.

I sighed and shook my head. There was a hell of a lot to do, and Nadu had said he could handle the guards for a time. Why hadn't he told us all this before? What were those loud arguments in the guards' lines after they received their pay, and why was Nadu's voice always the loudest in those arguments?

We told Nadu that, henceforth, all guards would report to me or to Ermias for duty and patrol assignments, and I said that if he, Nadu, had any more trouble with guards refusing to obey orders, he was to report to me, in writing, giving the exact details. We would warn them first, then fine them, then dismiss them if they repeated the offense. And I wondered. I had been in the Simien for two months now. Had the guards caught any poachers? Any forest cutters? Nadu said they hadn't. I grew more suspicious, and demanded to see the patrol reports. Was he sure he had dispatched patrols? If so, of what strength, and where to? Oh yes, indeed yes, he said. He had the reports in his house in Amba Ras and would bring them to me. He was lying.

Forest fires burned every night, scattered like the lights of towns over the countryside below. But there was no electricity within a hundred kilometers, and all the villages were dark and shuttered at night. According to Guard Tedla, the people were burning even the tree heather forest on the slopes at the foot of the escarpment, where the Walia went to graze. Although Nadu argued that this was not so, I believed Tedla, and went with him to a good vantage point where we could look down with binoculars. He was right. A three-man patrol was sent down, with a letter from me translated in Amharic, informing the villagers that the cutting and burning of the forest was against the law. I saw this destruction as the greatest threat to the recovery and survival of the Walia ibex, and to the survival of all the wildlife in the area except baboons, scavenging birds, and rats. I was sure that the forests at the top and bottom of the escarpment were vital to the Walia, as they were vital to the leopard, serval, colobus monkey, wild pig, bushbuck, duiker, and any other wild creature that might have survived the centuries of slaughter and abuse that the Ethiopians had heaped upon this country. And I knew, too, that without the forests on these slopes, the springs that seeped from the soil and rocks under the protecting canopy of the trees, which held that same soil with their roots, would surely die, dry out. This was the history of North Africa and the dried-out countries of the Mediterranean, repeating, repeating.

Nadu said that the patrol could do no good, that the people would never take any notice of our guards telling them to stop burning forest. Only the government in Addis Ababa could stop the people, and perhaps even the government couldn't do it. There was little time. Everything had been begun too late. The road was the key. With a road, we would soon get the park buildings finished, bring in tourists and money, and the fat-arsed, high-ranking officials of the government. We needed the road, but even before that, we needed quick legislation to declare the area a national park, and to fully protect the ever-decreasing forests and wildlife.

✕✕✕✕✕

It was December 21, when a long-absent game guard, Lemlem Gonete, came into camp. He was not in uniform. He was a dark, swarthy man, more heavily muscled than most of them. I called court in Ermias' big tent, with Nadu and Tedla standing by. Why had he taken so long to report for duty? He swore that he had been

73

sick, but, of course, could show no doctor's note. Anyway, said Lemlem, he had already done his turn of duty for a month. My ears
pricked up.

"What does he mean . . . he did his turn?"

Ermias questioned him. Nadu kept interrupting.

"I don't understand what he is trying to say, but I think they took
turns at guarding the Geech camp." Fair enough. "After that he says
he was on patrol in his home area, and that he has tried to take
many people to court, but the police and courts won't listen to him."

"Who sent him on patrol to his home? Where is the report?" Lemlem said Nadu had sent him. Nadu denied it, and they started to
quarrel. I shouted at them to shut up. It was some time before I
found out that Nadu had been taking bribes from the men in exchange for permission to stay and work their farms.

I ordered a parade.

The game guards lined up, a small band of men in ill-fitting
uniforms. Their faces seemed intent and serious. I gave them one of
the first of many, many speeches. "Ethiopia is one of the most beautiful countries in the world, and the Simien is the most beautiful
place in Ethiopia. In the Simien, there are animals, plants, birds that
are found nowhere else. Like the Walia. His Imperial Majesty has
understood all this, and has decided that the Simien must be a national park.

"A national park belongs to the country. It is like a garden,
though not made by men, but by God. The governments of all
countries like to show the most beautiful places in their country.
These places must be protected so that visitors from other countries
may come to see and admire. Each country's people are proud of
their own country's beauty. You are Ethiopians. You must be proud
of your country. Our job now is to develop and protect the Simien
so that people from all over the world may come to see it. The people call us the Walia soldiers. That is good. But protecting the Walia
is not our only job, and you must understand this. Without the forest and the plants the Walia will die, and so we must protect its
home as we would protect our own homes. Future generations will
bless you for saving this beautiful country. But if the Simien is destroyed and turned to desert, with no animals but the rats, the baboons, and the crows, they will curse you.

"We are the first. Like the soldiers who are first into a battle, we

74

are going to have lots of troubles, fighting, hardship. I know your troubles, but I promise you, that if you do your duty and work hard for the Simien Mountain National Park, I will do my utmost to improve everything for you. You are two things. You are soldiers, and you must be teachers. You must tell the people the reasons for our being here. They must understand that this is for the good of the country. If the park is established, many tourists will come and bring money to the country. We must fight and teach together for this park, so that we can all be proud of working in the Simien, and of being the first . . ."

I told them all this, and a lot more. High-sounding and flowery perhaps, but the game guards were visibly impressed. Ermias was a fine interpreter and a fine speaker. He went on for a long time.

If only it was all that simple. Governments don't set up parks because they know the country is beautiful. Governments are pressured into doing things like that, either from within or from without. The Emperor had seen some of the parks in East Africa and got ideas, but as far as I could see, he wasn't ever doing anything except issuing proclamations. Perhaps I was being unfair, but that was how I felt. I could go blue in the face telling a government official that the Simien was beautiful, but if he hadn't seen it, and didn't want to see it, it was hard to win him over to the conservationist's point of view. To most of those officials, progress meant fine buildings in the capital, not a lot of wild animals running around in the bush, making a nuisance of themselves in the crops. And the game guards? We could tell them that the cliffs and mountains were magnificent, the animals unique, the birds beautiful, the flowers rare and delicate, but could we make them feel it? Already I felt that we couldn't. And if we couldn't make our own men feel it, we surely never would get the peasants to understand. Damn the human race! Stand up and bray like a bloody donkey about enemies, and defending the motherland or the fatherland, or driving out the invader, or liberation, or shedding blood to the last drop on sacred soil, and people will get impassioned and ready to fight. But talk about erosion, desiccation, shifting deserts, pollution, and poisoning, and most of them don't give a damn. Wars can come and go and leave the face of a country unchanged, but erosion or pollution will completely destroy it in a century. And this kind of destruction seemed to come from two directions: either the blind ignorance of the uneducated, backward peasant, or the blind greed of the industrialist.

When Ermias had finished talking, Guard Lemlem stepped forward. "We thank God and His Majesty for sending you to us. Now we have a good master to teach us, we can know how to work for our country. Some of us have been lazy, but now we will work. You are a foreigner, but you speak as though you love the country; we must feel ashamed, and we must love our country too. We bless you, and hope that you will stay with us for many years."

I thanked Lemlem for his speech, and one by one, the other guards stepped forward to deliver similar speeches. Ethiopians seem to like speeches.

Guards Lemlem and Kasahun reported to the tent. They were given orders for a ten-day patrol to the lowlands, descending by the footpath below Michibi Ras. They were to skirt the land at the foot of the escarpment in the proposed park area and to report on the extent of the forest damage. If possible, they were to get the names of offenders, but if not, then the villages doing most of the cutting and burning. This time, no arrests, no arguments, just information. Since both Lemlem and Kasahun could write, we gave them pencils and notebooks and also some money as an advance against the patrol allowance which would be due them at the end of the patrol. They saluted and left.

They started off in the early hours of the following morning. But they did not go to Michibi, nor did they descend directly to the base of the escarpment as ordered. Instead, they went to Debarek and spent a few days at the house that Kasahun had rented for his wife, feasting on mutton and drinking talla. After that they took a bus to Adi Arkai, Lemlem Gonete's home area. Lemlem never returned to the High Simien while I was there. He stayed at home, swaggering about the village in uniform, showing off his rifle, and boasting, calling himself "Chief of Forests and Wildlife." It took me almost a year to get Lemlem officially dismissed. Old Kasahun came back to camp after a couple of weeks, with no report. He said that Lemlem had made the report. Then he got upset because I had found out the truth and wouldn't pay him his patrol allowance. It wasn't really his fault. He was from Tigre and did not know this part of the country, and I suppose he felt he had to take Lemlem's lead. All I found out from that patrol was that the guards generally couldn't be trusted on such a duty alone, and that there was, according to Kasahun, a lot of forest cutting in the Adi Arkai area.

Christmas Eve day. It seemed a day like any other day. The morning was bright and sunny, for the dry season had started. We left quite early, taking Nadu, Berehun, and Ambaw, and two mules. Our plan was to go to the head of the Khabar meadow, overlooking the Geech abyss, then travel down through the forests, through the deep valley of Serecaca, to the conjunction of the Khabar, with the Balagas River, the stream that carved out the deep gorge on the southeast side of Amba Ras. We would travel up the Balagas Valley, make our way onto the Amba Ras highlands, and then head back to camp from there. I was interested in those valley forests, but the principal reason for the journey was to find sand, which should be in the beds of those rivers.

The trail was narrow, through dense forests, green, shaded, hung with creepers and tree orchids. Birds trilled, and in the high branches, where many hives were wedged into the forks, bees hummed steadily. Animals must have been there in the undergrowth, but we saw nothing. Nadu and the other two guards kept up a continuous, shrieking, raucous banter, despite repeated angry orders from me to shut up. They seemed incapable of being silent, and it was as if they were nervous in the forest and made noise to reassure themselves. I fell behind, walking silently, looking from side to side at the thick undergrowth, glancing up into the leaf-dappled corridors of the forest way.

Halfway along the valley we came to a clearing in the forest. The people living there were afraid, and hid inside the compound. Nadu signaled us to wait, and went ahead, calling out to the people. On hearing who we were they came to welcome us, and invited us into the houses. These people were Muslims and could not offer meat to us, but instead we were treated to hot buttered wheat pancakes, with dollops of spicy pepper paste, to gourds of milk, and cups of strong, bitter coffee. I was struck by the beauty of the woman who served us. She had a face like a Greek goddess, and although her tightly braided hair was greasy with butter and a long, dirty gown hid her body, she was one of the most beautiful women I had ever seen. I never ceased to admire the physical beauty of the Ethiopians; it continued to surprise me. The man of the house pressed food upon us, telling of the troubles they had with the wild pigs which came to steal their crops and to break into the stores of wheat and maize. It would be good to come down here on a hunt, and I talked about it. I asked if they ever killed colobus monkeys. They denied it vigorously, and Ermias said he believed they had a superstition, or some religious reason, for not killing them. Way up the towering valley wall, below Michibi, there was a holy man, living in a cave, a Christian hermit who sometimes came down to the valley to walk in the forest and eat the wild herbs. If they harmed the animals, the hermit would curse them. But the grivet monkeys and baboons did much damage. I said that if we could, we would try to help them, although it depended on time and on ammunition.

Thanking them, and promising to come back, we went on our way; we saw many troops of little gray and white grivet monkeys. It grew hotter and hotter as we descended, and the vegetation changed. There were more clearings, with millet and maize, and irrigation ditches around the fields. All along the way people came out to greet us, both Christians and Muslims, begging us to come and drink talla or tedj with them. For many of these valley people it was the first time they had seen a foreigner. Children ran out, dodging through the woods, crying "Come! Look!" We stopped at only one other house and drank good, clear talla. At another place an old man ran beside me as I rode the mule, trying to pull me off, pleading with me to honor his house and to drink tedj with him. But it was getting late, and we had a long way to travel.

To reach the fork of the two rivers took five hours. The Balagas must have run deep and fast in the rains, for its bed was wide, and littered everywhere with boulders. A few brightly colored Egyptian geese stood in the shade of trees by the stream, and in the pools, small fish darted, all silvery. There was lots of sand.

"Ermias, does Nadu think we can get the local people to haul sand up to Sankabar from here? We will pay them a fair price, as much as we would pay a mule packer from Debarek." Ermias asked Nadu. He wanted to know how much sand we wanted, and how much money we would pay for it. Estimating roughly the amount of time which would have to be spent, the number of men and animals that would have to be used, I reckoned that four dollars a quintal (a hundred kilos) would be fair enough. With the amount of sand we needed, and for the time that the local people would take to get it to us, this would be an unheard-of sum of money for the Simien people. Nadu promised to get men to do the work, and I stressed that I wanted to make a contract with a particular man to haul a fixed amount of sand.

It was getting late. We went up the valley of the Balagas, past farms with irrigated fields. All along the way, people came out to greet Nadu. Halfway along the valley Nadu went off to look at his teff field, and to speak to the peasants about his harvest. A large band of men came along as we waited. They were all armed. Nadu and our guards went to kiss the leader, Nadu's elder brother Negash Worota. These were vigilantes, and they had come to see justice done in a land dispute. The Italians must have had a lot of trouble with bands of men just like these. Both the leader and I dismounted to shake hands and exchange greetings.

The ascent from the valley floor to the highlands of Amba Ras was exhausting. The guards wanted to stop and drink talla in the homes of their relatives, but it was past five o'clock, and the path was steep and dangerous, so I said no. It was a long way to Sankabar, and we had to go. I'd be damned if I was going to spend Christmas Eve being eaten alive by fleas in some peasant's house. Ermias and I had mules, and the path by which a mule could go was a long one, winding and turning. A man could go by a steeper but shorter route. We would go on, and Nadu and the guards would meet us at the top. We set off, warning them that if they were not at the top of the valley by the time we got there, five dollars would be taken from each man's pay.

Nadu had ordered a peasant, one of his servants, to guide us to the top. It took an hour, and we climbed over three thousand feet. When we reached the top, the guards were not there.

We were now on the Amba Ras. We could see our camp site across the mighty gulf of the gorge of the Khabar River (sometimes called the Wazura River). Our path was to the head of the gorge, then down to the meadow overlooking the Geech abyss, and on to the main trail leading to Sankabar. We traveled quickly, kicking the mules into a brisk trot along steep and perilous pathways. Stones slipped and bounced down the slopes and dropped out of sight over the cliffs. A slip would have meant certain death. The sun had set, but twilight lingered long enough to see us safely off the narrow gorge-top paths, out onto the turf.

By eight o'clock it was pitch-dark. My night vision is good, and Ermias had a flashlight, so between us we found our way, going down to the meadow, fearful of suddenly coming to the yawning chasm and going over the edge, stumbling along trails hidden in dense secondary growth of tree heather. A voice hailed us. Guard Berehun. He had run and caught up with us. The others, led by Nadu, had been drinking talla and were still behind. Typical. They left us to find our way in the dark, over trails they knew were dangerous and which they also knew we had never traveled before. Nadu considered himself too great a man to take orders. We'd fix him.

We got back to camp at nine or so, thanks to the steady, sure gait of the mules once on familiar paths. It was a five-and-a-half-hour trip from the sand deposits to our camp. Rough, but not too bad a track, certainly possible for donkeys. Until the road was finished, if it was ever finished, the Balagas Valley would be our main source of sand.

Christmas Eve. I ate a simple supper of canned sardines and black barley bread, and bid Ermias good night. To the Ethiopians, whose calendar is different from ours, Christmas falls on another day. Christmas has little significance, even to the Christians; they call it "Guna," after a game they play on that day, a game rather like hockey. For the first time in my life I was truly alone at Christmas, and I felt that loneliness. The tent was cozy enough, set up with everything I needed, warm in the light of the pressure lamp, but on that night, the cluttered solitude of the tent oppressed me. I pulled on my parka and climbed to the top of a hill at the edge of the escarpment, overlooking the silent darkness of the lowlands, dotted here and there with forest fires. Silent night, holy night, all is calm, and above, the stars piercingly bright in the thin mountain air. My gaze wandered to the guards, squatting around their campfire, talking in low voices. . . . *While shepherds watched their flocks by night, all seated on the ground* . . . Take away the rifles from this country, and the odd tin roof in the lowlands, and the distant, unseen road winding forty kilometers or more away and built by Italian invaders . . . as the Roman invaders built roads in those long ago and near times . . . take away only these few things, and you would have a situation, a country, and peoples almost identical to the times of the Bible. Ah yes, it had been easy to scorn and disbelieve when surrounded by sophistication, engines, noise, electrical comforts, but here one felt it definitely possible that a Christ child might be born in a stable.

Owls hooted, and my scalp tingled. I began to hum carols to myself, walking farther away along the cliff tops. And I sat on a rock, looking out at the fires, and above at the stars and the oft-traced lines of meteorites, thinking about my family and loved ones, and long-ago and faraway friends. Away, away, in distant cities that seemed more distant than that manger, there would be much lusty singing, boozing, feasting, dancing, kissing under the mistletoe. People would be gay and noisy, and perhaps think they had forgotten what it was all about. But I wondered. This silent land seemed to be all calm and waiting, and things were easier to believe, in the dignity of the hills. I worked today, and perhaps, if I felt like it, perhaps I would work tomorrow. But this was a special night, and I felt in this quiet land a kind of sad happiness.

I went back to my tent, lit the lamp again, and bawled for Abahoy. I said that tomorrow was Christmas for me, even if it wasn't Christmas for them. Nobody was to disturb me. Nobody was to come yelling and shrieking outside my tent in the morning. I kept a rifle by the bed. Any noise tomorrow and I would shoot through the tent in the general direction of the disturbance. OK? Ermias explained what I was saying. Abahoy laughed, and said that if I wanted him to make tea, I should call for him, and he would come without any noise. Fine.

I climbed into bed with a bottle of araki. The whole bottle was empty by the time the lamp ran out of gas.

6

LEOPARD-SKIN DEALERS, FOREST FIRES, AND A FIGHT

After Christmas we drove to Addis Ababa. No money for the project. No progress on the road. My dysentery getting worse. The back of the pickup was loaded with our luggage, a broken charging engine, and a fat wether that Ermias was taking live as a present for his father. With three of us in the front cab it was crowded, and I was in a bad mood. That morning, as we were fueling up, it came out that Abegas had spent a large portion of the money entrusted to him for fuel on food and drink, mostly drink. He didn't give a damn what promises he'd made, or whose money it was. He was surprised at my being angry. Why should he go hungry when he had money in his pocket? As a result, I had to pay for the gasoline and oil, and would be short of money on the trip.

At the headquarters, they were not pleased to see me. They didn't like the game wardens coming in from the parks, bothering them about things and making trouble. Major Gizaw had made a miraculous recovery and was back on the job, although nothing was happening except a flurry of letters here and there. Endless promises and assurances that things would be done, sometime in the future.

I felt that nearly everything was a sheer waste of time. My letters and reports, sent from Gondar, had not been read. Ethiopians were not the slightest bit interested in the park, only in the welfare of this or that person, and the price of sheep and eggs, and whether or not it was cold.

But the evenings were fun. Lots of friends and parties, and I stayed with good friends at the English school, a private school staffed by English people.

Leopard-skin dealers, forest fires, and a fight

Dr. Wan was in Addis Ababa at that time. Through him I met two Japanese, Mr. Yamada, a mining engineer, and Mr. Kurosawa, a judo teacher (these are not their real names). We got along well, the four of us, for we had a common language, and we were all a long way from our homes. We met in Mr. Yamada's hotel room, a cheap, dingy place on the piazza. He had a leopard skin and a couple of serval skins in the room. He'd bought them in the souvenir shops in the market. Now he wanted to know how to get a permit to take them out of the country. I promised to find out.

I went to see Zaudu, the licensing officer, the next morning. He leaned back in his chair, smiling.

"Does this man have a permit from this department? He cannot take the skins out or possess them without a permit, you see."

I'd already explained, but I tried again. "No, that's what I'm asking you about. He doesn't have a permit, and he wants to know how to get one."

"He cannot get a permit. He should have got one from us before he bought the skins. He now possesses these skins illegally and must surrender them to us."

"But how was he to know! The skins are on sale quite openly. If it is illegal for the tourist to buy them, it must be illegal for the dealers to sell them. You can't blame the tourist, it's our fault for not stopping the sale."

I was annoyed. It was stupid. The skins were on sale openly in a store. Yamada bought them in good faith, and now applies for a permit, which he can't get because he didn't get papers before he bought the skins. Ridiculous. If he'd brought the skins in himself he would have lost them, and a lot of money too.

"Look. The tourist brings money to this country. We mustn't discourage this admirable trait by penalizing him for our lack of control. Let's get the dealer who sold the skin and fine him heavily, then let us take the skin from the tourist, in this case my friend, and return it to him on payment of the fee. You can't blame the tourist. He doesn't know our regulations. Get the dealers."

Zaudu was adamant. The tourist should know, and if he doesn't the fault is his. Last year, they broadcast the wildlife regulations in English on the radio, and put them in the *Ethiopian Herald*.

"Idiot. Do you imagine that the whole world listens with bated breath to the Ethiopian radio? And do you think last year's *Ethio-*

83

pian Herald is going to have any meaning to a tourist who just got off the plane?"

But arguing was a waste of time. The tourist, he said, was to blame for buying the skin. It must be confiscated (no doubt for later auction to the same dealers who sold the skin to the tourist in the first place). I thanked him, told him the system was crazy, and took a copy of the rubber stamp the Wildlife Conservation Department used for marking licensed skins. This in itself was a ridiculous system, for anybody could copy and duplicate that mark with no trouble at all.

Later, I showed the mark to Mr. Yamada and told him of the outcome of my inquiries. He was annoyed too. The skins he had bought actually bore this mark. There was nothing for him to do but to smuggle the skins out in his luggage when he left the country, and to pretend ignorance if he was caught. And that was what I suggested he do.

By now, I had grave suspicions about the whole setup. It was just too easy for the illegal dealers. I asked Mr. Yamada to show me where he got the skins. We went together the next afternoon. I dressed in a dark suit and sunglasses, carried a briefcase, and tried to look like a visiting businessman. The shops were in the market, but there were not too many leopard skins there, mostly colobus rugs. However, Yamada had found out from the man in the shop where the dealer lived, and where it was possible to see many good, large leopard skins.

It was a dirty, narrow street a little way up from the marketplace, with fences of rusted tin sheeting and dingy mud-walled houses and flies, refuse, human feces all over the street. Yamada went in first and spoke to the dealer, who came out and looked at me. He was a Muslim, an ugly man, turning to fat, dressed in a threadbare suit, with an embroidered cloth cap on his head. We shook hands. Yamada told him that I was a Canadian interested in leopard skins. The man called for a boy who could speak English and showed us into the house. I told them that I was representing a Canadian furrier in Montreal, and that I was especially interested in leopard skins. The boy went into a back room and brought out a few leopard skins, salted and untanned. They were fairly good, but small. He asked four hundred dollars apiece. I said I wanted to see more skins, bigger ones, and asked if he could match skins in color and pattern. Bigger, finer skins were brought out. Five hundred dollars, seven hundred dollars. I took two skins out of the house, into the light. The dressing and salting were not good, but the skins would tan well enough. I said I was not just a tourist, but a businessman, and that we needed good-quality skins in large numbers. Kenya and the other countries were getting difficult, and we, in Montreal, were thinking of opening business with Ethiopia. The merchant was very pleased at this and took me into a back room. Wild animal skins in great piles—colobus, leopard, serval, civet, gazelle, a couple of lion skins, even python. I flipped over the pile of leopard skins, the most valuable of all, looking for the Wildlife Conservation Department stamp. Several of the skins were stamped, but many were not. They were certainly illegal, stamped or not. There must have been over twenty thousand dollars worth of skins in that room. What a place to raid! I thanked the dealer and went out, assuring him that our company would be very interested, but first I would have to make a report before starting any transaction. And one thing, how about exporting this stuff? Permits? Customs? The dealer spoke to the boy, frowning.

"What is the matter, don't you like these skins?"

"Oh no, it's not that, but I represent a very respectable company, and if we are to do business here in Ethiopia, we must be sure that there will be no trouble with your government, with the Wildlife Department. I'm sure that there must be regulations, licenses, permits, and so on."

The boy talked to the dealer, who laughed. "It is easy. We will arrange everything, for as many skins as you want. We know somebody in the Wildlife Conservation Department."

I wondered if that comment was as meaningful as it sounded. I thanked them and wrote out a fictitious name and address, promising to be in contact with them soon.

Naïve and foolish, I wrote a brief report about this case and gave it to Gizaw the next day. I suggested that I could go back, with guards and one officer, to raid the place. Gizaw glanced briefly at the paper as I talked.

"This is very good that you did this, Nicol; we will keep it on record."

"But we must do something, Major; we should confiscate all those skins. They represent more dead wild animals than there are in the whole of the Simien Mountain National Park. What is more, some-one from this office seems to be helping these criminals, and we must get him. It is no good chasing the peasants and small poachers, or the street boys; we must go straight to the heart of the problem, the big dealers."

Gizaw said he agreed, but it wasn't easy; we first had to get a court order before we could raid, and that would take time, and even if we got it, by the time we raided, the dealer would have been warned, and the skins removed. I was frustrated and annoyed, and didn't want to shrug it off.

"OK. I'll go in and trick the dealer outside the house with a leopard skin. We can arrest him, and I can go into his back room and drag out some more as evidence. Then we can seal the house and get a court order to confiscate the lot."

Gizaw didn't like this idea either. "No, this is what we do. You ask them to bring a leopard skin to your hotel, and when he brings it, we can arrest him there, call the police, and take the skin."

"But don't you see? We will get one leopard skin and one of his servants! We should get the whole lot, and the boss himself. Think of it! Twenty thousand dollars worth of skins at least! That's enough money to build three houses in the Simien. Let me do it! I don't mind the risk."

But it was no use. The Wildlife Conservation Department would do nothing about it. It was difficult. It was too dangerous. It was impossible. Neither Balcha, Zaudu, nor the game guard lieutenant wanted to hear about it, and they all avoided the subject and the consequent memos which I wrote. Bekele, the legal officer, argued that it was impossible, and we exchanged bitter words on the subject. I had not worked in Africa before, but I knew that this was not the way things were done in other African game departments. John Blower, senior game warden, was away. I would wait and talk to him about it. In the meantime, I did some detective work downtown.

It was a simple matter to get wild animal skins from the souvenir shops in the market, or from any street boy you happened to ask. I saw thousands of monkey skins in a week, and hundreds of leopard skins. Within four days I located two other big dealers, one by the post office and one up near the market. Any street boy could take you to their houses, and there was nothing secret about it. There was no doubt in my mind that our so-called Conservation Department was protecting the big men, and there could be only one reason for doing that. Wild animal skins were big, big business in Ethiopia.

When John Blower came back, I told him what I knew. He knew it all before and had been trying to fight this for two years, blaming the failure partly on the lack of regulations to enable us to act. He was resolved to go on fighting, and saw the new regulations, which he had drafted long before, and which were awaiting the signature of the Minister, as the biggest weapon in the fight. I vowed to do anything to help. I wanted to raid the dealers. But the more I found out about the Wildlife Conservation Department, the deeper became the feeling of hopelessness.

※※※※※

Dr. Bernhard Nievergelt and his blond, attractive wife, Esther, arrived from Switzerland in January. They were both biologists. Dr. Nievergelt was an expert on ibex, especially the ibex found in the mountains of Switzerland. His study in Ethiopia would be the first real examination of the population and ecology of the Walia ibex, and it would take a year. Such a study was essential to the planning of the proposed park. Dr. Nievergelt had been on one preliminary trip to the Simien, before I arrived in Ethiopia. His project was financed and supported by the World Wildlife Fund and the Swiss Foundation for Alpine Research. The Ethiopian Government had promised to provide a house and some facilities, which, of course, would remain in the park for later use by park staff or visitors. So the Wildlife Conservation Department was definitely going to come out well on the deal, what with the Land Rover that Dr. Nievergelt would buy new, use for one year, and then give to the park.

They were staying at the Ras Hotel. I went and found them, after ten minutes' argument with the desk clerk who said they were not guests at the hotel. They were having lunch. I introduced myself and joined them. What I had to say was depressing for all of us. On his first trip to Ethiopia, Dr. Nievergelt had been visiting the Awash when the Emperor came down and set up a fine camp there. He met the Emperor and told him about the project and the Walia. His Majesty at that time promised that by the time Nievergelt came back there would be a road, an airstrip, and a house waiting for him. Now he was back. There was no road, not even a survey for it. No airstrip. And not even enough money to start building a house for him. I saw the disappointment on his face and knew how he felt with his wife there with him; I felt partly responsible for it.

Of course, he complained bitterly to our department, and they promised, because they always promised, but he had to wield some bigger sticks than that. By the time I went back to the Simien, thirteen thousand dollars had been produced from somewhere to start work on the buildings, in particular the houses for myself and the Nievergelts. This was only a fraction of what was in the budget for the park, but it was something. And it was only due to Dr. Nievergelt's arrival, and outside pressure, that I got that.

Apart from the road, the money, the regulations, and the poor standard of the guards, I was seriously concerned about the enormous destruction of the forest. When John came back, we both went to see the Major. We wanted him to push through all channels for strong action to stop the cutting and burning. The forest laws were adequate for this. But his response was strange. He sat fiddling with a heavy caliber hunting shell.

"The forest is not your responsibility. You are to protect the animals, not the trees. That is the job of the Forestry Department, not your job, and you shouldn't interfere." John and I exchanged glances of amazement and exasperation.

"But Major Gizaw," began John, in his patient manner, "the Forestry Department have no people in the Simien, and don't even visit it. Mr. Nicol and his men are there. And if somebody doesn't look after the habitat, the forest, then the animals will go. You must see that."

"That is the responsibility of the Forestry Department, not yours. I will write a letter to the Director of Forestry."

We tried to explain, but Gizaw still insisted that the forest was not my responsibility, only the animals. I couldn't believe he was so stupid, and suspected his attitude might have something to do with the fact that the Wildlife Department was only recently separated from Forestry, with some bad feelings perhaps? We left. I would speak again to the Governor General of Begemdir, and get Dr. Nievergelt to come and back me up. Arguing was pointless. Once

88

Leopard-skin dealers, forest fires, and a fight

Gizaw stuck his heels in, he was almost impossible to budge. So forest was nothing to do with wildlife. Hmmm.

Driver Abegas did not return to Debarek. A new driver was assigned—a burly, jovial Gurage called Tesfae. He was in the black books for rolling a Land Rover. Tesfae didn't want to come to Debarek either, nobody did, but he was given no choice. We left Addis Ababa in the third week of January, loaded with blankets, mattresses, lamps, equipment, and with an American wanderer, hitching a lift with us to the Simien. It was good to get out of the city, with money to begin work, and dysentery cured.

Back in the Simien, the number and intensity of the fires had increased as the dry season progressed. Nadu was right, damn him. They ignored the patrols, the police and the courts ignored the charges, and everybody except John Blower ignored my reports.

The house building in Sankabar took most of our time, for we soon found out that the workers, including the so-called carpenter from Debarek, were quite incapable of retaining the most simple instructions in their heads for even a few minutes. Time after time, Ermias and I tore down the walls they put up, having ignored our guide marks. We then rebuilt the walls, while the carpenter argued, and I cursed at him to shut up.

Guard Tedla came and stood in the house as we worked, shaking his head. "But you do not know our country—it is cold, and it rains, and there is fog. The wind will blow in through all those holes!"

Ermias tried to explain about glass and outside shutters, but many of the Simien people had never seen glass and didn't believe in the worth of windows anyway.

Looking at my log, I see that I was often in a bad temper about the building, but now I remember and laugh, for the sun was bright, and there was man's work to be done, and there were many laughs and jokes. Materials were gathered, foundations laid, frames built. The kitchen was a complete puzzle to the Simien people, for it would have a sink, benches, stoves. And in the living room, against the big stone wall, we built a low stone pedestal to take the steel-cone fireplace which was being welded in Gondar. The workers asked what it was, and I said I would set a throne upon it, so that I could sit there in style when the guards came to speak to me. They believed it.

Stories of what I was doing began to spread over the Simien. People on the way to market stopped to stare for long, long periods at the house, and the camp, and me. They saw Ermias working, and they were amazed. How could he work like this? With a shovel, or a pick, or a hammer? He was a gentleman, and gentlemen never worked. Our men answered that Ato Ermias was a strong man and a good, hard worker.

"If our masters work, then we must all work too," they said with pride.

That a foreigner should work was really not so odd, for foreigners were mad anyway, and even did women's work, washing and cooking, and fetching water. But I was considered strange even for a foreigner. Each morning and each night I practiced karate, either formal movements, or striking the post embedded in the ground by our tents. Pads of grass rope were bound to the post, and within a month, calluses formed on my knuckles again. I also practiced with a white oak fighting stick and heavy wooden training swords, for these were excellent to build the muscles of the rib cage, and helped breathing at a high altitude.

Large parties of armed men often passed our camp on their way down to the court at Debarek, where they disputed land rights or sought compensation from feuds. Our guards had had trouble with some of them, and I decided to give another lecture. I told them that they must be tactful and speak gently to people, and treat even the lowliest peasant with firm courtesy. But the lecture did no good at all. The very next day another large party of people stopped near the camp and were preparing to spend the night. A guard went out, yelling and waving at them to move on. Ermias and I went over, dismissed the guard, and told the travelers that they were welcome to camp here, as long as they realized this was a park and that their donkeys must be tethered, that they should cut no trees, and that they should keep the place clean. They bowed to us and thanked us and blessed us, and I felt very righteous and good, and said, "See . . . this is the proper way to deal with the local people."

At nine at night, when Ermias and I went for a last stroll around the camp we noticed that over where we had told the travelers to camp there were nine or more big campfires, far too many for the available wood stocks. We went over to complain about it. Around the fires were well over a hundred people, sitting and eating their rations and drinking talla. The original party had been less than twenty, but more people had been arriving and quietly unloading their donkeys in the darkness. The donkeys roamed all over the place, and I could see that a lot of small trees had been cut. It was two or three hundred yards to our camp; many of the men had rifles, and all had sticks. Therefore Ermias, myself, and one guard moved from group to group, asking them to respect the rules of the park, to tether their donkeys, to be economical with the wood, not to cut any trees, and not to make so much noise. We remonstrated with the newcomers for not coming over to see us, and asked if a foreigner should ever have to ask an Ethiopian to be well mannered. And we said that we would have to protect them while they were here, for this was once a favorite place of the shifta, as everybody knew, and therefore we could only permit honest men to stay here. I cursed myself for being soft. The guards did things one way or the other. Either they shrieked and waved guns at everybody, or they showed complete indifference as to who came and went. The people all agreed to abide by my requests, and I went back to my tent, wrote the log, had cocoa, and went to bed.

After midnight, they started singing heroic songs in a nasal wail, interminable and, to me, unmusical. It was enough to wake the dead. I lit a candle. Maybe they would shut up and let us all have some sleep. But they didn't. The wailing and shrieking and shouting kept on, from fire to fire. I got up and went over. I took a rifle, in case of bad trouble. For a time, I stood in the middle of all the campfires, asking them to be quiet. They saw me and ignored me. I shouted for silence. Several of them cursed me, and the noise increased. I fired a shot into the air, and the crash of it cut into the noise and obliterated it. There was a brief moment of quiet, and then scrambling, yelling confusion, as they all ran hither and thither, fleeing into the bushes. The guards came running, and Ermias too, with his big .38. Techale came to me, and we rounded up the troublemakers, Techale using his rifle riot-squad fashion, quiet and disciplined. The Simien guards ran around shouting, bumping into people. Someone grappled with Guard Azezew, trying to take his rifle. They both fell down, the attacker on top, head swathed in a big turban, legs thrashing about under a long white robe. I clubbed the man in the kidneys, rolled him over, and dragged him off. He was the first one to start cursing me. I marched him and another to the camp, and called the guards to bring a few others. We formed a circle around the prisoners. I told them that they were ill-mannered louts and that they were all to get out of Sankabar. The moon was bright enough to see by. The man I had seized was a priest, a tall man with a hawklike nose. He was raging, threatening me, saying I would be whipped, and that I would go to jail for touching him, a priest. Techale yelled for a rope.

"Techale! Shut up! Ermias, tell this man that unless he wants to be handed over to Techale, he'd better get out of Sankabar, and not come back through here again. And he can tell all the others, that thanks to ill-mannered bastards like him, I am going to close this area at night. Let him go."

The priest fled.

The following morning several of the people crept back to camp to get treated for small injuries sustained during the brief skirmish or when they were rushing pell-mell through the bushes. Many of them had rifles, and all had sticks or knives, or both. Some men came and apologized. I wanted to sit down and laugh, for I had thought the shot, fired into the air in full view of all of them, would only have made them shut up. I had not expected the slapstick hysteria.

I wrote a notice to Dejasmatch Araya, telling him of the incident, and saying that in the future, Sankabar would be closed at night to unauthorized people, and that if the local people needed to stay there, they would need a note from either him or from one of the sub-district governors, and, moreover, they would have to report to me or to the assistant warden. Techale took the letter to the Dejasmatch, who laughed at it, agreed, and ordered that those responsible for any disturbance in the park area would be put into jail.

I thought a lot about this, wondering if I had been wrong. Later, the Dejasmatch said that the people had just been happy because there was no longer any need to fear robbers in Sankabar. If that was the case, I had acted with intolerance and a lack of understanding, but it seemed to me that the people had been testing me. No man in his right mind would dare to curse the Dejasmatch, or to disturb him, for he would have them thrown in jail and flogged. I had thought that only a gentle approach would work, though many people, including Ethiopians, had said that only a strong approach would work. How to strike a happy balance?

Leopard-skin dealers, forest fires, and a fight

As if the fates were giving me a chance to balance my actions, two days later a man from Addis Gey brought in his ten-year-old son, injured with deep cuts and contusions about the head and right arm. He had been beaten unconscious by a berserk priest, running wild through the village catechist school with a heavy club. The boy was weak, trembling, with a high fever. The man said they had caught the priest and locked him up until he recovered. Had he done that to my son I would have killed him. I treated the boy as best as I could, but he was in great pain; his father had taken a hot iron to the wounds on his arm, cauterizing them, but sealing in the infection. The arm was swollen, and there was a telltale lump in the armpit. I administered antibiotics, gave the father more, with strict instructions on how to use them, lent him a riding mule and saddle to take the boy home, and a warm woolen shirt to wrap him in. In truth, the boy should have gone to a hospital, but the father would not take him, and it was probably dangerous to travel. Guard Nagur went home with them and saw that the boy was put to bed.

By the evening of the next day the fever had passed, and the boy began to get better; in a week he was well, his wounds healing cleanly. The father brought the shirt back to me, with a present of a gourd of milk.

This story of the priest, and what I had heard and seen of the others, made me think of them as arrogant parasites, but I was hasty in my judgment, for later I did meet saintly men.

※※※※

The Nievergelts and their interpreter Berhanu arrived in Gondar in February. I went to meet them, and together we went to see Colonel Tamurat, the Governor General, to discuss park problems. He ordered the provincial police headquarters and all other officials to help us in controlling the forest destruction. Orders concerning this were drafted and sent out to district and sub-district governors.

That night I very much enjoyed the company of the Nievergelts at supper and afterward. Esther Nievergelt was worried about being all alone in the Simien, for their house would be in Geech, three hours from ours. Bernhard and I reassured her, and all the time I wondered how my wife Sonako would feel.

Sleep evaded me, as it often does in towns with their crowded loneliness. I got out of bed and dressed. My shoes were packed away, so I wore boots. Tomorrow, early, I was to go back to the Simien. The Nievergelts would come a day or so later. It was not so late, and the big iron gates of the hotel were as yet open, and the guard awake. I walked out and down the long flight of steps to the main street. Shadowy figures in shammas or gabis squatted in the bushes and in the groves of young eucalyptus. Ethiopians have a thing about defecating at night, especially the women. Any patch of grass by the roads or around the castles in the town was foul with human dung. It disgusted me. I felt a slight prickling at the nape of my neck. Somebody following? I stopped, turned carefully. No one.

Perhaps to go into one of the red-light bars alone, late at night, would be asking for trouble, and so I walked up to the Gondar Hotel, a cheap place, but brighter, with no dancing, where one could just go for a coffee. There were girls there too, very available, just like the others, but people in the bar didn't presume you came to bed the girls, and usually there were no comments. I ordered araki, and sat there, lonely, watching moths flitting around a bare lightbulb. A girl came to sit by me and I bought her a drink. She was very young, with a round, friendly face, a fine nose, huge brown eyes, and a compact, muscular body. She said she was sixteen. A gold cross dangled between two full, round breasts, and she wore no brassiere. Admittedly, the thought came to my head, but I didn't do anything about it, it wouldn't solve any problems. We talked. There were no other customers, and I suppose she was curious about the foreigner. The other girls came and talked about the kind of things girls want to know of strangers. The place closed at one o'clock. The streets were quiet, a few beggar urchins sleeping in the doorways, some drunken students going home, police patrolling.

I took the quiet, deserted back street that passed the high-walled compound of the Governor General's palace. It was rocky and rutted, more like a riverbed than a street, and along the way it was splashed with faint pools of yellow from lights on standards along the wall. One of the bulbs was broken halfway along, and I knew that there was a sidestreet, a few tall trees, and a broken stone wall hidden in the darkness. It would be better to walk in the middle.

I walked into the darkness a few steps, when a sudden insight of danger made me spin, raising a knife-hand block. There was a foot scuffle, a whoosh of air as a weapon came at the back of my head.

Leopard-skin dealers, forest fires, and a fight

With hips low, I blocked, barely in time, and took the man's wrist, turning into him, taking his throat with the left hand, throwing his body in front of me, stretching the weapon arm against my chest. There were two of them. The second, in haste and excitement, swung his club at me and hit his friend. I yanked the man's arm, forcing him to drop the club, at the same time stamping into the back of his leg behind the knee joint. He dropped. I let go and clipped a chop and a punch at the back of his neck; he fell on his face.

The other was swinging wildly, retreating. He was scared. I went after him, kicking. I couldn't connect with a thrust kick, the ground was bad and it was dark. I missed several times. Dodging and blocking the club, I charged, catching him with a front snap kick low in the guts, and a thrust kick in the chest, but he was still going backward and didn't take the full power of the kick. However, I got inside the swing of his club, and he couldn't use it. I hit him three or four times with punches, and once in the side of the temple with a snapping back fist. Damn, it was dark. He staggered forward and I caught his weapon arm, throwing on a straight arm lock as I had done hundreds of times wrestling and in a judo dojo. This man's arm was not strong, and it snapped at the elbow, going right back. The sound surprised and sickened me. I hit him again and he went down. I picked up his club. They were both using olivewood fighting clubs, the tips bound with iron. Bastards. I believed they meant to kill me. Certainly had the first blow hit me I would have gone down. I dropped the club and stamped on the left hand. He wouldn't be holding a club for a long time.

The first attacker started to get up. I ran back and caught him with a hard kick in the ribs, knocking him down again. Then I took him from behind and broke both his collarbones with a knife hand. I had to hit the left one twice. He wouldn't swing a club for a time either. I glanced up and down the street. Nobody. Sudden fear. Had I killed them? I knelt by each in turn, feeling heartbeats. All right. No excessive bleeding. They were ragged men, in shorts and tattered gabis, with shaven heads and bare feet, both fairly tall, but skinny. Probably hungry. I felt a bit ashamed, but then, they had tried to kill or injure me, and I got mad again. I ran softly back to the hotel.

Once in the room I saw that my hand was bruised and bleeding.

A couple of patches of skin torn off the back, probably from the iron tip of the club when I blocked that first swing to the back of my head. The hand was swelling, getting stiff. I sat on the bed, puzzled. Why had they gone for me? I didn't recognize them. Robbery? I had a vague feeling that they had been following me. This was the first time I had ever really used karate, and the result of the long training was gratifying. It worked. I was not pleased because I defeated the men but because I sensed and blocked the first blow in the dark, from behind. That insight of danger, a flash of understanding uncluttered by fear or hate or any emotion, was unforgettable. You see it in animals, but man buries it under so many thoughts and feelings. That was good karate. The rest was anger and savagery, and that would have to be beaten before I really made a good karate man. I washed the hand under the cold water tap and bound it in a clean handkerchief. No bones were broken.

We left in the early morning, and as we drove through the town I wondered if the police were looking for me. To hell with spending a couple of days answering questions and going to court to argue about damages. I had been strongly warned that if you got into trouble in Ethiopia and were a foreigner, you were wrong.

In Debarek, Dejasmatch Araya wanted to see us. Guard Chane Takalé was wanted for trial for cattle theft. Chane had given us a lot of trouble, deserting his post, arguing, going absent without leave, lying. I said I would disarm the man and order him down. If he didn't come, which I hoped he wouldn't, we could dismiss him from the service, and the police or the vigilantes could get him.

Once back in camp Ermias and I had tea and talked for a time, as we always did. We had become friends, although Ermias still called me "sir" in front of other people, and treated me with respect. Without him I would certainly have quit. He was reliable, good fun, intense, and honest. We had a standing joke about suntans, for I was always out in the sun, trying, and failing miserably, to get brown. We never quarreled or had a tense moment. I said what I wanted to say and never felt I should tread carefully because his tan was better than mine. I don't like people who are looking for hidden insults in everything you say in arguments, and good friends usually argue, for a man has to keep his wits smart, and arguing with a friend is good exercise.

I went for a walk at dusk. It was Ermias' turn to make the supper. On the south-facing side of the Sankabar ridge there was a stream with warm, shallow pools. At this time they were full of tadpoles and great gobs of frog spawn. This fascinated me, because I didn't expect to see frogs at ten thousand five hundred feet. There were lots of other creatures too, fly larvae, water beetles, caddis larvae in their cylindrical houses. What a fascinating place for a field course in biology! The Simien was such a mixture. It was the meeting ground for flora and fauna of Ethiopian, East African, South African, and European types. It had wild roses and ibex, ever-lasting flowers and jasmine, red-winged starlings, mountain chats, augur buzzards, and migrating harriers and kestrels which hunted over the open spaces here just as they did in Europe. And of course, there were spotted cats, baboons of two kinds, grivet or vervet monkeys, colobus monkeys, lammergeyers, Simien fox, and so many others. There were hundreds of Ph.D. projects here, and I dreamed of a time when there would be biologists all over the park, as there are in the parks in East Africa. I wondered how many animals had been exterminated by men in this area. Lion, elephant, buffalo, kudu, and others in the lowland certainly; Leslie Brown, in his book *Ethiopian Episode*, speculated that there had once been a large, bovine type of animal in the High Simien, for the thick-billed ravens had beaks that were adapted, and used, for turning over large dung pats to get at the grubs underneath. I looked over the hills, growing black with the setting of the sun, and imagined them as they were once, covered with thick forests of cedar, hagenia, olive, and full of game and birds.

Man changed the face of this land. Forest zones covered all the hills to the frost line, and the plains must once have been covered with grass, thick and waving, with great umbrellas of acacia standing here and there. The highlands must have been a bit like parts of Europe, with hundreds of crystal streams. Now the plains are scrubby desert, choked with weeds, thorns, annuals, lots of aloes and candelabra euphorbias with their poisonous, burning sap. The once-forested hills have become eroded and dry, bare and rocky, most of the wildlife gone, though some flourish. The hyena, the baboon, the vulture, and the raven do well, for the people of Africa graze too many cattle and other stock on any one piece of land, and the animals get thin, sick, starved, and die by the thousands in the dry season. Rock thrushes and chats like rocky places, and they increase, as do the pigeons, both the guinea pigeon and white-collared pigeon, for they love barley fields. And, of course, the rats. I had never in my life seen so many rats as there were in the fields of the Simien people, and in the meadows and moors of Geech and Amba Ras.

Mitiku and Ambaw were waiting back at the tent. They said they wanted an aspirin. I called Ermias to find out what was wrong. There was a woman, very sick. I took the lamp from my tent and went to see. She was lying in the bushes, outside the camp. It was dark. I put the lamp beside her and knelt down. She was delirious, babbling and shrieking and waving her arms about. An old woman, who must have been her mother, held her and moaned, begging me for medicine. The guards, and four men I didn't know, hung back, afraid to come near. Ermias was questioning them.

"Who are these people, and why is she here?"

"They are the relatives of this woman, her brothers, and they brought her to the camp because they say that our guard, Azezew, must look after her. She was living with him. When she first became ill, Azezew took her to her relatives and left her there. Now they have brought her back. They are afraid, they say she has the devil in her."

"Where is Azezew?"

"They say he left camp while we were in Gondar."

Damn him. He ran off without permission, no doubt over this business. I didn't know how to treat the woman, or what was wrong with her.

"Tell these men that they must take her down to Debarek and get her on the bus, or get the police to drive her to the health station in Dabat."

Ermias told them, and there was much argument, the four men shaking their heads, looking at the ground, and Ermias getting angry.

"They refuse. They are afraid, you see; they say she got the devil when she was with Azezew and we must take care of her." I didn't know what was wrong with her, and I hadn't even realized she had been in the camp. I told Ermias to order a guard to go to Azezew

98

with an order to come back immediately. Not even force would make the woman's brothers take her any farther. They feared the devil greatly. She lay on the ground, eyes rolling, shrieking, laughing, clutching at her mother, and in the darkness, strange shadows were cast on the bushes and the hollows of the ground, and the men stood around, leaning on their staffs in their ancient dress. Even I shuddered slightly, sensing the superstition and fear. I asked the guards to volunteer to take the woman on a stretcher down to Debarek, offering to pay their allowances. They all shook their heads. They were afraid, too. I said I would carry one corner of the stretcher, but still no offers. They brought her a blanket, and we tried to give her aspirin ground in water, but she couldn't swallow. The men all refused to go anywhere near her, and stayed at least five yards away, some of them saying prayers. To try to force the guards would have caused desertion. They gathered wood for the old woman and left her. We had no spare tents. I shouted at her relatives, the men, calling them cowards, but it was no good. They feared the devil far more than me, and they left her where she was.

I didn't know what to do, and asked Ermias for advice.

"This sounds bad to you, but I tell you that you can do nothing. You can't bring her into the camp or the men will mutiny. She is not one of our people, and it is neither your fault nor your responsibility. I warn you that if you arrange for her to go down to Gondar, or even just to Debarek, the local people will spread the news, and every person who is sick like this will be brought here, and they will make trouble for you if you help one and not the other. Also, the guards will blame you for any sickness in the camp after this if you force contact or try to force it. It is hard for you, because you have never seen anything like this. You see what it is like for my country, we do not have enough doctors and hospitals."

"But I can't just leave her out there to die, Ermias."

"What else can you do?"

What else? If I was a good Christian I would have taken her in, but I weighed what Ermias said—and I sensed to be true—against this woman's life. I sent out some food, and an old billy can, and left her where she was.

The next day Ermias stood by the path, beseeching the passersby to help this woman. I offered ten dollars each for four men to carry her to Debarek. She could not ride, and Ermias and I could not carry her down by ourselves. But the Simien people hurried on past, fearful of the place and the raving woman. The guard we had sent returned with word that Azezew had a bad leg and couldn't travel. Like hell. I sent further orders, to come or be dismissed, but his home was three days' journey, and all this took time. The woman lay in the bushes, under a rough shelter, tended by her mother. We fed them and tried to help, but it did little good. I set up buckets of disinfectant and ordered the men to wash their hands when they came in. I wondered what would happen if I got sick without Ermias around. It would probably mean death if I didn't treat myself, or get out in time. During the night, strong winds blew, and Ermias' tent was ripped.

The Nievergelts had moved up to Geech and were camping there by the low stone huts. I went up and walked over a few possible house sites with them, asking them to decide which they thought was best. Bernhard and I went out to spot Walia, but saw only one three-year-old male on the Marive Zemed Yellish cliff. He used a telescope and very powerful binoculars, but we couldn't find many Walia. Perhaps the cliffs were too dry, and the Walia were lower down in the Erica forest.

On February 17, Bernhard and I staked out the floor plan of his house on a beautiful site just across the stream from the huts which were there when I arrived. It would be a fine house, a double rondavel with a veranda and a kitchen annex, built of stone. Coolies from Geech began to gather stones and pile them at the site; the stones were good here, much better than the stone in Sankabar. The Geech stone was flat; because it was cracked by hot sun during the day and by the frost at night, it could be broken easily by a mason's hammer.

It was good to have the Nievergelts in Geech, to know that a project was being started in the park, to know there were some other people there interested in what was going to happen to the park and to the Walia. Bernhard said that he would make his observations morning and evening, and would be free to supervise the house-building during the day. Certainly someone had to do it, for the local workers could never build for even half a day without supervision.

We made radio contact with Addis Ababa, having brought in the charging engine by mule. I spoke to John Blower, who said he would visit the Simien, but that I should check again by radio the following Friday, and if he gave the word, I should come down to Gondar to meet him.

Back in Sankabar, the guards bought an injured cow from a Michibi peasant. The peasant could never have got the cow back to his farm. The animal had fallen off a cliff and dislocated its hip. The guards found it and hauled it up with ropes, then fetched the peasant and made the bargain. Only fifty-three dollars, Ethiopian. It was a young animal, and Ermias and I bought a share of it. It was slaughtered in Sankabar. That night Ermias and I sat out by a fire, roasting steaks over the hot coals under the brilliant stars and drinking excellent coffee. We talked about all manner of things until past midnight.

7

THE GEECH PROBLEM

John Blower confirmed by the radio in Geech that he was coming, and that I should meet him in Gondar. I rode the mule Abebich down to Sankabar from Geech, meeting villagers on the way who told me that some visitors had come and were waiting for me in Sankabar.

The visitors were Dr. Wan and Mr. Yamada. Yamada had a Colt .45 on his hip. They were both sneaking around, trying to get pictures of a big herd of gelada baboons on the hill above camp. I called to them, and we had a quick lunch together; I apologized, explaining about the need to go down to meet the senior warden.

"Look, I will be back in a day or so. There is lots of food in my grub box, and I will tell Abahoy to give you anything you want, and the guards will take you anywhere you want to go." They agreed, and we looked forward to having a good time later.

On a short trip like that, I didn't need to carry much down with me, for there was a suitcase with city clothes in the Iteghie Hotel at Gondar. I wore shorts, heavy socks, boots, a bush shirt, and a jersey, with a little money in my pocket, an ammunition belt with twenty rounds, a sheath knife, and a loaded .303. Leaving an hour for lunch to settle, I set off at a run, rifle at trail, switching it from hand to hand. Ineyu, who had come up with loads of roofing tin, caught up with me on the Michibi meadow, driving back the small herd of pack horses. The horses carried only their pack saddles; Ineyu was a fantastic rider, and he raced the animals, leaping from one mount to another as the animal tired, and whooping, yelling, driving the horses along the narrow, dusty, boulder-strewn paths, over rolling,

The Geech problem

green-turfed meadows, and up hills rutted with donkey trails, ducking under the low branches of giant heather and Saint-John's-wort. The galloping horses paced me, and I ran with them, leaping over boulders, with the sun burning down on my body, soaked with sweat and caked with dust. It was an exhausting run, but at the same time it was exhilarating, and I was glad that wind had at last come to me, and that my lungs, blood, and heart had adapted to the altitude. On a good horse or a mule, the trip from Sankabar to Debarek, a distance of about twenty-five kilometers, very rarely took less than four hours, and for most people it took five. My time that day was two hours and forty minutes.

I stopped running in the marketplace at Debarek. People were staring at me, and Ineyu shouted out to them as we went through, telling them of the run, and the time it took, for he had never come down so fast either. The beer in Berhanu's bar never tasted better. The horses were taken care of, and Ineyu joined me in the bar. We bought each other beers and told each other that we were brave and strong. A local hill chief in the bar was incredulous, staring at my filthy legs and face, at the rifle and ammunition belt. Foreigners couldn't run! They could hardly sit on a horse! No, no, old father, said Ineyu, this lord is not a foreigner, he is a Simien man. But my legs shook with the after-effects, and the beer, cool and delicious, went to my head.

Driver Tesfae found us and insisted that I come to his house, for his woman had prepared food for me. Tesfae had rented a tiny mud-walled shack for a couple of dollars a month, and had found himself a young woman to sleep with and to cook for him. She had a daughter of about eleven. Tesfae had laid on a feast, with much beer, injera, and wat.

Ethiopia has a tremendous variety of native foods, far more than most other African countries. One of the most delicious dishes is doro wat. Properly prepared, doro wat is made of chicken and hard-boiled eggs, simmered in an earthenware dish in a sauce of butter, onions, garlic, red pepper, various spices, salt, and probably a lot of other ingredients that I never discovered.

A big basket of fresh injera, made of white teff,* was set in front of us, and the hot sauce ladled into the middle of the pile of big

* The principal cereal of Ethiopia, producing minute red or white grains, from which large, slightly sour-tasting pancakes, called injera, are made.

pancakes. The little girl brought warm water for us to wash our hands before we ate. Tesfae and I shared the basket, as is the custom; Tesfae took choice pieces of chicken, picking them up delicately with a folded piece of injera and setting the pieces in front of me. Several times he took a wad of food in his fingers and placed it in the woman's mouth. This custom, called *gursha,* is a sign of affection and respect, and is surely as old as the human race itself. Food and beer were forced upon me until I could hardly move. At the end of a meal, warm water, soap, and a towel are brought for the men to wash their hands again, and Ethiopians swill out their mouths too. The woman prepared coffee and fanned a dish of coals and incense to fill the little house with scented smoke.

I needed to sleep, and sleep I did in the cab of the Toyota as we drove back into Gondar.

Doctors had told me that the sickness contracted by the woman in Sankabar was almost certain to be typhus. The disease is transmitted by lice and was very common in this province. As a precaution, I obtained chloramphenicol capsules and noted the dosage to be given.

John Blower and I reached Sankabar before the mules. John's stride was the long, straight-backed, unchanging lope of a British Army man, and his stamina was fantastic. No matter how much he sat in an office, he could still go out into the field and beat the youngest and fittest men on a march.

In camp, after a snack and a lot of tea, I had Abahoy build a big fire in the shallow, rock-ringed pit by my tent. He had slaughtered and butchered a fat young sheep the day before. I took the joints of mutton and wrapped them in aluminum foil, smothered in onions, garlic, wild thyme, wild sage, salt, pepper, and chopped-up pieces of the fatty tail. When the fire burned down to coals, I laid the foil-wrapped joints on top and covered them with a three-inch layer of earth and dead ashes. Over this I built another fire, not so big, but enough to do the rest of the cooking. With the meat and a few potatoes in the pit oven, John and I went off to try to spot a few Walia.

The Geech problem

The sick woman had come out of her delirium but was still not
normal. She had recovered from the first attacks of the disease, and
the medicine did nothing for her now. Azezew had still not returned. All the tents were dusted with DDT, the mattresses taken
out to air in the sun. Many spray bombs of insecticide were used on
them. I made pole racks and ordered that the bedding must be aired
every day. I told the men to keep their clothes washed. The Simien
men thought all of this a waste of time, and indeed injurious to
health, for, as they knew, the disease the foreigner called typhus
came, not as he claimed, from lice, but from the devil.

At the same time, many other problems had to be discussed: the
route of the road, and the urgency of it, the poor quality and training of the guards, forest destruction, erosion, buildings, boundaries,
legislation and control. With most of these problems, all we could
do was to go on pushing the Imperial Government, but as to the
guards accused of deserting, or being absent without leave and so
forth, John pointed out that I was in charge, and to hell with Addis
Ababa if all they could do was ignore reports and letters. John said
if he was in charge he would fire them.

Ah, that night we had a feast! Rough red wine from Asmara, and
whiskey, and a big earthen pot of good talla, with a dancing
campfire of dried logs under a clear night sky. Bats dipped and
squeaked. Dr. Wan and Mr. Yamada had cooked up a big pot of
spaghetti in a savory soup, which we had first, with Yamada slurp-
ing thunderously in the Japanese fashion, while Ermias and I
exchanged amused glances across the fire. The foil-wrapped meat
and baked potatoes were dug out of the coals and laid on a hot, flat
stone to be carved. The meat was done to a turn, tender, flavored
with the herbs and moist with juices. We ate the whole sheep and
drank three bottles of wine, a bottle of whiskey, and about two gallons of talla. Conversation became easy and jovial, though not foolish and raucous. I believe we all felt the companionship inspired by
fire, meat, the open sky and stars. From the first beginnings of the
human race, men have felt this warm communion in the act of eating meat around a campfire. Food under shelter is a woman's rite
and has always been so. We represented the races of three conti-
nents. Africa, where man began. Asia, where civilization began. Europe, where technology began. It struck me that if politicians and

diplomats were to meet in such circumstances and be forced to perform simple menial tasks like cutting wood and fetching water, instead of being behind their barricades of desks, podiums, ceremony, and prepared speeches, then they might see more of the similarities of man, rather than the difficulties and differences. But then, maybe I always see things too simply. I do know, however, that I have hunkered around hundreds of campfires, and I have never quarreled with any man who has shared meat with me in this way, and neither have I ever forgotten him. Can't say the same thing about meals in houses.

Yamada laughed at me as I gnawed on a leg of mutton and swigged wine from the bottle being passed around.

"This style suits you, Nicol, just like a pirate, with that fur hat and the rifle."

I looked across at him, hunched down and poking the fire with a stick.

"We are a nation of pirates and shopkeepers. But look at you—grow your hair a little longer, tie it in a topknot, and you could be a hill samurai of long ago."

There was a lot of tedious administrative work to get done the next day, and we worked at it in the big tent. There was also a list of men to be fired. We compiled this in the presence of Nadu and the senior guard, Tedla. They were told that if they had anything to say in the defense of the nine men we were going to dismiss, then they must say it, and what they said would be recorded. Much of the information against the men came from Nadu himself.

Most of the offenses involved absences. When most of the guards had taken the job, through the influence of this or that important relative, they regarded it as a special right; the position meant pay, a rifle, uniform, and importance. They swaggered around their home villages. They had no understanding of what a national park was, nor had they the will or interest to learn. They had become owners of rifles, government men, with many rights and privileges. Later, I learned that several of them had killed men in blood and land feuds. It is said, in the hills, that a man is not a man until he has killed another man, and perhaps this might explain their great obsession with the rifle.

John was sitting outside under the eaves of the tent, huddled behind a tripod, camera, and telephoto lens. He had wired sheep bones and staked them out around the camp area to tempt the lammergeyers. There is probably no other place in the world where this mighty bird can be seen and photographed as easily as it can be in the Simien. These birds are huge, with wing spans of seven feet and even more. Their bellies are stained reddish orange by the iron in the rocks; otherwise their plumage is russet and brown. On the ground they look fierce and beautiful, great eagle heads, with a tufted "beard." The lammergeyer is also called the bearded vulture, but it has none of the scrawny-necked ugliness of true vultures, and stands halfway between eagle and vulture. They take large bones and fly with them over the cliffs, dropping the bones on the rocks below, thereby breaking them so that they can get at the marrow.

As I typed out my report I could hear the rush of air in their pinions as they boldly swept low over the tent. Nadu said they were bad birds, sheep killers, yet I have often watched lammergeyers swoop low over sheep and never once did the sheep show fear, a good indication that the lammergeyer does little harm to a healthy animal, for an animal knows its natural enemies only too well. Nadu also said the big birds would sweep Walia kids off the cliff ledges. To this I said that if what he claimed was true, and indeed it might be, then this was God's way of making the Walia females take care of their kids, and of making Walia cautious on the cliffs. Certainly, if the big birds swept near female and young on the cliffs, the female would run to the young, and the young to the female. Nadu argued and said there was a local law that for each lammergeyer killed, the local people would give a sheep; I suspected Nadu of killing the birds himself. John overheard, and told Nadu that the lammergeyer was protected as well as the Walia, and that there would be serious trouble for anyone caught killing it.

In the afternoon John and I went over the Sankabar site, discussing the building needs and locations. So much could be done, with the money to do it! And the road!

We rode up to Geech the next day. There John, Bernhard Nievergelt, and I went off to spot Walia, but saw only one young male, though the lanner falcons darted about the cliff tops and delighted us.

Dr. Wan collected blood samples and ticks from upland cattle, and joked with Nadu, who wanted Dr. Wan to come and treat the people in Amba Ras.

"I'm a cow doctor, not a human doctor, but if your people are cows, then I will treat them."

John spent three nights in the Simien on this trip. Major Gizaw had been reluctant to let him come up at all, saying that the visit was unnecessary. But John could see the problems and suggested solutions on the spot, agreeing with almost everything I said.

We all went to Gondar together. Mr. Yamada wanted to go on up north, and Dr. Wan had to return to his duties at the office in Gondar. Blower and I were invited to see the Governor General at his home. Some military men were being entertained there too—two Ethiopian officers and an Israeli adviser. Conversation was polite, the same old things. I asked the Governor General to come and visit the Simien himself soon, and he said he would, although I knew he wouldn't. His wife, a granddaughter of the Emperor, was a charming lady, her English as perfect as her manners. Two klipspringers minced about the house on their dainty hooves, taking tidbits from the coffee table. The thought struck me that the worthy Governor General probably didn't have a permit to keep the animals, and I was vaguely amused.

John Blower left the following morning. It was March 3. I saw the police general and handed over a report on forest cutters. I went to see a Swedish friend, an engineer directing a Swedish aid program, building schools. He was designing furniture for me. Then I sent a telegram to my wife in Tokyo, asking when she could come, for I hadn't seen her for five months and it worried me.

A couple of mornings after John left Gondar, while I was waiting for an answer to my telegram and fussing around getting windows made and fireplaces welded, Kassa, our new clerk, sent from Addis Ababa, Tesfae, and I went out along the main road and caught a couple of poachers with serval skins and took them to the police station. They were poor peasants, barefooted and thin. Actually, I didn't believe much good would be done by jailing these poor men, and really only wanted to scare them, so that they would tell others of what happened. "You are poor men, and you know very little, you didn't even recognize the government badge on the car" —the police all laughed at this—"so this time we will not press charges against you, but a warning will be entered here, and the skins confiscated. The next time, you go to jail." I left and went out to the pickup. Tesfae and Kassa came out a few minutes later with the serval skins, a female and two kittens, probably killed together. The two released peasants followed us out and spoke to Kassa. He laughed at them and waved them away.

"What is it?"

"They want you to give them money for the skins, because they say they have spent much time today."

I shook my head incredulously. Kassa argued, and the peasants alternately pleaded and argued. We got into the Toyota and drove off. Nobody was convinced, nothing changed, and a morning was wasted.

Armed with an official letter requisitioning assistance for the survey of the Simien road, I went again to see the chief of the Imperial Highways Authority in Gondar. He was very nice, but said he couldn't possibly send surveyors, as all he had instructions to do from his headquarters was to give us "technical advice." I said that I thought this would include a road survey, to advise us where the road should run, but the chief did not agree. He said, however, that I was free to come to his office anytime to discuss problems. I thanked him and left, still holding my official letter with its magnificent array of stamps and seals.

Meanwhile, in Sankabar, the mother of the sick woman had contracted the disease, had become delirious, and died. Ermias knew that in my absence he would have to take care of everything, and get the body to hallowed ground to be buried. The guards feared to go near the body because of the devils, and Ermias entreated them as Christians. He brought out a bottle of alcohol and little wads of cotton wool. He soaked the cotton wool with alcohol and put it in his nostrils, saying that this was a sure preventive. The men trusted him and were impressed by this, for they themselves would put herbs into their nostrils against devils, sickness, vampires, and the medicine of Ermias smelled powerful. Ermias won them over, and distributed the cotton-wool wads. They wrapped the frail body in a mat and carried it eight kilometers to the church at Michibi. There the old lady was buried, with no sons, daughters, or grandchildren to attend her grave, for they all had avoided her and the sick daughter because of the devils that had possessed them. In death, the old lady was treated with more kindness than she had been during the last month of her life, for only when she had died could the men be persuaded to go near her, and for that act they were praised as good men. Her daughter still lay in a rough shelter in the bushes at Sankabar, tended by her twelve-year-old son, a thin, intelligent lad. We fed her, but Azezew had still not returned; people said he had injured his ankle and could not walk.

Ermias worked hard while I was in Gondar. The floors of my house were cemented, the frame finished, the roof ready for tin sheets. People came to stare at it and to walk around inside, marveling at its complexity and the design of the roof. They said it was as beautiful as a church, but were amazed that I would intend to hide the beautiful tin sheets later on with thatch.

Sonako sent a telegram to say she would come in May, and I was relieved and happy, and drank with Dr. Wan to celebrate. Peace settled over me, and I felt that now I could go back to the mountains and work hard for another month, my mind uncluttered by worries about my family.

I had to go up to Geech to pay the coolies. Two guards went on ahead with my sleeping bag and some rations and the cash box. At one point, a bunch of cattle blocked the narrow path; I tried to drive them back down, but they dodged and scrambled past on the precipitous scree slopes below the path. I picked up a rock and hurled it at one. The rock hit the cow behind the horn; its neck went stiff, eyes rolled up, and it fell and rolled about two hundred feet down the slope. An hour farther along, on the Amba Ras side of the Djinn Barr Valley, I looked back with binoculars and saw many vultures circling the spot.

About a kilometer out from the Geech camp one of the little valleys running down to the Djinn Barr echoed with the sounds of axes. I led the riding mule down through the tree heather and looked across the little valley at fourteen men and boys cutting trees on the side of the steep slope, right in the middle of the proposed park boundaries. Whips whirled and cracked over the backs of stumbling, paired oxen, as they strained to haul out the stumps. Clods of dislodged earth bounced and tumbled down the hill. I shouted at them to stop, but they merely looked up and went on working. Shouting, I went up to the camp at a gallop.

❈❈❈❈

The guards and Berhanu came out and stared at me. Even at the camp one could hear the *thock, thock, thockety, thock* tattoo of axes.

"Can't you idle, lazy, dirty, scrofulous, syphilitic sons of whores hear that?"

There was no doubt that they knew what was going on, especially guards Dawd and Hussein, two Moslems, who had relatives among the men cutting down the forest. Ordering them to follow, I took off at a run, carrying only rifle and ammunition belt. Guards Hussein, Dawd, Ambaw, and Amara followed, with Berhanu in the rear. We came down through the forest to the head of the slope where the men were cutting and working. Over three hundred trees had been cut. I shouted at them to stop, and they ignored me. I got angry and leaped down the slope in great jumps, leaped into the midst of them and sent one man head over heels into a pile of brush. Another shouted angrily and I threw him down the hill too. Yelling and cursing, I rounded them all up while the guards stood at the top of the hill, looking embarrassed.

"Berhanu, get down here with those bastard game guards and arrest these men." The guards came down, cautiously. "Tell them to put their hands over their heads." Reluctantly, everyone obeyed.

"All right. Now, Berhanu, you tell Hussein to pick out any boys under sixteen and send them home."

He did. That left eight men. We marched them up to the camp to be charged. On the way I knelt by one of the stumps and quickly counted the annual rings. Well over three hundred years for this particular patch of forest to grow and gather soil under its roots.

I had intended to lock the prisoners up in the small tool hut and take them down to Debarek in the morning. The leader was a man named Che Yenous, a Moslem of some standing from Geech, whose father was supposed to be a holy man, a man of great power in the village. Dawd and Hussein pleaded for their relatives, and begged me to forgive them and let them go home. I agreed, provided Dawd would sign a guarantee that he would be responsible for these men, and that they would all report to the court in Debarek when called, and would cut no more trees. Everybody promised, gathered tools, and went home, visibly stunned and subdued, even the arrogant Che Yenous.

In the early morning nearly all the men from Geech were sitting around outside, waiting for me. Acres of locals in gabis. The sheik, the religious leader, got up and gave a speech. He was an old man, with a scraggly white beard and a green silk turban. His eyes were rheumy, his robes torn and gray, but he bore himself with dignity and pride, and I felt rather young. As he spoke he fingered the beads around his neck.

"To sin is human, but to forgive is divine, and if you, a lord, can forgive these poor men for the wrong they did, then God will smile upon you and bless you, and these men will do no more wrong . . ." He went on for a long time. The idea was for me to drop the charges, and not report to Dejasmatch Araya, whom everyone feared.

"My job is to protect the national park lands. These men broke the law. I have no power to forgive, and for this they must state their case in court."

Dawd whispered to Berhanu that if I would forgive them, the people would give me a fat sheep. Berhanu spoke angrily to him, warning him not to ask me, but Dawd did, and I understood. I turned to Berhanu.

"Tell him that to bribe or to attempt to bribe a government officer is a serious crime for which I will see him jailed if he or anyone else tries again."

This idea was so strange that they gasped and stared. Berhanu explained that foreigners were not like the Ethiopian officials, and did not like to accept presents from the people, for it was not the custom.

The Geech people left, muttering curses at me and at the guards, but the sun was warm, and climbed quickly, and as I watched an augur buzzard patiently waiting on the top of a tall lobelia spike, I lost my irritation in the colors and life of the highland moors. I went for a walk until nine A.M., when I had to be back at camp for a radio schedule.

On the radio I complained to John again about the month's salary which the men had not received. He chased it up, and I heard that

The Geech problem

it was being sent through the bank from headquarters funds. The senior guard, Major Gizaw's relative, Amara, had stolen the money and couldn't pay it back. As is usual in Ethiopia, they then reasoned that if they dismissed him, he would not be able to pay back the money, so they kept him quiet, and us quiet, by paying out of other sources. In any event, the guards in the Simien would be glad to get their money at last. Of course, everybody had known all along that the man had stolen it.

When Guard Mitiku came back from his lowland patrol, he brought with him a lieutenant of the vigilantes, with a petition for us to take action against the baboons. At Shagné, a village below the Michibi Afaf, a big herd of olive baboons had been rampaging, killing goats and calves, destroying crops; they had even bitten children who had tried to drive them off with stones. The baboons were growing bolder, and the big dog-faced males were fearsome creatures. Ermias read the petition, and we asked who among the guards were the best shots. Nadu said that after him, Mitiku and Ambaw were best. I issued both of these guards five rounds of extra ammunition and told them to go down to Shagné and kill ten big baboons. They were to hang the dead baboons from trees around the fields, for I believed that this would give the people confidence, though I told them that the sight of the punished baboons would frighten the rest of the herd away. After the shooting, the herd would be wary of a man with a gun, and all a villager would have to do for some time after would be to walk out with his rifle and scare them off. I promised a bottle of beer for each baboon they killed, and demanded a bottle of beer for each time they missed. Guards Mitiku and Ambaw were delighted, and left before dawn the next day.

They killed the baboons easily by circling round and sneaking up on the herd as it raided a field of corn. The first shots, from close range, killed big males. Other males charged them, snarling and screaming, sacrificing themselves, whether deliberately or not, while the rest of the herd escaped. Twelve dead baboons were hung from trees, and the Shagné people feasted the two guards and sang songs of their bravery and skill.

Of course, ten was not enough; we should have had a proper control program. However, for that we would need better rifles, fast, accurate little guns powerful enough to kill a baboon with a body shot, but using ammunition cheap enough to allow a lot of shooting. We had neither the men, the ammunition, nor the time. All that the Shagné baboon killing did was to make that particular herd a little wary of guns for a time.

Leslie Brown, the famous wildlife expert and author, was visiting Ethiopia on a study tour. He was preparing a progress report for UNESCO on the state of the wildlife conservation program in Ethiopia. Before coming to this country, I had read, in his book, *Ethiopian Episode*, the description of a safari to the Simien. Brown outlined the awful problem of erosion, and suggested that the Simien would make a fantastic national park. I had wanted to meet him ever since I had read his book, and I was delighted to get an order over the radio to go down and meet him in Addis Ababa.

Brown had interviewed the wardens and assistant wardens of Awash and Omo in the field. He had not enough time to go to the Simien, so I was the last warden to see him. He appears to be a very fierce man, and his temper is legendary, as is the temper of his brother George, warden of Awash. His speech is precise and abrupt, and it was said that Major Gizaw and the other staff members dreaded him like a devil. He said what he thought, and he thought very little of Ethiopia's progress in the wildlife conservation field. It was Leslie Brown who often said, "In all Africa, no country has been more brutally ravaged by man."

The Emperor received a copy of the report, and minor explosions ruffled the still, calm waters of government apathy. It was pointed out that the department was ridiculously top-heavy, with the bulk of finances going to support headquarters, while the extremities, the parks, withered from lack of funds. Simien was the farthest extremity; the money I received for the park was less than my salary. All wardens complained that reports and letters were ignored, sometimes not even read. Conservation legislation, drafted by John Blower long before, was waiting for approval and signature by the Minister. At that time (1968), Ethiopia must have been the last country south of the Sahara to be without national parks, for the boundary and legislative declarations had not been signed. The situation was a complete mess. Headquarters grew and grew, but existed only for itself. And it was the Minister who once impatiently remarked, while being bothered about all this, "Wildlife conservation? It's a peculiar Anglo-Saxon disease." And I suspected that His

The Walia ibex.

ABOVE: *The Dejasmatch Araya.*

RIGHT: *The head priest of Deresghie in the Simien.*

LEFT TOP: *Mountain chiefs riding out to greet Haile Selassie in Gondar.*

LEFT BOTTOM: *Celebration of Maskal in Gondar.*

A herd of gelada baboons.

The mouth of the Djinn Bar Falls.

The Geech problem

Imperial Majesty's grasp of conservation did not extend much beyond the zoo in back of the palace; in this, too, he struck me, in my more desperate moments, as a medieval monarch.

I made the suggestion several times that if the government could not give me funds to develop the park, they might as well save their money and let me go. But it was as if the presence of a foreign game warden was magical and miraculous. His Majesty could be reassured that all was well, with the foreigners taking care of everything. Or perhaps real interest in conservation was the element that was miraculous?

The department was very upset that I had fired the nine men, and said I had no right to do it, the Central Personnel Agency would not permit it. I said fuck the Central Personnel Agency, the deed was done, and I wasn't going to deal with those men anymore. When Major Gizaw and Ato Balcha said I had never mentioned any trouble with the men before, I became angry and brought out the file with copies of the reports and letters I had written. The personnel officer was blamed for everything, poor man, and was called into the office to get raked over the coals and fined fifty dollars. With the exception of John Blower, none of the people in the office had read any of my reports.

Two of the nine dismissed guards were in Addis Ababa at this time to file an appeal against my decision. One was Guard Berehun, fired for going AWOL and refusing to report for duty, and the other, Guard Atakult, a cousin of Dejasmatch Araya, was the laziest, scruffiest guard we had. He was supposed to be the deputy chief guard; I had fired him for going AWOL too. Both of these men, I was told, came to Addis Ababa with signed notes from Nadu, saying that he had given them leave permission.

I was furious, and brought out the report, signed by Nadu and Tedla, accusing the men of being absent without leave. Nadu was the man who complained first about them, and gave the details. I pounded the desk, said that Nadu had no right to give anybody leave, and nobody could give leave for months at a time, not even Gizaw. I said Nadu was a liar, and that he must be called to Addis Ababa, questioned, and dismissed.

But arguing was pointless. The faked notes got the men off, and the department forgave them. I grew tired of argument, for there were so many other vital things on my mind. They promised that if anyone else stepped out of line, he would be fired. But I doubted it. The men all got jobs because of their relationship to an "important person," and in this kind of system, one could not rock the boat. I tried to make it clear, however, that if Nadu's word was to be accepted over my judgment, I would resign.

In truth, I didn't want to resign. The Simien Mountain National Park and the survival of the Walia ibex were more important than these quarrels, and at that time I believed that eventually I would win. I began to think a lot about Agafari Nadu Worota, and I began to watch him more carefully.

Meanwhile, in the Simien, most of the sand, cement, and other materials had been carried up to the sites. If the money lasted, we could perhaps get all the houses finished by the onset of the rains. The Nievergelts had been a long time in their tent, and it was hard on Esther, with the bitter cold of mornings and evenings. When I got back they were on their way out for a couple of weeks to take the car to Addis for servicing. I promised that we would modify one of the little stone huts and convert it into a small cottage with higher stone walls, a good roof, cement floors, a kitchen annex, windows, a sink, and stove. They could live in this little place until the big house was finished. Masons had already come up from Debarek, Tigre Province men, who have skill with stones.

Tools and rope had been stolen from the camp. It was probably our own men; we did not have a lock-up store at that time, only tents. The guards thought I should close one path leading by the camp on the north side, for the guards believed that passersby could easily pilfer while Ermias and I were working. I had tried posting guards, but that did not work. So we closed the northern path with a barricade, and widened and improved another path running just to the south, a path which was actually far better suited to pack animals, and which would not inconvenience the villagers traveling to and from the Debarek market. Guards were posted at the diversion of the paths, with instructions to ask the people, politely and gently, to use the southern path. Very few people objected.

But one morning as I was writing notes in the tent, a chief from Michibi passed through with his retinue of armed followers. The guard posted at the diversion could not bring himself to ask such a big man to use another path, and merely bowed and kissed his hand. Chief Mesfin was a rich man, with many followers and cattle and several rifles, and a house with a tin roof. He was greatly feared for his temper. On this day he brought only six or so men with him; they were on their way up to Amba Ras for a funeral. The chief, in his turban and gabi, swaggered ahead of the riding mule, led by a boy who also carried the chief's rifle. Simien game guards ran out to greet him, bowing, kissing his hand, exchanging kisses and long greetings with his followers.

Guard Techale stepped out into the path, blocking it, his rifle held across his body. He ordered the chief to go back and use the southern path. Chief Mesfin was astonished. Nobody in the Simien had ever dared to speak to him like that, least of all a man from the south. He roared at Techale to get out of his way. The Simien guards remonstrated with the angry Techale as if he were a child who had forgotten his manners, but Techale stood firm and told the chief that he would give him no more warnings. The chief tried to push Techale out of the way, and the followers surrounded him. Mesfin was a big man, but Techale moved with the speed and balance of a trained soldier, causing his assailant to stagger back. Mesfin shouted at Techale, calling him a coward and a Galla slave. Techale forgot his training, thrust the rifle into Guard Ambaw's hands, and pushed Mesfin in the chest, forcing him back again.

At this moment I saw the chief reach under the loose gabi wound over his shoulders to snap open a pistol holster and fumble for the old service revolver he carried. His face was twisted with rage. Two guards had pinned Techale's arms from behind, and the followers stood ready with their rifles. I thought he would kill Techale. I snatched for my hunting rifle, jacked in a round and knelt, as the Eskimo hunters do when they stalk seal behind a screen. The range was forty yards, and I was on a knoll. The big man's turbanned head was in my sights, and if he cleared leather and cocked back the hammer of his pistol, my soft-nosed hunting bullet would blow half of his head off before he could shoot. I had taken seal from greater range than this, from a moving boat, with fast head shots, and I liked the feel of this English rifle.

I waited for a few minutes. Perhaps the followers saw me, for they got between the two raging, cursing men and stopped it. I put the rifle away and went down the slope, very angry. Mesfin and his followers hurried away, hurling insults back over their shoulders, promising to return. Ermias came hurrying out.

I shouted at the guards and brought them to attention. This exhibition of disloyalty and weakness to their fellow guard disgusted me. I asked the guards what had happened, why the man had been allowed to pass. Techale spoke first, said that the man tried to pull out his pistol and threatened to kill him. I glared at the Simien men. "Well, is it true? Is it?" The Simien men all denied that such a thing had happened; they laughed and said it was all Techale's fault for being rude to such a big man. I threw down my hat with the government badge and tore out the gold Walia insignia on my shirt.

"Right. Ermias, you tell these lying swine this. I saw everything that happened, and I do not like liars. I am going to act like a man now, not a game warden, and I'm going to fight all five of these despicable cowards. Techale had better go back to his tent and stay there until you tell him to come out."

The guards looked down at their feet and muttered that well, perhaps the chief did put his hand down by his pistol, but he didn't really mean to use it, he only wanted to frighten Techale. I turned on my heels and left them. Ermias talked to them for a long time, for he was very angry too.

I reported the incident to the police, pointing out that had I been obliged to kill this man in defense of Techale, there would have been so much trouble in Simien that the park project would have to have been shelved. Certainly I could not have stayed there. The next time Chief Mesfin went into Debarek the police arrested him and threw him in jail for two or three days to cool off.

It was not really that the Simien men were cowards, for they were not. This had been proved time and time again during the Italian occupation. At times, they were fiercely brave, with a passionate temper. But Simien society was closely knit, and a man could not go against his relatives, friends, relatives of friends, or friends of relatives. That was why no arrests had been made. The term "brother" was used loosely, but carried many obligations. Land was tribal, or village property, with no clear definition of where this man's land ended and another man's land began. To defend the land was a sacred duty to Muslim or Christian, and to do this, a man would need the rifles of his friends and relatives. Strangely, by the same count, the greater number of killings that occurred in the Simien were the result of quarrels between relatives over land they owned jointly. My servant Abahoy, who knifed his cousin, was an example of this.

The Geech problem

It is a pity that the Amhara do not have a system of family names; rather, like ancient Europe, they use the Christian name of the father as the second name, so that names are not passed down. Thus, the son of Berhanu Tessema (Berhanu, son of Tessema) would be Wolde Berhanu, and his son would be Abahoy Wolde, and so on. Had there been family names in the Simien, I think it would have been found that there were very few original families, and that most of the Simien people were in some way related.

I had become extremely attached to the trees of the Simien. The shapes of the weirdly twisted giant heather fascinated me, and made me think of the tortured dwarf trees of Japan. The new tips of the foliage were vividly green, while the older foliage was duller, almost metallic, and the trunks bore intricate patterns, delicate as fine Japanese pottery, shaped from the lichens, grays, yellows, pallid green, and gentle brown, all on the blackish brown of the trunks. The wood of the tree heather was red and hard. Coming up from Debarek, I could recognize certain trees, like old friends, but each time I came up and passed my old tree friends, one or more had been mutilated by the clumsy axe strokes of the villagers, or cut completely, leaving sad, angry stumps like petrified dwarfs kneeling in circles of chippings.

The Simien people could never understand my rage, and I tried to hide it, tried instead to tell them, no, don't cut here along the paths and on the slopes, but cut where the trees are too thick, or cut the sick trees, like this one, or that one. But they always ignored me, for I was a foreigner, and knew nothing.

There was a place on the way up called Addis Gey. It had a beautiful little meadow with a clear stream that tumbled over small, rocky waterfalls. Slopes of tree heather forest came down to it, and there were many flowers and spiked lobelias. The villagers were always cutting there, having cleared all the trees from near their homes, and they were beginning to make the valley ugly with stumps and ensuing erosion; in the end they would kill the forest-shaded springs, and the stream would dry up. There are so many of these dead valleys, ugly, bare, eroded. Four times I had gone to Addis Gey and warned the people.

Then one day, when I was out with Kassa and Guard Ambaw, I heard axe blows in the Addis Gey forests. Moving quietly through the trees toward the sound, I found the culprit and several trees already felled. I told the man to stop and walked toward him. He raised his axe. I caught it and slapped him on the side of the head with an open hand, then took him by the collar and propelled him through the forest to where the others were waiting.

We marched him twenty kilometers to Debarek. He didn't want to go, but each time he stopped to argue I kicked him in the rear. Soon a great crowd followed us, brothers, father, cousins, friends, the local priest. They yelled and pleaded, offered us sheep, encouraged the young man to run away. As we approached Debarek the din behind us became horrendous. They could easily have overwhelmed us, for Kassa had no weapon, Ambaw was the only one with a rifle, and I had an automatic, a Walther PPK. I stopped and faced them, and told them if they were not quiet and did not stop trying to interfere with me while I was doing my duty, I would be forced to arrest them all, and take them all down to Debarek. Fortunately, none stopped to consider how I should do this, and the bluff worked. The people quietly followed us to Debarek, where I marched the prisoner into the Governor's office, laid the axe on his desk, and told him of the case. The Dejasmatch glowered at the cringing peasant and ordered his guards to take him over to the jail. I explained that we wanted just one man from this village made an example of, so that the people would know that we had the support of the Governor in our work. He promised his support, and we thanked him and left.

The prisoner was released in less than an hour. The people laughed and jeered about it, and Kassa was in a rage. The worthy Dejasmatch was richer by a sheep. What the hell.

※◈◈◈※

In Sankabar the sick woman died, and Azezew, who brought her there in the first place, never showed up. Instead, her former husband, and the father of her son, came once with a bag of ground barley, a little coffee, and some pepper. Then he took the boy away. She was crazy when she died. I had given orders by this time that

The Geech problem

there would be no women or children in the camp until we could properly accommodate them. Trying to make the guards keep their mattresses and bodies free from lice was almost impossible, for the Simien men washed only hands and face, sometimes their feet. They believed that to expose their bodies to the air and sun was injurious. Techale complained about them, especially the women, who were even dirtier than the men. I feared epidemics. Guard Mitiku told me that in Amba Ras alone, fifty children had already died that year. Dr. Nievergelt had ordered typhus vaccine from Europe, and we had antibiotics, but it was barely enough to keep ourselves and the guards in health, let alone a lot of women and children in over-crowded tents.

Dysentery was rife, and the local habit of defecating in the bushes was beginning to foul the camp area and draw flies. We had good, clean, pit latrines, with screens, and we explained their use many times. But the natives ignored the latrines and the buckets of disinfectant for their hands. Finally I threatened to grab the first man or woman caught shitting in the bushes and rub his or her face in it, and I meant it.

"Listen," I said one day, "whether Christian, Muslim, or Felasha, we all know that all that is good and clean comes from God, and all that is dirty and evil comes from Satan. We cast out dirt from our bodies. Flies, which are evil and filth, land on the dung of a sick person, and then they carry the evil that is in the dung to your food, or to your children's eyes, and thus you get sick from the evil that was in the dung. You must use the holes, and each day we will cover the dung with soil so the flies cannot come. You know that lice are dirt, they make your bodies itch. A louse takes the blood of a sick man, and the evil that was in the blood. The louse crawls to your body and brings evil with it, and you become sick from the evil that the louse carried. You must set out your sleeping garments in the sun, which is strong and clean, for evil likes darkness and hates sun, and the lice will die in the sun. And you must keep clean, and use the powder in the tents. The medicine that I have is not magic, I am not a sorcerer, the medicine is poison that kills only the evil in your body. As you are in my camp, then you must obey my orders, even if you say it is not your custom . . ."

Oh, they listened, fascinated, proclaimed that I was a prophet, a wise man, their father and mother and lord, and they would agree that I was correct, but still they could never overcome their conservatism.

I shuddered to think how my wife Sonako would feel about all this, with her fastidious Japanese cleanliness. I would just have to keep constant watch on everything that went on in camp.

Guard Dawd had been sent on a two-week patrol to his home area, partly because he had been a long time on duty in the park, and partly to get away from the influence of Guard Chane. He came back on the day promised, a rare thing, with notes in Arabic script of each patrol he ran out of his home. The largest group of Walia he had seen was six, a big male, two young females, and one adult female and kid. He saw Walia every day, but in threes and fours. Walia used to run in herds of forty, fifty, even sixty before the occupation. The same thing was true of bushbuck, klipspringer, duiker, and colobus. From Sankabar we could look down on the hills and cliffs that Dawd had patrolled, with carpets of remnant forest. I could not believe that game was so scarce, but I knew Dawd to be a good spotter and an honest man about the animals he saw. He saw no leopard, though he heard one. Baboons were increasing, becoming more troublesome, killing even young donkeys and calves, as well as sheep and goats, and their massed, organized raids were getting bolder. The people were cutting heavily, especially around Torowato, below the main escarpment, and also below Michibi. Dawd remonstrated with them, and the men blamed the children for mischievously setting fires. Everybody knew that was a lie.

So the people destroyed forest and leopards, thereby improving and extending the habitat of the baboons, and the herd perhaps was getting a little above its optimum size, quickly increasing to fill the extended habitat. Overgrazing would make for weakened stock, and therefore easier killing for the baboons, who were, after all, primates, and very adaptable to fresh food opportunities.

The great difference between Dawd and the others, especially Nadu, was that if Dawd saw six Walia, he would report the six, the date, and the make-up of the group. Others would say, "Oh, many, many Walia," and if they traveled the whole escarpment and saw several small groups, they would report the sum seen as one group. And if Dawd saw a big old male one day, then went spotting at the same place on following days, seeing the same animal, he would report seeing the same single male at the same place, while the others would count each sighting of the same animal as a different beast, make grossly exaggerated estimates of the population, and pass the estimates on to local governors, who would pass them on to higher officials, who would believe them. After all, these were local people, were they not? They had lived there all their lives, had they not? What could a foreigner know about the Walia? Two hundred? A hundred and fifty? Ridiculous! There are thousands, thousands of Walia left in the Simien. . . .

Several visitors came to the Simien during this time, from Sweden, Kenya, the United States, Switzerland, and Germany. The Simien was becoming known, and no longer did visitors have to bring an armed escort. Our guards kept the bandits away, even though the old patterns of violence still continued among the villagers themselves, and the stories, recounted to tourists, gave an extra tingle of pleasure and adventure. . . . Geech villagers, returning from market at night, were robbed at Addis Gey by men armed with knives. The thieves were Christians, from Addis Gey, and their chief later pleaded with the Moslem elders not to report to Dejasmatch Araya. . . . A Geech man said he would plow up land that was common grazing ground, and the others said he should not. One day, when most of the people were attending a funeral, this man began to plow the land, with his rifle slung over his back. His cousin had suspected what would happen and when he saw him he ran toward him across the field. The plowman fired twice. Both shots missed, but the cousin lay down. The plowman ran off into the forest, leaving wife, children, oxen, and plow. . . .

One evening in Geech, as I was going to fetch water, I saw the silhouette of a rider, stiff in the saddle, and knew it to be a foreigner. He climbed down and greeted me in Japanese. I answered him in the same language, and we both laughed. He was a freelance journalist, a young Swiss named Johann Dornbierer, who had traveled all over Asia and Africa. He was almost frozen, dressed in only shorts and a sweater. I ushered him into the tent where we had food and alcohol and hot tea, and talked for hours. He stayed a few days, and I was glad of his company. He spent a week in Simien, then went on to the Sudan. Visitors were very special, and we always went out of our way to entertain them. We had very few facilities, but there was always good mutton, strong coffee or tea, and a bottle of wine or araki somewhere. I like to think that visitors who came to the Simien at that period carried many good memories back with them, memories of comradeship in a place lonely and difficult to reach, and memories of shared campfire and meat.

8

A WARNING FROM
THE POLICE

Nadu and Techale had quarreled badly. Nadu came to me and threatened to resign if Techale was not sent away, and said that the Simien people would kill Techale, because he insulted their national dress. What Techale had actually done was to call Nadu and the other guards peasants for wearing the gabi over their uniforms. Nadu thought it was not necessary for him to wear a uniform, for he was an important man, and all knew him. Of course, we gave orders about uniforms, and they were sometimes obeyed, but it was hard to keep watch all the time, and certainly if we did not watch, they would wear the gabi.

Techale came to the big tent and snapped to attention. He was offended by the slovenly attitude and manner of these peasants. And the trouble was that the Simien men were indeed peasants, and their idea of a soldier was not a disciplined man, but a fiercely independent, swaggering patriot hill-fighter. They had received no training before putting on the uniform. They had become owners of rifles, and were thus above criticism.

Techale handed me a written report, stating the occasions on which orders had been disobeyed regarding unauthorized people staying in the camp. The Simien men always allowed their friends and relatives to stay, Nadu especially, and these friends and relatives came from typhus-ridden villages. I called Nadu, furious with him. He smiled and said that in future my orders would be obeyed. Techale spat on the ground outside the tent eaves.

Nadu came to plead for one of the guards I had fired and refused to allow in camp. It was his relative. Nadu asked me to forgive the man, as a personal favor to him. I replied that as far as my job was concerned I gave no personal favors and had no friends. Nadu had received a bribe to do this, it was obvious, but I had no proof.

Techale's quarrels got worse. He had called Azezew a sorcerer, accusing him of putting a spell on the two women who died; and he forced Azezew's relative out of camp at gunpoint. Indeed, he had quarreled with all of them in turn, and he had insulted Agafari Nadu Worota, and that was dangerous.

Very reluctantly, I ordered Techale to go down to Debarek and stay there until further notice. He was a good soldier, but had a terrible temper, and the continual threats of the others to see him killed bore heavily on me, for Techale was one southlander among many mountain men. So I took the easy way out, fearing that they would kill him, or that he would kill one of them.

Before Techale went down to Debarek, I tried to explain all this to him, and he thanked me. Within a week of going down he got into a quarrel in a bar, threw a bottle at a policeman and hit him on the temple, knocking him out. They threw him in jail, and I went down and begged for his release on bail. I lectured Techale, telling him that his own temper was his worst enemy, and saw, in Techale, a part of myself. It sobered me a little.

Easter is an important celebration for Ethiopian Christians. It is a great religious event, and marks the end of a stern Lenten fast which lasts over a month, and sometimes almost two months. During the fasts, they eat no animal products whatsoever, neither meat, milk, butter, nor eggs. Those guards who wanted to go home for the feasting I sent off, and kept only Abahoy, two Muslim guards, and two men whose homes were far away and who did not wish to return. I was expecting the arrival of two friends, Englishmen teaching at the English school in Addis Ababa. They were going to bring with them a German Shepherd pup named Mogus, a gift to me from an Ethiopian vet. Fifty bottles of beer and ten bottles of wine had been packed in two days before, and as the Englishmen, Peter Robbs and Don Harris, approached along the trail, people shouted out to them, and called out, "Nicol's brothers are coming. He bought fifty bottles of beer!"

A warning from the police

Peter said that the people spoke well of me, and that I was famous from Debarek out. We drank much, and they both fell asleep early, while I talked on, quite to myself, singing drunken solos deep into the night. The pup Mogus stole and ate two legs of roast sheep.

In the morning the men in camp danced, jumping and stamping, waving sticks and chanting that I was king of Sankabar, and they were my warriors. Of course they knew about the beer too, and I had bought them a sheep. But in all, it was gratifying, and made me feel like a feudal baron, or a bandit chief, or a hero from a boy's book. I grinned inanely and distributed a largess of beer. And ah, but the sky was bluer than any other sky, and the sun shone brighter.

I rode up to see the Nievergelts, who had returned and moved into the little hut. Bernhard had done a lot of work, fixing it up with shelves, a cooking bench, racks in the roof, peeled branches for light and coat hooks, and putting in the sink and a fine door, and a wind fence outside. Thick wool rugs were on the floor, and with the whitewashed stone reflecting the brilliance of pressure lamps, it all looked warm and homey.

At dawn, loaded with packs containing cameras, lenses, flower press, parkas, and raincapes, we set off to watch Walia at the cliffs of Metagogo and Amba Ras. We also carried a telescope and tripod. Bernhard and Esther were fit, and Berhanu was getting used to the Simien and didn't think it was sheer hell anymore. Guard Mitiku came with us; he spoke Italian and could converse in that language with Esther.

By the cliff rims of Metagogo we put down the packs, took binoculars and crept to the grassy edges, looking over, pointing excitedly as Walia were spotted. There were eleven on one cliff, one of them a female with her kid. The kid was butting her udder and suckling, unconcerned by the horrific drop. Two big males with back-sweeping horns grazed peacefully, chomping on plants and low bushes that grew on the precarious ledges. Almost directly below us, four thousand feet and more, the round thatched houses appeared tiny in handkerchief barley fields. Looking down, I spotted a tawny eagle, circling. Ravens croaked among the echoing cliff walls. Doves climbed in flocks, in laborious spirals, up and up to reach the feeding grounds on the plateau, while hawks, eagles, lammergeyers, and vultures glided with ease on the rising currents of air.

Bernhard told me about color changes in the Walia. He said the dark stripe on the legs of the young males would extend and go across the chest when the animal reached eight years or more. The beards were an indication of age too; the beards of old males grew thick and long, befitting their patriarchal air, heavy bulk, and massive horns. Estimating the age by the horns was not so easy as I thought at first, for each growth ring did not represent a year's growth—only, so I gathered, those rings that went right around the horn. I found that estimating the age of females, looking through binoculars, was rather difficult. Their horns are much smaller and thinner, although the muzzles get longer after they reach five years or so. Every time I saw the Walia on their cliffs, I was amazed at the ease with which they traveled across the tiny paths and ledges.

Huge areas of forest had been burned off below Metagogo, right to the foot of the escarpment. On the day of the burning, a huge column of smoke spread in a thick, dark umbrella over the moors, the fire roared, and heat and smoke billowed up the cliff faces. We had watched the smoke that day and felt so helpless. Now we were looking at what the fire had done. The destruction was enormous. In North America, or Europe, or Japan, fire-fighting teams would have converged on the blaze, and thousands of dollars might have been spent in fighting it. Here, in poor Ethiopia, the ignorant peasants had fired the forest deliberately on slopes too steep even to walk up.

We went on around to the Amba Ras cliff face, which drops absolutely sheer for three thousand feet, and then tumbles another fifteen hundred feet or so. Below lay little villages on terraces divided by deep, river-cut gorges. It was like looking over the edge of one world into another world below. I have no great fear of heights, but this face terrified me, and to look over I had to crawl to the edge, grasping the tough grass in my fists, my stomach heaving. Esther sat on the edge, legs dangling over, looking down with her binoculars. "There's one, a male . . . there's another . . . see . . . by that white streak, halfway down to the right . . ." I glanced at her and looked away, horrified. Mitiku stood right at the edge, looking down, while Bernhard set up his telescope. Berhanu didn't mind it either. Wind licked up the cliff face, and on a tiny ledge below, a thick clump of everlasting flowers rustled with the breeze. As I

looked over, fascinated, it seemed that the face was moving outward, outward, tipping me over to drop me down, down, down. I
backed away, shuddering slightly, and tried nonchalantly to disguise my discomfort. I found a warm rock and leaned against it,
turning my binoculars on an augur buzzard above us, with his
snow-white belly and upturned wingtips. Wherever I had traveled,
ever since I went on my first expedition to the Arctic at seventeen, I
had chosen a bird to be my totem. Here, in the Simien, the augur
buzzard was that bird. We stayed on the Amba Ras cliff for an hour
or more and then made our way to Amba Ras village, to Nadu's
home, where we had been invited for a feast.

During the feast, Mitiku read a poem he had composed about the
killing of the baboons, praising Nadu, me, and of course, himself
and Ambaw. I was surprised that the killing of a few baboons could
mean so much. A little girl was serving us, and Nadu nodded
toward her, promising a great feast when she got married, in a few
months. We looked at each other.

"Married? But how old is she?" asked Esther.

She was nine years old. The husband-to-be was eighteen. We
three foreigners were a little shocked and tried to hide it.

"They can grow up together," said Nadu, the girl's father. He
then said he would like the little girl to come over to Geech and
help Mrs. Nievergelt, and learn many things from her. I looked at
the little girl and wondered if, well, it could be a proper wedding.
Later, we were told that girls were often married at six years of age,
to young men, and that most of them were married by the time they
reached thirteen. It shocked us, but I remembered medieval Europe, and after all, the expected life span of a Simien Ethiopian was
about the same as that of a fourteenth-century European. An Ethiopian told me that when the girls were so small, the husband would
promise not to attempt sexual intercourse, though the promises
were not always kept.

As we were about to leave, Nadu's wife asked me if I would make
her brother a game guard, for we were good friends, and he was her
brother. So that was what the feast was all about! Nadu was looking
on. I said that by all means the young man should apply, and he
would be considered along with all the other applicants. Nadu's expression did not change, but I could see the anger and dislike in his
eyes. It was the last time I went to his house.

The time of Sonako's arrival was drawing nearer, and I had promised to meet her and the children in Cairo, where they had to change planes. To leave Ethiopia meant getting an exit visa, and this meant letters, visits to offices, come-back-tomorrow, tax forms, and trouble. I had to begin well in advance of the date she would arrive.

I was walking down the main street in Gondar, after coming from the post office, when General Seyoum stopped his car alongside me, called me over, and told me to come to his office that afternoon. I went, wondering if he was going to tell me of arrangements for police patrols to go into the Simien to stop the burning.

Colonel Azziz was in the big office, acting as an interpreter. The General told me that the police had received many complaints about my molesting the people and beating them, and he ordered me not to arrest any more. I said it was my job. The General got angry and repeated that I was not to arrest any more, and added that he was advising me this way for my own sake. Colonel Azziz spoke, smiling at me.

"We understand, Mr. Nicol, that you are trying to work for the Walia, but the General gives you good advice, and you must obey him."

"Does this mean that I am to watch the people destroying the forest and do nothing about it? What is your government paying me and my guards for?"

The General glared at me, and signaled that the discussion was at an end. He commanded a big, well-armed force of paramilitary police over a vast area, and he wasn't used to arguing with young men in shorts. A corporal showed me out. An old rage was boiling in me; I felt my stomach muscles contract and I clamped my mouth shut, nervous muscles twitching around my eyes. I left police headquarters and went down the road. Gizaw says the forest is not my responsibility. The local officials release prisoners. Guards turn a blind eye. Everybody ignores patrol reports, and yet they make promises when somebody like John Blower comes up. And now I am told not to bother the people, to leave them alone to cut down and burn all the forests in a national park that I am supposed to develop.

It was quite hot. There were many flies, and they annoyed me. I opened my mouth to swear, and managed to swallow one, so I then had to go into the nearest bar and swallow two double araki to sterilize my gut. Trying to fight a one-man war could achieve nothing, and at last I realized it. My tactics had been immature, impatient, and I would have to think of other ways. I borrowed a typewriter and pounded out an epistle called "A Letter to the People of Begemdir." It explained everything we were trying to do, about parks, forests, erosion, water, wildlife, all in simple, if somewhat Biblical, terms. My Ethiopian friends were impressed, and it was translated for me. I intended to get it copied and distributed among the Simien people.

The agricultural officer, Ato Alemu, read and approved of the work, reading it aloud to some of his workers. He said that it was a classical piece of writing, translated perfectly into Amharic, and he observed that nothing had been written for the people before. It should be circulated all over the country. I asked then if his office would copy it out. Yes, if His Excellency Colonel Tamurat agreed. His Excellency agreed, and praised it. But first, the Amharic translation had to be polished a little, then the secretary would type it out, and they would make copies on their machine. It took nearly eight months to get that done.

A year later, it was obvious that the letter had failed. Oh, those who read or heard it were impressed, but they forgot, or ignored, or didn't understand. One thing is sure—the pen is mightier than the sword in a literate country, but Ethiopia is perhaps the least literate country on the continent.

✕✕✕✕

While I was away, gone to fetch Sonako, Guard Dawd complained of a severe headache, and the others on duty in Geech asked Dr. Nievergelt for aspirin. Dawd had a fever, and a day later was delirious. It was typhus. Dr. Nievergelt sent down a runner to get chloramphenicol from my medicine chest in Sankabar, but while the runner was gone, Dawd's relatives came from Geech village and carried the sick man away, refusing to let him have the capsules which would have arrested the disease. He died within four days. After the funeral in the Moslem cemetery, Nadu had a squad of game guards fire shots over the grave, and all said what a fine, strong soldier Dawd had been, and wept for him. He left behind a wife and young children. Nadu gave Dawd's rifle, which was government property, to his brother, and the brother and wife returned to their home at the foot of the looming cliffs. Dr. Nievergelt wrote a detailed report about the death for Major Gizaw, but he didn't read it.

Nadu stayed away from the camps and never reported for duty. A bridge had to be built across the Djinn Barr, and a message was sent to Nadu to come and ask the Geech villagers to assist with the work. Ermias bought thick, straight eucalyptus trunks, and coolies carried them to the crossing place. Nadu did not come until a week after the construction was finished, and it was guard Hussein who asked the people to help. They did so very reluctantly, but together with the park coolies, Ermias, Berhanu, and Dr. Nievergelt, a fine, strong bridge was constructed well above the rainy season flood-level of the stream. Even loaded mules could cross with safety on the bridge, and within a day of its completion, many people began to use it. It was the first bridge in these highlands. The elders of Geech came in a delegation to Dr. Nievergelt to say that he should thank them for ordering the people to help with the bridge. The bridge was more theirs than ours; there were over six hundred people in the village, and a handful at the camp. Dr. Nievergelt would be there only a year, and the bridge, unless humans destroyed it, would stand for much longer than that. He told them to go to hell. Later they came to me to ask for money, and I said sure, we could pay them a little from the toll we would put on the bridge. The subject was dropped.

After seven months of separation, I met Sonako and the children at Cairo airport in the early hours of the morning of June 1, 1968. We had not seen each other since she left Canada and flew to Japan, after we had packed up our home in Montreal. It had been far, far too long. We stayed a couple of days in the Hilton Hotel in Cairo, with a room that overlooked the Nile, with its slow-moving Arab dhows. In the distance were the pyramids, all hazy. Looking down on that broad, muddy river, whose banks and valleys had seen the passing of great civilizations, it seemed incredible to think that a tiny part of it had come from the Djinn Barr stream, in the high, cool mountains of Ethiopia.

9

THE KNIFING IN DEBAREK

As the big jet passed over the checkered hillsides of the high plateau, Sonako gazed down, feeling that she had come to the farthest ends of the earth. The scenery was unlike any other she had ever seen, and she felt, looking out of the small window, that she could almost catch the smell of the country, strange and different. Below lay bare mountains with small, scattered clusters of round houses and irregular patches of agriculture, with few trees. It had been a hard journey with the two children. Kentaro was two and a half years old, and Miwako was only eight months.

Going through Customs and Immigration was simple. We took a taxi from the airport to the Genet Hotel, a sprawl of buildings that had once been the Italian officers' club. Sonako was disappointed with Addis Ababa. It was like a small, dirty Tokyo, and even from the airport the "New Flower" had a strong scent, like manure. As we drove in along the magnificent road from the airport to the town, she saw that the trees were mostly eucalyptus, standing in tall, unnatural rows. She found the hotel depressing, for the windows were high up and the rooms rather dark. The hotel servants were slow and clumsy, and seemingly insolent. When she tried to get hot water to make milk it was a long, involved, and frustrating experience, and when she tried to wash out the bottles, hot water came from both taps. She began to get angry. After having read some of my letters, plus a travel book about Africa, which had very little good to say about Ethiopia, she had not really wanted to come.

At dinner, she could hear a lion roaring, which gave her some feeling of coming to Africa. She didn't know the lion was in a small cage in the garden of the hotel. Only hyenas and dogs ran free around the city.

There was now a tourist camp in Awash Park, run by a friend of mine, Ted Shatto, who was also one of the few professional hunters in Ethiopia. Since I needed to talk with Peter Hay, the game warden, and was also anxious for Sonako to see some real African animals, I accepted Ted's offer to take us all down with him in his Land Rover. When Ted arrived in the morning, we were ready to leave, dressed for the dusty ride to Awash. Ted stood in the door, looking Sonako over from head to toe.

"OK. She'll do. Maybe slacks would have been better." He smiled and shook hands. Sonako laughed. She liked Ted. After an excellent Italian meal in the Villa Verde restaurant, we set off, all of us in the front of the canvas-backed Land Rover with the cross-eyed lion emblems on the doors. Ted played classical music on a cassette tape recorder. Although Sonako was enjoying herself, she was somewhat fearful. It was a lonely road. What would happen if there was an accident, and she was left alone with the children? How could she get water to make milk for the baby? What would the tribesmen do to her?

On the way we stopped by a peasant selling a baby dik dik (a pigmy antelope). Ted bought it from him, although I wanted to confiscate it.

"Oh come on, what the hell good do you think that would do?" Ted rejoined. I shrugged. So we took turns holding the dainty little creature on our laps, much to Kentaro's delight. Later, Ted gave the dik dik to a little Dutch boy from the sugar estate at Metahara.

The camp in Awash was a lot of fun for Sonako. At last she felt she had come to Africa. From the dining marquee one could watch the brilliantly plumaged birds in the surrounding trees, or see the monkeys, apparently curious about the visitors. Sometimes a hippopotamus snorted in the river, or one could see a crocodile lying on the bank. The beer was cold, the servants pleasant, and the food quite good. And Ted, with his grizzled beard, his pipe, bush shirt and typewriter, was always around somewhere to make a fuss over the children.

Kentaro loved Awash, and had two adventures there. One day he ran into the sleeping tent to announce, "There's a big monkey outside!" Sonako followed him out to see Kentaro and a big male baboon looking at each other from a distance of less than ten feet.

Kentaro's second adventure occurred in the dining tent. He went to pour himself some cornflakes from an opened packet on the table. As he tipped the packet (a big job for such a little lad), a small mouse popped out, ran three circuits around the bowl, then out, across the table, and onto the floor. Kentaro and his father laughed and laughed. Fortunately, Sonako is not a screecher, and is not afraid of mice. The next morning, and all mornings thereafter, Kentaro was most disappointed not to find mice in the cornflakes.

Peter Hay's house in Awash was magnificent. Built by a contractor, it had cost about forty-five thousand dollars. It was made of cut stone, with a high, cool ceiling, a huge living room, and a big, airy veranda meshed against insects. Sonako could hardly believe that people lived in such a wonderful house, so far from civilization. To have such a house in Japan one would have to be wealthy. With a house like this, surely the inconveniences of isolation could be borne very easily. I envied the Hay family, and at the same time felt guilty and sorry for my wife; I explained as best I could that our house would be nothing like this. The house in the Simien, when I finally got the money to finish it, cost about six thousand dollars, including all fittings and furniture. Whereas Awash had roads cut through the bush, Simien had only mule tracks, so that cement was double the price, and sand Lord knows how much more expensive. During the entire time I was in the Simien I got far less than forty-five thousand dollars to cover *all* park expenses, including houses. But then, His Imperial Majesty could visit Awash and there was no hope of his visiting the Simien. Not that this detracts in any way from Peter Hay's achievements, for he fought every inch of the way for what he got for Awash Park, but at least he had some chance of winning.

As we sat in the house, drinking tea, Mrs. Hay observed that a good house was vitally important for keeping the warden's wife and family happy, for it was the wife who had to spend all her time in the house. I agreed absolutely. I admired the house, everything about it, from the kitchen to the servants' quarters outside. I wondered if I would ever get the money to build a really good house. For even half the cost of this house, I knew I could build a beautiful cottage in the mountains.

Outside the house, a lion cub was tied up that Peter was hoping to release in the park. This appealed very much to Sonako, who wanted to have animals around the house too. We took a drive around the park and saw herds of gazelles and oryx, as well as waterbuck, kudu, and warthogs. We enjoyed tent life, even the long columns of small ants, forming moving black lines over the tent ridge. Kentaro threw his hat and a ball in the Awash River, and I suppose they both went over the falls below.

Once we visited the Danakil market, at Awash station. Sonako said she had never seen a place quite so dirty (but then, she had not yet seen Debarek). Camels complained, and vendors called out their wares: salt, cloth, grain, butter. The women were bare-breasted, and many of them beautiful. I suppose I must have that Anglo-Saxon fixation about breasts, for they fascinate and stimulate me. I would like to have taken pictures, but the Danakil object to photographs, and sometimes get nasty about it. The men, with their fuzzy hair, skirts, knives, and hostile stares, looked fearsome. When I mentioned that the officers of the law held public hangings in this marketplace, Sonako looked around and said she wanted to leave. To her, the place had a weird and ominous atmosphere.

We returned to Addis Ababa on the railway that the French had built, and took a room in the International Hotel, a cheap but clean place much frequented by Peace Corps volunteers, whose headquarters were two minutes' walk away. Even if we still had not been able to get Sonako's residence permit, it was time to go north.

Before we went back to Gondar, Sonako came with me to our headquarters. There she met Major Gizaw. He was immaculate in a light-colored suit, and as usual, he was charming, gracious, and gave a very good impression. This time, too, my conversation with the Major was a pleasant, affable discussion in which he assured me, as he always did, that everything was being taken care of, that there were no difficulties in solving all the problems of the park, that the money had been applied for, etc., etc.

As we were about to leave, he remembered something. "Oh, just a minute, there's a letter from Nievergelt. Something about aspirin. You ought to buy some before you go up to the Simien."

He rang the desk bell for the office boy, who went off and fetched the letter. The first few lines described the initial onslaught of typhus in Guard Dawd, and the request for aspirin. At the end of the typed page, Nievergelt described how Dawd had died.

I was shocked, and looked up at the Major. "This is not a letter about aspirin. It is about Guard Dawd Yussuf. The man is dead, from typhus."

"Oh, is he? I'm sorry. I didn't read all of it, only the first few lines." The letter had been addressed to Major Gizaw, and was marked urgent.

"What should I do about this?" I asked, thinking about pensions, insurance, and about the paperwork I should do when a guard died.

Major Gizaw waved airily. "Oh, you'll have to get another guard. Ask Dejasmatch Araya to find you a man."

"No, I don't mean that. I want to know about the guard's pension and so forth."

"I doubt if he has any, he hasn't served with us for long enough."

I left the office a little numb. I wondered how much, or little, this department would help me or my family if ever some disaster occurred.

As there was no road into the Simien, I had told the department that I could not take my wife and children into the mountains during the rains. And as my contract called for free accommodation, I got them to agree to give me a housing allowance of one hundred and twenty dollars a month.

Before leaving for Cairo, I had signed a contract to rent an old Italian house in Gondar which turned out to belong to the sister of Dejasmatch Araya. The Dejasmatch himself owned many houses, bars, and shops in Gondar. The husband of the Dejasmatch's sister was a certain Fitawrary Haile Selassie, another titled gray-haired relic of the patriot resistance. Although at one time the house and garden must have been very fine, it had not been maintained, and it was in a mess. To facilitate the painting and maintenance of the house before we came back from Addis Ababa, I had paid two months' rent in advance.

The DC-3 ride to Gondar was a bumpy one, and left an indelible impression on Sonako. The rainy season had begun, and the aircraft flew in and out of thick clouds. Looking down, she sometimes saw small hamlets of round houses on the tops of hills, with no roads leading to them. Rain pelted the aircraft, and sometimes, off one wing, there would be dense cloud, and off the other wing, bright sun. It was a slow run, with several stops on the way. Each time, it seemed to her that we had made a forced landing, for the airports were mere fields, with perhaps a mud and eucalyptus shack somewhere, and a couple of passengers with odd bundles. Gondar airport was rural indeed, a fifteen-minute drive out of town. Sonako felt lonely.

I hired people to clean the house before we moved in, for it was filthy, even though the previous occupant had been none other than the mayor of Gondar himself. On moving in, I made a list of twenty-one panes of glass that were either cracked or missing, and I sent a copy of the list to myself in a registered letter. The painters had not bothered to wash the dirt and grease off the walls before applying the paint, and they had used only one coat. The toilet and sink were blocked. The roof leaked. But worst of all, the house was infested with bed bugs. Sonako had heard of such creatures, but she had never seen one until one evening, while she was writing a letter, a bed bug strolled unconcernedly across the paper. Sonako squashed it and kept it in tissue paper for later identification.

We used many cans and spray bombs of insecticide on the house. The fleas were bad enough—one could never get rid of them completely in Ethiopia, but the bed bugs were intolerable. Sonako was allergic to them, and, wherever they bit her, broke out in great lumps and welts. They weren't in our mattresses, for they were new, and half-stuffed with DDT, but rather in the cracks in the walls of the house, especially the ceiling. If one switched on the light at night, one could find the damn things crawling down the walls. It was a nightmare. I used ten gallons of a lethal insecticide on the house, even crawling under the roof with the big spray pack on my back. It drove the bloody bed bugs under for a week, but they recovered. And then the rats began chewing at the baby's clothes.

The servants of the neighbors, and the people in the back, threw all their refuse out around their dwellings, and at night, people defecated in the alley running by the side of the house. Although our garden was cleaned of its accumulation of sheep bones and refuse, and we burned all our garbage, the flies still came in swarms. When the sun shone, and Kentaro wanted to go out to play, the poor little lad could only stay out a few minutes before the flies covered his face. He would become hysterical and run into the house, rubbing his face, waving his arms, crying, "Flies! Flies!" Of course, I had not known all this when I rented the house.

A few days after moving into the house I had to go up to the Simien. Driving to Debarek with Tesfae and Ermias, I opened the glove compartment and found a nine-inch wooden-sheathed dagger, double-edged and sharp as a needle. The sheath and the handle fitted together to disguise the weapon as a simple baton. It belonged to Tesfae. He liked edged weapons, and kept a long, sword-shaped spearhead under the seat of his car. He handled knives with a practiced ease, and I believe the men of his tribe were good with such weapons.

While I was away, Ermias had done a lot of work, using his own initiative. He had built two guard houses and a small stable, and of course, had helped with the bridge across the Djinn Barr. He was leaving now, his year of university national service completed. He would go back to Alemayu Agricultural College to finish his fourth and final year. I was truly sorry to see him go, and would miss his easy laugh and relaxed company. I gave him my old camera, quite a good one, to remember me by. The guards and Nadu didn't even bother to come to see him off, despite all that he had done for them.

On the trail from Geech to Sankabar, in a cold, driving rain and under ragged mantles of cloud, I saw a small black snake, the first I had seen at such an altitude. It moved sluggishly in the middle of the runneled path. Before I could stop him, Guard Amara smashed its head with a rock. The killing of the little black snake stayed in my mind, like an omen of evil to come.

When I left the Simien, I gave orders for the camp to be packed up and stored in the unfinished house at Sankabar.

The house we rented from Dejasmatch Araya's relatives had a gloomy air about it. Maybe this was due to the poorly painted walls and the trees all around it, but our servants believed the gloom to be an evil caused by spirits.

Getenish, the maid, tried to explain to Sonako that our neighbor (a pleasant, educated government official) had the evil eye, and turned into a hyena at night and ate human flesh. Sonako laughed, but the maid was serious.

Then one day, when Sonako was working in the kitchen, there was an explosion in the dish cupboard. Saucers that had been dried and stacked had shattered into powder and tiny pieces. When I looked, I could see no reason for it. Getenish and Abahoy were convinced that it was the working of a spell, and were terrified.

They also pointed to the great welts of bites on Sonako's neck, saying the same thing. I knew we would have to move, but a lot of things had to be done first. Having recorded it in my diary, I brushed aside the suggestion of evil, but I had cause to remember it later.

We had two vehicles and two drivers now. The second vehicle was a rugged, powerful little diesel job called a Unimog, built by Mercedes. Tesfae couldn't drive it, so they sent a tall, husky ex-soldier called Mamo. Mamo had seen service in Korea. I certainly didn't want or need two drivers, for we didn't have the money to buy the materials to haul, and thereby keep both men busy. But I didn't want to lose the Unimog, because it would be invaluable to us when work started on the road, as well as for taking goods up to Sankabar if the road were ever finished. I desperately wanted money to be able to buy building materials now, and haul them to Debarek, so that they would be ready to go up as soon as the rainy season ended. I thought of sending Tesfae back, but he begged me to let him stay. The department said that both drivers were now assigned to the Simien and should stay there.

In July I again had to go up to the Simien with the payroll for the men. The first day the rain pelted down, turning every path into muddy, slippery torrents. Mules slipped, smashing their pack boxes. Riding was out of the question. Half-blinded by the rain, we went as far as we could, but the swollen streams forced us to go back to Debarek. I determined to spend the night there and to try early the next day. I had rented a big, windowless, stone house in Debarek as a store, and Tesfae and Mamo lived there with their women. That night they killed a sheep. When they cut its throat, the blood ran out and formed a perfect cross on the ground. Tesfae took the small intestine, poured water in one end, blew into it, and then squeezed along the length to clean it out. He chopped it up to be grilled on the charcoal brazier. Tesfae ran around, laughing, grinning, saying that this or that piece was the best-tasting, and that we should all enjoy ourselves.

In the early part of July a small collecting expedition came from the French Museum of Natural History in Paris. They were gathering zoological specimens from all over the country, taking skins, skeletons, and skulls for the museum. Among their permits they had one for six gelada baboons. They came to our Gondar house to ask me the best place to find them.

We had received several complaints from the Lemalemo or Wolkefit Pass area. The people said the gelada were damaging crops there. Since it was on the main road, any baboons killed could easily be taken to a vehicle and driven back to Gondar for skinning and preserving. I offered to go with the party in their Land Rover and help them kill the baboons.

Knowing that rain would close the pass in the afternoon, we left in the early morning. The chief shot of the party, Andre Kalfleche, was using a shotgun that day. I took the .30.06. The guards were supposed to be in Debarek at that time, waiting for Major Gizaw to visit us. Nadu was there, and half a dozen of the others. When they saw me in the Land Rover, they thought it was the Major, and they all ran out. Having no assistant or interpreter at that time, I had to stumble along in my atrocious Amharic. I spoke to Nadu.

"These foreigners have letter. Wildlife Conservation Department. We go now to kill gelada in Lemalemo. One soldier come. Only one."

Nadu ordered Mitiku to climb in the back, and then got in himself. He obviously didn't count himself as being a game guard, and he obviously considered that he was so important that there was no question of his not coming along.

"Get out. One man. Understand?"

Nadu argued, and I had to shout at him. Grumbling, Mitiku was ordered out. Nadu took Tedla's rifle and ammunition.

We drove down the looping cliff road and stopped at a hairpin bend, partway down. There was a terrace there, not so wide, but very long. A man called Takale Wondeferow lived there, in a small village by the road. He was a member of the vigilantes and had once helped us arrest a poacher with a bushbuck and kid. (The Governor later let the poacher off with a ten-dollar fine.) We couldn't find Takale, but the other villagers told us there was a big herd of gelada on the land, and that they had damaged the crops. We said we would shoot the baboons, and they seemed very pleased. Theoretically, it was my job to control the baboon populations outside the park, but I had neither the time nor the ammunition. This day, however, I was determined that the museum people would get six good specimens. As this particular herd was giving trouble, we would kill as many as possible.

Sure enough, there was a herd of about eighty animals. We got up to them easily and opened fire. Nadu killed two with his first shot, for the .303 military ammunition passed right through the bodies. The museum didn't want the skulls or skeletons damaged, so I was making body shots, just below the sternum. My first shot ripped the guts out of a big male, but he fled to the cliffs and died there, out of reach. The females and young fled screaming to the cliffs, and some of the big males made mock charges. I stopped the leader with my second shot; the expanding hunting bullet blew him off the ground and spun him over backward. The herd fled to the cliffs, and we followed them, going along a steep path. Nadu killed a female and I killed another male, this time an immature specimen.

As the shots crashed about the echoing cliffs, Takale came down from his lands, where he had been tending his beehives. He followed us and found me, demanding to know why I was shooting, and who gave me permission. I replied that we had seen the permit, and if he wanted to see it too he could, but after we had finished. He tagged along suspiciously. I was impressed with this man, and thought he would make a good game guard.

The gelada were by now a hundred feet up the cliff, perched on rocks, weaving and bobbing, grimacing at us, and no doubt feeling safe. We now needed an immature animal, and two more females. I chose the targets carefully, ignoring the shouts of Nadu, Takale, and the villagers to shoot, shoot. The rifle crashed once, and a body hurtled down to bounce and roll to a stop way down the slope behind us. Another shot brought another body, this time almost directly over my head. The baboons were getting hysterical. More people came running along the path. I don't usually like the killing part of hunting, unless there is considerable danger to me in it, but for some perverse reason I was enjoying this. I chose the last animal and fired. The body hurtled head over heels and landed with a bloody thud among the watching villagers.

Nadu and the villagers wanted money to help us carry the dead animals back to the Land Rover. I picked up the biggest body and told them to go to hell. I would carry the whole lot back myself if need be, and didn't want or need their help. Nadu shook his head, saying, "Ah, Mister, Mister." As I started off, the villagers all grabbed the rest of the dead animals. As we passed the village the dogs barked, children hid, and women shrieked to see the dead animals, horribly grotesque in death, with staring eyes. They looked like misshapen, hairy dwarfs. We loaded them into the back of the car. There was some more argument about payment for carrying the baboons.

Meanwhile, Nadu had gone to Kalfleche, and asked for cartridges from the belt he was carrying. The Frenchman gave him three, each of which was worth at least three dollars in the Simien. Nadu said he wanted more. I heard, and got angry; I wanted him to return the cartridges, but Kalfleche said it was all right. But this had been Nadu's job, and what shells he had fired would be replaced by us, directly to Guard Tedla, from whom the ammunition had been borrowed. I was trying to record the use of each round of ammunition, in order to stop the existing black market in these valuable rounds.

Nadu was getting to be infuriating. Next he tried to argue with the leader of the party that because the villagers had helped us, we were obliged to carry some of them up the steep road to Debarek. Since the car was already overloaded, I shouted at Nadu to either shut up or get out and walk. He shook his head at me, saying over and over that I was not good, not good, and I was sorely tempted to kick his head. Threatened with a fine of ten dollars, he shut up.

We drove back along the road to Gondar, stopping in Debarek to let Nadu out. I ordered him to report to the police the reasons and results of the shooting. We had six dead gelada and several birds in the car. At Wokun village we stopped and weighed the gelada on a merchant's grain scales. The males were not as big as some I had seen. Two weighed sixteen kilos and one weighed twenty. The females weighed twelve, eleven, and nine kilos. At a guess, I would say that some males went up to thirty kilos, though not much more. They looked heavier, but a lot of that is due to their great mane of long hair.

Back in Gondar, in the garage of the Iteghie Hotel, the museum people skinned the animals and prepared the skins. As the gelada are vegetarians, I wanted to take some meat, which was probably very good, to boil up for my dog, but Sonako wouldn't hear of it.

Major Gizaw came a couple of days later, and Mamo went to meet him in the Land Rover, borrowed from Dr. Nievergelt. We drove straight to Debarek, where the Major intended to talk to the assembled game guards about their problems with allowances, housing, and work conditions.

Driving up, we discussed the road project. Major Gizaw assured me that it was top priority, and that the Russian earth-moving equipment, now in Awash awaiting the arrival of technicians from Russia, would come straight to us. I didn't really believe it, but my hopes were raised. This equipment had been donated to the Wildlife Conservation Department as part of a UNDP project.

"I'm glad to hear it, Major, but they must be ready to start work in September or October, as soon as the rains end. We'll need a lot of money now to haul up to Debarek, and to make some rough shelters for the equipment."

"I assure you, Mr. Nicol, I will do everything I can for the Simien. It is on my mind all the time. We have put in our budget requests to the Minister, and the money should come soon."

"I hope so," I said, thinking that if he was so conerned, why was it that neither he nor any of his Ethiopian officers had been to the Simien since I took the job.

The first person we had to see in Debarek was Dejasmatch Araya. He came out to greet Major Gizaw; he took his face in his hands and said that it was thanks to God that Gizaw had lived. He kissed him on both cheeks, and they walked hand in hand to the house, where the Dejasmatch had ordered a feast. Many things were discussed. The same old things. I was beginning to sound like a looped tape recorder. The Dejasmatch went over the old business that it was he who should say which men were good for me, and that he knew fine, outstanding fellows, not like the thieves, liars, and robbers who made up my present force. I quite enjoyed these feasts. Everybody was nice to everybody else, bandying flatteries about. It was fine as long as you didn't expect any of the promises to be fulfilled.

Dozens of people were trying to present Major Gizaw with applications for the post of game guard. He passed them on to me. Dawd's brother was among the applicants, and the Major talked with him, and gave him some money. I gave him some money too, quite a lot, but he didn't thank me, which was most unusual.

The guards had many complaints, most of them justified. Major Gizaw talked to them and promised many things. Nadu complained that I had refused to help him build his house in Sankabar. I pointed out that we had bought all the materials, and had already hauled them to the site. Nadu had previously promised that the house would not cost more than two hundred dollars. We had already spent about six hundred. And he had said that he could get the villagers to help him. At this time we had no park funds. All this, I had gone over with Nadu. The hostility between us was growing.

The Major stayed only a few hours in Debarek, and then we drove back to Gondar. On the way back he pointed to a spreading umbrella acacia tree, one of the few left.

"If I saw the owner of that tree I would give him a dollar, and tell him what a good man he is for not cutting it down." I was surprised at the sentiment, but wondered if it was the tree owner who cut down and denuded all the surrounding hills.

The Major visited my home for coffee and biscuits, and we talked for a while. He seemed lonely and remarked that he had no friends. This remark, I suspect, stemmed from an accusation made by certain persons that the Major hired only friends and relatives in the department. I couldn't help but feel sorry for him; I sensed that Gizaw was mostly good, but had perhaps tried to balance the old Ethiopian ways with modern bureaucracy. Although the way he did things annoyed me, he never annoyed me as a person. But one shouldn't feel sorry for the boss.

There was a lot of trouble in the department at this time. The senior game warden, Blower, while on safari in Eritrea, had uncovered evidence in Asmara to implicate certain wildlife officers—Ethiopians in the head office—in the illegal leopard skin trade. He reported it in strong terms to Major Gizaw, and within ten days was told that he no longer had a job, and that he should leave the country. This was a very transparent, foolish move. Moreover they had tackled the wrong guy. They couldn't fire him without either three months' notice or compensation. The case went to the Minister, who said it was all nonsense, and of course they couldn't fire Blower. At about the same time, the incident was going up before the board. Storm clouds were brewing for the Major. Most of us suspected that he had been advised by the so-called legal officer, who was a crook, and undoubtedly involved in or aware of the leopard skin business. He was the man who had argued with me so strongly about the impossibility of raiding illegal dealers in Addis Ababa.

As he was talking to me, the Major was sitting on a couch, over which I had hung a fine winter polar bear skin. It was an excellent skin, about seven feet long, with thick, lustrous fur. The Major stroked it.

"This is a big sheep, Mr. Nicol, where did you get it?"

I stared at him. "Sheep?" I said weakly, not believing my ears.

He looked at the hide he was sitting on, and at the great claws on it. "Oh, it's not a sheep, is it?"

But of course, he knew a lot more about African animals.

A few days after that, the July payroll came through and I had to go up to the Simien again; but I stayed up in the mountains only a couple of days. When I came back neither Tesfae nor Mamo wanted to drive to Gondar; they seemed to have important personal reasons for not wanting to go. I didn't press them. They said they had no money, and if I had insisted they go, it would have meant a long hassle over allowances and money, which I just did not have to pay them. Major Gizaw had ruled, quite rightly, that they were not entitled to receive an allowance merely for living in Debarek, when we provided their lodgings.

After exacting a promise that either Tesfae or Mamo would drive to Gondar the next day, I took the Toyota and drove back alone. I was worried about the drivers. With no money to start work they were idle, and they were drinking a lot. Tesfae seemed happy enough, but Mamo was brooding. But when I asked him if he wanted to transfer, he answered no. Perhaps I should despair of getting funds, and send Mamo and the Unimog back?

Neither Tesfae nor Mamo came to Gondar the next day, and I was annoyed, because they had promised. It was July 17, my birthday.

While I was drinking at home in Gondar, Tesfae and Mamo were boozing it up in a little bar in Debarek. They had been drinking all day. Tesfae left fairly early, and went home to sleep, but Mamo stayed on, and got into a fierce argument with some highlanders, probably about a woman. The Debarek men resented the drivers. Tesfae and Mamo were getting a large salary, far more than the local people, and as they had the money, they got the women. In addition the drivers came from the big city, and they scoffed at the local people, and at Debarek, and even at Gondar. They were big, strong, burly men of the world. Moreover, the locals were Amhara, and Tesfae and Mamo were not. During the quarrel, Mamo got

angry and stormed back to the house to waken Tesfae. He shouted
and shook him, saying get up, they are insulting us, these peasants,
we must go and fight them. Tesfae got up and stumbled into his
clothes. He was very drunk.

Together, they went back to the bar, to find the door locked.
Mamo could hear people inside, and he pounded on the door in his
rage, and kicked it in. Women screamed as the two big drivers
stormed in and beat up the smaller, skinnier highlanders. Neighbors
woke to the screams, curses, and roars of rage. Tesfae and Mamo
had both served in the army, and knew how to fight. They were big
and well fed. The Simien men had no chance. As Tesfae and Mamo
went out, a local chief, named Zenabe Takalé, from the High Simien, grabbed Tesfae around the neck. He had seen the fight, but had
nothing to do with the quarrel.

Tesfae was easily strong enough to handle this man, but in front
of six witnesses, Tesfae drew out the knife with the wooden sheath
and ran Zenabe through the back. He fell, and died within thirty
minutes.

Tesfae went back to his room, crawled into bed, and was asleep
when the police came to arrest him. They found the knife where he
had dropped it. He said it wasn't his and denied everything. Perhaps he was too drunk to remember.

Early in the morning, a policeman was pounding at the door. I
got up and answered it. He had a garbled verbal message in Amharic that I must go to police headquarters. I had a slight hangover, and I didn't feel like rushing about on the orders of the police.
After much tea, and breakfast with Sonako and the children, I decided to stroll down to see what the police wanted. I had gone less
than a hundred yards when Colonel Azziz's green Land Rover
stopped by me. The Colonel looked agitated.

"Why didn't you come quickly? A terrible trouble now! Your
drivers have killed a man in Debarek with a knife and the people
want to kill them."

"Where are they?" I asked, startled.

"In the police station, but we must take them away, the people
are very angry."

Three uniformed police, cradling automatic carbines, and an
English-speaking inspector named Hailu came with me. On the way
to Debarek we stopped in Dabat. They needed a certificate of

death, signed by a doctor or health officer. The Dabat health officers didn't want to come, they didn't want to take the responsibility, but finally they gave in and came with us.

As the Toyota churned and whined in four-wheel drive through the mud up to the police station, people gathered around the car. The police sat with guns at the ready. A mob had gathered around the station, some two hundred or more, mostly men armed with rifles, pistols, and sticks. They wanted to lynch the two drivers. The drivers were in chains, locked up in the crude eucalyptus and mud jail. Ten or fifteen police stood around the station, carbines ready. Dejasmatch Araya was there, waiting for us. His tall, broad, white-haired figure stood out in the crowd. I drove slowly through the hostile, angry people. They did nothing to the car. The Dejasmatch came forward to greet me. He said that it was a terrible thing, and that only God could help them now.

The police captain brought out a bloodstained knife, wrapped in cloth. Inspector Hailu asked me if I had seen it before.

"Yes," I replied. "I have seen it once in our car. It belongs to Tesfae." The inspector nodded, and they put the knife away.

The body of Zenabe Takalé had been washed and laid out in the captain's office. It was the Dejasmatch himself who had performed these last services to the dead man. The health officers issued a certificate of death by stabbing.

Outside, the crowd pressed closer, and some women relatives of the dead man danced a wailing, shrieking dance in front of the crowd. They shook their heads and arms, tore their hair, threw dirt on themselves. Dejasmatch Araya went out.

"Who are the brothers of the dead man?" Two men in front answered that they were his brothers.

"Come carry your brother to his grave," ordered the Dejasmatch. The crowd raised a great cry. The police glanced nervously at each other, for the people were in a dangerous mood, and they were becoming hysterical.

"Let those murderers come to carry the body!" they shouted. The old Dejasmatch roared with anger, and wielding his stick in both hands, he drove into the crowd, cracking heads and shins, pushing the crowd back with his weight and strength. Despite their numbers and weapons, they feared him terribly. He was one of the old warlords, an old lion.

The knifing in Debarek

"You boast before the women," he roared, "but let us see if you are really so brave. We are going to take these men to Gondar for trial. When we go out, why don't you boasters come and wait for us outside the town, where the women are not watching you. Then we will see!"

He turned his back on the mob and returned. With his stick, he marked a line on the ground.

"Now," he glared fiercely at them, "if any man steps over this line I will order the police to open fire!" There was a murmur in the mob, and the old Dejasmatch gave an order. The great-coated police cocked their carbines.

Dejasmatch Araya seized the two brothers by their necks and banged their heads together, even though they were grown men, and much younger than he.

"Are you going to carry your brother?" They began to protest, but he pushed them forward, kicking them to the door of the office, and flung them in, raising his stick to beat them. They carried out the body, wrapped in a white sheet. A wailing arose from the crowd, and the whole mob went off with the body to the graveyard. Rain began to fall.

Tesfae and Mamo were taken out of the jail and loaded into the back of my Toyota. The Dejasmatch and some of his armed followers escorted us to the outskirts of the town. There was no more trouble. On the way back to Gondar Inspector Hailu told me stories of the old Dejasmatch, about how his rival kidnaped his wife, and the lengths he went to get her back. The old lion was a legend in this area, even if he did serve the Italians for a time.

In front of the police headquarters at Gondar, Tesfae and Mamo climbed out awkwardly. They were wrapped in their blankets, and looked old and tired. I got out to speak to them, and they removed their watches, rings, and wallets, and gave them to me to give to their wives. The police looked on and said nothing.

I went home. Sonako was angry with me about something, but I didn't know what. I was preoccupied by the mood of the mob, an unjust, unthinking violence that no movie could capture. Before sealing the drivers' things in envelopes I opened Tesfae's wallet. There was a picture of his wife in her shamma, and a picture of a happy, round-faced little boy of about five, and a pretty little girl of perhaps ten or eleven. That would be his daughter, who once, so he had said, wrote him a letter, saying that until her father came home to them, she would not eat good food. There were tears in his eyes that time, while he held the letter. Sonako looked at the pictures and she cried, saying in Japanese, "It's so pitiful, so pitiful . . ."

It had been a dark, gray, evil day, with fog in the hills around the town. The murder convinced our servants that the old house carried an evil spell. Many months later, when the old zubanya (house guard) died, vomiting blood, Abahoy and Getenish nodded wisely, and spoke in low tones with other servants from the big houses nearby.

Sonako made food for the men the next day, and I took it to the police station jail. It was hell in that jail, but nothing like the dreaded "Bata," the fearful prison down in the Arab quarter, by the market. Tesfae and Mamo were weeping, begging me to mediate for them, to plead with the Governor General. They felt sure that if they paid blood-money to the family of the murdered man, they would be released quickly. I didn't believe it possible, but would try to get Dejasmatch Araya to mediate.

✕✕✕✕

Since, despite several letters, the owner did nothing to repair the house I had rented, I found another one, much bigger and cleaner, in the so-called gentleman's area where many high government officials and foreign doctors lived. The rent was three hundred dollars, the highest rent in Gondar, but the house was large, clean, and airy. The flies were bad, but nothing like the first place, and there were no bed bugs. The garden was huge, with big pine trees, false bananas, and eucalyptus. I sent another letter to Fitawrary Haile Selassie, informing him that I had canceled the contract, and requesting that he or his wife come and collect another month's rent.

There were many birds in Gondar now, and they delighted Sonako. Flocks of little red-painted fire finches and cordon bleus were so tame they sometimes flew into the house. Long-tailed whydahs danced their flickering flight among the garden trees, and there were many brilliant green lovebirds. Weavers built their hanging nests from our false banana trees, and we could watch them at any time, out of our windows. Hornbills visited us, and there were always kites and the odd lammergeyer scouting overhead for scraps.

The knifing in Debarek

Sometimes Sonako and I went out into the garden and tossed bits of chicken gut into the air, to watch the kites swoop and catch the bits in mid-air. Pigeons and doves hooted about the roof tops. From our big sun roof, we had a fine view of the hills, with ancient castles and churches nestling in trees on their crowns. At night, lightning flickered on distant mountains, and it was cool.

10

TAG'S FIGHT WITH NADU

There was no dentist in Gondar, and I had lost a filling, so we had to go up to Addis Ababa.

We stayed in the International Hotel again, and found it pleasant. I was in the lobby one morning, waiting for Sonako to come down, when a broad-shouldered, bearded young American approached me. He asked if my name was Nicol, and held out his hand.

"My name is Tag Demment. I'm a volunteer, assigned to the Simien. I was hoping to meet with you and find out a few things."

I was both surprised and delighted. Some time before, I had asked for a volunteer, but gathered that Major Gizaw was against the idea. This was the first I had heard of Tag. We sat and talked. I liked the look of him, big, strong, with hands that were obviously used to work. He seemed to have a lot of practical ideas. The last thing I needed was an enthusiastic aesthete who didn't know how to hold a shovel, and there were quite a few of those about. Tag had hoped, and prepared, to go to Gambella, which is hotter and more typically African, but he had been diverted to the Simien. I could really use some help, especially with the buildings, and Tag was a Harvard graduate in architecture. He was deeply interested in wildlife, and had fallen in love with Africa after spending some months the previous year in Kaffa Province. He was going to come up to Gondar in a few days, and I suggested that as it was still the rainy season, he could occupy himself by making pack boxes, and by drawing a map.

I didn't want to spend much time in Addis Ababa, but I did go to see Major Gizaw about the road. There was an idea in the air that the British Army might help build the road as a training exercise. Foolishly, I broached the idea to Gizaw, who burst into irrational invective.

"You don't know what they are like! They will come here, do a little work, and then charge us a couple of million dollars for nothing. Like this expedition. Do you know they think they should get duty-free fuel from us?"

The good Major's outrage was considerable. I reminded him that our department alone had received a lot of material from the British Army: tents, generators, and other valuable equipment, all flown free of charge from Aden. I also tried to point out that the results of the expedition would be made available to the Imperial Ethiopian Government, and would be of immense value to them if they had the intelligence to know what it meant. That time we didn't part on good terms.

I was told later that the Major had tried to prevent John Blower from going on the Blue Nile expedition, but had been informed by higher authorities that it was imperative that either the head of the department or the senior game warden should go. So Blower went.

When we got back to Gondar, there was a newly assigned game guard, named Zeleka Belaiy, waiting for me with references from John Blower. When he saw me, he saluted, and handed me the letter. I spoke to him at length. His uniform was smart, and he wore many service ribbons. He spoke English, Italian, Swahili, and of course, Amharic. He had been the chief game guard at Omo Park until he quarreled with the servant of the Ethiopian assistant. George Brown, the game warden, had been away at the time, otherwise I doubt if the assistant could have got rid of Zeleka. Ethiopian officers generally disliked him, sneeringly calling him "the foreigners' friend." Zeleka was a damned good soldier and received excellent references from all the foreign wardens, not because he was a boot-licker, but because he did an honest, forthright job, toadied to nobody, and bullied the guards under him into some semblance of work. He had served in the Korean campaign, where he had won decorations for outstanding courage, including the American Silver Star. He was a hell of a drinker, and a scrounger, but then, most old soldiers are. He had not wanted to come to the Simien, but had quarreled with the people at the head office, and this was their way of punishing him and getting him out of the way at the same time. I was glad to get him, and hoped he could drill the Simien men.

I sent Zeleka to Debarek, to live in the vacated storehouse. He could come up to the Simien with me at the end of the rains. After a few days he came back, with a story that some of the local men had threatened to kill him, saying he was a relative of Tesfae. I asked for details. Zeleka said he had no proof, and I didn't know whether to believe the story or not. But I had no reason to doubt Zeleka's courage, and I didn't want to risk any more serious trouble, so I kept him with me in Gondar, quartered in a shed in our garden. He shared the place with my servant, Abahoy.

In Debarek, the Dejasmatch and Nadu were trying to persuade the family of the murdered man to take blood money from Tesfae and Mamo, and not to press for the death sentence. The price being discussed was around three thousand dollars. The system of justice was a mystery to me, but I gathered that if the bereaved family would take the money, then they would tell the court that there was no bad blood between the two parties, and that they wished for forgiveness for the killers. Witnesses and judges could be bribed. A Gurage police major in Gondar had already come to me with Tesfae's brother and begged money to pay toward the compensation. At first they asked for three thousand dollars from me, then two thousand, then one thousand, then took what I gave them, which was considerably less. People in the head office in Addis were collecting too. But so far, the bereaved family were divided in their decision. The dead man's wife wanted to take the money for herself and the children, but his brothers were squabbling over their share of the blood money, and trying to push the wife out of the picture. There was a lot of litigation going on. It is the Ethiopian national sport.

A rumor was going around Debarek that I had taught Tesfae how to use a knife, and some were even saying that my evil powers had something to do with the killing. But generally, the people did not believe this, for being a foreigner made me an outsider in all things. There was little danger that this particular rumor would get out of hand. Nevertheless, I did resolve not to openly wear a belt knife in town, and when Tag arrived, I requested him not to wear one either.

It was not true that I had taught Tesfae to use a knife, but I was interested in edged weapons. Having met armed parties at close quarters in the Simien, I had considered many means of a fast and effective defensive attack—just in case things ever got nasty. With Zeleka, I practiced disarming a rifleman, but that would only work at a range of one, perhaps two meters. They usually didn't stand so close. Christer, a Swedish carpenter who was helping me on my house, had given me a set of three Swedish throwing knives, finely balanced, with six-inch blades and thin handles bound with leather. Taking a knife from the belt and then throwing it was too slow, nor could I throw underhand with any power. Instead, I stitched the sheath of one knife into the back of my bush shirt, using very light stitches so that the shirt could be washed and the sheath taken out. The knife would go down the back of the collar, just out of sight. With raised hands, I could slip the knife out and throw it with force, overhand, from the back of my head.

I practiced for many hours in the garden of our house in Gondar, and after some time I could bury a knife two inches into a pine tree at a range of three or four meters. The knife would be buried in a rifleman's heart before he could react and pull the trigger. At the moment of releasing the knife, I ducked and drove to the right side of the imagined opponent, in this case a tree, pretended that I blocked a swinging rifle, and chopped to the back of the imaginary opponent's neck, the tree in this case. Driving to the right rear of the opponent makes it difficult for him to swing his rifle around to fire. It would be much easier to swing to the left. Try it with a broomstick and you'll see. I worked out a dual knife-and-karate practice with Zeleka. He had seen a lot of hand-to-hand fighting with the Chinese in Korea, and knew the dangers of underestimating prisoners with raised arms. He told me that the move was effective, and only a very wary, highly trained soldier could counter it. I never hoped to use this technique, but having it, and knowing it was well practiced, gave me an extra confidence.

When you live and work in a foreign country you always go through cycles of feeling for the people of that country. Sometimes you love and admire them, sometimes you hate and despise them. Sonako and I were going through a very low period at this time. It was impossible for Sonako to go for a walk alone in the town. Gangs of children would follow behind her, chanting, "China!" "China!" and spitting and throwing stones, while adult Ethiopians laughed and jeered, encouraging the children, even though Sonako might be carrying the baby. She flew into a rage on a couple of occasions and hurled stones back, which was foolish. The only thing to do was not to walk in Gondar town.

Our German Shepherd dog Mogus was stoned by children while he was chained and could do nothing about it. The children climbed the garden wall to do this. Mogus developed a fierce hatred for any Ethiopian he did not know, and I feared that when he got older and more mature, he might prove dangerous. The children rarely tried any nonsense with a man, and on a couple of occasions when they tried it with me I ran after them and kicked their backsides. It was really the parents who should have been kicked, though.

And the fleas. Sonako could never get used to them, and we could never get rid of them. They came in from outside on my trousers and socks, and on the servants. Sonako caught all the ones on her legs and dropped them in a bottle of alcohol. Nobody in Japan would believe her if she didn't have proof. The Simien wasn't quite so infested, thank goodness.

At this time, the owner of the previous house was giving me a lot of trouble, saying that I was bound by the contract, and must pay. Pointing out that he was also bound by the contract to effect repairs was pointless. The old zubanya came around to claim that our son had broken the windows. Showing them a copy of my first letter, giving a detailed account of all the broken windows we found on entering was also pointless. Sonako was getting so angry that I had to hide the rifle bolts.

We were at home one day in Gondar when a man called Shiferaw Araya came to the house. Shiferaw was the son of Dejasmatch Araya, and a member of parliament for the Simien district. He claimed to be representing his uncle, and as I had once talked to him and his uncle about the house, I believed him. His English was good, so the story was plausible. I showed him various copies of the letters giving notice of quitting. I also said that his uncle could collect a month's rent from me at any time. Sonako didn't like Shiferaw. She told me so, in Japanese. She said that he could not be trusted.

Tag's fight with Nadu

The next time Shiferaw came with his uncle, and we argued; me, Sonako, Abahoy, Getenish, Zeleka, Shiferaw, and the old man. A little while afterward, Shiferaw returned alone and said that he would take the rent. Sonako warned me again not to trust him. But I trusted anybody and everybody, and was sick of arguing. And Shiferaw was a member of parliament, the son of a governor. I gave him the money, on the understanding that he would hand it over to his uncle, and he signed a detailed, dated receipt for it.

Not only did Shiferaw not give the money to his uncle, he denied ever having received it. The uncle came around several times to argue, and said that if I had paid the money to Shiferaw, it was my fault, I should have paid him. I told the old bastard to get stuffed, the contract wasn't with him anyway, but with another nephew who was now away in Addis Ababa. The old man couldn't write. They threatened to take me to court. I chased after Shiferaw to give him a letter about the money, asking him to pay it. He signed a receipt for the letter, and I had a carbon copy. But he never paid the money.

And thus I was taken to court. The courtroom was small and dingy, and full of people waiting for their cases. It was bedlam. Everybody was yelling in Amharic, even the traffic policeman waiting for the next case, and the judge could not make himself heard. The spectators joined in, choosing sides, and shouted and waved fists at each other, greatly appreciating the unique chance to argue for or against a foreigner. I understood nothing. My letters and receipts were all ignored. I had nobody to represent me. The judge decided against me, and said that I should go immediately up to the house and pay the rent. I left the court. Somebody who understood English informed me of the decision. I said a lot of rude things, marched down to the post office followed by the old man Fitawrary Haile Selassie and various hangers-on, and sent off a telegram to the British Consul, asking for advice, because I had been taken to a court where the whole procedure was in Amharic, which I didn't understand.

In less than twelve hours oil had been poured on troubled waters. From the Consul, to the Minister of the Interior, to the Commissioner of Police, to the Chief of Police of Begemdir, General Seyoum, who was quite put out.

"But why didn't you tell me?" he asked. "Why did you go to the

British Embassy? We are your friends. We have to help you." I pointed out that nobody could object to going to court, but that I must be aware of what is going on, and that I must have fair representation. The General was annoyed at the rockets flying over this rather less than major case. He said I should get the money from Shiferaw, and the case would be finished.

When I found Shiferaw, he was in a Land Rover with some friends. They were all armed with rifles, and the vehicle was loaded with luggage, some of it lashed on the roof.

"Where do you think you are going?" I asked, smiling, pulling the door open and squeezing in, unasked, beside him. He looked put out.

After some none-too-subtle persuasion on my part, we went together by taxi around the Arab quarter. Shiferaw stopped off at several bars and brothels, borrowing money here and there until he had the sum I had given to him. I gave him back his receipt and bid him adieu.

Ato Bekele, the legal officer, came to Gondar on the case of Tesfae and Mamo. I went with him down to the Arab quarter, to the big prison in which the two men were awaiting trial. Crowds of people sat around outside the gates, waiting to be let in. Uniformed guards with rifles and bayonets kept order. They let us in and took us to the warden's office. There was a lot of bowing and handshaking. As we sat talking to the warden, I heard a clanking sound, the sound of men shuffling in leg irons. Tesfae and Mamo were shoved into the office. They said Mamo had been fighting. They were both in leg irons and manacles, and they were emaciated, with dark hollows under staring eyes. Their heads were shaved, like all the prisoners I had seen, so many times, being marched in their chains up from the prison to the court. I looked in horror, not believing that these wretches could have been the husky drivers I had known such a short time before. There was a lot of talk about mediation, and Bekele made promises. Mamo asked me to give something important to his wife. I knew that this was his pistol, which I had kept. They said they feared the Debarek people would try to take revenge on their families. I nodded, and said I understood.

We were not shown the rest of the prison, but I got the feeling of it from the low clusters of buildings, the tin roofs, the crude high

walls, the black-bereted guards with their rifles, the hordes of im-
ploring relatives, the smell, the barbed-wire barrier where the prisoners were taken to see their families, and the two hideously ugly,
fat women guards who broke all the gifts of bread and food into the
prisoners' feeding bowls with their hands. They squatted on the
ground, these women. They looked loathsome. I sensed that a gift of
bread to a prisoner in this place was almost a sacred thing, especially if the bread had been made by his wife, or mother, or sister,
and had probably been grown on his land, if he had any, and yet
this gift must be profaned by these female ogres. Of course, I could
see why they had to do it. But still. The prison had a feeling of darkness, despair, horror, and evil. When we got out we found that
Mamo's wife, a tall, attractive woman, was weeping at the gates, for
the guards had not let her in. I remonstrated with Bekele, protesting
that we should go and ask the warden for permission for her to see
her husband. He said that she could come the next day, and spoke
to her; she nodded, and I felt sick to my stomach, and hated him.

A couple of days later I went back with Kassa, at visiting hours,
with a bag of bread and fruit. We pushed in past the crowd at the
gate and waited by the barbed-wire barricade. The prisoners were
being brought in a few at a time to take the food. For some reason
the guards were shouting at Kassa, saying we couldn't see Tesfae
and Mamo. But these were visiting hours, and we had been told by
the police general that we could always see them at this time. One
guard pushed Kassa, and tried to snatch the bag of food from him. I
rushed to him and swore. He threatened me with his long club, and
I must have gone a little crazy, for first I tensed, and then relaxed,
and my heart received a shock of power, and I decided that if he
touched me I would kill him. He was a big, paunchy man, with
angry but weak eyes. He backed off. God save me and all men from
places and situations like this. We got out of the prison yard. I
couldn't drive for a time. My hands were shaking from the anger
and adrenaline in my system.

"Kassa," I said, a little ashamed of myself, "I can't come here
again. Will you come tomorrow? I'll drive you down. If you have
trouble with the guards, just come on out and we'll go and complain
to General Seyoum. He is a fair man."

I had not enough courage to see men treated like animals, or to
sense the misery of this prison. It was medieval. I reminded myself

that in this country, this so-called Tibet of Africa, they still hung men in the market square, even in the great city, and the Emperor still had people flogged in public. Feeling it, I wanted to shout, to fight, to kill somebody or break something. The image of those chains stayed with me, and the memory of the sound, that clanking over cobbles in the rough prison yard. People, doctors, told me it was a living hell in that prison, and I felt that I could read as much in the faces of the men there. In an attempt to cleanse my soul of anger I practiced karate harder. It is said that through strength comes gentleness. I practiced with hands bound, and with narrow stances, and techniques of fighting and disarming while handcuffed. In Begemdir I never saw those modern handcuffs, the ones with the ratchet. They used a very ancient type, with heavy iron wrist pieces that don't tighten up on your wrist. You can fight with those things on.

What would happen to Tesfae and Mamo if mediation failed? Would they be taken to the marketplace in their chains and hung there? I have always thought that the law, on the whole, was just and good. But no man deserved the hell of the Gondar prison. Ethiopians I knew said, "But they are in prison to be punished. They cannot expect to be comfortable." The thought struck me that perhaps it would have been better if the men had died at the hands of that vengeful mob in Debarek. Why the hell had they not escaped? I didn't expect them to live for more than a few months, but they lived much longer.

Meanwhile Tag Demment was getting fed up with Gondar. He said he wouldn't mind living in a tent in the mountains, as the rains were tailing off now. He had met two travelers passing through Gondar, a big, effusive American by the name of Doug Martz and a thin, lanky, red-haired Englishman called George Beeby. Both were footloose, seeing the world. Hearing about the Simien from Tag, they wanted to go up. It was time to visit again, so I said fine, as long as they had their own sleeping bags and rain gear. It still rained sometimes in the afternoons, but there was a lot of fine weather, and the air was very clear, so it was a good time to go up.

Our house in Sankabar was unfinished, and I was eager to get it done and move in, but there was no money in the park account, not even enough to hire mules. I was using my own money, trying to hide the fact from Sonako, who was angry at me. She said it was

stupid to do this, throwing water on a red-hot stone. I was neglecting my wife and children, and putting all my spirit into the
park project. Interest from abroad was growing, and I was getting
letters from all over. From tourists who wanted to visit, from
somebody writing a book about climbing, from the International
Union for the Conservation of Nature. And I was writing and talking about the Simien, pushing for finance and support. I wrote to
Prince Philip, president of the British Appeal of the World Wildlife
Fund. I wrote to tourist organizations. But the Ethiopian Government, and especially our department, remained as apathetic as ever.
Only outside pressure could achieve anything.

After a day in Sankabar, we went up to Geech. Bernhard and
Esther had moved into the big house, now called "Swiss House."
Bernhard had painted Walia murals on the wall behind the tall, black
steel cone fireplace. Rugs and mats made the floor warmer, and
sheepskins were tied onto the chairs. The furniture, designed by my
Swedish friend and made by an old Italian carpenter in Gondar,
was sturdy and good-looking, in natural wood colors. It had been
constructed so that it could be easily taken apart for carrying. The
roof, with its pattern of converging eucalyptus poles, backed with
rush mats, was beginning to mellow with smoke; it was high, but
dissected by a semicircular sleeping platform, reached by a ladder
fixed to the stout center pole of the main room. There were pictures
about the place, and books on shelves, and crockery, and steam
coming from the kitchen. My rifle, Bernhard's binoculars and telescope, and various parkas and things hung from wooden pegs. The
fire blazed and threw out heat, and the room was illuminated by the
brilliant, hissing pressure lamps. We were invited to spend the
night. There was plenty of room for the four of us on the sleeping
platform. That night we toasted cheese and drank wine. George
Beeby entertained us for hours with epic poems like "The Charge of
the Light Brigade." He had an incredible memory for these poems.
He stood in front of the fire, a glass of wine in one hand, reciting in
his Yorkshire accent. I had a very warm feeling inside, and recalled
that awful first night I spent in Geech, wet and shivering, tired and
hungry. Here we were now in a stone house, with light, fire, and
wine. Bernhard had done a tremendous job, and we were both
proud. We had designed the house, chosen the site, arranged for
and instructed the workers, had all the stuff hauled in over rough

mountain paths, had the furniture, the windows, and everything designed and made to our specifications. And our finances had been very limited. In a house like this, even more than in a city house, one could sense the personalities of the people who made it. Bernhard and Esther's presence would be very strong here, long after they left. I could even sense myself in this house, and was pleased. Until the house was finished, Bernhard had gone out in the early mornings to spot Walia, then spent the rest of the day working. We slept comfortably up on the sleeping platform. It was warm up there, close to the roof.

We got up early the next day and went out Walia spotting. Doug was suffering from altitude sickness, and stayed behind. The weather was fine, and we spotted fourteen Walia and six klipspringers at Metagogo. The altitude was three thousand nine hundred and thirty meters here. The sounds of drumming and yelling reached us, fading and rising with the escarpment breezes. *Tonka tonka tonka tonk!* With binoculars we could see tiny figures in the village of Taya below us, and Berhanu, the interpreter, said that down there a Muslim medicine man was driving out the devil from a sick person.

The Simien was bursting with flowers and green plants. Tiny alpine flowers lay like jewels in the close moss. Towering battlements of ambas along the escarpment. Dog-tooth ridges and mounded hills like the bellies of monsters, with a faint hint of snow on Ras Deschan, highest mountain in the empire, and a two days' march away. The horizon was lost in distance; there were drum sounds below, and then, from another world, to the north and almost at our level, a couple of kilometers off the escarpment, the Gondar-to-Asmara DC-3 buzzed past, throwing sound off the mighty cliff faces. The echoes were confusing and loud, and it took time to spot the machine; when we did see it, it looked like a tiny silver insect, so small that it gave scale to the hugeness of the scene.

Three of us returned to Gondar the next day, while Tag stayed in Geech. Tag would be helping Bernhard Nievergelt in his research. He had brought up a pile of biology books to study, and was very keen.

People were coming. It was the beginning of the Ethiopian spring, and the fields were yellow and gold with Maskal daisies. I had been back in Gondar only a day when Dr. Kummer, a primatologist, came with his wife and three children. They were Swiss, and friends of the Nievergelts. He had been studying baboons in Awash, among other places, and now wanted to visit the Simien. They were going up to stay with the Nievergelts, and would be up there for about ten days. I gave them a little help, arranged for the animals, and lent them some sleeping bags and saddlery.

In the last week of September, a great parade was held in Gondar, and in cities all over the country. It was the celebration of Maskal, the Finding of the True Cross. The streets were filled with women in their new shammas, and with men swathed with bandoliers, and carrying their rifles proudly. Finely caparisoned mules jogged along the streets, their silver ornaments jingling and tassels dancing. The army marched through, and drove their jeeps in the parade, with howitzers and heavy machine guns, and at the sight of them, the women let forth their shrill cries. Priests in black robes and turbans danced in swaying lines under the huge, spreading shade of the great fig tree which King Fasilidas had used as a gallows in his time. The dance of the priests was as ancient as the time of the David who slew Goliath, and they chanted to the big drum and moved back and forth, silver-tipped prayer staffs over their shoulders. There was a big bonfire, with a tall cross of brushwood bound to a pole in the middle of it. As the service progressed, the crowd became excited and pressed closer around the tree, under which the priests danced, and the big men rested, in the shade. Silver cumulus moved slowly in a deep blue sky over the gray-brown battlements of Fasilidas castle, and over the swaying eucalyptus, the alien trees, and over the brilliantly colored parasols of the deacons and bishops of the Coptic church. At last the fire was lit. The place throbbed with drums and ululating cries. The flames weaved and danced around the cross, and the priests and bishops circled around the fire, and then the people. There was crying and shouting, and I saw a few women weeping with joy. The burning cross trembled and fell, and a shout went up. Whichever direction the falling cross pointed would get great fortune in the following year. As the fire got cooler, the people took pieces of charred sticks and marked themselves and their children with the ash.

All through the day and night, drums throbbed in the churches, and bands of young men and boys went around the shops and

163

houses, singing, shouting, and getting money, while the musicians, with fiddles and flutes, played their strange music and sang heroic songs. We had drinks on the veranda of the hotel. In another world.

Tag came down with the Kummers, who were full of enthusiasm about the Simien. Dr. Kummer wanted to give me money for the project, but I declined it, and said that it was enough to know that he enjoyed it and would talk about it to other people. His children had no trouble on the long trip, and came down even browner than when they went up.

They had stayed in the Sankabar house for one night, and my accountant, Kassa, had let the mule packers sleep in one wing of the house. Since Ineyu was his uncle, it was difficult for Kassa to refuse. But the damned mule packers had lit a fire on the bedroom floor. On the way back, Tag had found that his medicine chest, which he had left in the house, had been robbed of some two hundred and fifty capsules of tetracycline, as well as a couple of tubes of codeine. The house was kept locked, and the guards had the key, though it seems that for convenience's sake, they kept one window open all the time so that all of them could get in and out as they desired without having to bother to unlock the door. The warden's orders, after all, had just been to keep the doors locked; he had not said anything about the windows.

Nadu had moved his bed into the house, without permission. Nadu's bed had been placed right next to Tag's medicine chest. Coincidence? I knew Nadu had set himself up as the great benefactor of Amba Ras, and that there was a lot of sickness in the village at this time. Nadu once begged me for antibiotics, saying that it was for a typhus case. It turned out that the patient had been dying of advanced tuberculosis. Some months before, I had seen penicillin powder in Nadu's house. He was treating a villager for a sickle wound. He said that Guth, the previous warden, had given the powder to him, and I had no way of proving otherwise.

The theft of medicine filled with me with anger and disgust. If any of our people had needed medicine, all they had to do was ask for it, and it would have been given freely. In Gondar, one capsule of tetracycline cost a dollar. Two hundred and fifty capsules had been stolen. I was sure that a local peasant or one of the lesser guards had not taken it. Everything pointed to Nadu, though I had no proof. What could I do? Agafari Nadu had been appointed by

His Imperial Majesty, and could do no wrong. However, if I ever found out who the thief was, he would have a very rough ride down to Debarek. Zeleka would have to be on duty then. We could maybe arrange for the prisoner to fall off the mule a few times on the way down, because if it was an important Simien man, then he would certainly bribe his way out of trouble at court.

Tag also reported a very disturbing incident. He had been out near the Geech escarpment, on his way to do some spotting, when he saw a villager carrying a freshly cut tree. When Tag looked through his binoculars, the man threw himself down to hide in the long grass. Tag did nothing. I had asked him not to involve himself in control work. Later, when Tag had gone a little way down the cliff, the man came up behind and above him and began hurling down stones from a sling. The man's aim was wide, but there was no doubt in my mind that he was trying to intimidate Tag. If a stone had found its mark and toppled Tag off the ledge, nobody would have been the wiser. We would have presumed that he had slipped and fallen to his death. I wrote to Major Gizaw, telling him to take note and remember this incident, and pointing out that had it been me I would have been carrying a gun, and would not hesitate to shoot and kill anyone who interfered with me on the cliffs. Both of us being bearded, and white, we looked very much like Ethiopians. Tag had been a short time in the Simien, and had interfered with no one. I had a hunch that the man with the sling had been a villager whom I had arrested some months before. We would have to be very careful.

On October 6, I got a letter from Major Gizaw saying that my recommendations for the establishment of the park were good preliminary measures, and that he would take it up with the board.

On October 7, Thor Heyerdahl came to Gondar and gave an informal talk at the Iteghie Hotel. He had been filming the reed or papyrus boats on Lake Tana. These boats, called *tanqua*, were very similar to boats used by Easter Islanders. At this time, the great adventurer was planning his Atlantic trip and the building of the raft *Ra*. The papyrus for this raft came from Lake Tana, and I think the shipment was arranged by the Italian owner of the Iteghie Hotel. As it happened, I had just finished *Aku-Aku*; moreover, Heyerdahl had been my boyhood hero.

Heyerdahl was a big man, energetic and interesting. He was

dressed in long boots and finely pressed bush gear. When he spoke, there was depth and fire in his eyes. None of the Ethiopian big men had heard of the Kon-Tiki expedition. Few of them ever read any books. I was bursting with questions. The whole idea of the voyage, and of the possibility of ancients crossing both Pacific and Atlantic Oceans enthralled and fascinated me, and Thor Heyerdahl's enthusiasm was infectious. I was not disappointed in my hero. After the talk, I tried to persuade him to take a trip to the Simien. He said he was too busy, and sorry. I laughed and said there were pyramids up there, at which he promised that if this were so, he would come the next day, and I said we would build a small pyramid for him if he would come.

Later, I followed the voyage of the *Ra* with deep interest, and thought of him often. It is a great thing for a man to follow his dreams and convictions, and to do things that make people wonder.

Tag returned to the Simien a few days after Thor Heyerdahl's talk. Before he left I gave him a new padlock for the Sankabar house, and asked him to kick out any guards who might be using the place.

When Tag reached Sankabar, he found Nadu in the house. Nadu had been sleeping on my bed and using my sleeping bag. Tag told him to get out, and Nadu refused. Nobody had ever talked to him like that. Hot words were exchanged, and in the quarrel, Nadu reached for his pistol. Tag retaliated by a move for his broad-bladed Bowie knife. Nadu snatched up a rifle, but before he could work a shell into the breech, Tag had grabbed his bow, notched a razor-sharp hunting arrow and pulled it right back, aiming at Nadu's stomach. If released, the arrow would have gone straight through his body without stopping. Nadu dropped the gun and Tag dropped the bow. He seized Nadu by the shoulders, lifted him off the ground as if he were a child, walked to the door, and threw him out into the mud. Tag and Nadu were not good friends after that.

I heard the story from both sides. Nadu said that Tag went crazy and slashed at his neck with his knife, and tried to kill him, but God stopped the blade and saved his life. He said that he would forgive Tag, because he was young, and a foreigner, and did not know the customs of the country. Nadu's followers hated Tag, though they respected him, and never dared try anything with him. Nadu's version of the story was different from Tag's, but I knew both of them, and believed Tag.

An American sociologist went up to the Simien a couple of days after this trouble. On his return he told me that things could get dangerous for Tag, for Nadu had lost much face, and it didn't sit well with him. He also told me that one morning he saw one of the guards, almost certainly Nadu from the description, stop an un-armed peasant and rough him up. The peasant was just passing through, doing no harm. The American got the impression that this show of violence was for his benefit. He had been doing his research in Manz, among Amhara people very similar to the Simien people. Fear and violence were a part of their lives, and maintaining social status was vital. I learned a lot from this American. And I sensed, al-beit dimly, an ominous undercurrent of something which I had not yet fully understood.

11

MORE TROUBLE WITH NADU

Nadu came to the Geech camp with two of his followers, villagers from Amba Ras. They sought out Guard Amara Gebrew and accused him first of cattle theft, saying that Dejasmatch Araya had sent them to get him for this crime. Amara argued, and Nadu said that His Imperial Majesty had given him the right to arrest all thieves and robbers in the Simien. The quarrel grew loud, and Nadu tried to snatch away Amara's rifle; the others helped Nadu, and then Guard Ambaw, another Amba Ras man, joined in on Nadu's side, and all together they managed to wrench the rifle away. Amara was terrified, and ran up to Swiss House to seek Dr. Nievergelt's protection. Nadu rode off toward Amba Ras.

Bernhard Nievergelt was furious and sent people to call Nadu back. Surprisingly, Nadu came, and was lambasted by Bernhard, who warned him that this was going to mean trouble. Amara feared that Nadu was going to kill him. They all shouted at each other. Nadu still had the rifle. This meant the camp was undermanned and underarmed.

The Nievergelts were due to come down again from the Simien, en route to Asmara. They arrived after dark in Gondar and came to my house, bringing Guard Amara with them. Amara was mortified by what had happened, and by the loss of the rifle that meant so much prestige. Nadu had no right to take the rifle away by force. If it was true that Amara was wanted for a crime (and it was not true), then the situation should have been explained to me and I would have disarmed him, issued a receipt for his rifle, and given him orders to go down to Debarek. We had done this before, and

More trouble with Nadu

Nadu knew the procedure quite well. Actually, I believed that Nadu was after the rifle and ammunition.

Amara slept that night with Zeleka and Abahoy, and borrowed my rifle. Abahoy, my servant, was Nadu's relative, and he and Amara argued during the night until I had to go out and yell at them to shut up. Nearly all the guards had some connection with Nadu, and were loyal to him.

The next day, with the help of an impartial interpreter, a veterinary assistant from the agricultural office, I interrogated Amara. It was an amazing interview. According to Amara, Nadu had attacked him because he had been refusing to give Nadu a cut of his salary and field allowances. I pricked up my ears at this, for other men had told me this previously, but had refused to sign statements about it. Apparently all the Simien men paid Nadu about five dollars a month, more if they had been out on patrols and got allowances. If they didn't pay, Nadu would threaten them, saying that he could get them sent to Omo Park. The Simien men, having lived all their lives under such systems and such officials, did not question his authority or his right, and had not even thought of complaining to me. Techale, a southerner, had laughed at Nadu, and told him to go to hell. Techale would pay bribes to no one, and this was one of the reasons for Techale's quarrel with Nadu. But even he had not reported it. Techale had no social connections in the Simien, and could afford to stick his neck out, but Amara was different. All his family lived in the Simien.

So Nadu had been demanding and taking bribes from the guards ever since he got the job. He took money for special services, like the writing of those letters giving "permission" for men to be off duty. He also took "presents" from the local people, promising in return to use his "influence" with me to get them jobs. And, more serious, he was accumulating rifles and ammunition, taking them by force, and by other, more subtle means.

All this talk of bribery annoyed but did not deeply shock me. Bribery is a part of Ethiopian life. What hit me hard was Amara's testimony that Nadu was advocating the killing of the rare and beautiful Simien fox. This animal, with its red fur, bushy tail, and long legs, lives only in Ethiopia, in the mountains of Bale and Simien. These two mountain groups were so far apart that the Simien foxes found in Bale and those found in Simien were almost certainly different races. In our area, I believed the Simien fox to be in even more serious danger of extinction than the Walia. We saw very few of them, and the one that had been seen around camp was usually associating with golden jackals. Nadu had often argued about the fox, saying it killed sheep. Every biologist who had been into the Simien said that it did not kill sheep. Biologists are often wrong, but not this time. I myself had looked at hundreds of droppings of the Simien fox, and had found nothing but the bones and fur of grass rats. That the Simien fox ate grass rats was beneficial to the moorlands. I had also seen a Simien fox pass right by sheep without disturbing them at all. But Nadu argued and I got angry; I told him that if anybody shot or harmed a Simien fox there would be very serious trouble. In front of other game guards, right in the proposed national park area, Nadu, the chief guard, had shot at a Simien fox. He missed on that occasion, but boasted that he would kill them.

Amara testified that Nadu had told the other guards, "Don't listen to the foreigner. Listen to me. I am your father. The red jackal, the jackal, the leopards, the lammergeyers, and great birds must all be killed. They attack the sheep of our people. Only the Walia is to be protected. His Majesty gave me the right of protection of the Walia. The foreigner knows nothing. He is a usurper, sent by my enemies. You must kill these animals." And Nadu cursed some guards who were trying to take poachers to court. The poachers were snaring klipspringers, duikers, and serval cats. Nadu said, "Why do you persecute your own people? Leave them alone!" Of course, he had been bribed by the families of the poachers.

On numerous occasions I had explained the laws about the defense of property. If a wild animal damaged property, it could be killed, but it must be reported, and the skins turned in. I spent hours trying to explain, in very simple terms, the balance of nature, and said that it was a God-made thing, and that we would protect all wildlife. But each time, after I left, Nadu had scorned what I had said, contradicting everything. He repeated, only the Walia is to be protected.

And this, of course, became the general idea; even among the wildlife officers in our headquarters. Certainly it was the idea held by all local officials. Even the Governor General himself called me "the Walia foreigner."

Hearing all this, I realized that Agafari Nadu Worota had deliberately been destroying and undermining everything that I had been trying to do for almost a year. All of this explained why there had been no prosecutions or arrests in all the time that Nadu had been in control. Nadu had either ignored all crimes or had been bribed. In another time, another era, I would calmly have killed him.

He had been killing the great bone-breakers, the lammergeyers. He had advocated and perhaps killed the rare Simien fox, an endangered species, within the proposed boundaries of the park. He had extorted money and taken bribes. He had taken rifles, ammunition, and uniforms, and probably a lot of other equipment. He had attacked one guard and incited other guards to violence. He had lied, cheated, got off work, and undermined what I was trying to do. And he had even slept in the warden's bed and in the warden's sleeping bag. According to reports, he was gathering and arming his followers, and like his father before him, he fed them from his extensive barley crop.

As long as Nadu was in the Simien, the park project would fail. I wrote out the charge sheet, with Amara's signed testimony and my comments. I sent the lot off to Major Gizaw, and told him that unless Nadu's crimes were immediately investigated and punished, I would resign. I wanted them to suspend Nadu from all duties and pay until the investigation was completed.

I also wanted a letter from the Palace, refuting Nadu's claim to guardianship of the Walia, and explaining that the Simien Mountain National Park was under my direction, as the game warden, who was employed by and answered to the Wildlife Conservation Department, under the Ministry of Agriculture, under the Emperor. The Emperor's actions, or lack of them, puzzled me. I never got the letter I requested.

The Emperor had given Nadu the authority to protect the Walia when Nadu had gone to Addis Ababa with the three Walia, captured at General Nagur's request. The General was the former Governor General of Begemdir, and Nadu had been his Agafari. The Walia were presented to the Emperor for his private zoo. Many people had done this, to curry favor with His Majesty. I was puzzled.

Everything I had read about Haile Selassie indicated that he was a man of more than average strength and wisdom. History will record him as such. But some people in Ethiopia told me that the Emperor was incapable of admitting that he was wrong, or of getting rid of anybody who had ever done him a service. I preferred to think that knowledge of what was happening in the Simien was kept from him.

Some days later, I phoned the department and spoke to Ato Balcha, who was as vague and noncommittal as ever. I raged over the phone, threatening violence, resignation, and all manner of greater evils. Ato Balcha flapped, said he would have to speak to the Major about it. Very soon afterward, Major Gizaw phoned and promised that Nadu would be transferred to Omo. They felt that investigations would be long and painful, with little chance of getting to the truth. The other guards would perjure themselves, there would be much bribery and intrigue, and meddling by important personages. They wanted to take the easy way out and send Nadu to Omo, out of harm's way. I didn't believe that Nadu would go. I thought he would probably resign.

But whatever happened, and I stressed this, it had to be shown that the government and the Palace supported me, or what I was trying to do, against men such as Agafari Nadu. If not, there would be bad, bad trouble.

It would be great if Nadu went to Omo. It was hard there, and he would be far away from the support of his relatives and followers, a little frog in a big pond, under the not-so-gentle but very just care of the warden, George Brown, who was known by many who crossed him as "the foreign devil." If Nadu went to Omo, there was no doubt that he would become a changed man. If only he would accept the transfer!

※※※※

A boost to optimism came one day in the form of a huge, dull-red Russian bulldozer. It was part of the UNDP equipment sent to the Wildlife Conservation Department. When I heard that the low-loader was coming along toward Gondar, I drove out to meet it. The big truck roared along at a snail's pace, having come all the way from Awash. The relief driver took my Toyota back into town and I rode in with the truck to show the driver the turn-off.

The bulldozer was massive, square, and unrefined. Very Russian. People waved to us along the road, for many of them knew me, and knew that I had been pushing for a road into the Simien. The fat

172

madam of the Lumumba Hotel and bar stopped her little car and waved jubilantly. She knew too, for she was a close friend of the old Dejasmatch, and Ermias had often talked to her about the Simien when he stayed at her hotel.

In Debarek, the people clustered around the huge machine. Dejasmatch Araya came out in his black cloak and stood in front of it, holding my hand, boasting in a loud voice, so that all could hear and laugh, that if I now did not build a fine road all the way to the church at Derasghie, then he would hang me in the market square. I said the road would cost money, and the Dejasmatch said that they could get the money from the people. Somebody in the crowd, a bold man, asked what had happened to the money already collected for the road, a long time ago. There was some argument. But the Dejasmatch and the people were as elated as I was. At last it seemed that building would begin.

"When will you start work?" asked Dejasmatch Araya.

"When the Russian men arrive," I answered.

"We don't need them. We have the machine. Even I can drive it," he said.

But we did need the Russians. Nobody but the Russians knew how to drive this monster, and nobody but the Russians were supposed to touch it. The bulldozer was unloaded and parked outside the police station in Debarek, to await its masters, fuel, and spare parts. And a good survey of the road. The seats were taken out and locked up in our store. But we had a bulldozer! I hoped the Russians would come soon, and anticipated working with them with eagerness. Ah, we would work every day until the road head came up to Sankabar. At night we would have roast sheep and chickens, vodka, beer, and wine; we would get to know each other! The people would help us, respect us, and bless us for the road. What a dream!

On October 15, I went up again to Sankabar with Christer, the Swedish carpenter, and worked for four days on my house. We were lining the inside of the house with tarpaper or roofing felt, then putting up a frame, then paneling the inside of the house with plywood. It looked really fine. We fixed benches and shelves in the kitchen. Tag came to help. On the 17th, Yemanu, the headquarters accountant, came up too, and this astonished me, for he was the first head office man, other than John Blower, to come into the Simien since I had been there.

Christer, Tag, and I worked by lamplight until late each night, banging, cursing, joking, having a great time. Yemanu thought we were mad. At lunchtime, we took wine, bread, cheese, pickles, and canned meats up to the top of the hill for a picnic, and we fried sausages and brewed tea over a small fire, and gazed out at the tremendous view, now daubed everywhere with splashes of Maskal daisies and flowering sage. Yemanu said that he now understood why I loved the Simien, for it was beautiful. He went up to Geech and was impressed by Swiss House and saw that it was possible to live very comfortably in the mountains. He promised to strive for the Simien. He had, however, actually come to tell the game guards that they would not be getting any compensation for the long months they had spent in tents, and the guards were not happy about this. He brought some wild promises of money for the project, and I began to hope, although I suspected that it was all just another load of bullshit. Which it was.

We got most of two rooms finished before having to go back to Gondar. Christer had work to do, and I had to renew my foreigner's registration.

I told Yemanu of my intention to return to Japan to study there. He asked me why I didn't make more use of my opportunities to get allowance money for myself. My allotted per diem for safaris, town trips, and so forth was fourteen dollars a day. I said that when I went out, I applied for the money and got it from headquarters.

"But you have the park money. You can take it out any time you want to. You just write on the form that you went for a trip, sign it yourself, take out the money and sign a Form Six. It's very easy."

He was, in fact, advising me on how to cheat the government, and get money that I didn't earn. As far as I could understand, nobody really cared what I did with the park money, as long as it was all accounted for in one way or another on the required forms. Despite the mountains of papers, the Ethiopian Government would be very easy to cheat.

Stories about the fiddling at headquarters were rife. Major Gizaw's uncle-in-law had made off with my guards' pay. There was a racket going on with the "official" stamping of illegal skins. There was another racket involving the licensing officer, who was "renewing" hunting licenses with a stamp and a signature, on licenses clearly marked as being unrenewable. Rather a lot of these "renewed" licenses had been found, but no record could be found of what happened to the fee. There were also a lot of professional hunter's licenses being dished out, together with "honorary game warden" cards and badges, some going to the most unlikely people. As, for instance, the best-known dealers in illegal leopard skins! There were some minor fiddles going on with per diem allowances, about which everybody knew. However, none of this mattered much to the Ethiopian officials as long as the paperwork looked right.

Talking to Yemanu, and perceiving the way he thought, made me fully realize that what we thought of as "fiddling" and "bribery" was viewed in an entirely different light in Ethiopia. It seemed to be more a question of "cooperation" and "knowing the right people" and "doing favors" and "returning favors" and "getting one's due."

Simien's new assistant warden, Mesfin Abebe, arrived in Gondar at the end of October. He had been a member of the big British expedition that sailed and walked along the Blue Nile. He was a graduate of the Tanzania College of Wildlife Management, a unique school which gives Africans a superb training in this field. Mesfin came through college with an excellent record. He had also been a forest officer, and had done a spell in the Ethiopian Air Force. His English was impeccable, tinged with a soft British accent. When I first met him, he was extremely polite and pleasant, and there was a subdued warmth about him. I knew that we were going to be friends, and breathed a silent sigh of relief.

Mesfin was keen to get into the Simien. I was still delayed with my foreigner's registration renewal. Some French tourists came, spent a day in Gondar with us, and went up to the Simien with Mesfin. It was important for Mesfin to get into the mountains quickly, for Dr. Nievergelt was at this time preparing to go on a safari to Ras Deschan, the highest mountain in Ethiopia. En route he would investigate areas outside the park where the Walia were supposed to live. Either Mesfin or I had to go, and since I couldn't, it was up to Mesfin. The interpreter and Tag would be going along, and it promised to be a good trip. I was jealous as hell.

I had received a letter from *Life* magazine. A photographer was going to come to take pictures of the Walia, and wanted me to help. I was delighted. This was the kind of publicity that we needed badly. The same week a French lady reporter came from Nairobi to interview me about the Simien. She should have gone up to see the place, but claimed that she didn't have the time. Other inquiries from prospective visitors were coming in thick and fast. Meanwhile, the Ethiopian Tourist Organization, with their plush Addis Ababa offices and countless expensive plans and surveys, stolidly continued to tell visitors who asked about the Simien that it was impossible to go there, that police escorts were essential because of the bandits, that special government permission to travel in the Simien was needed, or that they just didn't know anything. Some people knew, of course, for I had sent letters to them, but somehow the news never filtered down to the strikingly beautiful girls and handsome men behind the inquiry desks.

On November 16, the *Life* photographer came with a Peace Corps volunteer who was working with the Ethiopian Tourist Organization. We went up to Debarek the next day to arrange for the mules.

I was anticipating some trouble from Nadu at this time. He had been ordered down to Debarek to give a statement about some of the accusations against him. Amara and Guard Chane had come down too, as had Berhanu, all of whom had witnessed some of Nadu's crimes. He came down with many armed followers, riding his fine golden horse. Where Nadu was concerned I didn't trust the Simien men, and I requested that the Dejasmatch recommend two men to go up with us. One of the men Dejasmatch Araya pushed forward was the same Takale Wondeferow who had asked about the gelada killing. The other man was his own nephew. Later I heard that Takale had presented the old bastard with two sacks of honey so that he could get his recommendation for a game guard's job.

The trip with the photographer was a miserable failure; he cursed everything, never got close to a Walia, and got an infection of some kind. He called it off on the fourth day, and wanted a helicopter to take him out. That was impossible, and he had to make do with a mule. It rained like hell on the way down.

I saw Nadu in Sankabar. He seemed embarrassed. With nobody to interpret, there was no point in discussing anything with him, and besides, I didn't feel like talking to him for a while yet.

The wife of our servant Abahoy had hung herself from a tree in the garden of our Gondar house. She was slowly throttling to death when Abahoy found her and cut her down. Being a girl from the mountains, she had been unhinged by the big city. I had to take her to the doctor to get some tranquilizers. She said that Abahoy had been beating her and flirting with the city girls.

We wanted to get our house finished and move up to the Simien, but there was absolutely no money left in the park account. When I phoned Major Gizaw, he said, "Why don't you use your own money for a while?" I replied that I had none, to which he replied he would send me five hundred dollars from his own account. I kept thinking about that magnificent budget that I thought the park was due, but which seemed to exist only on paper.

Tag, Mesfin, and the Nievergelts came back down to Gondar after their Ras Deschan trip on December first. I had dinner with Bernhard and Esther at the hotel, and afterward, over drinks, we discussed the Walia and its survival problems.

At one time, the Walia ranged over the entire Simien, for there are cliffs everywhere. Then men and their agriculture invaded the valley of the Takazze, following the deep valleys of the tributary rivers that dissect the great volcanic dome. At the time of the Fascist occupation, many people came into the mountains, and agriculture and wood-cutting increased. During and after the occupation, the men had rifles, and poaching was common, for the flesh of the Walia is good and not forbidden by their religion, and one Walia yields much meat. The formerly vast habitat of the Walia was cut off into several pockets, isolated from each other by deep valleys and cultivated fields. Forests were destroyed and erosion ran wild. Deprived of cover, the Walia became more and more vulnerable. Buahit, an area out of the park, which was probably the former center of the Walia's habitat and range was now a bare, eroded desert, with not a tree to be seen. Within living memory the Walia had been numerous at Walia Kind, and at Ras Deschan, but on the recent safari, not even droppings could be found. Within living memory the Walia had disappeared from the cliffs of the Balagas Valley, and at Silky Mountain, an area renowned for Walia, only twelve animals were seen after an extensive search. Three quarters of this group were under three years of age. The big ones had nearly all gone. Their little pocket of natural tree heather forest and tussock grass was dwindling rapidly. Silky was a long way out of the park, and with such a low density of population, and with so much interference, these Walia were doomed. In 1963, a German scientist named Werdecker made a superbly detailed and accurate map of the Ras Deschan area. Every hut was marked. Now, in 1968, Bernhard Nievergelt estimated that the number of the huts had doubled, and in proportion, the amount of agriculture and erosion had increased, and the forest cover had decreased.

Without a doubt, the largest pocket of fairly natural Simien vegetation remaining in the whole mountain area was that of the proposed national park, a mere two hundred square kilometers, including the lowland area at the foot of the escarpment. And the local people were cutting, burning, and plowing into this, and their goats were invading it.

The goats were potentially a very serious problem. Goats and ibex can produce fertile hybrids. This has been done with the European ibex, and in Switzerland, the authorities had their work cut out to kill off these animals. As the number of Walia decreased, it would become more and more difficult for them to find breeding partners, and more and more likely for them to crossbreed with the common goats that invaded their cliffs. Once crossbreeding began, it would be almost impossible to preserve the ibex as a pure and rare strain. Their refined genes would be tossed into the pot again with their common, domesticated cousins. The result of thousands of years of adaptation to the cliffs, the climate, the altitude, and the plants would be lost. The very nature of the Simien would probably not allow a strict culling program. If the Walia were to be saved, the park boundaries had to be declared within a year, and then the area would have to be clearly protected, and all local humans and their stock kept out.

Previous estimates of the Walia's population put them at around two hundred to two hundred and fifty animals. Bernhard roughly estimated them at a hundred and fifty or less. The Ethiopians ignored this. Villagers told the officials stories. There were always many, many Walia over the next hill. Old men remembered the way it had been when they were young. Young men heard them, and repeated the story, for the old men were bound to be right in the wisdom of their years. But where once the sight of forty or fifty Walia constituted a big herd, now the sight of ten Walia was a big herd. Colonel Azziz told me confidently that there were several thousand Walia in the Simien, and so did the old Dejasmatch. Neither of them came up to see or count. Nadu knew the truth, I believe, for he was not a stupid man, but he too persisted in saying that there were many, many Walia. After all, had he not been placed in charge of them by His Majesty? No matter what, the foreigners were bound to be wrong. But we were not wrong.

Bernhard Nievergelt had an idea that a good plan, possibly the surest plan, to save the Walia would be to capture a breeding nucleus of a few animals and take them to a country like Switzerland, where they could be bred in isolated and controlled captivity. It was a good plan. But would the Ethiopians like it? Would it not be a blow to their very considerable pride? The idea was that the captured animals could ensure the survival of the species, should the Simien Walia die out. Then, if the Ethiopian Government could ever assume responsibility for maintaining a park in the Simien, some animals could be brought back and released to start over again. That is, if the goats could be cleared out.

Simien fox were rare too. On the Ras Deschan safari they heard only one. In the park, one or two animals were seen, very often associating with golden jackals. Even there they were not safe from men like Nadu. Without any doubt, they had been shot all over the Simien. They were not particularly timid animals, and therefore an easy target for a rifleman. I feared that the numbers of the foxes were so diminished that they would soon become extinct in the mountains for which they were named.

While we were talking over our maps and notebooks, a big, loudmouthed Ethiopian, slightly drunk, asked what I thought I was doing in Ethiopia, and what I thought I could achieve by scribbling things in notebooks. His tone was challenging. He said that the Ethiopians didn't care what the foreigners said or wrote, we could write about the smell of their armpits as far as he cared. He sat at a nearby table with Colonel Azziz of the police. Colonel Azziz was a diplomat. He jumped up and introduced me to his loud companion, who turned out to be another police colonel, the chief of the transport and maintenance division of the entire police force. He was a big man, scornful of our work. Not to be browbeaten, I lit into him about erosion, soil and water loss, drawing simple pictures in my notebook. I did not bob and bow to the big man, and he liked this. He became interested, and then concerned. Colonel Azziz told him where we lived, how we traveled. The police colonel said he would give his life to help me. I complained about the lack of funds, and he said that Begemdir was always being forgotten. The people of Begemdir, he said, were good, quiet, loyal people, and they were the essence of Ethiopia's culture and history. Everything was going to Shoa, and to the south. He said he was proud to be from Gondar, to be a true Ethiopian, a clean Ethiopian. He was very drunk. He began to say things about other people who were not pure Ethiopians, and Colonel Azziz, not enjoying the way the conversation was heading, urged him to come home to bed.

The next day a letter came by hand from Dejasmatch Araya. Nadu had been talking to him. Now he was on Nadu's side, and demanded to know why I was sending Nadu to Omo. I wrote a reply saying that it was not me, but the Addis Ababa headquarters who were sending Nadu to Omo, and that they had every right to do this. He was a game guard and was liable to be posted anywhere in the Empire. I added that he had been accused of certain crimes and that these crimes were too serious for me to handle. However, Nadu would not serve in the Simien while I was there. I then requested that he direct any further questions to Addis Ababa.

I had been right. I knew that Nadu would never accept the transfer.

12

RUSSIANS ON MULES

Five Russians came up to Gondar from Addis Ababa with a driver from our department. My image of Russians was that of a hearty, friendly, hard-working people, relaxed and quick to laugh. On first meeting the five I was disappointed. Only the interpreter attempted to speak English. They declined invitations for coffee, and then for lunch. The international community of Gondar was to be disappointed. I had been promising a big party when the Russians came. We quickly forgot about that. They had come to look over the route of the road, and would spend a few days in the Simien Mountains.

"Where is your equipment?" I asked, thinking I could drive it up to Debarek and have it packed in ahead of them.

"What equipment?" asked the interpreter, a tall, blond, handsome young man.

"Sleeping bags, camp beds, mountain clothing, pots, pans, cups, plates, you know, camping gear."

"We have only what we are dressed in," he answered. I stared at them. Business suits, white shirts, ties, and city shoes. "Major Gizaw just told us that we should come up."

I rushed around town and borrowed sleeping bags, air mattresses, and camp beds from the American and Swedish volunteers. The Russians went out and bought a few blankets. Clothing and boots were a problem. I could lend enough for two men, and I suggested that just two should come up this time. They insisted that everybody must go. They were determined to go, business suits and all.

In an effort to break the ice, I laid in a few bottles of vodka and told them they must come around to my house. They did, and there they began to relax. They were nice fellows after all.

On the first day we drove up early to Debarek and looked over the proposed road route from Debarek to the top of the great ridge. We came back that evening. My job, apart from that of guide, was to pace out the distances. I strode along, counting and checking in my notebook. From Debarek to the church, one kilometer. From the church to the Lama River, three kilometers. From the Lama River to the top of the ridge, three kilometers. Along the crest of the ridge, three kilometers. The chief engineer of the party rode behind on a mule, noting the number of places where culverts would be needed, the degree of the slopes, the soil, and so forth. At the top of the ridge we stopped for a lunch of cheese, bread, olives, wine, and oranges. I was very tired. Walking was nothing, but to count each step, and thus to be conscious of each movement and effort, was terrible. Walking ten kilometers this way was more tiring than walking forty kilometers without counting.

Back in Gondar, Sonako was reading a book after lunch when our maid came in saying, "Madam, madam . . . Chinese, Chinese." Since Dr. Wan had gone home a couple of months before, Sonako thought that the new Taiwanese veterinarians had arrived. She went out and saw two young men in dirty, patched jeans, parkas, and crash helmets. They were almost black from the sun, and there was a certain air about the way they walked. They wore the red sun flag.

"Ah! You are Japanese! Welcome! How did you know where to come?"

They had heard about us from Mr. Yamada, whom they had met in Tanzania. Mr. Yamada talked a lot about his trip to the Simien, and about the English game warden who spoke Japanese and had a Japanese wife. These two young adventurers were touring the world on 250-c.c. Suzuki motorcycles. When I came home they were on the living room floor, playing with our children. We introduced ourselves. Their names were Mikio Maeno and Takashi Kasori. It was an easy matter to talk them into coming up to the Simien with us the next day.

Neither the five Russians nor the two Japanese had done much, if any, riding, and they sat awkwardly, clinging to the pommels of the high wooden saddles; the Russians especially looked funny with their red, sunburned faces, worried expressions, and crumpled suits. The chief of the party had stuck a piece of paper over his nose to keep the sun off. Another engineer wore a natty little city hat which looked like a chamberpot. But they were game for anything, and they kicked and wobbled and flapped their legs, and shouted, "Che! che!" at the suffering horses. The mule packer's men and our guards ran beside us and laughed delightedly to see the clumsy antics of the foreigners. We came down a hill and onto the wide rolling meadow before the Lama River, and I could not resist kicking my horse into a gallop and racing Mesfin. The weather was fine, the air like crystal, and the meadow smooth and dry. Mesfin was a good rider, but I had the better horse. We whooped and thundered along. Unfortunately, the other seven riding animals decided to race too, but not all in exactly the same direction. Ethiopian horses usually have hard mouths from the cruel iron bits that are used there, and as a consequence they don't respond to reins. Certainly the Simien horses didn't turn on the reins, but rather were turned by tapping the sides of their necks with a stick or a riding crop. Mesfin and I stopped and looked behind. First one Russian fell off, then another, and then one Japanese. The others jogged along in varying positions of precarious discomfort, hooting with laughter. Humans chased horses over the hills. But dignity was gone now. Everybody laughed and joked and fell off a few more times all the way to Sankabar.

The next day three of the Russians went back along the road to look at the last three kilometers to Sankabar, the part which skirted the great valley. Mesfin, Mikio, Takashi, the two remaining Russians, and I went along the cliff edge and watched a big herd of gelada. They were always my favorites. To watch the baboons was to see a caricature of one's own species. Their actions, visible emotions, jealousies, contests, and play are so similar to ours.

I soon found out that it was difficult to get close to the herds by sneaking up on them. Young males kept to the outer perimeters of their constantly moving territory, watching for suspicious characters. However, it was ridiculously easy to get near them by casually sauntering into full view. Once close to the herds, however, any movement would bring cries of warning. The females and adolescents are awful shriekers and are given to excited noise-making. If a movement seemed dangerous—if you lifted an arm, or walked toward the herd, the whole herd would bolt for the cliffs. The sound of the hundreds of feet was like thunder as they leaped and tumbled down impossible faces of rock and crashed with what seemed like suicidal abandon through the cliff-ledge heather trees. Their quickest way of getting down a cliff was to fall, occasionally arresting the fall by grabbing for a rock or a tuft of grass here and there. Once on the cliffs they would yell. It sounded like abuse. The adolescents in particular would bob and weave, grimace and shriek. However, if we just sat quietly, in full view, the herd would go about its business, and keep up a sort of reassuring grunting. During the daylight hours, feeding and grooming never ceased. They shuffled along on their bottoms, a foot or so at a time, digging for roots. Gelada are vegetarians. Their digging looked not unlike someone typing with the two-finger method, only they kept all their fingers together. After a herd of gelada had passed over a piece of ground, it looked as if someone had been at it with a hoe.

They kept close to each other, and at first sight looked like a jumbled crowd. But on closer inspection, one could see that there was definite order, with the young males on the outside, and the females with their young and the play groups of juveniles closest to the cliffs. There were family groups, each headed by a magnificent, long-maned male.

While we watched, a play group was contesting for a tree, playing "king of the castle." About fifteen young baboons scrambled and wrestled and shrieked, pushed each other off the branch, pulled tails, jumped, swung. We couldn't help but laugh to see them.

Several females had tiny young, which clung to their belly fur and fed from the breast. Gelada young suck both teats at the same time. The teats are rather long and point inward from the bare, red hourglass-shaped patch on the adult breast. This bare patch, which looks heart-shaped from a distance, has given rise to the gelada baboon's other name, "the bleeding heart baboon." In the big males and sexually receptive females, this chest patch is bright red.

Grooming went on all the time. Their fingers were quick and deft, and the big males enjoyed a lot of attention. There was also a fair amount of copulating. It was a very quick business, with the female on all fours, the male standing on his short legs at her rear, grasping her rump and penetrating her with quick thrusts. From the noises they made, it seemed to be a very enjoyable business for them too.

The youngsters were extremely curious and would come to peek at us. They sneaked up behind rocks or bushes and stood on tiptoe to look over; they would peer out, giving little cries of what sounded like a mixture of fright and delight.

When the herd moved, the big boss males trod majestically, and with their long manes and tufted tails, they were often mistaken for lions.

The Russians bought a sheep, and that night they made a kind of soup and shish-kebab. They were very much more relaxed now. It is almost impossible for men to share meat and fire in the mountains and still be aloof. We sang songs and drank, and talked about many things. It was a mixed group: Ethiopian, British, Japanese, and Russian.

We argued a lot about the road. Dr. Nievergelt and I had both told the Russians that we needed a small mountain road, not more than five meters wide. With a few lay-bys, even three and a half meters would be enough. But the Russians were talking about a highway some ten meters wide, even twenty-five meters wide including the shoulders. This was ridiculous. Such a road would look ugly in a mountain park. It would disturb too much ground, especially on the steep slopes. Economically, it didn't make sense. It would take too much time, land, and money. We did not want a road for touring cars, but for a dozen or so Land Rovers and one Unimog truck a day. I pointed out why we desperately needed a road, that if we didn't get it soon the project would fail. I said that time was short and that a small road would be ample for the needs of the park for the next ten or fifteen years, until the park could demonstrate that it was worth extra money. We needed a small road, quickly. They all talked. The interpreter looked at me very seriously and said, "In Russia, we do not build little roads."

I wanted to laugh. It sounded like something out of a comedy. We continued to argue. I felt apprehensive. They obviously did not want to work in the Simien. They wanted to work in Awash, which already had rough roads, and which was close to Addis Ababa and convenient for their families. They had been told before coming that they would work close to the city and that masses of equipment and men would be supplied by the Ethiopian Government. They said that they had not been told about the Simien.

"Well, how long would this road take?"

"With the equipment we have, about ten years."

"What? Have you seen what the Italians did in a few months just twenty kilometers from here on the escarpment face? They brought a road right up the cliffs, all four or five thousand feet of them. And they didn't have bulldozers. They built roads all over the country in three years. What you say is ridiculous. We need about thirty-five kilometers of road for four-wheel drive vehicles. Sure, we need culverts and maybe two bridges, and we will have to do a lot of maintenance on the road. But if this road is not built soon, the area will be destroyed, and there will be no point in trying to do anything."

But they were adamant. They said that when I got back to Gondar I should give them a letter telling them what I considered to be the requirements of the road. But by this time I knew that the Russians were not going to build it, and my old depression was coming back.

✖✖✖✖

We left at eight in the morning and came down along the route of the proposed road. When we got down to Debarek, a servant came to tell me that Dejasmatch Araya wanted to see me at his house. When I went in, the old Dejasmatch asked if I had eaten. It was just past noon. I said I had not and he called for injera, wat, and for tedj. Kassa was with me.

After the preliminary inquiries about the health of myself, my wife, and my children, and the road, he brought up the subject of Nadu. He leaned over and patted my arm, speaking in a confiding tone. He asked if I could not let Nadu stay until the road was finished, because Nadu had great influence with the hill people, and we would need his influence to get the people to work and cooperate with us.

"Nadu is a criminal as far as I am concerned," I said. "He must be tried, and if guilty, he must be punished. He has been accused of bribery, of theft, of shooting a rare animal that he was supposed to be protecting. He has been accused of encouraging the people to poach. He has been accused of killing a rare and protected bird. He does not do his duty. He thinks he is a great lord. He is a liar, he is disloyal. I trusted him like a brother, and he has betrayed me and destroyed my work. I would never work with this man again. On no account. If Nadu stays, I will go."

Russians on mules

Kassa translated. The Dejasmatch shook his head, saying that this was terrible, that he had not known. He changed the subject. He could see that there was no point in pursuing it with me.

Everyone who came to Debarek was supposed to go and see the Dejasmatch, but the Russians had not done so. He was annoyed and asked to see them. I apologized and told him about my two Japanese friends who were waiting for me.

"Go and fetch them!" he ordered, and two men ran out.

When Mikio and Takashi came in, I introduced them, and the Dejasmatch bade them be seated. His servants stared from the doorway, and several followers with rifles stood by here and there around the room. Both men were offered tedj; Takashi was a drinker, but Mikio was not, and he declined it. The Dejasmatch glared at him and said if he did not take the drink he would be thrown in jail. The riflemen around the room grinned. I believed that the old man was serious, and I told Mikio this. Mikio drank the tedj.

Dejasmatch Araya was talking about the war against the Italians. He said that he led four thousand men in the Tigre campaign at the beginning of the war. He was wounded three times. In that fight the Ethiopians had rushed the barbed wire and machine guns and tried to cut their way through with their swords. In the course of this campaign, the Italians had picked him up and treated him. In turn, he served them until the war began to swing against the Fascists.

He started insulting our guards again, saying that if they were good soldiers they would do sentry duty all night, be always by my side to respond to any wish I might have, and would never allow oxen to stray into the camp and rip the tents.

He said he knew that the Japanese were good soldiers, that during the great war they flew their planes into the American ships, and that when they were losing they cut open their bellies rather than surrender. Kassa and the Dejasmatch's followers were incredulous, but Mikio, Takashi, and I said it was all true. We got more and more tedj. Since I had eaten oily food previously, I wasn't getting drunk, but Mikio and Takashi were drinking on empty stomachs.

Mikio was red in the face. He called for injera. I laughed and said that they had not eaten, and the Dejasmatch said that I was a poor friend for not telling him, and for letting my brothers go hungry. His wife brought food for them. Mikio shouted for water. A servant

187

brought it, but before he could drink it, the Dejasmatch took the glass and splashed it in his face, saying that it would cool him off a little. The Dejasmatch asked if they thought they could drink more tedj, and Takashi said "one bottle" when he meant to say "one glass." A single bottle of good tedj can make a man drunk, and Takashi was already red in the face, laughing and gobbling his injera with a greasy-fingered, unrestrained gusto that was not really typical of a Japanese. The Dejasmatch was enjoying himself. He called for more tedj and set one bottle in front of Takashi. The servant started to fill our glasses from this bottle. The Dejasmatch stopped him.

"No. He asked for one bottle. He will drink it all. Bring another bottle for the others." Sure enough, he made Takashi drink the lot.

The Dejasmatch pounded Mikio on the back. "You must stay in the Simien. We will find you wives. Every day you can drink good tedj and talla, and eat good injera and wat. We will build houses and a road for you. Your children will grow to be strong men. Why go back to your country?" He pointed to his wife. "Do you have such beauties in Japan?"

The Dejasmatch's wife was younger than he, and very fat. Her neck and hands were tattooed. Her eyes were large and brown. Mikio cocked his head to one side. He was almost too drunk to talk. He said in Japanese, "No, we certainly do not have such beauties in Japan."

Mikio was now blowing and puffing, slumping against the wall, his eyes squinting and his face lobster red. Takashi was laughing and talking loudly. Mikio started waving his arms and calling for them to bring on the women, because he was ready. Maybe it was time to go. The Dejasmatch tried to get them to drink more. I stood up and said that I had to go back to Gondar. Mikio, Takashi, and the Dejasmatch bid affectionate farewells to one another.

It was only four o'clock, and still light, the sun very bright. I walked in the middle with Mikio and Takashi leaning on me. We weaved past the police station. Everybody was watching and laughing. They knew where we had been. I loaded the two drunken Japanese into the back of the Unimog where they promptly fell asleep among the boxes and bundles and two sheep which Guard Mitiku was taking back for Abahoy. I drank much black coffee, splashed my face with cold water, and drove the growling Unimog back to Gondar. There I got hell from my wife for not looking after our two guests better.

The five Russians went back to Addis Ababa and never returned to the Simien while I was there. When Mikio and Takashi recovered, they decided they liked the Simien so much that I suggested they stay longer and do some work on the house in exchange for food and lodging. They were delighted to accept, and went back to Sankabar with a list of jobs and a couple of boxes of supplies.

The rains were over, and the canopy was off the Unimog cabin. I liked best to drive alone, feeling the great power of this funny-looking machine, and singing to myself against the noise of the diesel engine. Everywhere along the way the people were harvesting, threshing, and winnowing. I saw dozens of threshing circles, surely unchanged in style since the days of Christ and even long before that. The men and boys drove their docile, hump-backed oxen round and round, trampling the barley stalks underfoot. They whistled and sang and cracked their whips, and round and round went the sad-eyed cattle. They tossed the broken barley into the air and sunlight glittered in the golden slivers of wind-carried chaff. The heavy grain fell to the ground. The men were all speckled with golden dust and bits of straw, and they sang their weird songs of heroes and good harvests. Thousands of green and yellow weaver birds, and bishop birds too, with their vivid scarlet wing patches, darted about the fields, and flocks of doves pecked about in the stubble and rose with whirring, clattering flight, making me wish for more time, and a dog, and a good shotgun.

When it got late, and the night drew in and brought out the brilliant stars in the purple-black sky, the roaring of the engine, and the rush of wind, with stars above and red dots of fire all around and below made me imagine that I flew a chariot through the sky, and I sang and sang. There were fires all over the hills. Along the escarpment edge I could look down and see those fires. The air was clear, and the visibility good. Men and boys stayed out around those fires, which flared up, brief and yellow-orange as the boys tossed on bundles of straw. They crouched around the fires, warming themselves, singing songs and telling tales and asking riddles, which they loved, rubbing heads of roasted barley between their palms, blowing away the husks with short, sharp puffs of breath. The roasted barley was good, and tasted nutty, crunchy, and slightly sweet in its freshness. And when I drove through the darkened roadside villages, for there was no electricity, the air was heavy with the tang of eucalyptus smoke. At such times as this I wondered about what the people felt or thought, and perhaps, as the noisy engine broke the peace of the night, they wondered about me.

It was such a night when I took a young schoolteacher from Debarek to Dabat. He had asked about the national park, and I was telling him what the whole conservation drive was about.

"You must stay here in the Simien for ten years," he said. "Then something will be achieved. If you go, it will all collapse."

"Nonsense," I retorted. "Mesfin will take over. He knows the park well, and he has had the best training. We foreigners have only come to get the thing going. Ethiopians must take over from us. That is the plan. You don't want us here all the time, telling you what to do, interfering, meddling, making social blunders, annoying people with our blunt manners."

He laughed. "We may not want you, but we need you. If you go, the park will be a failure. I know my people. I know myself. When we have had an education we do not want to live in the mountains. Why should we? We can work in the town, be close to the bosses, get promotions, have a good salary, have girls and fun, maybe get a car, and live in a nice house. Once we go into the bush they forget about us, and if we go, everybody thinks we have been sent there because we are troublemakers, or because we are crazy, or because something is wrong with us."

I knew that what he said about forgetting people in the field was true, and it was also true that most Ethiopians, having had a taste of the towns, did not want to return to the country. But Mesfin was surely different. I said so.

"Yes, but when you go, do you think those people in Addis Ababa will take any notice of what Mesfin says? They won't, I tell you. They will ignore him, no matter how good his training is. If you are there, in the Simien, they will listen to you, and Mesfin will get his house and his money. He gets his salary now, doesn't he?"

"Yes, sure."

"You see? I have not received my salary for two months. If you go, Mesfin will be in the same position. Once you go, they will forget him and the park. So why should he stay up there, without money, getting nothing done? He won't stick it out unless there is a foreigner there with him."

"I don't believe it," I said. "Mesfin is a tough, independent guy, he can take it. He knows what to do."

"Oh, you do not understand what I am telling you. Of course we Ethiopians are tough. But the government is tougher. Do you think that Mesfin or I could criticize the government? You can and do."

"But only when I think they are not doing their job," I answered. There was a clause in my contract saying that I should not meddle in politics.

"We only criticize when we think something is wrong. Let us face the truth. You know that there is much wrong, and much needs to be done, and so do I. We have been sent for education by our country, and when we want to change things, use what we have learned, then we either lose our jobs or get sent to some out-of-the-way place. Or maybe we land in jail. We love our country. No, I tell you, an Ethiopian cannot develop a park in Ethiopia. I am sorry to say it, and ashamed to say it, but it is true. I know my people."

"I just don't believe it," I said again, though sensing that much of what the young teacher had said was true.

It was not only the knowledge of the foreigners that Ethiopia needed, it was our drive, insistence, and general immunity from social and political connections. If I raved about somebody important, all they could do to me was to ignore me, give in, or kick me out. I had talked to many young Ethiopians. Without exception they were all fiercely proud of their country and their history. Most of them, but not all, respected and even loved the Emperor. But all of them felt some kind of discontent. With education and literacy, the discontent would grow. Something serious was going to happen in Ethiopia. With the growth of education, the old feudal system had to go, but it would not go easily. The Ethiopians are a rough, passionate, and often violent people. The educated young could not forever be kept down by old warlords and effete young aristo-crats. And the fact that the Amhara controlled nearly everything rankled a lot of people, including some young Amhara, who were more conscious of being Ethiopian.

At long last I got all our stuff hauled to Debarek and packed into the Simien. We spent a couple of nights in the Iteghie Hotel and left Gondar on December 23. Sonako had never ridden a horse be-fore, but she was quite good and didn't fall off. Kassa, who had ar-ranged for the horses, took Kentaro in front of him on his saddle, and I took Miwako. The children liked the ride, though it was long and tiring for them, and they got very sunburned. We stopped for refreshments along the way. Abahoy led Mogus on a chain.

The guards came out to greet me and my family. They were eager to meet them. They saluted Sonako, and later I told them that they need not do so. Mogus went wild with joy, and chased about every-where, marking his territory again, sniffing about and chasing the thick-billed ravens.

Mikio and Takashi were glad to see us. The toilet was built, the center poles rubbed and polished, the back steps built, the third rondavel ready for plywood panels. But there was still a lot of work to be done, and the place was a shambles from our unpacking. The glass panes had as yet to be put in the windows, so at night the shutters had to be closed. The roof needed thatch over the tin sheet-ing, shelves had to be built, painting done, walls fitted with panels. But at last my family was with me in the Simien, and we sat all to-gether around the fire. Kentaro was greatly amused by the sounds of the mice scurrying about in the walls.

The next night was Christmas Eve. We sat around the fire, drank wine, and talked of many things. Owls shrieked in the night. Forest fires burned in the lowlands. Sonako, the children, and I slept in one room. It was cold at night, and we had to cover the two children up well. We clung close to each other, whispering, listening to the owls, while candle shadows danced in the dim yellow light. I hid some books wrapped up in Christmas paper at the bottom of the children's beds. It was not much of a Christmas as far as celebra-tions went, but I enjoyed it and remembered it. There was a lot to be done to the house, but already it was beginning to look and feel like a home. Children's laughter and children's toys help to do that. I was not lonely in the Simien anymore. Jasmine was sweet along the path, and a bouquet of it in a vase filled the room with its scent. And every night we had picture book readings, and then long talks and many cups of tea in front of the fire after the children were in bed. The wind-brushed hills, the bright, clear stars in the black-velvet sky, the shepherds huddled around far-off fires, these were all unchanged; but there was no longer any need for me to spend a solitary, drunken Christmas Eve in a tent. Sankabar was home now.

NADU'S CAMPAIGN

After the long service (the guards told me), the priests and the elders and all the people gathered outside the round church in Amba Ras. They stood around, leaning on their prayer staffs, or sat on the ground to listen to Agafari Nadu. He had heard about his transfer to Omo and was giving a speech to the people.

"... Now they are going to send me to Omo, in the south, to Galla country, among the slaves and the Gallas. You are my brothers, and the children of my land. You must help me to get out of this. Help me to get to parliament!"

The people clapped and voiced their support for him, and inspired by this, he spoke for a long time against the national park project, against the foreigner who led the project, and against the Wildlife Conservation Department. He told the people that the land was theirs, that they could graze, cut, or plow it as they wished, and that nobody could stop them. He, Agafari Nadu, would lead the people against this foreigner and his soldiers, and together they would cut the trees. If the foreigner interfered, he would be swept aside. The Walia belonged to the people; they knew best how to protect them, and did not need outsiders to come and meddle in their affairs.

At last the feelings against the park project, and against us, were coming right out into the open. But there was still no visible support for us from high government officials. Nobody important had ever come into the mountains to tell the people what was going on. As far as the Simien people could see, I, the foreign meddler, was usurping Nadu's rights and demanding things I had no right or power to demand.

Stories about me spread. I was supposed to have caught and tortured villagers. It was even said that I had the power of the evil eye.

Negash Worota, Nadu's elder brother, and chief of the vigilantes, proclaimed that the people should do as they wished with their land, and by this he meant the virgin forests and the tussock grasslands of the park.

"The foreigner has built his house on a meadow of the Walia. The Walia used to come onto this meadow to graze. Now he has frightened them off."

It was true that the Walia used to come up onto the little meadow where I had built my house, but only very rarely. On the other hand, there used to be bandits and poachers in Sankabar, and now there were none. The Walia no longer came right up by the house, but fresh droppings could be found in the groves of giant heather just twenty meters below the house. Moreover, the protection we gave the Walia was beginning to make them much tamer around Sankabar than they had been for decades. The last shot fired on the Sankabar cliffs was fired by one of Dejasmatch Araya's tax collectors, and Ermias had caught him. In a few places, on the ledges just below the house, I had put down salt. In time, if things went on as they had, the Walia would grow tamer and would perhaps even come up onto what was now my back lawn.

So I let it be known to many people that I thought Nadu and Negash were full of hot air, that they spoke in farts, and that if they dared to try to cut the forest near me, they must accept the consequences. News travels fast in the Simien. And it gets exaggerated.

Gray-haired old Atakult Ferede was a cousin of Dejasmatch Araya, and through this dubious virtue had been made into a deputy chief guard. He came to Dr. Nievergelt and asked for permission to take a few days off to go to Amba Ras and give his condolences to Nadu, for Nadu's barley stacks had been destroyed by fire. The villagers had made a fire next to one of the stacks, while they were guarding it. The fire spread to the stack, and as they were fighting the first fire, the second stack began to burn. Bernhard guffawed, and denied permission. Atakult couldn't see what was funny.

One morning, while riding along the cliff path from Sankabar to Michibi, a man ran and caught up with me. He carried no gun, but from his fine gabi and turban, I could see that he was more than just a simple farmer. He was an Amba Ras man. He greeted me and walked by my horse. He asked if I knew Agafari Nadu. I said yes.

"Nadu is a big man. Very brave and strong. A very good man."

I replied in my pidgin Amharic, "Nadu is a big fart. A liar and a thief."

The man held his hand to his face. "Aaaeeee! That is not a good thing to say. Nadu is a very good man. He is my brother." He pointed back to Sankabar. "That is a very bad place for shifta. If Nadu is not here, perhaps the shifta will come. Nadu is strong."

"Nadu is a fart," I said.

He pointed to the boulders and to the trees and rocky ledges above the path we were traveling, and made a motion with his stick, squinting along it as if he were firing a rifle.

"One man up there . . . bang . . . dead. Nobody knows. Do you understand?" I understood well enough. I was sure that this man was an envoy of either Nadu or Negash.

I laughed at him. "Perhaps they shoot me. But His Majesty will send soldiers." I pantomimed a hanging and pointed at him. "Simien men are fools. I do not come to steal your land. I don't want trouble. But if trouble comes . . ."

I reined in the horse and stared long and hard between his eyes, as I had learned to do in the dojo in Japan. My face was without expression, and it unnerved the man. He looked angry and scared. I turned the horse into him and bumped him against a rock face. He ducked and dropped back behind me. Kicking the horse into a canter, I left him behind, no doubt wondering and worrying if there was any truth in the rumor about the foreigner having the powers of "Budda" . . . the evil one.

⬥⬥⬥⬥

The Sankabar house was beginning to look very nice. Our Swedish friends came up from Gondar for the New Year, and they helped us with the work, fitting windowpanes, making shelves, and tidying up.

It was very dry now, but it was a good time of the year, with fabulous weather. There was jasmine along the paths of Sankabar, and I wore a sprig of it in my hat. The house was all cluttered with picture books and toys, and when I came down the path I would hear children's voices laughing, and my young son Kentaro would come to the door to greet me.

Abahoy was overwhelmed by his new chores. He was forever washing diapers and children's clothes, airing mattresses and fetching wood and water.

Many visitors came during that time. A geophysical expedition came from Liverpool to bore cores in the successive lava flows. (It seems that in some places there were about one hundred and forty layers of flowers top to bottom of the escarpment.) These cores would later be sectioned and examined to assess their magnetic orientation. The lava flows were laid down over aeons. There was a great difference in age between the top and bottom layers. The scientists could tell the age of the flows, and by comparing this with the variations of magnetic orientation, they could gain information that might indicate shifts in the continent. They were an interesting party; they enjoyed my cooking and brought some whiskey. As this was a school vacation, many Peace Corps people came up to the Simien. Our house was always full of guests.

Mikio and Takashi had left after staying about a month. As far as we knew, they were trying to get into the Sudan by the northern road.

Nadu came into Sankabar looking very fine in a checked shirt, breeches, shoes, and a game guard's bush hat. He wore his old .45 service revolver in a Sam Browne holster. A servant carried his rifle and held the reins. Nagur, his big golden horse, looked magnificent with its jingling silver decorations and bobbing red tassels. Nadu bent down and tried to shake hands with me.

"When will you go to Omo?" I asked.

He said he would go next month. He showed me a letter from headquarters and said that it ordered me to give him money to pay for the transport of himself and his family to Addis Ababa. The letter was in Amharic script, and I had no one to read and interpret it for me. Mesfin had been gone over a month. However, I gave him some money for bus fares and got him to sign a receipt. I doubted if he had any intention of going. I asked him if he would truly go, and he said yes, he would truly go.

He then went up to the guards' quarters. Guard Zeleka, the Korean campaign veteran, and the only guard I trusted, was down in Debarek getting his rations. Nadu told the other Simien men of his plan to campaign for parliament. They all pledged to vote for him. I thought that Nadu had gone, and I was up on the hill, with binoculars, scanning the narrow escarpment path, when he came out of a guard's hut, with the men following him, kissing his hand, bowing, holding his horse. Nadu was their lord, and his father had been their lord before him. What could a foreign game warden do against him?

Despite this, three of the local guards were on bad terms with Nadu. They had fallen out with him over the bribes that he had been demanding and taking. These men, Amara, Berehun, and Chane Takalé would, they said, testify against Nadu if the case ever got to court. Hearing of this, and of the protection that I was giving these men, Negash Worota sent a letter. The letter said that they should forget their differences with his brother and not to do anything to jeopardize his future. I heard about this letter from Amara, who feared for his life ever since the fight, when Nadu and the others had taken away his rifle. Amara said that Chane had the letter, and Chane said that Berehun had it. Berehun, the most amazing liar I have ever met, said that the letter had been washed with his uniform jacket and was destroyed. The idea that Berehun's uniform jacket had been washed was, quite frankly, ridiculous. But there was no way I could get my hands on the letter. I was surrounded by duplicity. With such a letter I could prove to the department my claims that pressure was being brought to stop any action against Nadu. The men were afraid. If the department did not take very strong action against Nadu, then there would be serious trouble for the park.

We were invited up to Geech to stay for a while at Swiss House with Bernhard and Esther Nievergelt. It was really nice to be with them. Esther played the guitar, and they sang, and we talked and drank wine. We had lunch and breakfast out on the veranda, and we rode around on the horses. The children loved the sleeping platform, and after they had gone to bed we could look up from the easy chairs in front of the fire and see their sunburned little faces peering over the railing above us. It struck me that there was something special in our race memory that made high safe places especially attractive for children, just as they have a delicious, special thrill of fear when being chased up a tree, or up the stairs.

At this time, January, most of the male Walia seemed to be down in the forests at the foot of the escarpment. Bernhard said he thought that this might be due to some food preference during their molting period, or perhaps simply because the plants were greener and more moist down there under the trees during this dry time of the year. The females and kids were still on the cliffs, probably because of the safety that the cliffs afforded them.

It was our last night in Geech. Esther had prepared a superb meal, and we were halfway through it when Tag burst in. He had been away in Addis Ababa for about a month, and I had almost given him up. He was sweaty, dusty, and noisy with news.

"Do you mind if my lion comes in to get warm in front of the fire?"

We all looked at each other. A lion? At nine o'clock at night? At almost twelve thousand feet? But sure enough, there was a lion cub, spitting and hissing and very cross, looking out of a small cage which had been suspended from a pole and carried up all the way from Debarek by two stalwarts. Tag left the lion cub in front of the fire and rushed out again with a torch, saying that some people were left back along the path, and that they didn't have a light. He went out as he came in, like a tornado, leaving our heads spinning with a gush of news, stories, and incongruous facts—like a smelly lion cub in front of the fire halfway through a very civilized European meal. Ah, these Americans!

Somewhere in the darkness along the path between the Djinn Barr and this camp, five Peace Corps volunteers were stumbling along. It was potentially a dangerous situation. They arrived safely, although one girl had a specially hard ride up and was faint with cold and exhaustion on arrival. Tag brought her into the house to get warm. I was annoyed with Tag for a little while, for I felt that he should have advised the visitors to break the journey, and not to travel in the dark. I felt that he had been more concerned about his lion cub than about his friends. But Tag wasn't really like that at all. He carried himself and others along in furious waves of energetic enthusiasm and constantly forgot that not everyone was in such superb physical shape as himself.

He made sure the visitors had pitched their tent and gotten to bed, and then he came into the house to tell us some of the things that had been happening in Addis Ababa.

Tag had got money from USAID to build a guest house in the Simien. He had also extracted various promises from the Ethiopian Tourist Organization. The park badly needed accommodation for visitors. Without it we could not encourage people to come up. At least with a place to stay, we could get the more hardy souls to brave the long mule or horse ride. But with all that fuss and bother over pack mules, camping equipment, and argumentative Debarek muleteers, even hardy visitors were liable to get discouraged. Tag had great plans for the house. It would be big, round, built of stone.

✕✕✕✕✕

In the middle of January, John Blower came up to the Simien to discuss the park boundaries and other points with Dr. Nievergelt and myself. I had not known the exact date of his coming because the radio was out of order, and poor John had to come from Gondar to Debarek by the noisy, smelly, crowded bus. The bus arrived in the afternoon, so John was not able to hike all the way up to Sankabar by nightfall. He slept a few kilometers outside Debarek in the compound of the house of one of Nadu's relatives. He preferred this to the dubious comforts of Debarek.

He arrived on foot in Sankabar at noon the next day. After a shower bath and much tea, he did a flea hunt on his sleeping bag and netted thirty. Not bad. He would have captured many more if he had slept in the house instead of outside.

Major Gizaw's attempt to get rid of John had been a miserable failure. Some awkward questions were being asked. It was now known that Prince Bernhard of the Netherlands, the president of the Netherlands World Wildlife Fund, was due to visit Ethiopia and wanted John to accompany him on various safaris to see the situation of wildlife conservation in the Empire. His Imperial Majesty was hearing things. There were queries about the illegal leopard-skin trade. The licensing officer had been ordered to pay back a lot of money which he had cheated out of the government through his phony license racket. Minor tremors were beginning to shake the Wildlife Conservation Department. John Blower was not only one of the most physically tough men I had ever encountered; he was cold, calculating, and patient. Wars against the Japanese in Burma, the Mau Mau in Kenya, and numerous poachers and other undesirables in Uganda had put a certain edge on John that few men could match. Poor Major Gizaw wouldn't stand a chance; of that I was sure.

We had a pretty good idea of the boundaries now; the total area of the park should amount to about two hundred square kilometers, including the Sankabar ridge, Michibi Afaf, Geech highland, the Khabar Valley, the Djinn Barr Valley and the steep, forested slopes at the base of the escarpment. It seemed a lot, but in fact, if the park was ever declared, it would still be one of the smallest national parks in Africa.

John was concerned about the deplorable situation with Nadu, and he promised that he would try to get the fact across to the people who really mattered in Addis Ababa that this man Nadu had to be dealt with. If Nadu was going to campaign for parliament, then this action had to come quickly. If he was removed from the election race too late, the people would be up in arms. If he was elected, and I suspected that he would be, then nobody could touch him. I stated to John, very clearly, that if Nadu were not dealt with, I would resign.

✖✖✖✖

On January 17, we all went down to Gondar. In an attempt to drum up support for our project, we had arranged, a month before, to give a talk to the influential people in Gondar and to show them some of Dr. Nievergelt's slides. I couldn't leave Sonako and the children alone, so they came down too. Ato Seyoum, the bank manager, a big, friendly, well-spoken gentleman, had promised to arrange everything. We went down especially for the meeting.

January 18 was marked by the celebrations of Epiphany. The beautiful castle bath house of King Fasilidas (shortened in conversation to "Fasil") was filled at this time of the year with water, and it was here that the Coptic Church held a mass annual baptism. The streets were filled with processions of chanting priests; the deacons holding aloft the colorful, glittering umbrellas, the sacred books inscribed on the skins of goats, and the great silver, brass, and gold crosses. The hotels were filled with tourists who came in to see this celebration. Sonako, the children, and I had to stay with our Swedish friends for this night. We were not fond of crowds, and we arrived at Fasil's bath too late to see the service of baptism. But our friends said that it was a delight to see the big men of the town, the police chief, the mayor, and all the others, approach the bearded bishop with solemn, serious faces, receive baptism, and go away with eager, happy faces, free of a year's accumulation of sins. Even in such educated men, the faith of the Ethiopians runs deep.

By the time Sonako and I got to the castle, the water was full of naked little boys, at last allowed to splash around in the water by the overbearing keepers with their iron-tipped clubs. This was a special day. The small, elegant castle building threw its reflection off the water that surrounded it. Old fig trees twined their roots inextricably among the weathered stones and crumbling mortar of the surrounding walls, and tall dark cedars, older than the graves of the ancient kings, threw their coolness in dark pools around the lush grass. Bright green and red lovebirds, flittering long-tailed whydahs and noisy pigeons inhabited the trees. People were everywhere. The girls were gay and beautiful in their new white shammas with the colored borders, and everybody was happy and excited. Their glances at us were more friendly than usual.

It was said by the old keepers that the mortar of the bath had been mixed with the whites of thousands of eggs. And I had heard strange stories or legends whispered about the mad king, who had, so they said, drowned fair maidens in the waters of the bath after using their bodies in the pleasure house above, for the king was hairy of body like an ape, and did not wish the maidens to tell of his ugliness after having seen his nakedness.

But at this time the bath house was serene and beautiful. Nearby, there was a domed tomb. They said that the king had erected it over the body of a horse that he had loved. I thought about these stories and wondered about this strange, dark king.

And all night long the drums throbbed in the many churches, and the sound of chanting rose and fell; there was dancing and the discordant sounds of stringed instruments and the shrill cries of the women. The night was cool. The castles and ruins of Gondar hid in their stones and in their shadows a memory of such sounds; of the Portuguese builders and missionaries, of the bloody intrigues and wars of the old princes, of the songs and poetry of the priests and courtiers, and of the sudden and vile executions that had been enacted in the streets of this town, so unique in Africa. Bats squeaked and dipped, and a slight breeze bent and rustled the alien eucalyptus. We foreigners, isolated in our hotels and houses, illuminated with the electricity provided by the noisy generators near the road down past the tax offices, could feel little, if any, of the deep sense of continuity and history which the Ethiopians felt on such a night as this. I almost expected to see the lion-maned warriors with their curved scimitars, their round, hippo-hide shields and long spears metamorphose from out of the shadows of the dark stone walls. These mental images were vivid. The drums and cries and chanting both thrilled and bothered me; I went inside and had another drink. I was a European, and did not belong.

Ato Seyoum had arranged to hold the meeting in his own house. Bernhard and I went with the slides and were somewhat disappointed to find that few of the important men had been able to come.

The reactions of the Ethiopians to the color slides were very different from ours. To the flowers and scenes of mountain, forest, stream, and cloud, there was practically no reaction at all. They could not believe what we said about the prices paid in foreign countries for flowers, especially for such exotic flowers as orchids, of which there were hundreds of thousands in the Simien. In talking of the glorious red-hot pokers (Kniphofia), which are so common here, and so expensive in London, one man said, "Ah yes, my wife and children picked some of those flowers, but on the way home we threw them out of the car. They smelled."

There was some interest and questions when the pictures of Walia and klipspringers were shown, but the talk soon turned to hunting, and to the delicious wat that could be prepared from the meat of klipspringers. The pictures of gelada were of no interest whatsoever. Ato Seyoum, who was a very honest man, thanked us and said, "Tell me, Mr. Nicol, do you really think that visitors would want to see that?"

Bernhard and I looked at each other dumbly. Then we both said that visitors surely would.

Our talk, the slides, the urging, had no effect on these men. They neither cared nor sought to understand, and these were the more educated Ethiopians. What could we expect of the mountain peasants? As far as these men in Gondar were concerned, erosion was inevitable. Animals, flowers, and scenery were of little interest. They did not appreciate nature as we did. They did not see it. In fact, I was told that there was not even a word for "nature" in the Amharic language. We were talking into a void. The Ethiopians felt that kind of sentiment only for those things that had a direct, pragmatic meaning to their life. Like young cattle or new shoots of grain, or land brought under the plow, the ownership of a rifle, the words and teaching of the Church or of the Mosque. Bernhard, myself, and many other foreigners were misled by the seemingly perfect English and the apparent understanding of our Ethiopian hosts. Indeed, they knew, in English, what we said, but we lived in different thought-worlds. Bernhard and I had a few drinks and left; we didn't say very much on our way back to the hotel.

※※◇※※

We reached Sankabar at six P.M. It was a very hard ride for the children, and they cried as they came up the big hill on Sonako's horse. Sonako had to lead the horse and I had to walk by its side, making sure the two children did not fall off. The hill was too steep for us to ride up with the children in front of us on our saddles.

But when we got home we found the house neat and clean, with a big fire burning, and a pot of fresh tea. Abahoy was a prize. A tank of hot water was ready on the kitchen stove, and on the table there was a basket of fresh injera and wat, prepared for us by Abahoy's wife. Mogus the dog was happy to see us back, and wanted to be made a fuss of. I loved Sankabar. On the way up I had relished the profusion of blues and whites, and the sometimes red, orange, or yellow of the many flowers. Jasmine entwined itself in the giant bushes of wild roses, and its heavy scent mingled with the faint, delicate perfume of the fragile rose flowers. I noticed how red were the new shoot branches of the roses, and how it contrasted with the green of their leaves and the white of their flowers.

The moon was full. I went out after supper and watched the small owls, and tried to imitate their shrieking. I got out the telescope and looked up at the moon for a long time, until my eyes watered.

While we were away, Tag's lion cub managed to fall into the latrine. It was a deep pit, and well used, and the lion went in up to her neck. Tag had to go down on a rope to get her out, and during the rescue operations he got badly scratched. The lion spat and hissed in the mire, and clawed at Tag. I suspect that Tag's comments must have been as choice as the atmosphere of the pit. But he managed to grab the cub by the scruff of her neck. He hauled the befouled beast out and hurled her into the stream. Then he had to clean himself and treat the wounds on his hand. He used to refer to that day as "the day the lion fell into the latrine." I'm glad I wasn't there. I might have been asked to help.

For a hundred Ethiopian dollars I bought myself a big chestnut gelding named Shoeke. I got him from a priest in Michibi. He was a big horse, strong and quite fast. Sonako had her own horse too, a very gentle gelding named Brook, smaller than mine, but very hardy. Now we had five mules, two horses, and a donkey. We needed a stableman or muleteer to look after them. My servant Abahoy was too busy, and not particularly good either. The guards were useless. Any riding or pack animal left in the gentle care of a guard on a trip would come back with bad saddle sores. When the guards took the animals to Debarek they usually neglected to feed them, and later produced grubby faked receipts on scraps of paper from their patrol notebooks for the barley that they were supposed to have bought for the animals. Guard Zeleka was not dishonest that way, but he was not a highland man, and didn't know much about horses and mules. So I had to do everything myself, apart from the feeding; Sonako liked to do that herself when the animals were in camp.

At the end of January we had two special visitors, Dr. Lewis and Dr. Belcher from Gondar. Dr. Lewis, an Englishman, was a medical missionary to the Felasha people. He was a big, broad, soft-spoken man with an excellent command of Amharic. Dr. Belcher was an

American doctor from the Health College, a big, gentle man, well liked by his students. They were our friends.

Unlike so many foreigners in Ethiopia (including myself in times of frustration), these men never wasted time in slandering comparisons of the people, but rather tried to think of solutions to problems, and to grasp their underlying causes. But we could all see that any change in the ways of the peasant farmers would come very slowly, if it ever came at all. I was of the opinion that it would be too slow, but Dr. Lewis felt that it could not be rushed. More and more teachers were needed in the field, as was a lot of money.

Dr. Lewis was telling us of an experiment that he did in Dabat, at his mission there. "We plowed this field and marked it off, and then showed the local men that we were using fertilizer on one of the marked patches. None of them believed that this would do any good, but they watched politely. The results were fantastic. You could see the difference as the wheat was growing. The fertilized stuff was much higher than the rest, and the dividing line between the fertilized and unfertilized crop was clearly visible. We got the locals to watch as we harvested, and we showed them very carefully the yield we got from the two different patches. When we weighed it, we found that the fertilized patch yielded four times the amount of wheat."

"Were they impressed?"

"My word, yes. But we'll see next year if they were impressed enough to use the fertilizer themselves."

"What about the cost?"

"That's a problem. It's about fifty dollars a field, I think. But of course the yield of grain would give them a tremendous profit."

If only I could get an agricultural officer to come up and demonstrate some fertilizers in Geech, and pay the people to build a few soil-retaining terrace walls and sensible drainage ditches. I wouldn't mind subsidizing a few fields for one year myself, if I could get some barley out of it for our animals. It would be worth it. The Geech people had to be shown, not merely told. They didn't believe anything a government official said.

"That's what the government should be doing all over the country. Not farting about with big imported tractors and model farms on the road from Addis Ababa to impress visitors and themselves.

Look at Geech. They are all farmers up there, but they can't even grow enough barley for themselves to eat. And the situation is going to get much, much worse. At the present rate they will soon destroy all the land and won't be able to live up there anyway. What a lot could be done with one good man and a few thousand dollars for work and fertilizers!"

"Perhaps it is not that easy though. I heard a story about a couple of Peace Corps volunteers," began Dr. Belcher. "These guys were agriculture experts and had a lot of really good ideas. They were stationed in a little town, and hired a local gardener. They dug some special plots for vegetables and demonstrated the use of fertilizers. Their gardener didn't want to have anything to do with it, and they had to threaten to fire him before he would do what he was told. Of course, they grew enormous vegetables, bigger than these local people had ever seen in their lives. But somehow the locals never reacted favorably and were never really interested in what was going on. The volunteers wondered why. After they had been in the village for two years they felt a bit sad, I guess. When they left, some locals saw them off on the bus. Just as they were about to get on the bus they overheard their gardener shooting his mouth off to all the locals: 'See those suitcases the foreigners are carrying? They are full of Ethiopian soil which the foreigners are going to take back to their country so that they can have better crops.' So what can you do?"

Indeed, what could you do? The problems of malnutrition, the lack of education and understanding, the poor farming and erosion, the disease and corruption were all in their turn problems of the national park. They were all interrelated, just like the complicated blood-relationships of the local people. Doubts welled up in me again. Could it be done? Could a park be established here?

※※※※

A day after the doctors had left, at about four in the afternoon, Mikio Maeno, our Japanese motorbike-riding friend, came walking back up to Sankabar. I met him on the path, and he called out felicitations for the New Year. He and Takashi Kasori had some trouble getting a visa into the Sudan. It was all very complicated. They had to buy an air ticket, show the ticket to get the visa, and then one of them had to hitchhike to Addis Ababa to cash in the ticket and get their money back. While Takashi was away in Addis Ababa, Mikio would stay with us. They would not be able to go by the northern route. It was closed. They would have to cross into the Sudan by the rough Metema route.

"Ah, Nicol-san, we were lonely as we rode up the Asmara road, and we looked back on these cliffs, and we thought about you. I like this place better than anywhere else in Ethiopia."

They had had a rough time with stubborn officials and with a certain lack of money. Mikio told us of how, one night, while sleeping in some open place in the city, he felt things in his sleeping bag, slight sensations like those caused by one's body hairs suddenly standing on end. He investigated, and caught one hundred and two lice in his sleeping bag.

Mikio and I were painting the living room. It was a Sunday. Tag came down from Geech with his horse and a guard's rifle. He was very angry. Guard Amara had come very late with the pack mules, had refused to stay on duty in camp, and had followed Tag down to Sankabar. On the way, Amara had thrown a rock at a pack mule and had sent the skittish animal running over the Geech barley fields. Tag got mad at Amara and threw a clod of dirt at him, hitting him on the shoulder. Guard Amara complained to me that he had been wounded by a rock and showed his shoulder to me. There was not a mark on it. Tag had disarmed Amara. Amara wanted to make trouble. I ordered him back to Geech and gave back the rifle. He went. Tag went on down to Gondar in a bad mood.

It was good to have Mikio around. He made a second bookcase in the central room of our house and dug a vegetable patch close to the spring. He was an easy guest, good-humored and not fussy about anything. And of course, Sonako was pleased to have him with us. I think the Japanese enjoy each other more in a foreign country, where the social pressures of home are off them.

Sonako gave Mikio a haircut, and Abahoy washed his clothes. He borrowed a bush shirt and shorts from me, and had his photograph taken in a pose with my rifle, bandolier, battered hat, and Walia insignia.

The guards liked Mikio and Takashi, and loved to talk with them. Especially Guard Zeleka, who had once spent a month in Japan recovering from bullet wounds received in Korea. Zeleka considered himself an expert on Japan and would hold forth on the customs and manners of the people. Only it seemed that he either had it confused with another country or had gathered the wrong impression about some things.

"In Japan, the wives of the very rich men wear a long dress with a big lump on the back. They ride around in carts pulled by dogs. (By dogs? . . .) Yes, low carts pulled by dogs. The Japanese eat rice with little sticks. The police are very bad men . . ."

✕✕✕✕

At the end of January, Prince Bernhard of the Netherlands came to Ethiopia. I received a letter, dated January 25, to tell me that the Prince would not be able to come up to the Simien. He would visit Awash and Omo, and he would push the wildlife conservation bit with the Emperor. The foreign wardens had long been awaiting an event such as this. At last we would be able to get our grievances through to the Emperor, through Prince Bernhard, who was, after all, president of the Netherlands World Wildlife Fund. I was very disappointed that His Highness would not be able to come to the Simien this time, but he was sending in his stead Dr. Vollmar, who was the secretary general of the WWF. Dr. Vollmar would come to the Simien for a few days and then present a report to the Prince, who would no doubt pass it on directly to Haile Selassie.

John was very optimistic about the results of all this. In his letter he discussed some of the points which I should emphasize to Dr. Vollmar when he came. One of them was the fact that if a park was to be established here, then there was no alternative to the removal and resettlement of the people living within the proposed area of the park. Geech especially. He said that this could be done; that in the past week Awash had been proclaimed a park and two thousand five hundred people, together with their cattle, about twelve thousand of them, and their camels and goats, had all been moved out of the Awash Park area by the police. Their villages had been burned to the ground. This was all because Prince Bernhard was due to visit the park. But I wondered how long the people would stay out of the area after the royal visit was over.

However, news about Awash and the way the people had been

kicked out got to the guards, and then spread over the Simien. Guard Zeleka rammed it down the throats of some complaining Geech elders while passing through Geech on patrol, and he told them that if they gave us trouble, they would be thrown out and the village burned. This of course was an exaggeration. The Awash people were nomads, whereas the Geech people were farmers, whose village had stood for a long, long time. I made use of all this by telling the locals that the only way to deal with us was not by threats or violence, for that would only anger His Imperial Majesty and cause him to send in the police, but that the people should present their grievances in a calm, civilized way in a petition to the Governor General of Begemdir. But the stories spread.

The Nievergelts had gone down to Gondar to meet Dr. Vollmar and his wife. I sent down horses, guards, and saddlery for them. They came up on January 29. Dr. Vollmar was a youngish man, tall and athletic, with a precise, military bearing about him. His wife was a very attractive woman, and they were both very friendly and interested people. On our arrival at camp, the guards turned out and stood at attention while Dr. Vollmar inspected them. For once they looked almost smart, despite the dreadful baggy uniforms and unpolished, much-scuffed boots. Both Kebede and Zeleka had been drilling the men every day for a couple of months. Esther Nievergelt almost burst with laughing, for she had never seen our men doing this sort of thing. Dr. Vollmar gave them a pep talk, which was translated by Ato Berhanu, and then came to have tea at our house. I took him around the camp, showed him the awful mud hovels which the men had to live in, and explained what I would do if ever I got the money to build with. Later I showed him the files of reports and letters requesting funds or equipment, or the firing of corrupt and dishonest guards.

Of course, there were endless projects, plans, and reports on paper, but we had no power, no real authority to back us in our work. No money, no laws, no directives to the police and governors to support us. In most cases, the local officials were actively opposing everything we tried to do. We needed the Emperor to make an official proclamation about wildlife conservation, and to have this published. Then perhaps the officials would take notice of us. The governors, police, and armed forces were the worst poachers in the country, and often boasted about it. (Incidentally, various embassies and the US Mapping Mission were well known to us as poachers too.)

We heard that His Imperial Majesty had been assured by the worthy Major Gizaw that the illegal traffic in skins had been stamped out. When Prince Bernhard arrived, he sent an aide into town to ask about leopard skins. Within a very short time the aide returned, with illegal leopard skins, which could be bought very easily almost anywhere in the city. These skins were taken and shown to the Emperor, who must have been very angry.

Everywhere the Prince went, a great camp was readied for him. He is by all accounts an outdoor man, a great hunter and sportsman. He no doubt enjoyed the company of John Blower, with whom he had been on safari before. I wondered how Major Gizaw felt. He had tried to dislodge John Blower. Now an important figure in the wildlife world, no less than a royal prince, came flying in to look over the place, and asked that John accompany him. We also knew by this time that Prince Philip was going to come in for much the same thing the next month.

Dr. Vollmar saw and photographed Walia, Simien fox, and the big predator birds of the Simien. He was thrilled with the park area, and greatly impressed with its possibilities and the urgency of the situation. He promised to do what he could to help.

We were all very confident that big things would happen. And both Dr. Nievergelt and I stressed that Agafari Nadu Worota must be dealt with before things got out of hand. If he got into parliament he would be even more of a hero, and he would spread wild propaganda against the park. Dr. Vollmar promised that the Emperor would hear about this.

And he did hear about it. But Haile Selassie seems incapable of removing someone from office once he has decided that the man is good for the job.

As they traveled out of the Simien, Dr. Vollmar and his wife stopped again in Sankabar. I had staked and wired bones out around the house, and the lammergeyers were swooping down for them, a magnificent sight which the doctor could photograph while drinking his tea. I gave him a detailed report about the Simien, which he incorporated in his report to Prince Bernhard.

As I waved good-bye to the Vollmars, a string of pack animals, heavily laden with brightly painted fiberglass boxes, came round the Sankabar path. It was a large Polish mountaineering expedition. They were well equipped, and even had a doctor with them.

Mikio left the morning after the Polish expedition arrived. We were sad to see him go, and promised to exchange letters and to meet again in Japan. Takashi had arrived in Debarek, and he made the long walk up, just to say good-bye.

※※※※

I was busy every day. Apart from the park work, patrols, and administration, I had to stop everything every now and then to weigh a donkey-load of sand. Villagers were bringing hundreds of loads, and these had to be recorded and paid for. There was much arguing. I needed the sand for construction work, the first of which would be a large Japanese-style bath for me.

This was the height of the dry season. Every day small groups of migrants from Tigre Province, north of the Simien, passed on foot over the mountains on their way to seek food and work in the south. They were all thin, emaciated people, their clothes in rags and almost black with dirt. During this time of the year their own country was too dry to support them. Every year they walked southward for hundreds of kilometers.

Long ago Tigre had been covered with cool forests, running with countless streams that never failed. But the people had destroyed it with their bad farming, and erosion had turned their country into a desert for their children.

The Tigreans are fine stone workers, and we stopped parties of them and asked if they wanted work. They had never dealt with a foreigner before, and they tried to demand wages that were four times higher than they could hope to get anywhere else. One party became surly and insolent when I talked to them. Our dog Mogus was very prejudiced. He sat by his kennel and growled. I offered the men good wages and said they could begin work after lunch, for it was now noon, and we would pay them for half a day's work. These men were stupid and tried to insist that they get higher wages and a full day's pay for this day. When I told them to go, they began to yell at me outside the house. I slipped Mogus off his chain, and they didn't stop running until they got out of camp. The guards came out and screamed insults after them.

The next party of Tigre migrants was led by a man of about forty or fifty. When I offered them an excellent wage, they tried to kiss my feet. The other men were all in their twenties, but so thin and stunted that they looked like children. They had hardly any food to eat. But despite their weak appearance, these men worked with a will, and they broke and carried rocks for eight hours a day, never complaining, nor bothered by the thin air. They carried no food with them so we gave them barley, pepper, salt, and oil. I tried to give them some mutton, but they did not trust me when I said the animal had been killed by a Coptic Christian; they feared the meat was tainted by my unbelieving hand. Yet they must not have had any meat for many long weeks. They slept at night under the stars, on mats which I gave them. They had no blankets, and the frost lay on their thin cotton robes in the early morning, yet they did not seem to suffer. I wondered how men got so tough.

During the work, I took time out to talk with the Tigrean men about their country. Kassa, my clerk, interpreted for me. The other day laborers, men from Geech, Michibi, and the Khabar Valley, stopped to listen.

The men said that in Tigre many people had to walk three days to water their cattle, and I said that the same thing could happen to Begemdir in a few generations if the people did not take better care of the forests and water sources. I gave the same old lecture, embellishing it with stories from the Bible, slightly altered perhaps to suit my arguments. I promised that God would send a drought upon the land, as he had upon other lands, and that there would be plagues of rats, baboons, and pigeons. All this would happen if they continued heedlessly to destroy God's handiwork—the forests, the wild creatures. I tried to tell them that the land was given in trust to them, and that if they used it badly they would be punished. Kassa and I demonstrated to them that soil held water, that roots held soil. The people were fascinated by this and marveled at my wisdom, and they nodded sagely. Yet at the end of the discourse they remembered nothing. It was not that they had actively rejected what I said but rather that they just could not absorb the reason for this simple cause-and-effect argument, no matter how clearly it was explained.

I turned to the guards and asked them, "Why must we protect the forest?" Only Zeleka knew. None of the others had learned anything, not from our speeches, our many talks, or my explanatory letters, translated into clear Amharic. The Simien men especially seemed incapable of learning.

After my speech about God holding the water in the soil, under the shade of trees, and letting it out in pure streams, and about how the soil was washed away and dried into dust when the trees were all destroyed, the old Tigre man began to tell his version of why a certain hill went dry.

"There is a hill in my country. It once had forty-four streams and springs. Then one day the shifta killed a Moslem on the hill, and as he died he cursed them. The streams all dried, and now not one spring runs."

The others nodded wisely and said that this was true, for the Moslems knew such magic. I asked if there was forest on the hill when the streams were flowing. He said there was. I asked if the people had cut off and burned the forest and plowed the soil. Yes, they did, a few years after the murder. And then, after the people had destroyed the forest, the springs all dried up? Yes, he was emphatic; the magic of the Moslem was powerful.

I looked at Kassa. He was exasperated.

"You see, sir? It is impossible to teach these men. They cannot learn anything. All they believe in is this magic."

That night, as on all the other nights of that month, fierce, man-kindled forest fires blazed in the lowlands. The people were encased in their weird world, a thousand years out of date, a world of the vague and all-powerful will of a demanding god, and of magic. Could anything ever get through to them?

✳✳✳✳

Guard Mitiku came back one day with a letter from the hospital. His baby son had died of a heart disease. The child had been admitted once before with pneumonia, had been cured, sent home, and then taken in again. Mitiku was the first of our men to take a child to the hospital. Had the child lived, the others might have come to believe that hospitals were good. Mitiku was a wiser man than the others, and he knew that the doctors had done everything possible for the child. He said that God had wanted the child, and he shook his head and smiled sadly. The death of a child was not a rare thing in the mountains; nearly all of our men had lost children.

✕✕✕✕✕

The Geech elders were claiming that they knew nothing about the park. I became angry. We had sent many letters to them, held discussions with them, and Hussein Hassen, the Geech-born game guard, had been told to explain everything to his people. Bad feelings were simmering in Geech and Amba Ras, and I felt sure that Nadu was behind it.

"I do not understand you," said Sonako. "You keep on talking to these peasants, over and over again, the same things. You are wasting your time. You will stand and talk with a peasant for two hours, and forget your family. It makes me angry." She was right, in a way, but I had to keep on trying.

It was a clear night, and the moon was full. I remembered a promise I had made to the guards. I promised to show them the mountains and craters of the moon. At nine o'clock I set up the telescope and called the men. In this high, thin air the moon was almost white with light, and crystal clear. Ato Alemu, the Polish expedition's interpreter, came out and interpreted for me.

"Why does the moon fade away and come back each month?" I asked.

"It crumbles at the edge," said Guard Berehun, "and then it grows again."

"Is the moon very big? Is it as big as Ras Deschan?" They thought that this was a very stupid question. Anybody could see that the moon was very small. I asked how big the town of Zarema was, and they told me, and then I said no, Zarema is so small that even an ant could not pass in the streets, for we could see the town forty kilometers away from the top of our cliffs. The guards laughed and said it looked small because it was far away.

"Even so. The moon looks small because it is far away. In truth it is larger even than the whole of Ethiopia. Look closer through this telescope. You can see the mountains and cliffs."

Abahoy, my servant, became tremendously excited and said that the master spoke truly, that he could see them. Another guard

215

looked through and said that the moon was full of windows. I laughed, remembering the green cheese story.

The coolies came and clustered around. They all tried to look through, and most of them had great trouble focusing the image on their retinas. But when they saw it they cried out, and laughed and giggled like small boys. This was a memorable experience for them, and they talked about it for months afterward. They had seen. They discussed what I had said. Perhaps the foreigner spoke truly about the moon, and perhaps it was a great land in the sky. If only we could demonstrate other things so clearly to them!

※※※※※

More and more vague rumors and threats were reaching me through the guards. Nadu and Negash would come and cut the forest, sweeping us aside and killing us all. A hundred extra rounds of heavy .30.06 hunting ammunition had come into my hands. I mounted a telescopic sight on my rifle and bore-sighted it on a paper target at a hundred and fifty meters. After ten shots the bullets grouped inside a two-inch circle. I put up a fresh target. The guards watched closely, not understanding what I was doing. The target was on the side of a hill, and the soil there was dry and dusty. The rifle boomed four times, and dirt and small stones exploded at the target. A man ran to fetch it, and they exclaimed at the four holes in the black circle. I put up another target and paced off three hundred meters across a hollow. From a kneeling position I slammed a fast shot into it. With a good, well-sighted rifle, this was not difficult. Not as difficult as hunting seal. I filled a big tin can with earth and stood it on a rock at a hundred and twenty yards.

"That is an enemy's head," I said to the guards, grinning, and holding the rifle at the slope. "He waits behind a rock like a Simien shifta, with his old dirty rifle. But I see him. Zeleka, do you see him?"

Zeleka grinned and elaborated on the theme for the benefit of the rest of the guards. I turned quickly, raised the gun, and fired, blowing the can of earth off the rock. The mushrooming bullet blew half of the can to shreds.

"Zeleka, tell these men that if any fool wants to try to touch the forests or the Walia at Sankabar then he had better not get too close to me. I will blow off his head."

Zeleka told them. He also said that one bullet from this rifle could blow off an arm or a leg.

Some of the guards took the rifle and squinted down the telescopic sight, marveling at the cross-hairs and at the way the target came so close in the tube. I explained something slowly to Zeleka, who had seen telescopic sights before, and knew them. He grinned broadly and told the men what I had said.

"This gun bears the mark of the cross. If the mark of the cross should rest upon an evil man, he has no chance. He cannot escape." The guards looked with wonder at the rifle, and asked how much such a weapon would cost.

We did some firing practice with the guards. They had .303 carbines. Each man fired three shots lying, three shots standing, and three shots kneeling. Those men who had received some training in the army were quite good, especially Zeleka and Mitiku. Mitiku had been in the Italian Army. Guard Ambaw was formerly a notorious poacher, and he was quite good too. But the rest of the Simien men were terrible. The biggest boasters turned out to be the worst shots. I remembered an argument with Ermias, my first assistant, and with the army captain who was a relative of Nadu. They swore that every Simien man was a born marksman. I said that a rifle was a tool, and that skill with it was learned through proper shooting methods and practice.

Most of the Simien men had done very little if any shooting, even those who carried a rifle every day. Ammunition was very expensive, so when a Simien man shot at anything, he would rest his gun against a rock or a tree and get as close as he could to his target, an excellent hunting or ambush technique.

The Walia ibex is a very easy animal to shoot if one has time and patience, and if one knows its feeding ledges and paths. And of course, these specifications fitted the Simien men perfectly.

Great white hunters had come in the past with expensive rifles and dozens of men, and made a big issue out of killing a Walia. The Simien men, when they hunted, would either ambush the animal, or would have seized the chance to shoot when the opportunity presented itself, for they always carried their rifles wherever they went.

Tag, our Peace Corps volunteer, had stalked and hit Walia with his bow and arrow; the tips of the arrows replaced with an old plastic syringe filled with paint. This way Tag marked the Walia to help Dr. Nievergelt identify them for his studies. Shooting a bow on the cliffs is a damn sight harder than shooting a rifle.

So the fact that the Simien men had killed many Walia did not suggest to me that they were all good shots.

✕✕✕✕

At night, while fetching water from the spring, I saw a big frog lying still and mottled green among the stems of watercress. I fetched my young son Kentaro, and we both stood and watched the frog, its eyes shining in the torchlight.

Around the house, and especially about the spring, trees of giant Saint-John's-wort were ablaze with yellow blossoms. All day long the bees hummed loudly, and I wondered where they went at night, for I had never found a nest. The men said bees that suckled in these flowers gave a poor honey, but that if they suckled in the tiny white flowers of the giant heather, the honey was delicious. Zeleka was trying to set up hives near the camp, promising that we would have good tedj together.

The Polish expedition left, but before leaving, the doctor treated Sonako and the children for a throat infection. I had made a promise to Sonako that if the children ever got sick in the mountains I would take this as a warning and send them home to Japan. My heart was heavy. We had no road, and this was no place for anybody to get sick. We might have had trouble had an expedition with a doctor not happened along. I thought and brooded about this a lot.

On February 11, 1969, Bernhard and Esther Nievergelt came down from Geech. Their study was completed, and they were leaving the Simien. We spent a happy-sad evening together in Sankabar. They had mixed feelings, for they would miss their round stone house and the wild and beautiful Simien, but on the other hand they would be happy to see Switzerland again. We knew we were going to miss them badly. It made such a difference just to know that they were up there.

After supper, Bernhard drew Walia in strong black lines on our white living room walls. We talked about a hundred things. They had heard recently, almost by accident, that one of our guards kept a slave woman. On questioning some of the locals, it appeared that slavery was common in these hills, despite the severe laws and penalties against it. I had known that the Amhara here always called Negro people "slaves." I had been in villages and had noticed Negroes working, and people pointed and laughed, saying "slave." I thought that this was merely the bad language of ignorant and insensitive men. But it seemed otherwise.

According to the story, these slaves were kept away from the notice of police or officials. This was easy to do here. The slaves themselves knew nothing. The children of a slave woman were liable to be sold by their owner to a known and trusted person.

The story had come out when a certain guard, a Moslem, had brought a little girl to Bernhard. She had lodged a coffee bean in her ear, and the ear was infected and swollen. He tried to dislodge the bean, but could not get it out. She would have to go to the hospital. The guard balked even more than usual at this. It seemed that this little girl was a slave, and on no account could she go to a town. Slavery was a hanging offense. I don't know what happened to the little girl, but it is likely she died.

I asked many people and most of them denied slavery existed, though the local men gave evasive answers. I was inclined to believe the story, for I had heard many similar stories, even in the environs of Addis Ababa. If it was true, it was a heavy irony. Ethiopia hosts the Organization of African Unity and fancies herself as a leader in Africa against the colonialistic and imperialistic despoilers.

In the early morning we went along to the "morning lookout." This was my favorite spotting place in Sankabar. It was a small, grassy ledge that jutted out to give a commanding view of two main cliff faces. The path to it was hidden in the trees, and the ledge was backed by a slope of fine old giant heather, so our approach was obscured and muffled. A few big trees leaned over and shaded parts of the ledge.

The weather was clear, and the vast panorama of rolling hills, steep valleys, and sheer-walled, flat-topped ambas stretched out below us. It was a dizzy height, but we were all used to it. Flocks of doves and chats circled up in the rising air currents. A pair of lanner falcons weaved and turned near the ledge on their scimitar wings. Immediately below, a whole troupe of colobus monkeys leaped about in the tops of tall trees. The pure-white and jet-black markings were distinct against the varying green of treetops, and their gruff, whirring voices echoed among the cliffs to be answered by another group of monkeys somewhere below my house.

With our telescopes and binoculars we spotted two big Walia males among the trees below us, and two females with five-month-old kids on the escarpment over to the left. They grazed peacefully, unaware of our presence.

The sun glinted through branches that were festooned with fronds of old-man's-beard, and sparkled on drops of dew in the grass and plants about us.

I took lots of photographs of Bernhard and Esther. They seemed so close to each other; the sun lifted over the slope, flooding the ledge with light, and somewhere nearby a troupe of gelada began shrieking at each other. It all seemed so perfect. The young were feeding and playing. One of the females was standing up on her hind legs and grazing like a goat from a bush. I saw her and was about to say something when she went down again.

We did not say too much on our way back to our house. It had been a fine morning to end a year's work. Bernhard and Esther had a quick breakfast, saw to the loading of the pack animals, and then they left. I followed them for a while, taking photographs, waving, calling out promises and entreaties to write. In twenty minutes their tiny figures, strung out in a line along the path, gradually got farther away until they were out of sight over the brow of the slope that leads to Michibi.

The guards were shaking their heads and sighing, tutting, saying what a good man the doctor had been. Mikio and Takashi had left. Tag was in Addis Ababa or somewhere, and Mesfin, the assistant warden, had been away for almost two months. And now the Nievergelts had gone. Sonako wanted to leave too. Walking back to the house, a sadness came over me. A whole year had flashed by in an instant. I looked around and realized how little I had achieved. It was a heavy feeling.

14

DINNER WITH PRINCE PHILIP

The stone bath house was coming along very nicely. The mason was doing a good job. He was an Eritrean, now living in Debarek. During the war he served the Italians, and from them had received the title of Grazmatch, an Ethiopian military title. He chose to retain it, and that was what we called him.

He was an outspoken old man, and I liked to work with him and listen to his stories. One day he told me he didn't like the English. They were thieves and robbers, stealing the country from the Italians, who were strong workers, and giving it to the *habasha* (Ethiopians), who were lazy good-for-nothings. The Italians built fine roads, bridges, buildings, wells, but the Ethiopians destroyed them or neglected them. Look at Asmara, he said, so clean and so fine! The Italians made Asmara. But look at Addis Ababa. He spat on the ground.

Old Grazmatch was by no means the first Ethiopian (or more precisely, Eritrean) who had said this to me. Many of the artisans, the mechanics, drivers, cooks, masons, and carpenters felt this way, and believed that the country would have been better off left in the hands of the Italians. When I asked about the people killed by the Italians they brushed it aside, saying that "many more were killed by their own people, or by the Gallas."

Of course, the younger, educated people were full of the fire of liberty and freedom, and were swept away with the whole complex of anticolonial beliefs. No, it was always the people who worked with their hands who thought in terms of work and pay and not in terms of liberty. These people, many of them, had known better times when the country was full of work provided by the invading Fascists.

And Dejasmatch Araya? Was it not true that he had been an Italian soldier too? The old mason ranted about him, about the way he would demand work from people and then neglect or refuse to pay, and about the way he would bully money out of them and take presents of honey, sheep, cattle, and grain.

To say some of these things in the town would have been very dangerous. I told him to be quiet, because I was a foreigner and should not hear these things.

"You are a good man," the old mason said. "I do not worry about my pay. I know that I will receive it, even if you do not have it now. We love to work for you. We want to work. But if we work for our own people they cheat and lie to us. One man cannot believe another man."

Afterward, in the house with Sonako, I talked over these things, and wondered what created or brought about the seeming distrust among the local people. I came to the conclusion that this distrust was directly linked to the landholding system. But the other side of the coin, turning up perhaps only in dire emergencies, was a bond of brotherhood. A mixture of love and hate.

The Amhara of the Simien highlands held common land with their blood relatives. The land was shared out by the elders of the village. It was the right of any male of the clan to receive his share. A long-lost relative could come from afar after twenty years or more and claim a portion of the clan land. However, these land shares were not marked out on the ground. Consequently, there were frequent squabbles, which often flared into fierce and bloody fights, over land, grain, and livestock. It seemed to me that nearly all the murders in the Simien now were those of relatives, over land, like the attempt of my servant Abahoy, who had stabbed (but did not kill) his cousin in a land quarrel. These people lived at a bare subsistence level. Each grain was vital. Each square foot of uneroded soil was vital. With this system the men had to wheedle, cheat, and argue with their relatives continually in order to feed their children and wives. It was almost expected.

But the land belonged to the clan. One man could never sell or otherwise dispose of clan land without full permission of all the elders. Should one disagree, the land could not be disposed of. The people often referred emotionally to each other as "child of my country," and the word "brother" could mean almost any degree of relationship. The complicated social duties and restrictions sprang from their ties to the land. The people got more emotional over their land than over anything else. Certainly they quarreled among themselves continually . . . but let an outsider interfere and he could expect nothing but the combined rage of all clan members. And, of course, I was that kind of outsider.

✦✦✦✦

A patrol caught a man cutting wild hops on the ledges where the Walia fed. He was an Amba Ras man by the name of Melese Makonnen, and he had worked for us previously. We had treated him very well, giving him free medicine for his children, and a good wage. He left of his own accord because of the harvest. As I berated him, he hung his head, for he knew that we did not permit anybody to disturb the Walia. There was no need for him to cut wild hops there anyway, for in the Khabar and Balagas valleys there was an abundance of the plant, and it was closer to his home. It was not impossible that he was setting snares; francolin were quite numerous and the people loved to eat these birds. He might even have been setting snares for larger animals. Anyway, I confiscated the wild hops and let him go.

The new guard Kebede, another ex-soldier, had caught the man, and I spoke to him. "Take this stuff. Burn it in your house stove. I will come in ten minutes to see that it is burned." It must not be said that we took the hops from the peasant and used it to flavor our own drinks. The man left sulkily. At no time during this incident did anyone lay a hand on him.

Within a month, the story had spread over the Simien. It was said that some guards and I caught the man innocently cutting grass (in some versions it was hops, but the hops didn't fit into the main theme, so grass was substituted). I raged at him and, at gunpoint, forced him to kneel, stand, lie (according to the whim of the teller) while the grass was piled around his head. Then I set fire to the grass. Dejasmatch Araya heard the story and told it many times, with booming, indignant relish to entranced audiences who took his word as law.

No one who heard or retold this story ever bothered to ask about the poor peasant, who would presumably have been burned and disfigured, if not killed, by this treatment. I was now a legend. A veritable ogre.

Mesfin, the assistant warden, was still not back from his Christmas vacation. Major Gizaw had sent him to Awash, ignoring my pleas to send him back.

Tag had returned, with a letter from the department to say that he was now an assistant warden. This presented problems, for there could not be two assistants unless their jobs were clearly defined; a warden or assistant warden had the right to arrest, to seize arms or trophies, to search, and to inspect licenses. This meant carrying a gun, at times, at least. The Peace Corps was not supposed to do that sort of thing.

Tag was having trouble with the guards. He had also lost his lion cub. It had escaped and made its way down to the valley, where, no doubt, the locals would shoot it. He was very keen to get on with the building. Swiss House was now open to visitors, and already four people were staying there; two Americans, one Canadian, and a Dane. Tag was taking care of all this. I had to go up and talk to him about the house rents and the new buildings.

A precipitous, narrow path girds the upper slopes of the Djinn Barr Valley and the Geech abyss. From it one can see part of the tremendous waterfall of the Djinn Barr, which falls about fifteen hundred feet into a deep, sheer-walled hole that lets out into an incredible valley. As we rounded the path we saw an Amba Ras peasant whipping his team of oxen, trying to make them drag a plow across the path. Although made of soil, the path was hard as concrete, for it was mixed with dung and trampled into a cement mixture during the rains, then pounded into a rock-hard texture in the dry season. The man hunched low, sweating, cursing, whirling and cracking the whip, while the oxen struggled and rolled their eyes. About two hundred meters of the path had been broken up into jagged clumps of dirt over which our horses and mules stumbled and slipped. Barley could never grow there. No other route was possible. The guards cursed, and I yelled at the man, demanding to know why he plowed the path. He ignored me until I took the whip from him and shook him by his tattered long shirt.

Dinner with Prince Philip

"It is my land, both sides of the path. I plow to connect it. The path is my land."

But there was no other way for the path to run. Only a few years before, the path had run through a thick tree heather forest. This man had cut it down and now claimed all of it. Moreover, the next day was a market day in Debarek, and within twenty-four hours his plowing would be trodden down again by the feet of a hundred farmers and the hooves of their laden donkeys. This peasant intended to spend all day plowing the path for nothing, and yet he would never do anything about the huge erosion gullies spreading like veins all over his land. The stupidity infuriated me, and I wanted to shout at him, do something to turn all this incredible work and energy into some really worthwhile farming. But I didn't bother. The guards told him that this was a path, and all people had right-of-way, and that it would be trodden out by the next day, but as soon as we left he went on trying to plow up the path, whistling, cracking the whip, shrieking in a high, hysterically shrill voice.

Various worries and strains were telling on me. When visitors came I drank and talked too much, and bored my wife, who had heard it all before. Two Englishmen, friends of our teacher friends in Addis, came and camped in our back yard. Their company was a relief; they didn't mind my talking, and we all laughed a lot.

Threats against our camp made me nervous about leaving my family alone in Sankabar. People who had not been into the hills, Ethiopians, assured me that there was no danger, but I knew that the hill people were often violent, and no other foreigner had lived in the Simien as far as I could discover. I also knew that if any obstreperous people came waving guns around when I wasn't there, Sonako would not hesitate to shoot and kill, whereas I would probably try to bluff it out first.

I was lying on the grass after lunch, thinking about what to do, and getting too angry inside, worrying about the anger, and about it coloring the way I reacted to people. Being without an interpreter and assistant for so long had a lot to do with it, for the assistant would act as a buffer between me and the people. Without the buffer I was beginning to wear down. Peasants passed on their way to market. Disembodied voices rose and fell in their chants of heroes, as they strode along the path that was hidden from the house by trees. The ground and air were very dry now, but on the north-facing slopes the tips of the tree heather foliage were brilliantly green. I stared at the house I had sweated to build for myself and family, and then beyond it to the far-below sea of hazy hills. Being so high above hills, and lying thus on the ground, hearing those weird voices, filled me with a sense of unreality. My thoughts, feelings, physical position, did not jibe in my mind, and I felt strongly alien. Realizing this, I got up suddenly and went into the house to fetch my binoculars and telescope, determined to find a Walia to look at, to remind myself of why I was here.

The park bank account was still low, and one friend who visited us, and who worked in the Ministry of Finance, told me that the whole country was low on funds, and that the Emperor had gone to beg money from the United States to pull the government out of trouble. The army was agitating for its pay, and the poor teachers had not received their salary for months. You can't achieve anything here, Sonako was saying; it's all a waste.

※※※※※

Guard Chane Endeshaw arrived in camp. He had been absent without leave for ten days, and claimed that he had been attending the funeral of his uncle. It was a lie. When he had been ordered to go up to Geech to replace another guard, he had refused to go.

"Why?"

"I cannot go. A long time ago I was with a man, standing by him, when he killed a Geech man. If I go they take revenge and kill me."

The Geech camp was the center of the park. If a guard could not or would not go there, he was no use to me.

Chane had also been specifically ordered to come up with the clerk, Kassa, because Kassa was bringing up a month's salary for the men. Kassa had searched Debarek for Chane, but Chane had avoided him. It was rumored that he was doing something for the old Dejasmatch. There were no other guards in Debarek at the time, and Kassa had no gun. Moreover, it was widely known that he carried money, and until fairly recently, the path was infamous for its ambushes. In the end, Kassa came up alone with the money.

Guard Chane lied himself into knots, and I got angry, disarmed him, and ordered him out of camp. This man was always sneaking off in Debarek and hanging around the old Governor. I told him he would be fired or sent to the south.

Later, while I was eating lunch, guards Tedla and Berehun came to the door of the house, bowed down by the big rocks they were carrying on their shoulders. As I opened the door they bent down, still holding the rocks, and tried to kiss my feet. They had come to plead for Chane, and all this was a sign of humiliation, the rocks being the great load of the problem or petition.

"Stand! Act like men and soldiers!" I listened to what they were saying and told them to give it to me in writing, and I would put this in with my report about Chane to headquarters. My Amharic was very bad, and it always took me a long time to say anything, which merely increased my anger.

Kassa, who had gone back down to Gondar, returned that evening with a letter from John Blower. The letter said that I was to come to Addis Ababa, and from there go to one of the Rift Valley lakes, Lake Abiata, to be presented to Prince Philip, the Duke of Edinburgh. His Royal Highness was coming to Ethiopia to see and photograph wildlife, to look over the conservation situation here, and to encourage the British wardens in their endeavors. (There was, by now, a game warden of Eritrea, the ex-consul, Major John Bromley, also British like John Blower, George Brown, and Peter Hay.) It was no secret that Major Gizaw hated British wardens by this time, for they were troublesome and stubborn.

With two royal visits following one another so closely, things were getting shaken up in Addis Ababa.

Before leaving, I had to go up one more time to Geech. I went up with Kassa and a game guard. It was sunny and quite warm, with high altocumulus and cirrus clouds. Along the way we caught three groups of Amba Ras villagers cutting tree heather in the Djinn Barr Valley.

As we came up the last series of bare, dusty slopes leading to Geech, a delegation of village elders came to meet us, led by their religious leader, a garrulous old man in a green silk headscarf, torn robes, and beads. They had come to say that they could not live without cutting wood for fires and fences (something that I had never once argued about or questioned), and that if His Imperial Majesty thought it was possible for the people to live up there without a fire, then he should come and try for himself. Obviously true, and no doubt His Majesty would agree. But again I thrashed out the old criteria of not destroying the forest to claim land, not cutting big trees, not cutting near the escarpment, not cutting along stream banks or at the heads of springs. I told them that I would report their situation in detail, but that they should cooperate with us.

After three hours of talking in the sun and the dust, we got them to promise to cut only in zones which we would mark out and show them. This would be a temporary measure, for if the park was to be established, then there could be no cutting, and the Geech people would have to be moved out. But having got this promise from them, I felt at last that we were getting somewhere, and Kassa seemed to think that the people were pleased by the talk.

Up at the camp, Tag and I talked over park business. With Mesfin still not back, and me away, he would be left in charge. I was feeling nervous about it. Vague threats against Tag were being circulated. He had made an enemy of Nadu the day he picked him up and threw him out of the door of my house. I left a rifle and ammunition for him. The cutting was our main topic that day, and the fact that Nadu's villagers seemed to be the worst offenders in the highland. It seemed to us then that they would never stop.

At the end of February, Sonako, the children, and I came out of the Simien. She was pregnant again, despite all kinds of precautions. An obstetrician in Gondar said that on no account should she ride a horse or a mule until it was all over. So we knew then that she and the children would not go back to the Simien. At first she said she would stay in Gondar, but for a hundred reasons we knew it would be no good.

A promise is a promise. They would go back to Japan, and I would take them, and then return.

If the road had been built, there would have been no difficulty. The road, the damned road.

The drive from Addis Ababa to Lake Langano is very pleasant, the road is straight and paved, perhaps the best stretch of road south of Eritrea. Speeding along in the World Wildlife Fund Land Rover, inherited from Dr. Nievergelt, I wondered if the road was good because all the Addis big-shots used it on the weekends. Langano was a big pleasure resort, and the lake, which was slightly salt, was one of the few around that was free from Bilharzia, a disease-producing parasite, and therefore safe for swimming.

The royal camp was a few kilometers away, on Lake Abiata, back along the main road, about four kilometers from the road on the opposite side from Langano. I drove along, and found a Galla herd-boy to show me the path.

Thousands of flamingos made the lake border by the camp all white and gentle pink. And there were so many other kinds of water birds that I stopped my car and watched for an hour, forgetting what I had come to do. Ungainly pelicans swam in beak-dipping flotillas. Egrets, herons, and storks stood patiently in the shallows, while baleful-eyed marabou storks strode with deliberate steps like lanky headmasters.

The great funnel of the Rift Valley formed an important migration route for birds, and there were many European birds around the shores, mostly ducks, pipers, and waders.

I had never seen so many species of herons, egrets, storks, spoon-bills, and other water birds. And apart from these there were eagles, and other birds of prey, and many small birds I did not recognize.

The flamingos were the most striking; taking off and landing in clouds, exposing the pink under their wings so that white would change into pink and white, moving and spreading so that white and pink blended into each other and threw reflections off the still surface of the lake waters.

Standing in the shallow waters up to their waists, native fishermen worked their nets. Boys herded skinny zebu cattle around the lake edges, where the acacia spread their wide and thorny parasols.

All around the camp, smart Imperial Bodyguard troops stood guard, stopping all cars. They let me pass, seeing the mark on the vehicle, and I drove up near the camp, stopped the car by the resident biologist's tent, and walked up to find John Blower sitting by a table, drinking fine tea and writing. The Prince was out. He had been gone all day, crouching behind a camera in a stuffy blind by the lakeshore. John had much to tell me, so I joined him and we talked.

The Prince returned at about five o'clock. He got out of the Land Rover with a big canvas bag of photographic equipment. His was a familiar figure. I had seen his picture hundreds of times, and watched him on television. But this time there was muck up to his knees, and he carried a heavy bag, which made me think that somebody should go and take it from him, but then again that seemed silly because he didn't look like the kind of man who had to have his bag carried. He stopped by the table and asked if there was any tea left for him. Then he went into his tent, changed out of the muddy trousers, and came out again, picking his way over the thorn-strewn grass in his bare feet and making cracks about English lawns. John Blower spoke. "This is Nicol, sir, the warden from the Simien."

I bowed slightly, and the Prince held out his hand with a smile.

"Glad you could come, Nicol. Sit down here and let's have a talk."

It was all rather overwhelming for me. I come from a royalist family. My father, a Royal Navy man, is liable to express all kinds of rude thoughts about the government, but to him, and to all our family, the royal family is sacrosanct. Respect for the Crown is a very real thing. Yet none of our family had ever been presented to the Queen or to the Duke of Edinburgh, and here I was, dressed in shorts and bush shirt, sitting next to him, drinking tea, and talking about my work.

The Prince remembered every point I had raised in that long letter I had written to him about the Simien. He knew the animals and birds as if he had already visited the place. Of course he had talked for a long time with John Blower, but to remember all that information is not so easy. I talked to him for about an hour that day, with John Blower sometimes adding his comments or confirming what I said.

Before I went back to the hotel, Major Buxton, who was in charge of the camp, invited Sonako and me back for dinner with the Prince the following evening. His Royal Highness would be out in a boat on the other side of the lake all the next day, so John said I should come in the afternoon, bring the family, and look around at the birds.

Dinner was served under the marquee, which was open-fronted and faced the lake so that we could see the flights of water birds as we ate and talked. John Blower said the camp and the marquee reminded him of the old crusaders' camps. It was a small party, with the Prince, his security man and personal servant, and a few biologists and conservation men. I was the only one wearing a tie, having changed into pressed trousers, white shirt, and tie in John's tent. It was a very relaxed affair. The Prince wanted to hear more about the Simien, and so I was invited to sit next to him again.

It was an excellent meal, though I can't for the life of me remember what it was, for it was the conversation that was the most memorable. It ranged from specific topics and problems of conservation in Ethiopia to the whole conservation picture. There was a lot of laughter, and people were at ease, though the Prince was not the kind of man one would care to step out of line with. It was easy to see why the press loved to seize upon his comments. He is a direct man, with a fine sense of humor, though I would guess that he is very often quoted out of context. The only other people that I had ever met who knew as much about wildlife as Prince Philip were either biologists or wardens.

At dusk, myriad lake flies swarmed around the lights. The meal was finished with all the lights inside the tent turned off. The lake was thick with algae, on which the flamingo seemed to be feeding, and there was a certain not unpleasant smell.

Prince Philip said that he would like to visit the Simien quite soon, and I urged him to do so, knowing that he would enjoy and appreciate it.

I knew by now that the British Army was planning to come and look over the Simien, and that a preliminary road survey would be done in a month or so by a few officers. If everything went as we hoped, the sappers might come and build the road to Sankabar as a training exercise.

The party ended at eleven that night, when Prince Philip retired to his tent.

The road from Abiata to Langano was so thick with flies that the lights of cars were dimmed, as if in a thick fog. Insects splattered thickly over the windshield, and I had to drive very slowly, stopping now and then to scrape off the mess with a piece of wood. I was singing, swallowing an occasional fly, feeling exhilarated, for I had just talked for a long time with our Prince, the Duke of Edinburgh. Ah, I would be able to talk of this when I became a doddering old man!

He had urged me not to give up on the job in the Simien, and had said how important it all was. Of course, I knew this, but his saying it reinforced my belief in the importance of my work. I could not give up now, despite personal difficulties, trouble with officials, lack of funds, and obstreperous peasants. If and when the Prince came to the Simien, he would see that I hadn't given up!

Getting out of Ethiopia was as difficult as getting in. We needed exit visas, and that, for me, meant forms and letters from this and that department, and for Sonako it seemed that she must bring letters from Gondar. I had been in Ethiopia long enough to know that exploding in offices did no good. Knowing that I had been called by no less a greatness than a foreign royal prince raised my importance momentarily in the eyes of officials. A few words in the right places got the visa through, without my having to fly to Gondar to get the letters.

We arrived in Tokyo on March 18. Once through customs and immigration, I went to find a taxi. A driver took our bags.

"That car is cheaper than mine. If it pleases you, please take it. But my car is perhaps more comfortable for you with the children after your journey. You must be tired." No squabbling and haggling. No beggars. Nobody fighting to grab the bags. No arguing about the fare. My sense of relief was enormous.

A month in Japan relaxed me, and I was able to see the problems of the Simien in their proper light. Tokyo swallowed me up. In the Simien I was a very big frog in a small pond, but in Tokyo I was a tadpole in an ocean. Stick your nose too close to the mirror and you'll see only the pimples.

I saw old friends. I went to the karate dojo where some of my contemporaries were now full-time teachers. The training was just as hard, and watching it made me feel five years older. Tokyo's filthy air had affected my lungs, and I was unable to practice. Don Draegar, an old friend who is perhaps the foremost Western expert in the field of Japanese martial arts, asked me to get photographs of Ethiopians using the "dulla" or fighting stick. I said I would try.

I gave a couple of lectures, using a film loaned to me by the Ethiopian Tourist Organization. I showed it once at the National Museum. My zeal in attempting to influence people about wildlife may have seemed a little fanatical. There was some polite interest, but Japan has its own problems.

Dinner with Prince Philip

Ueno Park was full of tipsy, sake-drinking people who had turned out to see the cherry blossoms. We went to the zoo and saw some small gelada baboons huddled silently in the corner of a tiny cage.

Tokyo had changed. Many new, high buildings, twice the number of cars. The dirty air made us all sick; the stream behind my mother-in-law's house was now a stinking sewer of blackish gray muck, mostly from detergents. Tokyo was the most exciting and the dirtiest town I had ever been to. It is the only big town I have lived in, and I knew it well. Being able to speak Japanese reasonably well afforded me freedom of movement. There was no pressure on me here. Until I got out of Ethiopia I had not realized how badly the constant attention of beggars and street boys affected me. In Tokyo people in bars and shops smiled at me and were kind and polite, which they rarely were in Ethiopia. Police seemed smart and gentle, and officials seemed human. I did not carry a gun, nor a throwing knife stitched down the back of my collar.

The month passed all too quickly. In an inn at a hot spring resort in the mountains I made the final decision to return to Ethiopia. The inn was sheltered and screened by tall trees and bamboo; blossoming trees grew in the stone garden, and a pure mountain stream rushed over rounded boulders down behind the inn. There were great hot baths, two of them formed by natural stone in the open air. It was all so relaxing. I drank sake with my wife and questioned my soul. Was it right to go off and leave her alone again? Could I let go of the park and all that went with it? Was I returning due to a false pride? Or because of the elevated position of game warden? Or was I genuinely devoted to trying to do an essential job?

The decision to go back was made, I think, on the basis of a duty to myself and the people, no matter how few, who believed in me.

Sonako did not come to the airport to see me off. We hated good-byes. I fought back tears at parting, for I believed that this time it would be for a year and a half. Japanese friends saw me off.

"What troubles you, Nic-san?"

"I do not believe that in my heart I want to go."

"Then stay in Japan."

"No, my heart stays here, but in my spirit it is essential to do this work."

So I went; I arrived in Addis Ababa in brilliant sun and pure air on April 25. Riot police and soldiers were all over the city. The gov-

233

ernment was having trouble with the students. The taxi driver tried to cheat me and I had to shout at him. The wind gently bowed the high tops of the eucalyptus, kites circled, wood fires made smoke like thin blue veils over tin roofs, and it all seemed like so long ago.

15

RIOTS AND A ROBBERY

The university and nine secondary schools were closed. Truckloads of police and soldiers were moving all over the city, and twice I saw jeeps with mounted 50-caliber machine guns. The students were not allowed to gather, even in small groups, and hundreds had been arrested. Wild rumors were heard and repeated . . . there was going to be a coup d'état . . . some students had been thrown into a cess pit and drowned by the Imperial Bodyguard . . . the army was poised outside the town, ready to come in and take over . . . five young people had been jailed for five years' hard labor for distributing pamphlets . . . this time, the foreigners were going to be wiped out. . . .

The atmosphere was tense and uncertain in the city, and nobody knew what was going on, for the government outlets told us nothing. We knew only that there had been riots and that the schools were calling on each other to strike.

At the English school, where I was staying with my friends, the Robbs, classes were going on as usual, despite some threats. Here and there in the school compound, soldiers in battle gear, with their automatic weapons, were lounging around on the grass, grinning at the older girls.

In Gondar there had been riots too, and a police Land Rover had been turned over and burned. The police with guns faced the students, and a teacher friend of mine heard shots, though we heard no reports of woundings. Police dragged students out of their houses and beat them with clubs while parents looked on, pleading. Many students were arrested, and the situation was at boiling point. Then came the anti-Arab riots.

The Eritrean Liberation Front, the northern, anti-government guerrillas, had been blowing up planes and generally making trouble, and just recently they had been linked to Syria. Outraged editorials blasted them in the press. A huge "spontaneous" anti-Arab parade was held in Addis Ababa, with the lion mane headdresses, the round shields, spears, curved scimitars—the whole Amhara warrior show-off. In other cities and towns all over the country, Arabs were beaten up, and Arab shops were stoned. Part of it may have been due to a dislike or jealousy of the Arabs, who were the predominant merchant and tradesman group in the country; but to me, all this "spontaneity" seemed suspiciously like a politically convenient red herring.

Nothing was put in the newspapers. Headlines continued to proclaim that "His Imperial Majesty Grants Audience" or that the British, the Americans, the Portuguese, the South Africans, or the Rhodesians had committed yet further crimes against liberty and humanity.

People were agitated. Several cultured Ethiopians approached me, asking me if I could get guns or ammunition for them, and an English friend told me that he had been at a party where a very educated Ethiopian, slightly in his cups, had said, "Too long have the students been our conscience. Now is the time to get our guns!"

Feeling very conscious of the tenseness in the city, I went to our headquarters. A letter from Tag was waiting for me. Opening it, I began to read.

"Dear Nic, I hate to greet you with bad news, but there is no choice. Swiss House has been ransacked and robbed . . ." From his letter, I learned that Tag had gone down to Gondar on April 8 to get money for masons and coolies. As he often did, Tag returned at night, on April 9, reaching the house in Geech at eleven thirty P.M. He found that the kitchen shutter had been forced, the window broken, and the place wrecked. It was in absolute shambles. Shelves and cupboards were tipped over, boxes emptied out, letters torn, food and medicine cartons ripped open and their contents scattered. The hooligans had smashed bottles and other things, and had urinated and defecated all over the house.

Some four thousand dollars worth of goods had been stolen, including a rifle and ammunition, a Nikon camera and various lenses, a pair of binoculars, a cash box and cash, a Zenith radio, saddlery, and various clothes, blankets, and small items.

Tag said in his letter that he didn't have a clue as to who had done it, but on Wednesday, the day it must have happened, many people had been traveling across the Geech plateau from the market down in Debarek.

The previous week there had been a big fight in the market. The Ethiopians had started beating up Arabs, so the Governor, Dejasmatch Araya, closed the market down. Consequently, the next market had been very crowded and very rowdy.

Tag sent a report to our clerk, Kassa, who translated it and handed it over to the police captain in Debarek. It was a big theft, one of the biggest in the worthy captain's area, and probably the biggest theft since the war in the whole of the mountains. But no action was forthcoming. Tag needed a note from the police to say that he had reported the theft, for he wished to report the loss of his cameras to the insurance company. The police refused to give the note.

While Tag was away, four men, game guards armed with rifles, were supposed to have been on guard duty: Guards Chane Takalé (who formerly was suspected of and charged with cattle theft, but who got out of it by bribing the right people), Guard Amara Gebrew (who had quarreled with Tag), Guard Atakulte Ferede (who was a cousin of Dejasmatch Araya), and Ambaw Achanafi (who was very loyal to Nadu, and who had formerly been a servant in Nadu's father's house). None of the guards was any good, but I was highly suspicious of two things. One was the loyalty owed to Nadu by two of the men. The other was the lack of action by the police, who must have reported to the Dejasmatch, and the recent tie-ups between Nadu, troublesome peasants who wanted us out of the area, and Dejasmatch Araya.

The thieves must have made a hell of a lot of noise when they wrecked the place. Why had the guards not heard them? Tag had been away only a day, and although the Geech people could have seen him go down, and would know that he and I were both away, it did not seem likely to us that they would have acted so quickly.

The thieves found the rifle, an Mk. 5 Lee Enfield .303 jungle carbine, and they also found the magazine and the ammunition, all of which had been very carefully hidden by Tag. The only people in the area with this type of rifle were our guards. And what would local peasants do with a camera? How could they dispose of such things? I knew of only one man living in the Simien who could get rid of such things. He lived only a few hours away, in Amba Ras.

What was Nadu doing at the time of the robbery? No, no, it could not have been him, for he was in Addis Ababa. But I was still suspicious. Nadu had many followers. He knew the layout of the house and what was in it. He was also closely connected with the Dejasmatch, and Nadu's elder brother, Negash, was the chief of the vigilantes. And they, and his brother, wanted us out.

As I expected, the four game guards said that they knew nothing. The value of the stuff stolen represented about eight years' salary for one of our men. The theft of a government rifle was an especially serious crime. Why had the police done nothing?

Angrily, I reported the contents of the letter and some of my thoughts about it to Major Gizaw, who phoned the Governor General in Gondar. Immediate action was promised, but absolutely nothing was done.

And, I asked, what action had been taken against Nadu? When I left for Japan, his case had been brought, through the auspices of both Prince Bernhard of the Netherlands and Prince Philip of Britain, to the notice of the Emperor. Nadu had not returned the rifles, ammunition, and other equipment he had acquired, and neither had he cleared himself of the charges of bribery, extortion, and shooting rare animals. So what had been done? Headquarters tried to evade the issue, offering various excuses, but I found out soon enough.

Nadu had been given three months' leave by the Wildlife Conservation Department in order that he might run for parliament, for the Simien seat. Nadu had beaten us, as he said he would. The foreign game warden was powerless against this man. And the local people, the officials, and the game guards of the national park knew this very well now.

I went to see the Minister of Agriculture and complained about everything. He promised to do something about Nadu. Within twenty-four hours, fifteen thousand dollars had been deposited in the park account in Gondar. The Minister, a tall, thin, gray-haired aristocrat who had formerly been with the Ethiopian Embassy in London, said that a great part of my troubles had been due to the failure of the government to explain to the local people. They should, he said, be sure that a high-ranking Ethiopian went up to talk to the people and tell them about the park. I agreed. I had been saying as much in my monthly reports for a long, long time.

I got further news from the Simien. Sonako's horse, Brook, had been killed and eaten by hyenas. The game guards had neglected to stable the horse, and had left him hobbled outside for several days.

One Sunday, before I left Addis to drive up to Gondar, I decided that I wanted to see Ted Shatto, the hunter. His big house was up a narrow, muddy road, past the Italian Embassy, overlooking the town. As I went up, a cloudburst sheeted water down, making the reddish-yellow clay road up to Ted's house very slippery. I drove slowly, less than twenty kilometers an hour. Down the hill came a peasant with a host of donkeys. I eased the Land Rover to the side of the road to let them pass, but the incline at the side was steep, and slowly the car slithered into the ditch. I got out and, with an entrenching tool, began to break up the hard soil near the wheels. Hostile people came from nowhere to stand in the driving rain and stare.

A boy about fourteen or fifteen years came from a nearby eucalyptus grove. He was screaming and groaning, clutching at various parts of his body, telling the crowd that I had been speeding up the hill and had hit him, nearly killing him. Only the donkey man had been on the road at the time, and he had gone. I said the boy was lying, and went on swinging the tool. Another man joined the boy, saying that he was the boy's brother, and that he had seen the accident. I continued to work.

"Go and fetch a policeman, you dung of an animal," I said. Another man came from a house some fifty yards back along the road. He had been drinking talla, his breath smelled and his eyes were wild. He shouted at me, telling everybody that I had smashed his fence. The car had gone nowhere near the fence, although it was indeed broken. The fence looked as if it had rotted away many years before. The man said I must pay him immediately, and he pulled at my shirt, demanding two hundred dollars. The crowd encouraged him.

"Ten dollars eucalyptus," I said. "Three dollars nails. You, liar, fart, drunkard. Go!"

I looked at the man and he stepped back. People began to pick up stones. It was a very lonely road. During the riots, street boys had stoned a foreign university teacher and he had lost an eye. A Walther automatic was hidden under my shirt, and in the car, just behind the seat, was a heavy, well-sharpened machete. What I thought was stupid and suicidal, but I despise mobs, and I was far too frightened to feel anything like fear. These lying bastards wanted only a chance to get at a foreigner, and they took advantage of my misfortune.

Two English-speaking students came along and asked what happened. They listened to me above the clamor of the crowd. They could see that I told the truth. They helped me to get the car out. It had gone into the ditch so slowly that there was not even a scratch on it.

Once the car was out, and the crowd saw that I could drive away, they started shrieking and darting for stones. The students, who knew Ted Shatto, said he was out, so I could not expect help from him. I drove up the road and turned the car around. About fifty people blocked the road. They wanted money, or me. They screamed that I had almost killed a boy, and smashed a fence.

"If the boy is hurt, he must go to the hospital," I said, opening the door and hauling the boy in, protesting. The "brother" got in the car. The others started rocking the car, and I reached for the machete. The ones nearest to me backed off. Soft foreigners didn't fight, but this one looked crazy. The students intervened and argued with the people.

"Go," said one of them, "before they get more excited. You do not know our people."

At the nearest hospital I ordered the two of them out of the car; I dragged the "brother" when he resisted. An Indian lady doctor was on duty in the out-patients' section.

"What has happened? A traffic accident?"

"Yes, this boy claims that I hit him with my car. But he is lying, he was nowhere near the car. Since the crowd seemed angry, I had to bring him here. If he has any injury, I will pay to treat him."

Two attendants washed the mud off the boy's legs. The doctor examined him very carefully.

"There is absolutely nothing wrong with this boy."

"Are you sure?"

"I have seen so many of these cases I do not care to count.

Riots and a robbery

Usually the driver, if he is a foreigner, is worried, and pays money immediately. I will give you a note about this, in case they talk about going to court."

I thanked the doctor, and paid a little money. She gave the boy an aspirin. The "brother" began to argue and shout, until the door guard came and took him out.

Once outside, the boy and the young man were shrieking at me and whining, and the young man shook his fist. I seized his elbow, and foot-swept him, dumping him on his arse in the mud. Then I grabbed him by the collar and dragged him to his feet.

"Baboon. See this car. Remember the mark. Later I will come with soldiers to find you."

Remembering the boy who started it all, I grabbed him. So nothing was wrong with him, eh? I kicked him as hard as I could in the seat of his ragged shorts, and hurt him quite badly. From the steps of the hospital the door guard looked on and laughed toothily, saying, "That is good, that is strong, they are liars!"

Remembering that I was, after all, in Ethiopia, I gave the young man a dollar, saying in a loud voice, loud enough for the guard to hear, that he should take his brother home by taxi. And then I remembered to give the door guard a two-dollar tip. It probably would not have been necessary for him to remember me, but now I could be sure he would.

My clothes were soaked and filthy with mud. I was sweating and tight in the guts with tension and rage. Why in the name of hell had I come back to this lousy country?

But later, at my friend's house, while listening to tranquil music in a bright, warm room, I thought about it all, and I pitied people who had such darkness and desperation in their hearts. Surely, the Simien people were not like this.

❊❊❊❊

Despite the friends, parties, people to talk to, excellent restaurants, and good shops of the big city, it was a relief to get on the road to Gondar. Tag had come to Addis Ababa in the meantime, and we went back together.

I had been informed, through the military attaché at the embassy, that British officers were going to come to look over the road site. I had to arrange animals, equipment, and saddlery for them. Could it be that the park would actually get a road?

The weather in Gondar was superb. I stayed overnight with our former neighbors, an American doctor and his family. The big house which I had rented through the previous rainy season was empty and lonely. A semi-tame monkey with a broken lead chattered in a tree in the garden, and doves gargled mournfully. Gondar was unchanged, but so lonely now, and I wasn't looking forward to going back to my empty house in the hills.

But back I went, the long and tedious ride that I had made so many times. The game guards at Sankabar seemed happy to see me return. Now they would be assured of getting their salaries. None of them had believed I would come back, and they knew how strongly I felt about the business with Nadu.

Children's toys and my wife's things were scattered everywhere in the house, for we had left in a hurry, only taking a few essentials. The house was cold now, and slightly damp. Thought-ghosts lingered in the shadows, and a kaleidoscope of memories spun through my mind. I picked up my son's picture book, looking for a long time at a childish scribble on the cover, and I thought of my children and missed them like hell.

Abahoy busied himself tidying up and brewing tea, asking about the family, asking about Japan. God, could I stand it here all alone now? I had built this house mainly on the hopes and anticipations of living in it with my family. I had worked alone here for eight months before they came. Now they were gone and would not return. I looked at the table. There were six chairs around it, and two high chairs, cut to the size of Kentaro and Miwako. I had designed them myself, had them made, had them carried all the way up here. God damn!

I could feel tears coming to my eyes, and feeling ashamed to show emotion in front of another man, I went out and climbed to the top of the hill. Looking out over the lowland hills and the great black-shadowed wall of the escarpment, I said small and personal prayers into the wind, and asked the gods, or God, for an omen. I have asked for omens many times before, something to fasten my concentration onto, to assure me of direction.

Down below, the smoke from my chimney wafted over the three

*The view from the path to Geech—with the Djinn Barr falls, Geech abyss,
and, above, the scattered tukals (round houses) of Geech village.*

*Guards Tedla, Mitiku, and Amara
with sheep.*

LEFT TO RIGHT: *Game guard Chane Takalé.
Game guard Zeleka. Game guard
Amara Gebrew.*

John Blower discussing problems with a local resident.

Lowland villagers, vigilantes, and our guards, also Mesfin.

A patrol camp at Dohara, at dawn.

The escarpment—from the lowland village of Antola.

Geech men carrying eucalyptus poles for our building projects.

LEFT TOP: *The Simien ramparts—approached from the north.*

LEFT BOTTOM: *Flamingoes at Lake Abiata.*

The house at Sankabar, a triple rondavel linked by corridors.

Tag with a lion that did not want to walk.

C. W. Nicol at Michibi cliff.

Sonako and Kentaro.

Kentaro, Miwako, and Mogus playing in the tree heather.

A boy and a mule, at Geech.

Simien shepherd boys making hats.

*Amba Ras shepherd boys at
13,000 feet.*

Forest fire, set by villagers, below Sederek peak.

Forest destroyed near the sources of the Zarema River. The land is too stony for farming, so the destruction is willful and pointless.

Geech villagers ploughing a typical stony slope.

Fasilides bath at Gondar.

At Debarek, ready to leave for Simien.

round, yellow-thatched roofs of my house. Abahoy was in the kitchen, cutting up meat, garlic, onions. Guards were shouting to each other in the camp. Could I really spend a night, a week, a month, a year, in that deserted house? Even my dog, Mogus, was still in Gondar, for soon I would go on a long patrol and didn't want to take him.

I saw a guard, in his khaki uniform, come down to the house, looking for me. Soon some foreigners came down the path. Visitors who had trouble with their mules? Who wanted a guide? Or wanted to camp here? Or just to say hello?

Getting up from the lee of the big rock where I had been sitting, wallowing in self-pity, I dusted the gritty stones from my shorts, and whistling, I hopped down over the rocks, down through the grove of trees to the house. My family, my children, were all safe in Japan. Here was here. Now was now. There was no time for all this. There was much work to do. The Simien National Park would perhaps be one of the best in Africa, and I was the warden of it. Here indeed was an omen. A foreign visitor in a bright red jacket.

Morning is a very delicate time of day for people like me. Dreams and brilliant ideas of the previous evening and night are torn down and shredded by the cold, Anglo-Saxon common sense of morning. Reality glares me in the face. One of the reasons I hate shaving is that I can't bear staring at myself in the mirror. Ugly, wrinkled, and with eyes red-rimmed, it is hardly a sight to start the day on.

Saddlery and camping gear had to be readied to be sent down to Debarek for the visiting British Army officers. I was the only one who could do it. The store was in a shambles, with gear scattered everywhere. The guards had been using the gear. Saddle blankets and pads were matted and stiff with gore and muck from the saddle sores. I cursed, for when we went to Japan the animals were in fair condition. Now that our pack animals were inflicted with sores, they would have to be rested, and this would mean hiring local animals, which we could ill afford, despite the fifteen thousand dollars deposited in the bank.

I worked all morning, cleaning, checking, sorting, and packing equipment. Each item packed and balanced in the boxes or bundles was recorded in my field book. By lunchtime I was almost done.

A very large cup of tea reminded me of a biological need. Retiring to the very fine toilet built by our Japanese friend Mikio

Maeno, I got an unpleasant shock. The formerly clean, bleached, glass-papered wooden seat was gritty and black with the mark of feet and boots, and all around it was caked with hardened filth. My prolonged and highly obscene bellows of rage brought Abahoy and two guards running to find out what had happened. Abahoy had to spend the rest of the day cleaning the john. I don't know if it was he who had been standing, or rather squatting, on the seat, but he should have guarded it. I was glad I hadn't seen it first thing in the morning. The shock would have incapacitated me, left me unable to face the mess in the store, and sent me off over the hills with binoculars to watch birds and gelada for the rest of the day. The state of the john can affect the average Englishman's thinking for the entire day.

Mesfin, the assistant warden, had also returned to the Simien by this time. He had come back with a long list of jobs, given to him by me, and most of them he had completed. One of the jobs was to mark out the cutting zones for the Geech people, just as the village elders had promised before. Now the elders had gone back on their word and refused to take any notice of the zoning. Just as before, they continued to cut where they pleased. Agafari Nadu had been encouraging them in this, asking them what right the foreigner had to tell them where to cut wood and trees.

Mesfin and I went down to Debarek together, and then on to Gondar to meet the British officers, who would be coming with John Blower and Major Gizaw. For the first time since I had taken over the park project, the Major was going to come up into the Simien.

We met them at the airport in the morning. Three British officers came, two majors and a colonel. One of the majors was concerned with the logistics of the possible road-building operation, and the other was an engineer. From the airport, we drove into town and waited for a while, for Major Gizaw wanted to talk briefly with the Governor General. Guards and mules were waiting in Debarek, and we reached there in the late morning.

Saddling and loading the ten waiting pack animals and six riding animals took a lot of time. Mesfin tried to hurry the packers on, amid the screaming, squabbling confusion of boxes, bundles, saddles, and quarrels over who should use which particular piece of rope. John Blower, Major Gizaw, the three British officers, and I sat in Berhanu's bar, drinking hot sweet tea from small glasses and eating the fresh rolls baked in the town.

The police captain was in the bar. I reminded Major Gizaw of the robbery, and that the police still had taken no action. Major Gizaw talked to the captain about it, and the captain said he was under-manned and could not send men into the Simien unless the Dejas-match ordered him to do so. Which was a complete lie. I said that we would take the matter to the police general in Gondar if he didn't get police up to Geech soon. He left the bar.

John Blower was itching to get going. He suggested we start walk-ing and leave orders for the rest to meet us at the river en route. I went out to tell Mesfin.

Mesfin was having a rough time, but was coping well enough with the squabbling muleteers, each of whom wished to load his own animal with the lightest load. I told him that we would walk on ahead, and that he should come on with the pack caravan and guards.

"We will follow the proposed route of the road, not the normal trail. We will camp tonight at the river, where the Imperial High-ways Authorities decided that a bridge should be built."

"Do the guards know the way?"

"They should. Berehun has gone over the route twice with me."

Mesfin asked the guards, and they said yes, yes, we know.

"Don't make a mistake," I said. "This route is the one that Ato Ermias and a highways engineer followed last year. They marked stones along the way with red paint."

Mesfin asked again if the guards knew this route, and they said they did.

Colonel Randle, Major Downes, John Blower, and I started walk-ing. The other major stayed in Debarek, asking questions about fuel, supplies, and whether or not the local bakery could provide bread for a hundred or so soldiers. Major Gizaw also stayed behind to wait for the mules. He preferred to ride up to Sankabar, and not to camp with us.

The weather was fine, and we took only our notebooks. Our in-tention was to walk for three or four hours, by which time we would reach a fine camping site on the banks of the Angoba, a small river which would have to be bridged if a road was going to be built.

I looked forward to the evening, anticipating a pleasant camp, a few drinks before supper, and a good chat before turning in.

We got to the site early enough and waited for the others. We waited for a long time, until it began to get dark, and still there was no sign of them. I went back along the path, meeting three villagers with bundles of firewood.

"Have you seen my mules, boxes, soldiers?" I asked.

They bowed and pointed back to the long ridge.

"The mules and soldiers have passed, lord, over two hours ago."

Having ascertained the direction the train had taken, I realized that they had taken exactly the route I told them not to. They were heading straight for Sankabar.

Ashamed, I went back and told the others. I should have known better than to trust the damn game guards. We had no food, and we were hungry. It was too late to retrace our steps to Debarek, and anyway, it was as far from the Angoba to Debarek as it was from the Angoba to Sankabar. We started walking.

Stars began to climb up the darkening sky. There was no moon. We had no flashlight. We stumbled through the dark for a couple of hours, passing a village. Dogs barked. I called, but for a long time the people stayed in their dark houses, afraid to come out. Eventually, some men did come out, and after a hassle which lasted thirty minutes, I bribed three men to show us the way as far as the Michibi meadow, where I knew the path well enough to be confident of it in the dark. I did not know this part of the plateau well enough to lead people in the darkness, for there were steep and dangerous cliffs all around, dropping off without warning, and the trails branched confusingly.

I was younger than the others, and they had been traveling from Addis Ababa since the early hours of that morning. None of us had eaten lunch or had any kind of food since the tea and bread of that morning. Major Downes had been suffering from a stomach upset, and he was exhausted, in a cold sweat. The paths were rocky, steep, and black as hell. We skirted cliffs and maneuvered horrific paths in the darkness. It was an unpleasant introduction to the country for the two visiting officers. Our guides kept up an insistent, high-pitched, infuriating barrage of comments and questions, nearly none of which I could understand. But nobody complained.

I don't know exactly how many hours we walked through the

darkness, but it was five or six, or more. At last we came out onto the Michibi meadow, and we threw ourselves onto our bellies and drank the water from the stream greedily. Our guides began to agitate for their money, but in hoarse whispers, for they were afraid of hyenas, which were known to kill horses here.

A horse snorted somewhere across the stream. I heard a low voice, and shouted a greeting. It was our men and mules. They had stopped here at Mesfin's command as soon as he discovered that Guard Berehun had decided that it would be better if he ignored my orders and came by the normal route.

Mesfin had asked him several times if the road they were taking was the route described by the warden, for he had seen no red paint marks on the rocks. When they arrived at Michibi, he knew that there was not going to be a big bridge here, and he asked Berehun again if this was the route of the proposed road. Guard Berehun, the incredible, buck-toothed fool, finally admitted that this wasn't the route. He could give no reason for misleading them, and only nodded, saying, "Yes, lord, that is true, that is true," when Mesfin got angry with him.

Taking the stupid guard with him, Mesfin went back to search for us. By this time it was dark, and we were stumbling toward the village.

At Michibi, I unlashed the grub box, the camp beds, the mattresses and sleeping bags, and set them up, urging Major Downes to get into his bag while I brewed up hot, sweet tea and a makeshift meal. John Blower found and opened a bottle of Scotch. Ah, nectar! We would sleep under the stars, for it was too dark and we were too tired to try pitching the tents.

Mesfin came back very, very late, picking his way carefully in the darkness by the weak yellow light of a hurricane lamp. He was greatly relieved to find us, and was so furious with Guard Berehun that he could hardly speak to him. Mesfin was an efficient man in the field, and this affair had wounded his pride, especially knowing that two visiting British officers and the senior game warden had been inconvenienced and even placed in danger. I got up, heated the tea, and told Mesfin to forget it, but promised that this fiasco would cost Berehun a month's pay.

It was hard to get up in the morning, with the frost on our sleeping bags. Colonel Randle had to go back to Debarek. I sent a guard with him and apologized profusely for the terrible night, trying not to make too many excuses. Colonel Randle laughed and said it was nothing, and inside I felt rather proud, for although he was not a young man, he was a British officer, tough and cheerful, and it made me feel good. Major Downes was in good spirits too, anxious to get on with the walk.

When Major Downes, John Blower, and I reached Sankabar, Major Gizaw was in the house. Apparently he did not intend to go up to Geech, but had sent word for the village elders to come down to the Sankabar camp to talk to him.

By the afternoon, over fifty men had gathered at our camp from the surrounding villages. They wanted to hear the words of Major Gizaw, for he was an Ethiopian, and a big man, and held authority over the foreigner and his soldiers. The Major was to tell them about the cutting of the forests, to explain that it was against the law, and why. He was also to explain to them the reasons for establishing a park here, and by what authority it could be done, and how it could benefit them and their country. I had explained all this, but why should they believe me, a foreigner?

Major Gizaw talked to the people, and they asked questions and argued a little, and at one point he conceded, according to later reports, that the villagers could cut "small trees." They seized upon this business of the "small trees," and the word spread rapidly all over the Simien. They took it to mean what they wanted it to mean. To the peasants, the great weeping cedars and spreading sycamore and fig trees around the churches and mosques were big trees, and "small trees" came to mean any of the highland species; the giant Saint-John's-wort and the giant heather. Yes, these trees were small, for were not the great trees on holy ground much bigger? And if the Major says we can cut the "small trees," what right has this foreigner to try to stop us?

The elders also raised the question of jackals and hyenas. They said that the government must help them to protect their cattle and sheep from these predators. (In the Simien, both these animals were predators, as well as being scavengers, for the jackals killed sheep and goats, and the hyenas killed horses, donkeys, mules, and cattle.) Major Gizaw called me and told me, and I said that if I had time and reliable people to assist me, I would try poisoning the jackals and hyenas outside the park area, if he thought it would do any good. But at the same time I suggested that it might be a good idea if the villagers did not forever let their domestic stock wander unprotected through the woods, especially in the park area where they were a damned nuisance. There were outcries of rage at this. "Screw your bloody cattle," I thought.

As soon as he had finished his talk, Major Gizaw had his mule saddled and left, while game guards trailed him along the path with their complaints and petitions, and while he kept repeating that they should take everything to the game warden, and that he had so much work to do in Addis Ababa that he had to hurry back. I asked when he would come back and suggested that when he next came he should bring his wife and stay here for a few days to really see the Simien. He assured me that he would like to do this and that it was very likely that he would, after the road was built. But, he added, he might not be coming back here as the general manager (i.e., director) of the Wildlife Conservation Department. So it was as we all thought. There was going to be a change sometime. But when? And would it do any good? Would the new director be any better? Or could he be worse?

Going down, the Major passed four visitors on the way up. The visitors were two ladies and two men, all English. They had come to look over the possibilities of hotel building and tourist development in the Simien, and were employed on contract by the Ethiopian Tourist Organization. One of them, Robert Marshal, was a well-known architect, who had designed some of the best tourist lodges in East Africa.

By this time, Major Downes had told us that it would probably take about six months to get a rough road into Sankabar from Debarek, but that to take the road on up to Geech would take much longer and would cost a lot of money. I had always said this anyway. Major Downes could not say much more about it, but we were all very optimistic.

We took our guests to the top of Michibi Afaf, on the proposed border of the park. This point was at ten thousand six hundred feet and commanded a breathtaking view of the lowland hills and of the escarpment to the east and west. There was water nearby, and it would be easy to get a road into the site if the access road was going to be built from Debarek to Sankabar. Round about were pleasant little hills and knolls, with many Afro-Alpine flowers and plants, and coppices of highland trees. The meadows were fine for riding or walking, and there were some good spotting points for Walia ibex. The site overlooked the park camp at Sankabar, and although it was not too close to be a nuisance, it was not too far away to inconvenience a guest who might have business with the park officials.

Below this peak there was a magnificent virgin forest of olive, cedar, and other trees, one of the last forests of this kind left in the Simien. It showed how the area looked a hundred or two hundred years ago; the place at the bottom was called Adermas, which means "the place of the elephants." The last elephant was said to have been killed there eighty years ago. Now only leopard, bushbuck, colobus monkey, and wild pig were left, but with care and protection, no doubt other animals could be reintroduced.

But we would have to act quickly. From Michibi Afaf we looked down on the tin roof of the house of Bogale Mersha. Bogale was the owner of six rifles and a pistol, and he had six sons and henchmen. He had moved to the sloping terrace just below the escarpment only seven years before, and in that time he had cleared over six square kilometers of forest. A friend of Bogale's, a priest, had also moved in, and he too was felling and burning. Bogale had either threatened or ignored all our lowland patrols, and had told Guard Tedla that he would kill any man who interfered with him or his land. Bogale was a close friend of Dejasmatch Araya, and besides that, the guards said that the bandits who sometimes ambushed the cars and trucks along the Asmara road always called on Bogale, and could be enlisted to fight for him if he called them. John and I would call on him.

The tourist development people were delighted with the site and said that the Simien seemed to have the greatest possibilities of all the places in Ethiopia. I could imagine a hotel here, just a pleasant walk from my house. It should have great wide windows to watch the scenery, and from a comfortable chair one should be able to look at some of the most fantastic and changeable scenery in the world. I could just see myself sitting by one of these windows in clean clothes after a good day, watching the setting sun striking the hills and drawing out the shadows, and sipping a cool drink, making conversation to interested, interesting people, nonchalantly letting them know that I was indeed the warden of this fabulous place. Ah, was it only a dream?

Riots and a robbery

Major Downes left, but our four other guests, John Blower, and I went on up to Geech. That night, in Swiss House, I got drunk. It had been a grueling day for me, for I had been trying to make sense out of the guards who had been in camp at the time of the robbery. The others went to bed early, and I sat alone by the fire; I could hear the ladies, Mrs. Wales-Smith and another beautiful English girl called Leila, giggling in the adjoining bedroom. I was in a whimsical mood and recited nonsense poetry and sang foolish songs. A bottle of vermouth, a bottle of gin, and the remnants of a bottle of Scotch were challenging me. I could not have gone to sleep, for my mind was in a whirl. Optimism and dreams about roads, animals, and plans for bringing in animals to reintroduce into the park jousted with worries and frustrations over political corruption, stupid guards, and obstreperous peasants and chiefs. It was a warm and merry time that I spent in front of the fire, and the tide in the bottles receded, and the house was in a glowing haze, and I watched the dancing flames in the fireplace, and felt good and bad, happy and sad, all at the same time.

Despite the excesses of the previous night, I woke early in the morning. After swinging a fighting stick for about twenty minutes, I went and doused myself in the icy stream. The guards were wandering around, getting ready. John and I would take our guests to see the view from Metagogo, and then we would leave on a ten-day patrol around the foot of the escarpment.

The rolling golden moorland was strange with scattered ranks of tall, still lobelia plants, carrying their ruffs of spear-bladed leaves. As we walked and chatted, I enjoyed the feel of the tall, coarse grasses against my legs. Then I saw the awful blackish-gray smoke-mushroom, towering up several hundred feet above the escarpment and spreading in a slight morning breeze. Forest fire. A big one.

We hurried to Metagogo and stared down with horrid fascination at the huge fire which raged up the cliff faces and steep, wooded slopes of Sederek. This fire was one of the biggest I had seen at the foot of the escarpment. Even though it was at least three kilometers distant, the roar of the fire throbbed among the curving cliff walls. Orange flames spread in sheets through the forest, snake-tongues leaping and dancing through the top branches, racing all the way up to the narrow ledges on the sheer cliffs, firing bracelets of tussock grass, already scorched by the heat and dry as tinder. The heat on the cliffs above the fire must have been tremendous, and I knew, and John knew, and all our men knew, and the villagers who set the fire knew, that these cliffs had been a favorite habitat of the Walia ibex.

It was the people from the Moslem village of Antola who were responsible. Only a week or so before, one of our patrols had gone through and had warned them not to touch the forests. Yet they had cut the trees, let them lie on the ground and dry for some days, and then set fire to them. The fire had spread up the slopes, which were so steep as to make it impossible for a man to walk straight up, unless he went on hands and knees. The cliffs chimneyed the heat, smoke, and flames. How many Walia females and kids had been on those cliffs? Had they escaped? And how many eagles, falcons, ravens, lammergeyers, doves, chats, and other birds had been on the cliffs? And how many klipspringers? And now that the protecting cover was destroyed, how long before the rains would wash the pitifully thin, centuries-gathered soil from those steep, rocky inclines?

John and I took many photographs. We intended to show them to the Minister. But I knew it would do no good. Our guests gazed at the fire and shook their heads. As I had said, the destruction of the Simien was going so fast that if action was not immediate, strong, definite, and permanent, the worth of the place as a national park would be gone. If this sort of thing continued—and now that they saw it for themselves, the fact was brought strongly home—there would be no point in advising anybody to put any money into a hotel here. John shook his head and cursed. He had read my reports and knew that I was speaking the truth, but this was a vivid demonstration.

"You see," I said with sarcasm, "this is what the Ethiopian officials continue to accept as my imagination. That is a grass fire, they will say. The bastards do not choose to believe me. They only believe the Dejasmatch."

Through binoculars, I could see tiny man-figures running around at the foot of the fire, carrying and spreading it further. Seized with rage I fired a couple of shots down at them, hoping that the hiss of the passing bullets would make them aware that somebody was watching. They knew damn well that this was illegal, but they had been urged on by local chiefs, headmen, and governors, who would get a few years' tribute in barley from the eroding soil before it was gone and bare. Almost two years of talking, patrolling, and beseeching had achieved nothing. Nothing.

The rifle shots echoed and re-echoed, and drew themselves out into a whisper lost in the steady roar of the forest fire.

We said adieu to the visitors and set off on our long trip. We would call on the villagers of Antola. Mr. Wales-Smith promised to see Colonel Tamurat, the Governor General, and tell him of the fire and of what it would mean to the future development of the Simien as a park if this sort of thing went on.

John strode down the tussocked slope on his long, green-shorted legs, and I followed him, down into the head of the valley of the Djinn Barr, just below Metagogo, where our donkeys and the game guards were waiting for us. I didn't look back at the giant smoke-mushroom.

16

THE LOWLAND BOUNDARIES

It began to drizzle as we came over the Amba Ras and looked down into the huge, steep-sided valley of the Balagas. At this end of the valley there were no trees left, and I counted about a hundred and fifty round houses clinging to the plowed, eroded slopes. We had hoped to reach Chenek, at the head of the valley, but it was getting dark. We had to camp somewhere, and this was a problem, for the sides of the valley were steep, and we were forced to keep to the path. We marched for a long time before we could find a level space. The valley was a depressing sight, so bare, so eroded, all brown-gray and filled with an atmosphere of poverty. Within living memory the valley had been thick with forest, full of game. The grazing had been good, and the people kept fine hives in the high forks of the trees and took much honey from them. The valley was stepped with sheer cliffs, and Walia had been numerous on them. Now there was nothing, only flocks of barley-eating doves and crows and vultures, and the odd jackal, and myriad grass rats.

Halfway to Chenek, we passed a rifle-bearing man on the path. He wore an army raincape of the type issued to our game guards. This type of cape could not be bought, and our men were the only men in the Simien to be issued with them. I stopped the man. "Where did you get this cape? It belongs to the government. You are not a government man."

The man sneered, and answered, "Agafari Nadu gave it to me," and then he turned and went on his way.

As we came up above the frost line, at the head of the valley, the agriculture gave way to tussock grass, alpine flowers, and lobelias.

The lowland boundaries

A few groves of tree heather were standing, and a clean stream babbled over its rocks and pebbles. This was Chenek. In the future, we hoped to build a rest house and guard post here. Chenek was an important control point, for it commanded the head of the path leading down into the lowlands and was also on the route to Ras Deschan, the highest mountain in Ethiopia. Many tourists passed this way. Chenek was on the edge of the proposed boundary. From Sankabar it was a full day's march, through Amba Ras, Nadu's village. It took two days if one detoured through Geech.

Not so long ago, this path had been another notorious ambush place. For hundreds, perhaps thousands of years, this route had been used by the trading caravans crossing over the Simien. There were only a few places where a donkey or mule could scale the mighty escarpment. Merchants were forced to take this path, and robbers, often from neighboring villages, would ambush them. The robbers were rarely caught, for there were so many escape routes, and there were no police. If we built a control point here, with a handful of armed guards, I had no doubt that the people would have been very happy, as they were when we built a control point at Sankabar. That is, before Nadu began agitating against us.

On the approach to Chenek from Amba Ras, one climbed up a narrow path, very close to the cliffs. However, for a time, the sight of the drop was hidden by a long bluff or outcrop. But along the way there was a seven-meter-wide gap in the rock, a sort of natural window, letting out onto a sheer cliff which dropped for a few hundred meters, then tumbled in a series of drops for a thousand or more. It was a beautiful, horrifying place. Through it one could see a fantastic view of ambas, cliffs, spires, peaks, and hills. It was right at the edge of the path, and the suddenness of it was terrifying. It was called Korbet Metaya, and it was a place of horror, sadness, and ghosts for the local people. The bodies of many had been hurled out through this gap by the bandits. The last murder occurred only two years before, and up to seven years ago ambushes had been common.

Now the bandits were gone, or greatly reduced, and it was said that Nadu had been responsible for clearing them out. Nadu was a strong man. The bandits feared him. I took photographs through the rock window, but it was dark and gray, fitting the mood of the place; the photographs turned out dark too.

Before descending the steep, winding path, we stopped at the top of the cliff to rest and tighten the lashings of the donkeys' loads. The wind at the edge was cool and refreshing, and we stood to look out and down. Guard Zeleka sat with his legs dangling over the cliff rim, looking down with binoculars. Voices were coming up the path. Zeleka cried out that the voices belonged to two of our men returning from a patrol.

Sweating from the climb, guards Nagur and Kebede saluted and gave their reports. Two Walia ibex had been shot and killed by Amba Ras people on these cliffs some two weeks before. The guards had been to all the neighboring villages, but nobody would give information as to who had done it, though it was obvious that they knew. The people were afraid to talk. However, the poachers came from Amba Ras, and that was Nadu's domain. If a man brought back meat or horns, anybody would know what it was and the word would get around. There was in the village probably not a single man of twenty years or over who had not eaten Walia meat. From the time of the war, and until quite recently, they had been killing off the Walia for meat and horns. (The horns were molded, after softening in boiling water, into fine, tall drinking cups.) If this report of poaching was true, and I believed it was, then Nadu must have known about it. He had been boasting that if he did not protect the Walia, then they would be killed off. Nadu himself had shot at the rare, protected Simien fox in front of other guards in the park area, and I was sure that any Walia-poaching being done was being done with his full support and approval, if not at his urging. No man in Amba Ras would dare touch a Walia without Nadu's approval. He was known to whip men who displeased him, and to lock them up in his own private jail.

The guards told us that shots were being heard quite often now. I nodded grimly. I had heard shots around the cliffs myself. I had expected and predicted all of this. Nadu had been allowed to get the upper hand, and he was now confident that he could do anything.

The two guards returned to Sankabar with a message for Mesfin to join us at the bottom of Chenek. Mesfin had taken Major Downes to Debarek. He was badly needed, for with my lousy Amharic and Zeleka's army pidgin we were not going to get far in our meetings with the village elders. John and Zeleka both spoke Swahili, and that helped, but I was not sure if we could express ourselves well and lucidly enough to the stubborn, argumentative peasants.

At dawn, the shadow of a far line of hills moved slowly down the cliff wall behind us. The size of the cliffs was overwhelming. From the bottom, looking up, the cliffs are so high that they seem to be a part of the heavens; they seem to lean over, threatening to crash down and swallow you up. The cliffs dominate the sky and call to mind magic worlds and giants' castles. Looking up with binoculars I could recognize outcrops of rock near the top which were higher than city blocks, yet from down below they were mere points. Photographs cannot capture the feeling of the Simien, one negative cannot convey the sheer size of those cliffs without dwarfing and compressing it in the lens.

After breaking camp and packing up, we called the village people together, and John gave them a lecture, telling them that if they did not stop this cutting and burning, and interfering with the Walia, the government would be forced to move them out. He also said that if they cooperated, then the government would help them and give jobs to the men of the village. It was a long speech, but I had said it all before. The people made the usual promises, which I now knew they had no intention of keeping.

By late afternoon the next day, the rising of hot, moist lowland air against the cliffs had caused thick clouds to gather at the head of Amba Ras and Metagogo and spread, darkening, along the whole of the escarpment top. Lightning had begun to flicker and stab at the rims of the cliffs, and the thunder rolled like the drums of the gods in this massive sound chamber. The storm broke as we reached the village of Torowato, and the rain drove down, stinging us, making donkeys dash for cover. John and I marched on, marveling at the ferocity of the storm, and at the dark clouds which piled up against the escarpment, rolling, twisting, changing shape, giant sky-dragons with forked tongues and god-voices. To the north, the sky was clear, and there was brilliant sunshine, but the clouds were dark, overhanging eaves of the escarpment, and it was cool, slightly chill. We could hardly hear for the noise of the thunder.

We retraced our steps the following day to take photographs and estimate the extent of the destruction of the forests below Metagogo and Amba Ras. Then we went on to Antola, passing the remains of the forest fire which we had seen from the top.

Our camp was made here on a wide, grassy terrace dotted with hagenia and fig trees. It was about seven thousand feet above sea level here, and pleasantly warm. As dusk fell, Mesfin caught up with us, having climbed down by a path near Sederek with old Guard Kasahun. We were glad to see him, and celebrated his arrival with drinks.

Sunset gave us a fabulous view of silhouetted dog-tooth hills, and of distant flat-topped ambas, tall spires of old volcanic plugs, and the looming wall of the great escarpment, tinted with delicate pastel colors of the setting sun.

I had sent for the chief, wanting to talk to him and arrest him if need be, but villagers came to say that the chief was not in the village; he had gone to Debarek to pay taxes.

The villagers seemed to be avoiding us, and in the morning I went with Mesfin and the guards to the middle of the village and stood waiting while the guards went around the houses, shouting and bullying the men out.

Sullenly, they gathered. I berated them for disobeying the laws and firing the forest, even though we had warned them before. I warned them that nothing but serious trouble would come of this, and that we were going to bypass the local officials and take the matter directly to the Minister. Fourteen men had been responsible for the destruction. They argued in the obtuse, ambiguous, and infuriating manner of the Amhara peasant.

"We wish to plow the land for farming, not to destroy forest."

I pointed out that to plow the land the forest stood on, they always destroyed the forest first. They insisted that to destroy forest was not their intention, that to plow land was their intention, and some of them tried to twist the argument further to say that they had not actually destroyed the forest, they had only cleared it for farming. We pointed out that we had seen and photographed the cutting and burning. A man called Alem Worota sneered and said, "If you tell us not to cut the forest and plow the land, you must give us other land!"

This was what I hoped for. I told them that we would suggest to the government that different land should be found for them; then they could be moved away from here. However, if they wanted to stay, they had better not cross the government, and they had better obey the forest laws. The older men glared angrily at Alem;

they did not want to move off their land. Some of the older men promised that they would cut and burn no more. Then others asked if they might plow the land already burned. I refused outright, and said that if they touched that land they would all go to jail. At this they said they had nothing to eat, which was probably true, for their land was so badly eroded that it could barely support anything. Telling them that the steep slopes they were destroying now would only give them a few years' crops would mean nothing to them and achieve nothing. These peasants cared only for the present, not for five years hence, and if they were good Moslems, they could be assured of a place in Paradise. If the land gullied and washed away in the rains, then it was the Will of God, and not theirs to question.

We marched on, stopping to talk at every village along the route. At each village the story was the same. The people claimed not to know the law, despite the patrols. No high-ranking government official had talked to them.

There was no game. With the exception of baboon, the rare timid klipspringer, bushbuck, or colobus, the game had been killed off or had gone with the habitat.

At one village, I saw some fine trees that had been bark-ringed and killed. I asked why they did this, and a headman said that they cut the bark to bleed the tree for resin, which they used to make glue. I asked then if they wanted to kill the tree, and they replied no, there were so few of these trees left. With my knife, I showed them how to make a sloping cut in the bark of the tree, such as the rubber gatherers use. I took an old can and showed them how to fix it at the bottom of the cut to gather the resin. The villagers marveled at my wisdom.

"Ah, lord . . . that is a wonder. You know many things. That is very good, very good."

I asked if they would do it this way now, and not kill the trees.

"No, lord, it is not our custom to do it that way, in our country . . ."

After five days' marching we reached the Sanka Valley and made a camp at six thousand three hundred feet, by one of the loveliest streams in the Simien. Waterfalls over great, smooth rocks made pools, some of them deep enough to swim in. In the valley bottom, tall trees with vivid red blossoms carried round hives in their forks.

Swallowtailed butterflies were plentiful, and there were birds and semitropical plants. The descent into the valley had been dangerous. The donkeys had to go a long way around, but we climbed down a series of crude wooden ladders on the cliffs. It was a gorgeous valley. But in the past three years, half of the forest had been destroyed by the Moslem villagers of Muchila. Game Guard Dawd, who had died of typhus the year before, came from this village, and had reported nothing of the activities of his relatives.

During the day we had been treated to the sight of many beautiful waterfalls, gushing out from high rock spouts and hanging hundreds of feet in long silver ribbons. Any one of these waterfalls alone would have been a major tourist attraction in most parts of Europe.

In the warm sun of the valley John and I splashed about for a long time in the pools. I swam after a frog and caught it. Guard Mitiku was the only Simien man to take a bath, and Zeleka joked with him about it.

As we left in the morning, John borrowed my rifle and bowled a baboon off a rock. Villagers had been complaining about the baboons down here. Passing through the village of Muchila, Dawd's brother tried to give me a goat, but I refused it, for I was angry with these people for beginning to destroy this wonderful valley.

Another day's march brought us to the village of Shagné. Riflemen accompanied us, saying that there were sometimes bandits in the valley which we crossed, and that a man had been shot and wounded a short time before.

There were a few burrows on the way. I asked what they were, and the people answered that they belonged to an animal called an "Ouch." This animal, they said, was a wicked beast, and it would dig up the bodies of people in the graveyards and devour their flesh. None of the people could give a description of the animal that jibed, but they all said it came out only at night. I wondered about this beast for a long time, until I realized that it was an aardvark. I was able to confirm this later. Of course, the aardvark does not have the unpleasant habit of devouring bodies, but the peasants were adamant. I rationalized this belief of theirs by figuring that somewhere, at some time, an aardvark had burrowed in a graveyard and given way to jackals or hyenas, who do eat dead people. If this was the case, then the aardvark had been blamed for the work of hyenas. Aardvarks, as far as I know, are predominantly termite-eaters.

From the bottom of the Chenek descent to a river gorge just below Shagné, we had been passing through Moslem country. Now we were among Christians, and our Christian guards began to boast about the difference in hospitality. As we were setting up our camp, men brought us delicious gourds of yoghurt and earthen pots of talla and injera. They came around the camp to pose for photographs with their rifles.

I could look up to a tiny notch in the rim of the escarpment. This was the small meadow and hollow which hid my house at Sankabar. As I gazed up, I imagined how an explorer would feel if he were looking up there, and wondering if it were really possible for someone to live up there, so high, way up with the gods.

That night, under a big, spreading fig tree, Mitiku, who was a learned man, and very religious, told us again the legend of Kedus Yared, the Ethiopian saint who brought the evangelical books from Jerusalem on the backs of the Walia, one thousand and one hundred years ago. The local people believed this story implicitly, and we thought that it could help us. There were several monasteries and churches in the cliffs, some of them very old. If we could get someone like a bishop to reissue a statement about the Walia and the cliffs being sacred, it would do more good than a hundred laws.

The ibex always had special significance for Ethiopians. Once I saw a beautiful bronze figurine of an ibex, perfect in detail, dug up in Ethiopia. It was supposed to date from the times of the ancient Egyptian empires that had flourished in the south, beyond the mountains. I wondered what legends had been woven about the ibex before the times of Christianity.

By lunchtime the next day, we had reached Adermas. We camped in a deep, forested valley, by a stream, below the terrace on which Bogale Mersha lived. The game guards were slightly nervous. They had been to warn Bogale three times, and the last time he had threatened them.

Colobus monkeys, about six of them, moved in the high branches of the trees near our camp and looked down on us with mournful eyes. Their beautiful black and white markings were strikingly attractive against the green of leaves.

Once the camp was set up and we had eaten lunch, John, Mesfin, the two guards, and I climbed our way up the steep path to the terrace.

Seen close, the destruction was incredible. The place looked like a First World War battleground. Everywhere the ground was thick with hot ash, smoking debris, charred stumps, and partially burned tree trunks, lying about willy-nilly. Some of the felled trees had been sixty feet and more in height, and now they lay burned on the ground. I could hardly believe that a few men, with simple, blunt iron axes had felled so many huge trees. Cedar, olive, hagenia, Podocarpus, euphorbia, and many others. This year alone, Bogale and his sons and followers had cut and burned about three square kilometers of forest.

Angrily, we called for him, but he and four of his men had gone to Debarek.

The value of the timber destroyed must have been stupendous. And this fool had used none of it. He had not even taken some to his house to use for firewood. It was all burned on the ground. Wherever there was a big trunk, they had simply piled branches around it and kept the fire going until it ate through the log. Some of the large standing trees had been killed by fire around the bases.

As we walked to the charred, dying trees at the edge of the burned patches, verging onto the living forest, a beautiful bushbuck stepped out and stood poised for a few seconds before dashing, all golden and dappled, back into the trees. There were grivet apes and colobus there, and we saw a duiker.

Mesfin went into the house and looked around for traps, because we knew that Bogale trapped leopard here, although we had no proof. He found nothing.

I warned Bogale's son that we were going to make serious trouble for them, and that this matter was going to be taken to the Minister. We had taken enough photographs to convict all of them. I also warned him that to threaten my men was foolish. We represented the government.

Disgusted, angry, and sad, we turned to go back. I would have liked a good showdown with Bogale and all his men, and I felt cheated. I would dearly have loved to put my telescopic sight cross-hairs on him. Dogs threatened us from the houses, and I took out my pistol, inviting the people to set the dogs on us. They didn't, so I put the pistol back, and we walked along the path, with John in front. Suddenly, two dogs burst from a clearing by the side, darting through the gaps in a crude log fence. By the time I had cleared my pistol from its holster, John had spun round in a fighting crouch and slammed machine-fast shots into the dogs. One died a few feet from him, and the other scrambled away, yelping. My shot, much slower, hit the dying animal. John slipped his heavy nine-millimeter Browning automatic back into the holster and turned to me.

"That's enough," he said.

We went on our way. I was grinning, thinking of the astonished expressions on the faces of the guards behind me. A little farther along the path, John turned and said, "Do you know, I'm sure that dog was rabid."

"Yes, I'm sure it was," I agreed. But I wish it had been Bogale Mersha himself.

We followed the sources of the Zarema River out to the main road, dropping in altitude. It got very hot. All along the way the people had been cutting and burning the trees that sheltered the river, and the river was already below its normal level for the season. The land was so stony that it was absolutely useless for growing crops, so the destruction was willful, pointless, and stupid.

The river was full of silvery fish, and at noon we stopped for lunch and bathed.

It must have been great country for elephant, buffalo, kudu, leopard, and other animals, and we talked about how fine it would be if the park were developed properly, the people moved elsewhere, and we were able to reintroduce animals. We could set up lodges down here, and then we would have two parks in one. A highland park, with an Afro-Alpine flora and fauna, and a lowland park with more typical African ecology. And two different angles from which to view the escarpment and the animals that lived on it.

Where the trees had been spared, the scenery was fine indeed. Big trees spread cool green shadows, sometimes flashing with the vivid colors of birds like the touraco. Grivet monkeys were numerous. There were tall stands of bamboo and acacia trees.

The town of Zarema, on the main Asmara road, is at about four thousand two hundred feet. We arrived at one thirty in the afternoon and marched up the main road. People stared at us. John, Mesfin, and I all had the same thing in mind. Beer. In the nearest, scruffy, mud-walled and earthen-floored bar, we flopped onto rickety benches and swigged down Mellotti beer from bottles that had been kept cool in a tin bath full of water under the counter. The young harlot who served us stared with ill-concealed amusement and wonder at the two sweaty, dusty, sunburned foreigners.

It was Sunday, and there were buses. However, the malaria eradication people were camped in the town, by the river, and we hoped to persuade them to give us a lift up to Debarek. We had passed their Land Rovers parked under the trees. John and I went to see the officer in charge, rousing him from a Sunday sleep. John gave the man his card and explained who we were. We asked if he could give us a lift up to Debarek. We would pay for the gasoline and for any other expenses. I could see immediately that he was not the type to help anybody. A conceited young man with a rudimentary college education. He said he would not help us unless he had permission from his superior, and his superior was in Addis Ababa. It was no good pleading with him. Pointing to the USAID signs on his vehicles, I said I wished there had been an American in charge. He shrugged and went back into his tent to sleep.

We camped at the opposite end of the town, on the banks of the river, just below a fine stone bridge, adorned with Fascist symbols.

In the tree above where we wanted to put up our sleeping tent, the men saw a green snake. Zeleka took a .22 rifle and shot at it. The snake dropped to the ground and slithered rapidly away to a hollow in the bole of the tree. I shot the snake again with a pistol and pulled the body out. None of us knew much about snakes, so we couldn't identify it. We didn't think it was a poisonous type though. I wanted to take the skin, and had to argue with Guard Kasahun, who wanted to cut off its tail.

"If the tail of this snake is not cut off, the snake will grow wings in the night and fly off to find the man who attacked it. Once it finds him, it will kill him."

Mesfin laughed as he translated this, but Kasahun was serious, and predicted disaster when I would not heed him.

Old Kasahun and all the others were full of weird and wonderful animal tales. If Mesfin or I told them other things, they would refuse to believe us. They said that a hippopotamus defecated through its mouth, that a ground hornbill was the devil's horse, that there were "water sheep" in the Omo River, a strange woolly animal that looked like a seal, and of course, the usual African stories about all lizards being deadly poisonous. I had heard hundreds of these stories. The curious thing was that if I told them a fact about the biology of an animal, none of them would believe it, but if they heard some truly weird, supernatural story about the animal, they not only believed it but repeated it as gospel. On the whole, the people seemed very ignorant about the wild creatures living about them. Having lived and traveled with Eskimos, I found this curious.

We loaded our gear onto the roof of the bus and let the donkey drivers walk their animals back up to Debarek without any load. It was a noisy ride. The bus bristled with the rifles of the men passengers and smelled of the butter in the women's hair.

On reaching Debarek we tried to see Dejasmatch Araya, but he had gone to Gondar with his important guest. Mesfin returned to the Simien, and I drove John to Gondar. Throughout the last long and hot marches we had been promising each other cold bottles of Tüborg beer when we got to the Iteghie Hotel.

It had been, on the whole, a good safari. We had decided exactly where the lowland boundaries should run, and we had gathered a lot of information. John talked about trying to put together a pamphlet about the forest burning. He said that in twenty years in Africa he had never seen such destruction as this. I had been exhilarated by the possibilities and depressed by what was happening. We now knew that there was hardly any game left in the lowlands. In ten days we had seen only one bushbuck, one duiker, a few colobus, and some baboons and grivet monkeys. We were trained observers, and had game been abundant we would have seen much more. The number of rifles held by the people boded little good for the wild animals.

Disaster was surely inevitable for the Simien people. They had raped the land, the soil was impoverished and eroded away. Streams and rivers were dying and springs killed. Baboons were on the increase, together with rats and crop-eating birds. Already the people were barely surviving on what they raised. By destroying what remained, they could not last more than fifty years. Starvation, drought, and disease would cull off their numbers in the end. Surely it was better to have the people moved away now, while there was still time. A national park would benefit the country, and would be of lasting value.

If only the government would truly back us! If only the Emperor would openly show his support!

17

THE DECISION TO LEAVE

The villagers of Antola traveled two days to reach Debarek to talk with Dejasmatch Araya about the words of the foreigners. The old Governor listened to their complaints and pleas and gave a grandiose speech, designed to impress the villagers and all who gathered to listen to him. It did indeed impress them.

"Do they think they can stop the poor people from farming? Is this not your land, and the land of your fathers? The foreigner is here to watch after the Walia, and not to chase with his soldiers after poor people who wish to plow. Without barley, how can we live?"

Bogale Mersha came into Debarek with his men, and he too spoke to the Dejasmatch about the land, and the Dejasmatch said much the same thing to him.

The word spread around the Simien. The foreigner had no right to interfere with the people.

After all the fuss, charges, and complaints I had made against Nadu, the Wildlife Conservation Department once again made only a few false moves to make it seem that they were following up Nadu's case. They sent a man called Araya (no relation of the Dejasmatch) to Debarek to investigate and place charges against Nadu. This man was supposedly an assistant lawyer. In fact he was a game guard, and not nearly important or influential enough to do anything against Nadu.

The department also assigned a new chief guard to Simien, to replace Nadu. This man, also called Zeleka, though no relation of our ex-Imperial Bodyguard veteran, was renowned as a troublemaker, and had been kicked out of the other parks for inciting mutiny. Once he had pulled a knife on a British officer while taking part in an expedition, and nearly lost his life at the hands of an Ethiopian officer on the expedition who wanted to take him behind a bush and execute him with a .45. This man, Zeleka Asfaw, had a powerful relative or friend somewhere in Addis Ababa, so Major Gizaw could do nothing against him. However, Zeleka Asfaw, though he made trouble often, was known for speaking his mind, and was unafraid of big men.

Zeleka Asfaw was as much of a dandy as Nadu. When he reported to Mesfin and me in Sankabar he wore a tailored uniform jacket and a shiny brown leather belt with bullet pouches. His trousers and boots were of better quality than those issued to our men. He said that he was to take over the chief guard's job and to investigate Nadu's case. He said that the "assistant lawyer" sent from Addis Ababa had returned to Addis Ababa without placing charges against Nadu. Zeleka told us that this man had gone to see Dejasmatch Araya and had there been dissuaded. The old Governor was supposed to have asked, "Why do you want to charge Nadu? First you fired him from his job, and now you try to stop him from running for parliament. The case was a year ago (sic) and you should have charged him then. If you deter him from parliament, how can you run the park without him? If he is prevented from going to parliament he can kill you all and destroy all the animals."

What this Zeleka was telling us rang true. He had no reason to lie. Nadu and the Dejasmatch were as thick as thieves now, and it was known that the Dejasmatch was supporting Nadu. He had sent a letter to me, some months before, trying to get Nadu off, and had once tried to talk me out of pressing charges against Nadu.

And there were these reports of Walia killings, and the wild rumors about me and my men.

Zeleka reported the spread of an alarming rumor around Debarek. It was being said that the government in Addis Ababa had sold the Simien land to the foreigner. To me. This incensed the people. And recently the Dejasmatch had gone on a tax-collecting tour of the hills, but he had very carefully avoided the park area, even though the Geech people had been collecting money, some for taxes, some as a present to the Dejasmatch in the hope that he would do something to prevent the establishment of the park. I figured that Dejasmatch Araya did not want to show either open support of or open hostility toward us. Should he show himself to be openly against us, the government, and particularly the Emperor, would be displeased with him. He was an old fox.

This latest rumor about the selling of land to a foreigner reminded me of a story told to me by my Swedish friends. In another part of the Dejasmatch's district, near the Takazze River, the Swedish volunteers had begun to measure and lay out markers for a new school. A rumor was spread that the land had been sold to foreigners to build a hotel. One night some locals crept up to the tents and blazed away with their rifles. Only the Ethiopian site supervisor was around at that time, and unknown to the raiders, he had slipped out and was staying with a friend.

The two stories, of the school land and the park land, were suspiciously coincidental. I began to take very great care, and slept at night with a loaded pistol under my pillow. The German Shepherd Mogus was my guard.

About a week after John and I finished our lowland safari, Bogale Mersha and his men fought with another group of farmers, jealous of that sloping terrace. One man was shot dead. This kind of story was on my mind, and seemed to point to what might be developing for us.

However, there was nothing I could do at this time except get on with the building, be prepared, and hope that John could drum up support in Addis Ababa.

I was worried a lot about Tag too, for several guards had reported that "certain people" had told them that they would kill Tag. Tag was working hard, and driving his laborers to work as he did. He did not go out of his way to be polite to locals who were squabbling over who should work for him and so forth. Rumors about Tag were wild and dangerous, and I was sure that the ones responsible for starting them were our men. Tag was not popular with Nadu either, ever since he picked him up and threw him out of the door of my house.

To fully understand the problems of the village of Geech, bang in the middle of the park, a census had to be carried out. Mesfin and Kassa did this while I was in Japan. The people were suspicious, so at my suggestion, Mesfin and Kassa told them that they were gathering information in order to present the people's case to the government and to plead for relief, schools, and hospitals for them. This was only a half lie, and we didn't feel bad about it. For the interest of the reader, I set out some of the figures:

Geech village: 1967 to 1968

Total population	619
Adult males	148
Adult females	135
Children of school age	222
Children under three years of age	114
Children who were sick last year	87
Children who died last year*	49
Children born last year*	71
Children remaining alive of those born last year	61
Number of houses	122
Number of cattle	1,034
Number of sheep and goats	1,937
Number of donkeys	114
Number of horses and mules	37

* This would not include children born dead or children who died soon after birth, as these figures were impossible to obtain, owing to local superstition.

These figures opened my eyes to the desperate situation of the Geech people. And from what I had observed, heard, and recorded, I didn't think that the conditions would vary so greatly from one highland village to the next. They were surviving, but that is all. The death rate of the children was shockingly high. From these figures, presuming that the birth rate was roughly the same each year, it would appear that 70 percent of the children were dying before they reached adulthood. In one year, 87 children were sick, of which 49 died, and 71 babies were born and living, of which 10 died before they were one year old. Victims of typhus, tuberculosis, pneumonia, influenza, dysentery, and God knows what, all magnified by malnutrition.

I talked with our guards, and they all said how many of their own children had died, and how many of their brothers and sisters. One guard had lost six children, another five, others two or three.

To a wildlife man, the figures indicating the number of domestic animals living in the park were terrible too. It meant what was only too obvious to see, that the land was being overgrazed, hopelessly overgrazed. The Geech people, on the whole, kept their stock on an area of about forty square kilometers. Doing some rough calculations, I figured to the first decimal place that the Geech highland was supporting per square kilometer no less than 15.5 humans, 25.9 cattle, 48.8 sheep and goats, 2.9 donkeys, and 0.9 horses and mules. And on top of that, a few hundred gelada baboons, billions of grass rats, and a few wild ungulates. It was incredible to realize the pressure put on the land. Of course, in the dry season, the stock would decrease, either by being sold, or through death. Valuable plants were being exterminated, and inedible plants were thriving. Thorny Sodom's apple was spreading, and so were some types of coarse grass. The people burned the dung of the animals for fuel, not allowing even that to return to the life cycle of the land.

The Simien needed a team of ecologists to begin to sort out some of the problems that were going to arise.

Mesfin and I talked about what all this meant in terms of biomass and cover, and speculated on how the park would be if the village of Geech was moved, lock, stock, and barrel, and the land allowed to recover. Grasses and other plants would grow back, animals would invade and multiply. We could introduce wild animals, keeping a tight control on the balance. A few leopard and servals. Mountain reedbuck. Kudu in the Djinn Barr Valley, maybe even mountain nyala. The highland would become a small paradise of seas of long, waving grass, millions of flowers, delicate ungulates, gliding leopards, majestically stalking servals. The Walia would multiply to a couple of thousand on the cliffs, and would grow tame. It would be a beautiful, peaceful place up there in Geech, with no noisy cars, stinking fumes, ugly clutterings. It would be a place of peace and beauty for those who were willing to get up there, for the kind of people who would seek it. This was what I came here to develop, and the dream came back to me.

But neither Mesfin nor I believed, at that time, that the village of Geech could be moved.

We were building in Sankabar, trying to beat the rains. The warden's bath house was completed and functioning, and now I could treat myself to deep, hot baths as frequently as I could get

Abahoy to gather wood for the stove. We were building an annex to this, to make a store, and we were also improving the two guard houses now in use by giving them stone walls instead of wattle and poles. Mules, horses, and coolies were carrying in a lot of cement and tin roofing sheets from Debarek, but the rains had begun, and I doubted very much if we would continue to work much longer.

One day in Sankabar I received a visit from a missionary. He was a thin young Englishman, fired with extraordinary zeal. He had been traveling by the cheapest possible means all over Africa; a sort of hitchhiking evangelist. I invited him in and gave him tea. He had brought hardly any food with him, and was expecting to stay and live off the local people. When I suggested he stay in Swiss House, he complained that our charge for a night was excessive, although it was less than one American dollar. I did not want him to try to scrounge off the locals, so I gave him a few eggs and some barley bread to see him through the night. I also warned him that I would take a very dim view if he distributed his tracts around Geech. Geech was of the Islamic faith, and the last thing we needed was for the people to feel that we wanted to interfere with their religion. Any foreigner coming in was presumed to be an agent or relative of mine, and I was ultimately responsible for what foreigners did in the area.

I was quite prepared to have the missionary arrested and thrown out on his ear, and I warned him, which pleased him little. When he left, a guard trailed him to make sure he didn't make trouble.

When he came back down, it happened that Mesfin and I were due to make a trip to Gondar. We traveled down together. He was a nice enough fellow, though I am suspicious of people who seek to change somebody else's religion without first getting to know and understand what it is all about. Once out of the park area he began to hand out his tracts again. He did not understand Amharic, and they were written in that language. When asked, he actually confessed to not really knowing what was written in the tracts, even though he had been giving out hundreds of them. What is more, they had been printed in South Africa. We watched some illiterate farmers take tracts from him.

"What is this?" asked one farmer.

"It is a paper," said his companion. They both sat down on the grass and looked at the paper, first upside down. Mesfin and I were seated too, eating a lunch of barley bread and cheese. Mesfin showed them the right way up.

"You know, they will probably put it on the wall of their house, and be quite happy, even though they don't understand. They like pictures."

Later, along the path, the wandering missionary and I had an argument, for I suggested that there were many ways to skin a cat, and limitless pathways to God.

In the meadow just outside Debarek, there were thousands of mushrooms. Taking off my sweater, I tied the sleeves to make a bag and filled it with mushrooms to take to Gondar to share with friends.

We had many things to do in Gondar, so we stayed for three days. The roof rack of the Land Rover was broken and needed welding. I took it to a small garage and waited around until the job was finished.

In Gondar a group of four young men came down the road, two of whom I knew. They were students, doing a year of national service as teachers before their final year in the university. They came over to exchange pleasantries.

"Well, Mr. Nicol, how are things doing in the Simien?" asked one.

"Not too well."

"Why?"

I looked at them, and shrugged. "Oh, the usual troubles. No funds, no support, dishonest officials, apathy, people in office with no interest or responsibility—that kind of thing. You know about them. But I guess there are more important matters than national parks."

The students wanted to talk. They were bitter, angry, and frustrated. One of them had recently been in jail. One day during the student disturbances he had been walking down the main street in Gondar, and had remarked to his friend, "The law is not only for the Emperor and the police, the law is for everybody." He was overheard and picked up to be interrogated and beaten. Then he was let out with a warning. He was a small young man, with a shock of wild hair and an active, intense face. I knew of him because he had been asking Mesfin if we could give him help to bring a party of school boys into the Simien. All the students resented the restriction of basic freedoms, the strong censorship, the corruption and nepotism of the government.

About a month later we learned that this wild-haired young man boarded an Ethiopian Airlines domestic flight in Bahar Dar with a group of others, and with a pistol in one hand, a knife in the other, forced the pilot to fly to the Sudan. It was said that they wanted to go to China. People who knew him were shocked, and shook their heads, pitying him and his family. But there were a few who admired his courage, and drank to him. If steam is not allowed to escape from a boiling vessel, the vessel will explode.

The cities were still tense. I felt that trying to get anything done for the park was untimely, for the government was in the throes of a political and financial crisis, partly due to a change in the tax system, against which the people of Gojjam Province were revolting. Some people laughed the tenseness off, saying that it was just the seasonal madness of students.

✕✕✕✕

When we went back this time I took Mogus, who had been staying with a friend. The easy life in Gondar had made him soft. The long walk up from Debarek blistered his paws. It was good to have him back, and Abahoy and the game guards made a fuss over him.

As I had been in Japan for a month, spent some time fussing about in Debarek, and then come back to go straight on a long patrol, the problems of the guards had been neglected. The beginning of the rains brought a flush of sicknesses; many were caused by the damp and cold, but some had no connection at all. With Dr. Nievergelt gone, Tag and I were the only medics.

Guard Azezew had been off duty for almost two months. It was now said that he was dying of an infection of his nose, ears, and throat, that a lot of pus was coming from his ears and nose, that his neck was all swollen, and that he lapsed in and out of consciousness. The local magicians had failed to drive out the devils, and his grave had been prepared. His wife was already in mourning. Azezew had been sick on and off for a long time, but had refused to go to a doctor, preferring the village medicine men. When I heard about this, I sent off two guards with a lot of tetracycline, instructions on the dosage, and a message to say that I would hold the relatives responsible for his death if Azezew did not take the medicine. The memory of Dawd's death from typhus was still fresh in my mind.

The decision to leave

It took the men two days to reach Azezew's village. When they got there he was barely conscious. He took the antibiotics and made a miraculous recovery. Two weeks later he rode into camp. After a couple of brief words about God's blessings and his thanks, Azezew began to complain about not getting his pay for the two months he was absent. I said he would get the money if he went to a doctor and got a doctor's note, and I left him grumbling.

Guard Mitiku brought his youngest son to me. The child's penis was swollen and infected around the glans after a crude circumcision, done with a dirty knife. It was not much good being angry with Mitiku, for this was their custom, so I dressed the penis and fed the boy antibiotics. He came every day for cleaning and dressing. In ten days the swelling had gone down and the wound had started to heal.

On asking who had done the job, Mitiku hung his head and told me that it was Agafari Nadu. I swore. That bastard was everywhere.

Despite a total lack of medical training, Tag and I made some remarkable cures. I had picked up a smattering of first aid on Arctic expeditions, and had a little book, but that was all. A lot of our success was no doubt due to the fact that these people had not been stuffed full of drugs all their lives, so when they took a drug, it worked. But some of my success was due to witchcraft.

Guard Tedla came running one day to tell me that his wife was bleeding from her vagina and had started to have contractions. I went up and found her on a bed in the hut, groaning and writhing around. I felt her abdomen, but if there were contractions, they were not so strong. She was six months pregnant. She had been suffering with dysentery for a month, and it was my guess that this had something to do with the abortion that seemed about to take place. The people in the hut, guards and wives, looked at me with worried faces. I had to do something. She could not possibly go out to a health center. The only way would be by mule or on a stretcher, and this would be too long, too rough, and too dangerous. I paced around the hut. Both Kassa and Mesfin were away. I called Zeleka and asked him to help me explain. I did not want to use my bad Amharic.

"Zeleka," I said, "tell Tedla that I have some very good medicine, but this medicine is very, very strong." Zeleka told him and Tedla nodded.

"I am not a doctor, but my friend, who gave me this medicine, told me to be very careful. I am afraid to use it, because it is too strong." Zeleka told them and they begged me to try the medicine.

"If I give this medicine to his wife, he must not blame me. The medicine is so strong that if she takes it she will be unable to move. All pain will fade away, and she will sleep." They nodded as Zeleka told them. He was enjoying himself. He told them of the powerful medicine that soldiers have in the war when they are badly wounded. I said yes, that is the kind, only this is better, and is not given by a needle. I said that she would not be able to move, and would sleep, and her belly would relax and not push out the baby.

They pressed me to use this strong medicine, and after a show of doubt, I went back to the house and brought back some small white tablets that stopped diarrhea as effectively as half a bag of cement. With these I gave Entero Sediv, to work against the dysentery. Then, with a great show of concern, I produced the powerful medicine . . . two aspirin and an ascorbic acid tablet. After she had swallowed the other pills I told her to suck the Vitamin C tablet, and as she sucked it I told her that she would feel sleepy, that the pain would go, that she would lie still. I made her breathe the way my wife had to when she gave birth to our son, and I put a pillow under her hips.

Several times during the day I went up to give her medicine and to see how things were going. After three days, the bleeding had largely stopped. Two weeks later she was well enough to go down to the health station in Dabat. The dysentery was cured, and the unborn baby was doing well.

A few months later she gave birth to a fine, healthy boy, and I was as proud as if I had been the father.

✦✦✦✦

The clouds of the rainy season were marching over the hills, and Sankabar was increasingly damp and foggy. Guards there were forced to share houses, for the park money had not been given to us during the dry season, the time of building. By the time we got the money it was too late to build quarters. Sankabar boasted three guard houses. Two and even three men and their wives and children lived in a single house. The fog and the rain kept them inside, around the wood-burning stoves, and the women quarreled, and the quarrels were passed on to the men.

When Tedla's girl child became sick with dysentery again, four guards came to my house, with a secretive air about them, to tell me that the sickness had been caused by Guard Berehun. They said that Berehun had put the evil eye on the child, and on other people in the camp. They said that Berehun must leave or a serious accident would happen.

I saw the child, saw her stool, and began treating her for dysentery. Once again I admonished the women to use the latrines and to wash their hands in the bucket of disinfectant which I placed by the latrine. The women were worse than the men, and ignored my orders, so I roamed around after dark, when it was the custom of the women to go out into the bushes, and threatened that if I caught anyone not using the proper place I would treat them as a puppy dog is treated.

Zeleka ranted and raged at everybody. I discovered that they had been feeding the child on peppery wat and injera, so I prepared a dish of rice, milk, and honey, all sloppy and good. Zeleka fed it to the child, and the child loved it. For a week, rough, loudmouthed, war-hardened old Zeleka came down to my kitchen to cook up rice and milk and take it up to the child. Neither Tedla nor his wife, parents of the child, believed that such slop was good for her. But the child got better, and developed quite a taste for rice boiled with milk and honey.

However, although Zeleka accepted on one side the reasons for the sickness, the other side of him continued to believe that it was caused by Berehun's evil powers.

Gradually, things began to settle in the camps. It was early June when Guard Mitiku handed me a letter, much folded and creased, from the top pocket of his battle dress. It was a long letter, written in fine Amharic and stamped with a seal in the form of a large, ornate cross. Mesfin was living with me at this time, and he took the letter, asking Mitiku about it.

The letter had been given to Mitiku one year before. It was addressed to me and Nadu, and was written by a hermit priest who lived in a cave in the cliffs of the Khabar Valley. Mitiku said he was sorry, but he had forgotten to deliver the letter. Mesfin spread it out, and I copied his translation into my log book.

Greetings to Mr. Nicol, Agafari Nadu, and game guards:
From Sankabar to Debre Abo I have been protecting the forest, and accusing the offenders up to this day. Now, since I have been fasting and in prayer, I was told by people that the valley villagers are cutting and burning forest. I was very disappointed that you didn't stop this. At the beginning I was very glad that the Wildlife Conservation Department came here to protect the forests and the animals. Even more so was I glad that the Simien people have been employed to do the job. Let us now protect what is left. I need your help badly. If you do this task honestly, God will have a refuge for the animals. I think it is better to protect the forest first. For example, if a person raises cattle he has to prepare a barn for them, and for the wild animals, their barn is the forest. But if the forest is destroyed the land becomes barren, and the animals have to go away to another place. For this same reason, forest protection is most important. In the long run, the government is likely to visit this place, and will see what kind of protection has been given to the vegetation. The Forestry Department and the Ministry of Agriculture have always tried to tell the people about the law. They also let the people know that no tree is to be cut without permission. This should not be forgotten. But since the people do not take advice, frequent control is needed. Otherwise they will not stop breaking the law. Please answer my letter and tell me whether you can do this control or not. Then I will be able to report to the Ministry of Agriculture.
Aba Finote Salem Kalema Worq.

Mesfin looked up. "This is an excellent letter. He understands the problem."

"Yes, damn it," I said, thumping the table. "And this letter has been in bloody Mitiku's pocket for a year. He read it, and he must have known what it would mean to us. Now this priest thinks we don't care. This man sounds educated. He is a priest, and the people will listen to him. He could have been our strongest ally. Why the hell didn't Mitiku give us the letter?"

The decision to leave

But Mitiku could not explain his default. He apologized, and said that he was a foolish man. I asked when we could go to see Aba Finote Salem. Mitiku replied that the priest only came out of the cave on Sundays and on great church days. We could see him then.

The church was on the edge of the gorge. Below, on the cliffs, there was a narrow path leading to a cave. This cave had been used by holy men for centuries.

Aba Finote Salem, the hermit priest, was held in awe by the people. He fasted, spent his days in prayer, and endured great privations. He never slept on a bed, always on the floor. Christians from all around came to hear his sermons and to seek counsel. The highland people preferred the counsel of the priests to the dubious honesty of the town judges, and Aba Finote Salem was a very special priest.

When Mesfin, Mitiku, and I arrived, about a hundred people were gathered outside the church. The service was finished, and Aba Finote Salem was hearing out a land dispute. He sat on a chair, facing the people, while they sat on the ground. One old man stood to give his story, gesturing dramatically, and raising his voice in a high singsong.

This hermit monk was a young man. He wore a shirt of yellow silk, over which was a long, black cape such as all priests wear. Black, embroidered jodhpurs tapered to overlap a pair of brown leather city shoes. His hair hung down in long, untidy braids, and he wore a big black and yellow turban on his head. He was a bizarre figure, but his face was serene and handsome, and he looked on us with eyes that were deep and steady.

Mitiku bent to kiss the outer wall of the church. We sat and waited under a tree for the litigation to finish, and after a while an acolyte brought us a basket of bread that had been broken and blessed. We took it and ate. Mitiku said a prayer, but I noticed that Mesfin did not.

Quite unlike the scene at the court in Gondar, the people here were quiet and orderly in their litigation, and nobody spoke out of turn. Speeches were impassioned, yet not abusive, and throughout, the priest asked questions in his soft, calm voice, and one by one the men stood to answer him.

When it was all over, Aba Finote Salem came over to us. An acolyte brought the chair. Guard Mitiku stood, bowed deeply, and kissed the silver hand cross which the priest carried. He begged for forgiveness for not having delivered the letter until two days before. We rose and greeted the priest. Mesfin gave our thanks and apology.

For years, the forests in the Khabar Valley had remained unharmed. This hermit had protected the forest, for he loved it, and during his periods of fasting and meditation he would walk under the great trees, seeking herbs to eat, and to be close to God. Fearing his curse, the people left the trees alone, while all around, the land was cleared. But now more people were moving in from impoverished areas, and they were selfish and heedless of the holy man. Some of them were Moslems. When they began to fell the trees, the hermit complained and carried their names to the officials, who did nothing.

"This forest is holy," he said, "and must be protected, and the animals in the forest belong to God and must not be harmed or God will be angered, and great evil will come."

As we talked, I felt that for the first time I was talking to a hill man who could understand what I was saying. In his simple way, he could understand the delicate balance of nature and saw it as God's work. I asked him to help us, and to speak with the people, and he said that he would after the long fasts were over. Even as we spoke, the villagers were all around us, listening, and listening with respect. He made a sweeping gesture, encompassing the people.

"Our people are poor, and without education, and they do not understand the value of the forest and the wild creatures, even though I have tried to teach them. They must be taught, and if they do not learn, then they must be forced, but gently, gently. They are good people, and very proud, but they learn slowly."

This man, I was sure, could carry our words and reasons to the people in a form acceptable to them. The locals would not believe me, a foreigner, nor Mesfin, a city man. But they would believe this holy man. Had we received that letter when it was sent, a year before, a lot of trouble with the people could have been averted. Even Nadu would hesitate to speak against a man as respected as this one.

We went reluctantly, leaving a present of tea and sugar. He was going into his cave for a month and would not come out. He would have no contact except with the acolytes who brought his food and water.

The decision to leave

Villagers invited us for coffee. This had not happened for a long time, and I was very happy. We went through the yard of the nearest house, while a boy kept the dogs at bay and I tried to avoid the thickets of tall nettles around the house. We ducked under the stone doorway into a very large house. The high roof beams in the single room were black with wood-smoke tar, and long, dust-coated cobwebs hung and swayed. Our host ushered us to low olivewood and cowhide chairs. The women blew the coals to raise a flame and roasted coffee beans on the flat iron pan. While one woman pounded the beans in an old brass shell case, a girl served us yoghurt and roasted barley.

The owner of the house, a gray-bearded patriarch, was trying to convince Mesfin that it was the leopard that had killed off all the Walia, and that all leopards should be trapped and killed. I asked if the leopards in the Simien always wore gabis and carried rifles, and they all roared at the joke.

On the way home, we came across a lizard sunning itself in the path. With a curse, Mitiku reached for a stone to kill it, but the lizard scurried swiftly to safety. I said nothing. They were all convinced that these harmless, attractive lizards were poisonous, and nothing I said could produce any change.

✖✖✖✖✖

Abahoy had fried up some mutton and brewed coffee. Mogus strained against his chain, delighted to see me back. The fog began to roll in.

Night. Drinking coffee and sipping araki or whatever. Talking to the dog. Thinking of Sonako and the children. Writing purple passages in my log book about the waterfalls, especially the mighty waterfall of the Djinn Barr, which was one of the highest in Africa. Wind creaking a shutter. Cumulus clouds hurrying in fantasy shapes, great hulks of galleons and monsters across the sky. Me, stiff all over from too much exercise, mostly on the coarse leather, rice-filled bag which I used to punch, kick, and chop. Mesfin lying on his bed, reading a book.

Mesfin read more than any other Ethiopian I had met, more than most Englishmen too. We had been together for a few weeks, and had never had an argument. He was going to move up to Geech and live in Swiss House, which was now closed to visitors. He said he was thinking of taking a wife.

One morning a light aircraft circled us. We thought it might be a high government official and got excited. It circled low over our camp, and over Adermas and Shagné. Maybe Bogale Mersha got worried.

By this time, Bogale Mersha had plowed over the burned land. So had the Antola villagers. Could the plane have something to do with John Blower agitating in Addis Ababa?

Mesfin and I had to go up to Geech to pay coolies, get some administrative work done, look over the building, and talk to Tag, who was still working on his big house.

We found that the Geech people were seething with anger and resentment. As we went through, nobody cried out greetings to us, and the men gave us dark, ugly looks.

According to the guards, Dejasmatch Araya had been talking to them. He had told them that they would soon have to leave their land. They were simple people and could not imagine such a thing, and one man cried out that he would never leave his land, but would die and spill his blood into the soil that his fathers had tilled.

"Go ahead and die," said the irascible old warlord. "And then perhaps you will grow into a tree!"

Anger and worry filled me when I heard this. Although it was true that we wanted the Geech people moved out, the subject would have to be approached at a high level, and with extreme delicacy. If the reports were true, the situation could grow dangerous. Hopes I had been nurturing since the talk with the hermit dissipated.

The radio was out of order, and now we needed it more than ever. Tag and I spent a day fiddling with the charging engine and a new aerial. But it was no good.

As we worked on the engine, and had the parts laid out on the veranda of the Swiss House, a woman with a small baby came to us, accompanied by a tall old man. They bowed and mumbled honorifics. Tag left to go over to his house, and I called Mesfin to translate. The woman was a wife of Guard Ambaw Achanafi, and her father had brought her along from their village to complain that for a year she had received no support from her husband. I was surprised, for I knew that Ambaw had a woman and a small child living with him in camp, and that another woman, a third, was suing him for breach of promise. This third woman had been a Geech Moslem, but she had converted to the Coptic faith when Ambaw promised to marry her. After she had converted, thus separating herself from her family and friends, he had gone back on his word. And now there was this woman, with a child.

We called Ambaw and questioned him about it, although there was nothing we could do. We paid his salary every month, and made him admit this in front of his father-in-law. We told him that we thought poorly of a man who did not support his family. It was an ugly scene of bitter accusations and surliness. The woman, who was less than twenty, wore rags, as did the child which sucked on her breast. Ambaw said he had sent money via her brother, but nobody believed that, and he looked at the ground, his eyes shifting. I grew sick of it. I suggested that the old man come back with his sons, the girl's brothers, and I in turn would ensure that Ambaw had no rifle that day.

Our guards were the best-paid men in the Simien, apart from the masons who worked on contract for us. And in addition to their elevated government positions, these men wore uniforms and bore rifles. Most of them were regular Don Juans, seducing girls in all the villages, promising to marry them, escaping from their wives and children, and taking a new woman when they came to our camp.

Now that the people knew me, and knew that I never took bribes, I was regularly getting complaints and problems of this kind brought to me.

Ambaw, the young woman, and her father went away, shouting at each other. Ambaw had promised to support the child, but there was no reason to believe he would keep his word. I went into the house and sat staring at the work roster sheets. A hundred men, only a couple able to write their names. I started thinking about them, about the way they lived, and their poverty and the desperate life they led weighed hard on my thoughts. I could not get the image of the young wife and the breast-sucking, runny-nosed child out of my mind. Now she would go back to her village, live as a servant to her father and brothers. The child would probably never go to school or see a picture book or eat a candy. Anybody could see that Guard

Ambaw didn't give a damn. He had infected the woman currently with him with gonorrhea; had he infected the young mother too? Damn and hell.

I don't really know how long I sat there, head in hands, elbows on the table, thoughts jolting through my mind. Noise outside. Some boxes had been brought up from Michibi by horse. Half a day's journey. I paid the horse owner, and he began complaining, demanding money for two full days. Mesfin explained, but the man, a husky, handsome young fellow with an iron-tipped stick, refused to listen. For no good reason, rage suddenly rose in my gorge, and I grabbed the man by his neck and elbow and hurled him from the top of the veranda steps out onto the grass in front of the house. He picked himself up and raised the stick, but as I came down the steps he backed off, silent.

Tag, bless him, brought a bottle of bourbon over, and we all sat in front of the fire and talked of all manner of things. There had been so many visitors and guests that we had had little time to talk. We were all a bit depressed.

Dawn was a clamor of dreams which lingered long after wakening. That day I intended to talk with the guards about the positioning and designs of the new quarters. Mesfin and I walked over to their huts, and they came out, carrying their rifles. We started walking and talking.

Just in front of the guards' huts was a little wooded knoll. It had been arranged with rocks, grass, and a few old and twisted giant heather trees by nature, and it reminded me of a Japanese garden, though with no water. Then I saw them—four freshly cut tree stumps. With my knife I cut the bark back from the stumps and felt it. It was still damp with sap. Four trees, old and beautiful, had been cut just twenty meters in front of the guards' houses. My facial muscles tightened in anger. I asked who had done the cutting, knowing full well it had to be the guards themselves. Guards Atakult and Chane Takalé began to spew out justifications, excuses, and blame. I turned to Mesfin.

"Mesfin. Do me a favor and keep these men away from me for the rest of the day."

Slowly, I climbed back up the hill and crossed the stream to the Swiss House. For almost two years I had been teaching, preaching, pleading, cajoling. Now my own men had cut old trees right in front of their houses. They had been told a hundred times that if they needed wood to make something they should tell us and we would try to get it for them. We had a stack of eucalyptus up by the building sites. Part of their duty was to patrol the Geech highland and try to stop the villagers from cutting trees.

Slowly, as I thought, my rage subsided. And with the rage went a whole complex of feelings, hopes, fears, plans, designs, doubts. What I had tried so hard to do had failed. The Simien might be developed, but from now on it would not be me who did it. I made the decision then to resign.

✖✖✖

It was time to go down to Gondar again, and Tag had to go too. We stayed overnight at my house in Sankabar. We had a workout together on my punching bag and sparred around outside. Tag was fast and strong. Once in Addis he had floored the Ethiopian Olympic boxing contestant. We worked up a lot of sweat and wallowed afterward in the deep bath.

Once again, the long trip down. A quarrel with a mule driver in Debarek. Too much wine at dinner in the Iteghie Hotel. I stole a dozen rolls and went out with pockets bulging under the amused scrutiny of the waiters who knew exactly what I was doing. A night on the town with Mesfin. Tag in the hospital the next day with dysentery. And then, another, wilder night on the town with a Swede, him wearing Ethiopian national dress that had recently been presented to him. I had to wait two hours while he was out in the back somewhere. Talking about bulldozers and the price of sheep with a burly truck driver. Bats, dipping and squeaking around the lamp lights outside. Beggar boys huddled up by the wall and sleeping on the sidewalk. Letter from my wife and from John Blower and a new copy of *National Geographic*. Strange, tight feeling in my chest every time I thought about leaving the Simien for good.

18

BALLOT BOXES ON DONKEYS

"I can promise you this," said Colonel Tamurat, Governor General, "there would never be any chance of the Simien people shooting you. You have no need to worry."

"Perhaps you are right, sir," I said, "but the rumors in the Simien are getting wilder, and now that Dejasmatch Araya has been telling the Geech people that they will have to get out, the whole area is getting inflamed. These people will fight for their land if pushed too hard, and if they really thought that a foreigner was trying to steal it from them, well . . ." The Governor General nodded and picked up the telephone. He ordered to be connected up with the office of the police chief, General Seyoum. I had already handed a report to the police. I was now seeing the Governor General to inform him that I thought the rumors being circulated in the Simien could lead to violence, and as the police and government had not shown any support for the park project, I was alarmed. Everybody knew that a big robbery had occurred, yet nothing had been done. Everybody knew about the charges against Nadu, but nothing had been done. The peasants had been encouraged to kill game, to ignore our patrols, and to go on clearing land. No government official had really made it clear to the local people what was going on, and Major Gizaw's trip had been too short and too vague. I felt no confidence in the government and this was what I had been saying. I don't think that many government officials in this province put things as bluntly as I did.

When the telephone rang, the Governor General spoke briefly with Seyoum.

286

Ballot boxes on donkeys

"Please go over and discuss this case with General Seyoum. He is waiting to see you. When you have finished with him, come to talk with me again. I hope we can sort out this problem soon and make you reconsider your resignation." I thanked him, bowed, and went.

The agricultural officer came with me to the police headquarters. General Seyoum had not read my report yet, as it was not translated. Inspector Hailu, the officer who went with me when I picked up Tesfae and Mamo from the angry mob in Debarek, was working on it. Once we were ushered into the General's office, the agricultural officer was effusively polite. He never directly translated what I said, and lathered it with apologetic honorifics, but General Seyoum, though reluctant to speak English, had traveled in America and England, and had worked with British officers on the borders, and he knew what I was saying. He looked at me shrewdly. He was a big man, his head shaved bald as an egg. He had a reputation for toughness. When I finished, he spoke quietly. He said he could send police now, but it was the rainy season, so how could they travel; I shrugged.

"Well, sir," I said, "do you mean to tell me that your men are not as tough as mine? We travel all the time. It's our job."

He looked at me with no expression in his eyes. All right. The police would go. He would get the translation of my report by tomorrow and would see me again.

"You not resign," he said, extending his hand, and indicating that the interview was over. "You stay. This we can fix."

The next dry season, he told the agricultural officer, the police would establish an outpost to take care of all this sort of bother. We would work together. We thanked him, bowed, and left the room, with the agricultural officer bowing many times and thanking me and apologizing in flowery Amharic.

I saw the Governor General again the next day. He told me that Dejasmatch Araya had denied telling the Geech people that they would have to move off the land. That was not all. For two years he and Nadu, and all the other sub-district officials had sworn that the people did not cut forest, only the odd limb of a tree to fashion a plow or a roof beam. And I was told also that Major Gizaw had returned and had told the Governor General that he didn't see any forest-burning in the Simien. It was the truth in his case though, for he had not looked.

287

I passed some photographs of our last trip, photographs of the ravaged forest at Adermas and of the big fire near Antola, across the desk. The Governor General looked at them, nodded, thanked me, and gave them back.

"They have been lying, haven't they?"

"All you have to do, sir," I said, "is to take a light aircraft and fly anywhere in the province. You will see cutting and burning at any time in the dry season, anywhere where there is any forest left to cut. I have no reason to lie about this. Why should I tell you and the Minister that something is happening when it is not? Your officials have reasons. They are taking bribes from the people, or, like Nadu and the Dejasmatch, they have ordered their own servants to clear land for them and they wish to continue to do so."

The Governor General said nothing. He knew that I spoke the truth.

Just after lunch, at the Gondar Hotel, a thin Ethiopian approached me and asked in perfect English if he could talk. He knew my name and my job; and he introduced himself as Ato Berhanu Asarase, a cousin of Agafari Nadu. He had come to tell me, to warn me, that Nadu was a strong man, and would be capable of many things if I tried to prevent him from going to parliament. I listened to him, getting angry.

"Do you imagine that I am afraid of Nadu? I will fight him and anybody else who tries to block the development of the park." Then I said a lot of wordy things about the way it was with Nadu, Nadu's brother Negash, and me. When I had finished, Ato Berhanu began to talk.

"I have known Nadu since we were boys together. I was brought up with him. He is not a bad man. I did not know all of this, but I can tell you that a lot of the trouble being caused is not coming from Nadu himself. He does not understand what this national park business is about, and he sincerely believes that what he is doing is right for our people. On many counts he is wrong, and I admit that, but he is the right man to represent the Simien people in Addis Ababa, I can assure you of this. He is a good man, a brave man, but he is uneducated. He has been telling me that you have got something against him, and that you are trying to keep him from going to parliament. Don't try to do that. Let me talk with him. I promise you that I can make him see what is happening, and what you are trying to do for the area. Leave him alone now and I will vow, on my life, that he will not do anything against the park. This is our country, and the park will be ours. You do not understand Nadu, but I do. I will talk with him."

"Talking to Nadu is a waste of time," I said. "He will merely nod and agree and then do exactly what he thinks he should do. If this were an honest country, Nadu would have gone to jail. He takes bribes . . ."

The man put up his hands. "Are you really so naïve? You have been in our country long enough to know that there is hardly a single man who will not take a bribe. It is wrong to you, but not to them. You cannot judge him on this alone, but I will talk with him about it."

Thus we talked for over two hours, and I became impressed with this hollow-eyed, skeleton-thin man. He was direct and intelligent, proud but not arrogant. Ato Berhanu Asarase was educated at the Wingate School in Addis Ababa, a school to which only the most intelligent boys in the country go. Its teachers tour the countryside, giving examinations, so that even the poorest student, if he is brilliant, has a chance.

Following the attempted coup d'état, he spent five years in jail, though whether or not he was a revolutionary is not known, not by me anyway. He had come to Gondar to try to establish a cotton gin in the town, and was, among other things, trying to find land.

After I left him, some doubts and questions crossed in my mind. Perhaps Nadu was not entirely wrong, entirely bad. This man Berhanu was seemingly a man of influence, and he was backing Nadu. I suspected all along that I, Mesfin, and the Simien people talked on different levels, and that we could not understand each other. What was "bribery" or "corruption" to me was not at all the same thing to them. They thought in terms of presents and tokens of respect. But when we left, I said again, "I will fight anybody who tries to obstruct the park, anybody in this country—with only one exception, and it is by his decree that the parks are being made. Tell Nadu that."

General Seyoum had read the translated report, and had told me to meet him at eight in the morning in front of the police headquarters. Together we would go to Debarek and meet with the captain of the Debarek police and with Dejasmatch Araya. I rode in

General Seyoum's Land Rover, together with him, his son, Inspector Hailu, a corporal, and a driver.

On reaching Debarek we were ushered by the Dejasmatch into a room in the police station. It was a dark, cold place, with bare cement walls and no glass in the windows. Pigeons clattered and cooed on the tin roof, and diamonds of light shone through nail holes in the tin.

As General Seyoum read out the translation of my report, Dejasmatch Araya grew angry and tried to snatch it from him. At one point he shouted, pulled out his revolver, and laid it on the table in front of him. He glared at me, and I returned the stare, unflinchingly. General Seyoum spoke sharply to him, and he put the pistol away. When the reading was finished, the Dejasmatch burst into a flood of invective. With a slight smile, Inspector Hailu translated.

"It is all lies. Lies, lies, lies. He only sits in Sankabar. There are no Walia in Sankabar. His job is to guard the Walia, not to sit in Sankabar or Geech. The Walia are on the cliffs. He has two camps, but he should have many, all scattered around. And it is I who should choose who should be a game guard here, it is my responsibility to know who are the good men. Why does he not get out and guard the Walia?"

The old man raged on for a while, accusing me of neglecting my job. I could not see what this had to do with my report about theft and dangerous rumors, nor did I bother to try. I pushed my current field book across the table to Seyoum.

"This is my field book. Please look at it."

He picked it up and skimmed through the pages of rough, infield notes, patrol accounts, equipment lists, animal and bird sightings, sketches, rough maps. He passed it back to me.

"I know," he said.

He began to talk to the old man, who quieted down. I answered specific questions, and went over my plans for the park, the reasons for doing what I did, for placing the camps where they were placed. It had all been said before. I even suggested that they come and look for themselves to see whether or not there were Walia in Sankabar. It had all been said and written, many times before. Dejasmatch Araya began to praise me, completely reversing what he had been saying earlier. Nobody raised an eyebrow at this.

Ballot boxes on donkeys

Promises were made that after the rains, General Seyoum, Dejasmatch Araya, all the sub-district governors, and I would go up to the Simien and talk with the people. We would show them the boundaries. After this, the people would not bother me in the park, and I would not bother them outside the park. I nodded. At this stage, there was no point in arguing about a game officer's responsibility to all wildlife. I also pointed out that the boundaries we had drawn up had not yet been approved by the council of ministers. General Seyoum said that would not matter for the time being.

Finally, we got around to the subject of the big theft at Geech. Captain Asafaw of the Debarek police was called in and questioned. He emphatically and repeatedly denied having received a report of the theft. All I had with me was Tag's letter about the crime, plus a list of the missing stuff and the names of the men on duty at the time. The Dejasmatch also stoutly denied that this theft had been reported, although I myself had spoken about it twice. He reasoned that any report of such a large crime would have come to his notice, for he was in charge of the area. Yes, surely he would have heard about it.

General Seyoum looked annoyed. Clearly he believed the captain, and that I was making a fuss, when I was at fault for not having reported the theft. I called for Kassa, our clerk. When he came in I asked him if he had given a report about the theft, and he said he had, and that he had handed it directly to Captain Asafaw, who had signed it. The captain again denied it, calling Kassa a liar. General Seyoum stopped the argument. He glared at me, and spoke to Inspector Hailu, who said:

"The General says there is no report. You should have been sure that it was reported immediately. Now the captain will take the details and he will investigate."

"I have spoken to Colonel Azziz about this robbery. I have also spoken to Captain Asafaw and to Dejasmatch Araya. I was present when Major Gizaw asked the captain, and he said . . . oh, what the hell! Here, this sheet gives you the details. This is the serial number of the stolen rifle, here are the numbers of the camera and all that."

Now, they said, the police would investigate the crime. The security situation in the Simien would be ensured, and we would all work in close cooperation from now on. Now that we were on fairly amicable terms, we were all invited over to the Dejasmatch's house for a feast.

We sat around with a few drinks before the meal. Captain Asafaw was looking nervous. Kassa had left the station as mad as hell and was now looking through the files left here. Kassa came over to the house and was admitted by an armed guard. He brought a file with him. He handed it to me, and there were copies of Tag's report and the translation of the report. At the bottom of each was Captain Asafaw's signature. I stood up and handed the file to General Seyoum. Dejasmatch Araya said nothing, and pretended to ignore what was going on. The air was tense. Kassa was breathing heavily from having run up with the file. When General Seyoum looked up there was cold fury in his eyes. He spoke sharply to Captain Asafaw, who stood awkwardly and stiffly at attention. He ordered him to go and find the originals. The captain began to mutter about a lack of men, about too much work, about forgetting it, but General Seyoum spoke sharply again, and he hurried out of the room. Seyoum turned to me.

"I am very, very sorry; this is our man's mistake. He will be sorry."

The nervous captain was back in under ten minutes. Knowing the mess he'd put his office in, I had little doubt that he uncovered his file in an instant. He had known exactly where the file was.

I congratulated and thanked Kassa, who was now slandering the captain for lying, and for calling him, Kassa, a liar. Dejasmatch Araya said nothing, and avoided catching the frequent sideways glances of the now frightened Captain Asafaw.

We were called to the table by the Dejasmatch's wife. The table was spread with fresh injera and all kinds of wat. Servants waited with tedj and talla to serve us, and others brought legs of roasted mutton to be cut with the curved knives on the table. There were dishes of raw minced meat and of finely chopped stomach, liver, and spices. A bottle of Black and White whiskey graced the center of the table. I had by now developed a great love of Ethiopian food and ate like a hog, while the Dejasmatch, General Seyoum, and Inspector Hailu plied me with drinks.

It was not long before the old man had recovered his aplomb. He became jovial. The talk turned again to Walia, and the Dejasmatch said that the Simien people would kill him before they would kill this animal. Why, they knew His Imperial Majesty had ordered it to be protected!

From Walia, the talk turned to leopards. I ranted about the illegal trade in skins in Addis Ababa and Asmara, and said that I had been unable to find any dealers in Gondar, thanks to the police. I said the criminal dealers made vast profits, while the people made little, and I said that something had to be done about it. Dejasmatch Araya said something and they all laughed.

"He says that you are a troublesome fellow," said Hailu. "You make all this trouble about Walia and trees and a few bushbuck, and then you say you have to make more trouble in Addis Ababa."

We left on very friendly terms, the old Governor now lavish with praise for me. He held my hand as we walked up to the Land Rover. Could I do him a favor? Could he borrow our Unimog for one day, to haul the ballot boxes up from Adi Arkai? I agreed.

On the way back, General Seyoum talked with me. He now saw a few of the reasons for my anger.

"Now we will have good cooperation. If you have trouble, you tell me. You will not leave Ethiopia now. Everything is good."

I thanked him, but it all made no difference to my decision to leave. Resignation was not a lever to blackmail people into doing things. The sobering thought came to me that by resigning I might be doing more good for the park than I had in two years of work.

With a new determination not to be angry or bitter, I returned to the mountains. No guards came with me, and I carried only a small pack, a rifle, a knife, and twenty-five rounds of ammunition. Dave Priestley, an English tourist I had met in Debarek, walked up with me. I had invited him to spend a few days with me in Sankabar.

As we reached the series of low hills just after the big meadow outside of Debarek, a party of riders and walking riflemen came along the path, heading for the town. It was Nadu and his followers.

He reined in his big horse and, dismounting, greeted me. He extended his hand and I took it. I had not seen him for a long time. I noticed that two of his men carried the type of rifles issued to our game guards.

"You," I said, pointing at Nadu, "have no head." His followers stared with hostility, but Nadu grinned and asked why.

"This place will be national park. Emperor's orders. All animals and trees. Do not fight. Speak to your brother, Ato Berhanu Asarase. Speak to me after. Big trouble if wild animals are killed. Those rifles"—I pointed to his followers—"government rifles. Those are peasants, not government men." My Amharic was too poor to say what I wanted to say, but Nadu gathered that I had been talking to his cousin, and he seemed to understand.

"We will talk," he said, and put out his hand again. Gone was the time of threats and counter-threats, and I for one was very glad.

"Those rifles belong to the government, and these men only carry them for me. Later we will settle about that. Where are your guards?"

"I have no guards, no followers. I am not a big lord. I am a worker." I grinned and tapped the rifle I carried. Nadu laughed and said I was brave and strong, then swung up into the saddle and rode on.

✕✖◇✖✕

Back at the house, Dave and I ate and talked, while Mogus lay in his corner by the fire, chin on paws, looking at me with his beseeching eyes, begging for me to toss a bone onto the floor for him. I had gotten that way since my wife left. Like a feudal baron.

Thunderclouds enveloped Sankabar, and the lightning flashed for several hours. Toward ten at night the storm had moved away from the escarpment and was rumbling and flashing some miles away, in clear view, over the lowlands. The bottoms of the clouds were at our height, and I took out a camera and tripod to try to take some photographs. Dave stayed inside. Soft, muffled strains of guitar. Light from the house shining through the windows. Looking through from outside, passing my eyes over everything in the house, I decided that even if someone else had built it, it would still look great.

Dave stayed a few days and I welcomed his company. Mesfin had moved up to Geech. I was getting lonely at times. Kassa was waiting to be transferred to Addis Ababa. He'd had enough of Debarek. He was being replaced by an amusing, podgy old woman of a young man by the name of Tsehai, a name which means sunshine.

On the second day of Dave's visit I took him down to see the waterfall of the Djinn Barr. It gushed out through a cleft in the rock and fell sheer for hundreds of feet into the Geech abyss. When wind whistled up the abyss, the water trailed into feathers and spumes of mist, tinted by rainbows and caught by the wind to be blown against another rock wall, there condensing and rushing down again in a waterfall that roared into a series of deep basins and minor falls. Any one of these minor falls was remarkable in itself. At times the sun kissed the falls with three rainbows, and after heavy rains the water would shoot out from the cleft with awful force, clearing the rock walls and dropping in a white column that thundered so loud in the sheer cliffs that it was hard to hear speech. In the dry season, when water levels were low, the falls would lose themselves in a mist that stimulated luxuriant emerald-green foliage on the ledges of the cliffs around. I never tired of those falls. On foggy days, I would sometimes wait, staring into the white opaqueness of the mist, to be rewarded, all too briefly, by a sudden glimpse of the falls when wind or sun cleared the veil.

That day, the Khabar meadow was all yellow with large buttercups, and green with clover and tall green grass. There was a plant like watercress in the boggy ground at the head of the streams, and around the edges of the meadows were hundreds of mushrooms. Big, black-gilled umbrellas, and tiny, firm buttons with undersides of a delicate salmon-pink. Falcons, augur buzzards, and a pair of eagles graced the cliffs; sometimes, in the fog banks, I could not see them, but could only hear the rush of wind in their pinions. Chestnut-winged starlings flashed their brilliant shoulder patches in noisy flocks, and a pair of klipspringers jumped with their delicate, tiny hooves over mist-wet rocks.

Dave went back the next day, and it was just as well, for we were shrouded in a thick, wetting fog which swirled in through the doors of the houses if they were left open. And with the fog, a depression came, and I brooded deeply over the failure of the park project, and thought that I should hurry back to my family. When night came, a solitary owl squeaked outside; rain blew against the windows, and I thought about Tag, thinking that he too must be lonely up in Geech. Guards returned from another lowland patrol with bad news. This would probably be the last one until the end of the rains.

Tsehai, the new clerk, had come up, and was telling me of how his parents had opposed his coming into the Simien, so far away from home, but he had said that he must take this chance to see another part of Ethiopia. Tsehai was twenty-four years old, five years younger than I. His happy, somewhat inane chattering began to cheer me up and cause me to laugh again. He was a lot of fun, good at cooking, and bullied Abahoy in the kitchen.

Typing out the monthly report for June brought depression back. Even in daytime, the fog made it as dark as dusk, and the damp and cold invaded everywhere. The fire burned badly, for the wood was wet, and there was no view of mountains to lift my soul. Usually, I managed to lose bad thoughts in the view, but the fog hemmed them in on me, and I began to suffer a sort of mental claustrophobia.

As soon as the report was finished I put on a parka, called the dog, and went out for a walk along the rim of the escarpment. At the cliff edges the wind was soughing and gusting, and clouds formed against the cliffs and swirled up and over in thick, wet banks. Turbulence against the cliff walls buffeted the air up and caused the actual cliff edges where my dog and I walked to be calm, though overhead the fog banks swirled and tumbled until they flattened grass and plants and bent the branches of trees some yards away from the cliff rims. Noisy choughs played in the turbulent air, doing acrobatics, landing and balancing with clownish skill on overhanging rocks. Francolin stepped and pecked with a fussy, intent caution, though the rush of wind so deafened them that I was able to sneak very close. Water droplets formed on tree branches and fronds of old-man's-beard, then blew off in a fine rain, so that it was wettest under the trees. And the flowers, ah, the flowers. They bloomed everywhere. Tiny white ground orchids by the thousands. Violets, red-hot pokers, yellow daisies, and a hundred species whose names I did not know.

I sat on a rock and looked down into the milky denseness of the fog, and suddenly it cleared, exposing a breathtaking view of clouds, forming and changing along the other cliffs, and between the gaps in the clouds I could see patches of green hills, dotted with tiny houses and veined with streams and a hundred waterfalls. Speaking into the wind, I said, "I am lord of a magic island, sailing above the earth and above the clouds . . ."

Back to the house. Sun shone weakly through the fog, but the day laborers had all quit working. Too cold and damp for them. Having nothing particular to do I called Tsehai out and gave him some lessons with rifles, using the .22 training rifle first, then the big rifle. He was quite good. I started to teach him to use the pistol, but found he did not have the strength or coordination to cock the hammer with his thumb, and had to use both hands. I told him if he could not do it with one hand I would not let him waste ammunition. So he didn't get to fire the pistol. On hearing the shots, the guards came down, then stood watching and giving raucous advice, most of it wrong. Actually only the ex-soldiers could cock the pistol hammer without using both hands. When I told them that Sonako had no trouble doing it, they laughed and taunted each other.

All day, and all night, the thunder rumbled.

Guard Zeleka, the Korean campaign veteran, returned from Debarek with his rations and several bottles for me. He confirmed a rumor that Major Gizaw had been replaced by a certain General Mabratu Fesseha. This new chief of the Wildlife Conservation Department had served before with both the police and the navy, and was well known.

The delight shown at this news was perhaps unfair to the Major, but now, with a new chief, we all thought that really big things were going to begin to happen.

That night, all the guards in Sankabar came to my house for a party. The health of the new chief was drunk many times over, and talk flowed as freely as the locally distilled *katikalla*. The men all knew by now that I had decided to leave, and they asked me not to go. Mitiku said that I was their father, and that I must stay with them for many years. Guard Azezew said that they regarded me as a kind of apostle, a prophet, and that given time, all the mountain people would listen to me. And I wondered how many of the apostles had such a capacity for alcohol and vanity.

"Yes," said Nagur, "our people take time before they come to trust a stranger."

"Do not leave us," said Kebede, "but punish us for what we have done wrong, and stay with us. We need you, and the park needs you. Without you to look after us we will have nothing, just like before, no houses, no salary, no uniforms, no blankets, nothing."

Zeleka was quite drunk, and leaning back in his chair he said, "We know when we have done wrong. We know we do not always obey your orders, and we pretend not to understand. This is because we like to trick people, but in our hearts we know that what you tell us is good." And he began to expand on the theme, giving examples of their deceit. The others quickly shut him up, while Nagur tried to steer the talk around to baboons, and to the plague of baboons that I predicted for the lowland area.

"Yes, truly," said Zeleka, "and they are as cunning and as intelligent as men, for in truth, they are men. At one time, long ago, they were like us, but God punished them, and they grew the way they are now. He punished them for their greed. We guards are greedy, although we are poor men, and when we go on patrol we are thinking of our allowances."

As a man, the rest stood up, thanking me hastily, and hurrying the tipsy, talkative senior guard away with them before he said too much. Even as they closed the door, Tsehai and I were hooting with laughter. We had known of these things, but the abruptness of the leaving and the worried looks on the guards' faces were too much for us.

We laughed on and on, perhaps as a relief against the tight feeling of those fog-shrouded days, or perhaps because we had got a new chief, or perhaps simply because of the *katikalla*. Out in the kitchen, Abahoy brewed strong coffee, and the dog Mogus shifted on his blanket and groaned at the folly of humans.

❈❈❈❈

The bad weather continued, and one day, in the rain, we were astonished to see Captain Asafaw and two constables come along the path from Debarek. It was late in the afternoon, and Asafaw's heavy greatcoat was soaked and weighty. He must have had a hell of a rocket from General Seyoum, otherwise nothing would have brought him up here in this weather. We made him welcome, despite the feelings I had about his lying about the report.

Ballot boxes on donkeys

When we first invited the police in for hot coffee and a drink, they seemed very afraid of my dog, and wanted him chained up outside while they were there. But Mogus lived in the house with me now, and it was too damp outside. He eyed the police suspiciously, not wanting to let them in.

"Mogus—good dog. It's OK." The dog relaxed and looked at me. "Go in. House. Go in." He went in. "Sit, Mogus, over there, sit." He went to his blanket by the fire and flopped down, still eyeing the uniformed police with their guns with snorting, complaining suspicion. The police sat down for coffee. I called the dog over to me and told the men to hold out their hands. Timidly, they did so, and Mogus sniffed them over, still not particularly liking it. Then he went back to his corner.

Captain Asafaw was amazed. By a dog lover's standards, Mogus was very badly trained, for I had been away from him too much, and the servant Abahoy had looked after him. But the police, and the locals, and indeed, most Ethiopians, had never seen a dog obey orders like that before. And Mogus was a fine-looking animal, blackish-gray, big, heavy-shouldered, and with the intelligent-looking up-pointing ears of the German Shepherd breed. The locals had only seen the cringing, savage curs around the native houses, poor beasts who knew no kindness, and who were stoned, kicked, and beaten merely for the crime of existing.

"Mogus is my guard," I said. Captain Asafaw spoke some English. He asked if the dog would warn me if a robber came. I told him to watch, and called Mogus, making a noise indicating that something or somebody was outside. The dog jumped up and rushed to the door, listening and growling. I opened the door and made the noise again. The dog charged out, snarling and barking, and tore around the house, then rushed to the bushes, checking for the imaginary prowler. It was an impressive performance, though in truth, Mogus was a very gentle dog. I went out, picked up a stick, and went for the dog. It was a game we often played. He charged, jumped, took my arm at the wrist, pulled it down, and bit just hard enough to make me drop the stick. The policemen exchanged comments of wonder, and proud as a peacock I ordered my dog back into the house, made him sit by the chair, and then gave him a biscuit.

"He is like your brother," said Captain Asafaw. "I think he is more good soldier than some of my men. He obey order very good."

"This kind of dog is used by the soldiers and police of my country," I said, thinking to myself that I wished I had devoted the time to train the dog well, for he had been getting out of hand recently.

❈❈❈❈

Tag had to attend a Peace Corps conference at Lake Langano, and I had to send off some accounts, so we had agreed to go to Gondar together. He came down and spent another night with me in Sankabar.

He reported having seen a Simien fox mounting a female golden jackal, attempting to mate with it. Another golden jackal came and drove the Simien fox away. Later that day, Tag saw three jackals and the fox together in the same area. An animal will not mate with another species unless it is unable to mate with one of its own kind. This was a bad sign for the population of Simien foxes, but we had been expecting it.

Again, we spent a good night, talking, eating, drinking coffee, working out. Tag walloped the punching bag so much he took all the skin off his knuckles. His boxing punches seemed to glance on the bag, while karate blows did not.

It was the time of the elections, and Nadu's campaign had been going well for him. He was acclaimed all over the hill country. His handbills, with some writing saying how he had driven the shifta out of the hills, his photograph, and, ironically enough, the sign of a big tree, were all over the place. They decorated all the bars in Debarek, and the walls of our guards' quarters.

During his tour of speeches, a dramatic incident had occurred which greatly enhanced his esteem with the people. A young man of a certain village had been lost, and Nadu and his followers arrived in time to take part in the search. They found the body at the bottom of a cliff; the people thought the man had fallen, but Nadu suspected something. He washed the body, finding many stab wounds. He took off his fine white gabi, wrapped the body of the young man in it, and carried it to the police to report the murder. He was assured of all the votes in that area.

Ballot boxes on donkeys

The campaigns were drawing to a close, and the gray ballot boxes were being readied in small towns and mountain villages all over the country.

When I returned from Gondar on July 10, the rain pelted down in Debarek and turned the paths into a morass. I trudged up to the police station to see how the robbery investigation was progressing, and learned that the four guards at Geech had sworn that they had had no orders to guard the camp, which was utter nonsense. Moreover, they had said that when they tried to guard the house (Captain Asafaw could not see the contradiction in this), Tag would drive them away. Which was also nonsense. Captain Asafaw tried to tell me that the window had been forced from the inside, which was impossible, for nobody was in the house when Tag left it, and the doors, very strong, had been locked. All the windows were latched and shuttered. From my own inspection, and Tag's, it was obvious that the thieves had wrenched the shutter open, then broken the window. Tag said all the broken glass from the window lay inside. But Captain Asafaw was illogically adamant and would not listen to reason. With an idiot like that on the job, I was sure that absolutely nothing would be discovered.

However, he did do one good job up there; he arrested a man for cutting trees and charged another thirty-eight men with the same offense. They were to be brought down at a later date for trial.

Rain forced me to stay in Debarek that night. Kassa, the clerk, was preparing to leave, but had stayed on in the town to help a brother-in-law with his election campaign for the Debarek seat. It was this brother-in-law who first got Kassa the job with the Wildlife Conservation Department. That night Kassa and I went around to see Dejasmatch Araya at his house. I was going to tell the old man that I was planning to leave, and why. Maybe the next warden would not have such a rough time with him.

We stumbled and slipped through the mud. It was dark as hell, for there were no lights in the town. From behind the locked door of the Dejasmatch's house, a man shouted to us to identify ourselves and state our business. Hearing who it was, the Dejasmatch came to greet us. He was delighted to accept the bottle of whiskey I had brought with me. The big room was illuminated by candles and lamps and sparsely heated by a couple of charcoal braziers, which did little good, for the ceilings of these mud-walled, tin-roofed houses were very high, and the heat escaped.

After the normal round of greetings, I got around to discussing my leaving. He seemed distressed about it, and held my hand, repeatedly urging me to change my mind, saying he would not let me go, but would lock me up in the jail until I promised to stay. I said that if he wanted to put me in jail he must do it himself, because his men were not tough enough. He enjoyed this and pounded me on the back, promising that he would do it himself. Armed men, sitting on low earth or wooden benches around the walls, stared at me, wondering, and knowing the reputation I had built up, which had been grossly exaggerated in the telling.

The old man brought up the name of Zeleka Asfaw, the man sent from Addis Ababa, and accused him of all kinds of felonies. I had little doubt that this Zeleka was a scapegoat, even though it was true he got drunk and quarreled with harlots. The latest trouble between Zeleka Asfaw and Dejasmatch Araya was that Asfaw had accused him of using a government vehicle, namely the Unimog, which Araya had borrowed from me to haul charcoal. Of course, Dejasmatch Araya indignantly denied this, even though there were bits of charcoal all over the truck bed. He had borrowed it, he said, to carry down the ballot boxes to the lowland. This was true; he had. But he said he had not carried charcoal, which was not true. He did both, and I personally gave not a damn.

However, Zeleka would find himself in jail one of these days, and neither I nor his powerful friends in Addis could help him against this old lion. It was best he go.

The Dejasmatch was in a talkative mood, and we went on late into the night, talking mostly about the old, old subjects, although now he was admitting the possibility of danger from the local people if they were aroused.

". . . My people have tempers like fires. Recently, in the hills, a man grew angry with a neighbor at harvest time and chased him over the field. From behind he slashed the running man, hamstringing him. Then he cut the man's throat with a sickle.

". . . My own servant was plowing in Zarema when a peasant insulted him. He drew a knife and leaped on the man, but by the grace of God another man pulled him off.

Ballot boxes on donkeys

". . . These uneducated hill people and the whites always get into arguments.

". . . This man Nadu is a bold man, and he and his brother are greatly feared by the shifta.

". . . Worse than a thief or a murderer, is a liar. A liar can cause trouble, he can make bad blood between friends, and even cause brothers to kill one another. When I was a young man, I walked one day past the house of the Governor with another man. This man asked me if I knew who lived in this house, and I said, yes, of course I knew. Later, this man, who was jealous of the favor I held with the Governor, told the Governor that I had been ignorant of who lived in the house, that I, Araya, had been ignorant of the name of the Governor. This caused bad blood between the lord and me. I grew fierce in my anger. I followed the man one day and found him plowing. I seized him and tied him to his plow, then I took his own ox whip and lashed him with it. I warned him that the next time he lied I would kill him. Men have made lies about you, Nicola, and if they do this again, I will punish them. They fear me. . . ."

And I said that I too despised liars, and he retorted that I was not a foreigner, but a Simien man, brave and strong, that all knew my skill with a rifle, a stick, a knife, and that I rode and fought and traveled like an Ethiopian, and that we were brothers, and from now on we would work together to make the hill people understand the wishes of the government.

He praised Kassa, and said he was a brave boy, and an honest, faithful boy, and promised to write him a letter of recommendation to take to Addis Ababa with him.

That night I was wearing a sealskin jacket, Eskimo-made, of hides cured in the Eskimo fashion. It was a fine jacket, but in Japan's damp climate I knew it would stink, and that my wife would complain. The Dejasmatch had been admiring it so much that I took it off and gave it to him. He was delighted and said that he would always remember me. He had given me a hell of a lot of trouble, but I now believed that, at any given moment, he was sincere in his own way, and that he did right by his own cultural standards. The same probably applied to Nadu, if I was mistaken in my suspicions about his link with various thefts. It seemed almost certain that Nadu would get into parliament. For the sake of the park, there was no point in trying to flog a dead horse. Nadu had been untouchable, just as the Dejasmatch was untouchable. For the sake of the park project all I could do in my last three months would be to try to make them allies.

That night, I slept in our store, and was tormented by bed bugs and by a sheep which bleated all night in the spare room.

The dawn hours were clear and bright, and I set off, alone, with a pack. Hills brilliant with new, dew-sparkling grass and flowers. Peasants leaning their plows into rain-softened ground, oxen slipping in the mud on the steep slopes, men sweating, shrieking, whistling, cracking whips. Air crisp as a fine white wine, and streams running with silt like cold chocolate milk.

Debarek was filled with a great excitement over the elections. Dejasmatch Araya's son, Shiferaw (the one who cheated me out of the rent of his uncle's house and got me sent to court a year before), had run for a seat in the lowland Adi Arkai region. Nadu, of course, had run for the High Simien, and another ex-game guard, the verbose Lemlem Gonete, had run for another part of the Simien, below the northern escarpment. Kassa's brother-in-law had run again for the Debarek seat.

At the bottom of the big hill, a line of laden donkeys and a party of armed men and police crossed the stream. They were bringing down the ballot boxes with the votes of the mountain villagers. The boxes rode high on the animals' backs and bounced precariously. Nadu was there too. He led his horse across the rain-swollen stream. The water welled up against the animal's legs and belly, and it snorted. They looked very fine, the man and the horse. He wore a new gabi and a turban, and he seemed happy and confident. There was little doubt that when the votes were counted, Nadu would have a clear majority. He greeted me jovially and posed with his armed followers. Then we went our separate ways.

I watched them go, and had a funny feeling inside. The significance of it all came to me. Ballot boxes on donkeys. Here was the first germination of the seeds of democracy that Haile Selassie had sowed, here was what the tough old lion was leading his people toward, and it was a magnificent achievement, even if there was still much wrong with the Addis government. Stopping for a moment to take photographs, I thought of the Emperor and pondered the tremendous load he had carried for such a long time. The thought made me just a little humble.

19

NADU IS ELECTED

Now it seemed vital to gather images and impress them on my mind. Simien was a once-in-a-lifetime experience, and in three months I would be gone.

Now the present became more important. Most of the time I was alone with my dog, and he did not interrupt my ofttimes mutterings. I became egocentric. I read every book I could lay my hands on, including the Bible and the Koran. Outside, I walked, watched, observed, noted.

It was the season of clouds, and often I would go out to the escarpment, where the wind rushed and hissed up cliff faces, sounding like the suck and rush of a far-below sea. And from the edges, I looked down on clouds, sometimes catching glimpses of tiny fields. Clouds, always moving, rushing up the escarpment walls and boiling over the rims. Below-land obscured. Lord of a sky-island, I stood and watched, as the clouds and the fog swirled around, and the island seemed to sail at great speed through the heavens. In the belly of the sky, thunder rolled and rumbled continually, and the ponderous black thunder-heads stomped over lowland hills, charging the battlements of the High Simien, ripping out their bellies on ramparts and towers, bursting rain down upon the hills and turning trickles into rivers. Fog banks twisted and tumbled about my house, closing it, and me, and my dog Mogus in on ourselves. In the daytime gloom of thick cloud and fog, people in gabis looked like ghosts, and the mules and horses grazed slowly, snorting sometimes, like weird, dark monsters. As I sat at my desk, writing, women came past the house, silently, barefooted, carrying water pots; the dog growled softly, looking at me.

Clouds swallow the house. Thunder is a presence. For a few brief minutes the sky clears, and always the eagles and the bone-breakers are wheeling, circling the house. Then darkness again.

It is eleven A.M. I am writing a letter . . . and I can see only thirty yards out of the window. Guards' wives are shrieking at each other down by the spring, arguing about a bucket. The dog is groaning. Impatience? Abahoy bought a sheep for supper, and the dog no doubt waits for it to have its throat cut. It has been dark, foggy, gloomy, for over a week. Water dripped constantly from the eaves, and clusters of small, orange toadstools grew on the thatch. Flocks of wattled ibis poked around in the wet grass on the hills, flying in the fog with harsh, throaty cries.

Strangely, I no longer feel lonely. I am all cocooned in the cotton wool fog, inside my house, and am conscious of my own little territory. The stamp of my personality is everywhere. Thinking about everything and nothing.

For a while, I had begun to worry, feeling that I was hating too much, in my despair about the park, the forests, the ibex. But now, having accepted, compassion came. I realized that I hated almost all Ethiopians as officials and liked them as people. I find the capacity to hate and like, to respect and despise the same person. People change. We are all actors, in changing roles, but these Ethiopians seemed to play more roles than others. The thought came that perhaps the officials are all ancient feudalists with a thin veneer of bureaucracy overlying them. But I think that they were not too secure in their offices, and they reacted accordingly. It must be difficult to remember who is who. They were nearly all arse-kissing sycophants to superiors, and bullying, arrogant bastards to supposed inferiors.

And then, at home, they turn out to be warm-hearted, generous, and emotion-filled humans.

One day, I go out of the house and look at the spring. The water is cold, clear, and delicious. Fog condensed in my beard. When the rain stops, and the wind ceases, the high-pitched metallic whine of cicadas is deafening. They bothered me. Who ever heard of cicadas singing in the cold and fog? But they were cicadas, sure enough.

When I first heard the sound, I asked a guard what it was, and he indicated with forefinger and thumb that it was a tiny insect, less than half a centimeter long. For a while I believed him, and told Tag that it couldn't be cicadas, because they were too small. But my curiosity was not satisfied. The sound was too familiar, and I went often to try to find the insect. Under the wet trees, my ears ringing with the loud buzz, the sound all around me, and yet I could see nothing but wet lichens and branches. The noise would stop and start erratically. One moment they would all be buzzing in the damp fog, and the next moment they would all stop and the fog would be silent except for the dripping of water.

One afternoon, coming back from a walk with the dog, I stopped by the path through the trees, hearing one of the insects very close. I crept closer. The sound came from low down on a big Erica tree, and it was deafening, bothering the dog, who kept turning his head from side to side, whining. I looked, scanning the trunk and the lower branches inch by inch, until I saw it, less than two feet from my nose.

Sure enough, it was a cicada, a beauty, perfectly camouflaged, and buzzing and singing as loud as it could. It was colored dark brown, with a wet-looking sheen, and its body was blotched with pale, yellow-green markings. Its wings were semitransparent, and the whole color and design was that of wet tree heather bark and lichens. I had been looking directly at the tree on which it rested for more than two minutes before my brain registered what my eyes saw, and had it not been for my refusal to go away from the incredible noise in front of my nose, I might have missed it. It sounded like a high-powered electrical tool. All around, thousands of them were buzzing steadily. But that was the only one I ever managed to find.

I never heard the cicadas in the dry season. When I asked the guards, they admitted that they had never seen one, but they had found a singing grasshopper one time and presumed it to be the same thing. They could not understand my small joys of discovery.

Up behind the guards' houses was a little wooded gully. It was here that Azezew's woman died, half mad from typhus. The place took on an eerie atmosphere in the fog, and the guards seemed to avoid it. Up there, under a bush, lay a scrap of the woman's shamma, and in the strangeness of the sounds and feelings, I almost expected to see the woman's ghost lying there under the bushes where she died.

We had contracted with a man called Adana to haul sand to Geech for us. He was fairly honest and hard-working, and he agreed to our price. The other men tried to dicker for a higher price, and were astonished and greatly put out to find themselves out of a job.

Within six weeks we got thirteen thousand kilos of sand hauled up from the beds of the Balagas River, two days' journey away.

However, not content with the situation, the other men ganged up on Adana, saying they had the right to haul sand too. At first they came unasked with their loads, and we turned them down. Neither Mesfin nor I could be bullied. But poor Adana was forced to agree to let twenty-five other men share the contract with him. I could do nothing, for if I tried, they would only take it out on Adana, outside the park. When we paid Adana, it was enough money to feed him and his family for a few years, but he then had to go and dish it out to the twenty-five pirates, all of whom had tagged along at pay day, not trusting each other. It sounded like a riot in a monkey cage. We weighed and recorded each donkey load against the name of the donkey owner. They had to figure out how much this man should get with one hundred and thirteen kilos, how much another should get with two hundred and sixty-five, and how much another should get with sixty-seven kilos. As not a single one of them could work it out on paper, because they were unable to write, the whole thing had to be done by mental arithmetic. It was bedlam.

On July 16, the news reached us. Nadu had been elected to parliament by a clear majority. Mesfin said that many of the people were afraid not to vote for Nadu, and when I said that this could not be so, for the ballot was secret, he retorted that everybody knew just who voted for whom. Three thousand five hundred people voted for Nadu.

I had predicted it, and had resigned largely because of it.

Tsehai, the new clerk, came up from Debarek, bringing a letter and a bottle of araki from Kassa. Kassa was saying good-bye, and thanking me. He was now going to go to Addis Ababa. He said that I was his dearest brother.

"Tsehai, did you see Nadu?"

"Yes, I saw him. Oh, he is so happy. I saw him in the bar, inviting everybody. He even kissed me."

Outside, Tag's lion cubs Ruby and George, which he got to replace the lost female, were roaming about. They were getting quite big now, and they loved to play. Ambush and charge was a favorite game. We were in the house when they came to the veranda, yowling for food. Tag was away. Mesfin went to open the door to let the lions in, and Tsehai jumped up, snatched a machete, and bolted up the ladder to the sleeping platform. When the lions came in, Tsehai squeaked with fright, waved the machete, and shouted *"Hid! hid!"* (Go! go! in Amharic). The lions took no notice, but headed for the kitchen. Tsehai, his head draped around with a pink bath towel, flapped arms and legs from the high perch. The cubs bullied their way around the house, pulling cushions and sheepskins off the chairs, knocking over the garbage can, climbing over the furniture. Each cub was twice as heavy as my dog, and infinitely more stubborn. Mesfin got them outside again with a leg of mutton each. Tsehai came down and bolted the doors, then yelled abusive comments at them through the closed window for the next hour.

The next day was my twenty-ninth birthday. I read some poetry by Dylan Thomas and then packed a rucksack and started down, thinking about my own boyhood in Wales, and of the heron-priested shores and the knock of boats on net-webbed walls that he wrote about.

The Djinn Barr was swollen, and my dog could not wade across. After wasting an hour trying to coax him over the bridge I lost patience and threw him off the bank into the river. He got to the shore all right.

Guard Amara Gebrew was following me and irritating me. Mesfin had taken his blanket from him that morning. All guards had been ordered repeatedly not to wear blankets on duty. They looked like hell for a start, all swaddled from head to toe in khaki and green, with only the tip of the nose and their eyes showing, and besides, the blankets got wet, then they slept in them and got sick. I was wearing shorts, a bush shirt, and a light sweater, while the guards had shirts and heavy woolen uniforms. But Amara had chosen to ignore orders and report for duty in his blanket. Now he was following me, begging me to get it back for him. After throwing Mogus in the river I suggested throwing Amara in too. He shut up and went back to Geech.

Did the fog cause everyone to be irritable? A dead horse lay by the trail. Cold and brown with its insides all gone. As I approached silently in the fog a vulture came out of the hollow skin and flapped clumsily away.

As we were expecting a visit from our new chief, General Mabratu, I had to make another trip down. I ran down at scout's pace, getting to Debarek just after noon, before the clouds and rain came in. Some guards followed with horses, but I beat them. I went into Berhanu's bar and ordered some beers for myself and the guards. Berhanu's brother was behind the bar. He didn't like foreigners and was wont to be snide. After finishing the second beer, I bought several more, paid for them, and told him that they were for the soldiers who would come down soon, after me.

"What soldiers?"

"My soldiers. The Walia guards," I replied. "They will come. The beer is for them. I have work now."

He sneered and raised his voice so that even people outside the bar could hear. "Who are you to say that you have soldiers? They are Ethiopians. They are not your soldiers. I do not know what you are talking about."

But of course he knew. I tried to explain and he began to make fun of my language, which was admittedly poor, but I did not choose to have him insult me, especially as I knew his courage was mainly due to the fact that Nadu had won. Nadu had been drinking and boasting in this bar after learning of his victory. Tsehai told me this. Everybody knew that I had tried to get Nadu into court, thereby disqualifying him from running for the election. For no reason, other than the fact that many people had gathered at the door to watch, he began to make a show of taking back the beer. I said he should give me the money back, and he wouldn't, so I went behind the bar and helped myself. He grabbed my wrist, so I twisted my hand, locked his wrist, and forced him onto his knees. Then I pocketed my money and went to the other side of the counter. I was going to leave, but he shouted something nasty at me, so I seized him by the collar and lifted him across the counter and whispered something even nastier into his ear. Then Guard Takalé came in. He shouted at Berhanu's brother and insulted him. I told the girls to serve them beer and paid for it. Two other guards came in, pushing past the crowd at the door.

"Fool," said one of them, "do not make quarrels with our captain."

Nadu is elected

Berhanu's brother went out to the back, muttering threats which everybody knew he was incapable of keeping. Takalé followed him, hurling the choicest of insults about his parentage.

Meanwhile, after some bread and tea, I went up to the police compound to where the Land Rover was parked. Just as I passed the jail house, made of eucalyptus poles and mud, and full of prisoners, somebody pushed his nose through the crack and said, "Good morning, Mr. Nicol," in very fine English. It was by now the middle of the afternoon, and the whole thing suddenly struck me as a comedy. I sat in the Land Rover, laughing.

✕✕✕✕

His Imperial Majesty arrived in Gondar on July 19. The town had been whitewashed and painted, and arches of greenery and bunting were erected all over the place. The police and other officials were very emotional about the whole affair; they rushed about in cars, ordering people to line up properly by the roadside and they berated an old man who was trying to walk his firewood-laden donkeys through the town just before the cavalcade was due to arrive. Some hours before, I had parked my vehicle on the grass verge by the Swedish engineer's house. A little green police Volkswagen came by and two officers got out, waving and shouting at me to move the car. I had every intention of moving it before the Emperor arrived, but their histrionics annoyed me, and I responded by making rude noises and vulgar gestures with one hand.

The Emperor finally drove past in a Land Rover, with his little white dog on his lap. The people by the roadside were talking excitedly about the great number of cars that had gone out to greet him. No less than forty-nine! Forty-nine cars, all strung out. I was more impressed by the group of hill chiefs, galloping by on caparisoned mules, singing heroic songs.

Among the hundreds of big men who had come into Gondar from the country around were Nadu and his brother Negash. The Emperor was going to address them. Rumor had it that the address would be about the preservation of forest and wildlife.

All government officials and foreign workers, including volunteers, engineers, doctors, nurses, and advisors of various sorts, had been invited to various civic functions. Only one government official and foreign advisor was not invited: Nicol. I suspect that my reputation for saying what I thought had something to do with that.

The night of the Emperor's arrival, Tag and I were having drinks at the Iteghie Hotel, and talking to Dr. Han, a serene gentleman from northern China who had been the first director of the Public Health College. We were joined by Commandatore Buske, the dapper, talkative, and volatile Italian owner of the hotel, as well as several other hotels and the Navigatana boats which carried tourists to the islands on Lake Tana.

He recounted the tale of his shifting one of the great obelisks from Axum to Massawa, whence it went to Rome to be erected in front of what is now the FAO building. He said it was shifted in five pieces, the biggest weighing ninety-one tons. The trailers he used were meant to carry only twelve tons, and they kept breaking on the way, every four kilometers or so.

". . . And every day the Fascists say they want to shoot me. They say I am, how you say, sabotage the obelisks. They want to shoot me. Every day! Bing! Bing! Me! Buske! Understand?"

But in the end he got the pieces to Massawa, over some fantastic country.

Apart from that, he had brought some big boats, six meters across the beam, overland from Massawa to Tana. During the occupation, when the Italians were building, he once hired and bought twelve hundred donkeys to carry cement up from Zarema to make the Wolkefit Pass road. Another of his ventures was to farm two hundred and fifty hectares of castor oil plants, but that was terminated by angry locals.

And, of course, he was getting papyrus from Tana and shipping them out to make the *Ra*—Thor Heyerdahl's raft.

That night I read a copy of *Newsweek* magazine, dated July 14. The issue was banned in Ethiopia because it said some things about the country, the government, and the royal family. I thought the article was very fair.

The Emperor was about to return to Addis Ababa. John Blower came on July 22, but General Mabratu thought he should wait in Addis until after the anniversary of the Emperor's birthday, which was on July 23. It was the custom for all the big-shots to go to the palace to pay their respects.

Tag and I went to a dance at the Cinema Bar, along with our

Nadu is elected

English friend John Rivers, an English nutritionist now doing research in Debarek. John told us that Brian Jones, of the Rolling Stones, was dead. Brian and I both went to Cheltenham Grammar School, and although we were never really friends, for he was younger than I, I knew and liked him. The last time I had seen him was some ten years before, when we sat in a coffee shop, talking about Eskimos and Lapps. Brian had said that he wanted to spend a summer in Finland, and live with the Laplanders. Having been on a couple of expeditions to the Canadian Arctic, I considered myself some kind of expert, and was telling him a whole lot of things about equipment and so forth. And now Brian was dead, and a band from the local army base was trying to play rock music, and Tag was talking about the Stones, and I was thinking about Brian when his hair was short, and about all those long-ago boytime days, while drinking in a lousy bar in Africa, with big-eyed, dark-skinned girls flitting about excitedly. I became morose and thought of things, and brooded in my heart and uncovered feelings unfit for bars and cheap liquor.

Despite the hangover, I went along with John Blower and Tag for a drive to Bahar Dar. We stopped just out of town at the church of Gorgora. The car was parked under tall trees. I got out and breathed deeply, looking around. Lovebirds, brilliantly green; doves in the branches over the stone and cement grave heads and mounds. The outer walls of the church were of somber stone. Low sounds of chanting came from inside. The effect, however, was spoiled by the tin roof, topped with a garish metal thing, all spiked, with ostrich eggs impaled on the spikes.

On the road to Bahar Dar we saw so many birds—crested cranes, saddlebill storks, Egyptian geese, tawny eagles, and egrets by the hundreds.

When we got back, there was a big party going on at the hotel. They had all been to the last reception for the Emperor. Somebody told me that he had given a speech to all the local bigwigs, telling them of the need to preserve forest and wildlife.

General Mabratu finally arrived on July 24. He spoke excellent English, and was a relaxed, friendly sort of man in his late forties or early fifties. Yemanu, the accountant, came with him.

As it was too late in the day to set off, we stayed another night, but Yemanu and I went up to Debarek to off-load gear and to tell the guards to be ready with the animals early the next day. General Seyoum and the Dejasmatch were entertaining General Mabratu, telling him he was crazy to go up to the Simien in the rains, telling him to wait until the dry season, telling him how terrible it was. Yemanu and I did not talk too much. We were not on very good terms. However, we did have a brief conversation about national dress.

"I think that you educated people should wear national dress more often, especially on festive occasions. Instead, you feel you have to copy us, wearing these ridiculous suits and ties."

"I often wear it," said Yemanu. "Why do you not wear our national dress? There are many foreigners who do."

"Ah, come off it, Yemanu. I can't wear your national dress unless it is given to me by an Ethiopian. Then wearing it would have meaning. Don't you see that?"

"Yes. But I have an idea. You see, you can buy it from your allowances. If you fill out the forms, I will arrange everything."

"That is hardly the point," I said. We had been through this before. Having something fiddled out of the government was not an honorable thing to me, even if it did go toward buying national dress.

All along the hillsides too steep for plowing, the red-hot pokers were in full bloom, great red, yellow, and orange rods of blossoms. Everywhere else was either brilliant green with young barley or gray and red with erosion patches. The sky, full of rain clouds, was all colors: salmon pink, dark gray and pearl gray, blue, purple, and black. On the way back, the sun shone between cloud banks and glinted off the surface of Lake Tana as from a mirror.

I saw a marsh harrier by the road, and cried out with pleasure, but Yemanu grunted, said yes, and did not even turn to look.

General Mabratu had some trouble getting up in the morning. Dejasmatch Araya had poured on the hospitality at his Gondar house until very late. The Dejasmatch came to the hotel soon after six in the morning to see if he was all right. We got off at seven thirty.

Since I had taken over the Simien job, nearly three hundred visitors had been in. Some parties had been quite big, others small. Many organized themselves, but it was I who stabilized the prices and protected the visitors from any trickery on the part of the muleteers. Many parties were organized by myself, or by Mesfin, Ermias, Kassa, or Tag. Nobody ever helped us, or offered to help, or needed to help. We were fairly good at getting things done now. But General Mabratu was a big man. General Seyoum ordered the police to do the organizing in Debarek, and Dejasmatch Araya had ordered Nadu, of all people, to do the organizing. Our men ignored all other directives, and the animals were ready when we arrived, but the party had swollen in numbers. By this time we had General Mabratu, Yemanu, John Blower, Captain Asafaw, two other police, Nadu, three game guards, two coolies, Dure the muleteer, and two of Ineyu's men, plus a man with a petition for a driver's job, Tag, and myself. All going up to the Simien. Had it been the dry season I am sure the numbers would have been trebled.

I hate traveling in big groups, and Yemanu annoyed me by yelling at me, telling me how to handle my own horse, which way to go, where to mount and dismount. He had traveled the route once before, and looked absurd in his city suit. I shouted back, suggesting that he disappear up his own rectum, but he didn't understand the word, so it had to be put in simpler terms. General Mabratu grinned broadly, and Yemanu jogged along in sullen silence.

Tag was as disgusted with the crowd as I. I was especially disgusted with Nadu, dressed to the hilt, smiling genially and giving the impression of the ideal tour conductor. So we split off. By lunchtime, Tag and I had reached the meadow of Addis Gey. I was carrying a small pack, with a lunch for five people. Red wine, cheese, bread, smoked fish, cans of things. Tag and I finished the lot. By hitting the cork, Tag broke the bottom of the wine bottle, a thin, bulbous flask. Deftly, he tipped the bottle up, and we had a fine wineglass. While we ate and drank we debated what I should do if I found Nadu sitting in my house when we arrived.

On the hill trail leading to the wide meadow of Michibi, there had been two beautiful giant Saint-John's-wort, old trees, bearing a mass of large golden blossoms in summer. One of them had been hacked to pieces some months before. These old trees were the only survivors in several hundred square meters, for all the others had been cut long before, and the ground was eroded and ugly. When I passed them I gave them silent greetings; I knew every twist of the trunk, whorl of bark, and bend of branch. They were truly beautiful, and would have graced any garden. Some of my Japanese friends would have gone berserk over them if they could have them by the house, in a rock garden. Perhaps they had survived because their trunks were so twisted as to be useless for building, and because they were surrounded by boulders.

But this time, after having been away for a few days, I saw that the second tree had been cut. Nothing remained but two stumps and a lot of small chippings. Blunt axes. There was a peasant on the hill, building a fence. I say building, but in fact he was just laying an untidy pile of branches around a plot of barley. I wanted to go up and beat his brains out. I yelled all the bad Amharic words I could think of, and he looked dumbly down, not understanding what the crazy foreigner was angry about. I had looked on so many individual trees as friends, and one by one they had been cut. The demise of the last one I took as an omen.

General Mabratu, Yemanu, John Blower, Tag, and I spent a night in Sankabar and then traveled on up to Geech. The guards were delighted to at last have a senior Ethiopian officer who could listen to their complaints and worries, and who would look over their living conditions and realize why the warden had been asking for money to build quarters. The very fact that he came up into the Simien so soon after being elected to the post encouraged everybody.

In Geech, General Mabratu met with the elders of the village, who came to our camp. He knew how to handle people, and they listened to him. They wanted to know if the government thought more highly of the animals than of them. He answered that of course the government thought first of them, but that the Walia was very important to the country, and that while the people could move, the Walia could not. Three Walia had been taken to Addis Ababa, and cared for in the Emperor's garden, but they had all died. The people nodded. They knew this. One of the Geech men had died in the attempt to capture Walia for His Majesty. General Mabratu said that young people need land, that they need to expand, and that this highland was too small for them. He related how men had gone from their homelands to cross wide oceans to build new, rich countries, countries so rich that they could send men to the moon. Then he told them that the government had rich land for them, if they would agree to move. First they should look at the land, and then they could decide. After a long talk, some of the men said they would go to see the new land, and that if they liked it, they might agree to

Nadu is elected

move. But most of them said they did not believe that there was any better land than theirs.

A month before, I would never have believed that anybody could talk with the Geech men about moving from their land without incurring wrath and violence. The General had a magic touch.

Nadu rode over from Amba Ras. His followers carried a large jar of the finest clear talla, a basket of fresh white injera, chicken wat, and a fat, castrated sheep.

General Mabratu conferred with Nadu about moving the Geech people, about the park, about who had stolen the things from the house, about everything. Nadu was the man who had told the people that he would lead them in the fight against the park, the meddling foreigners, and Nadu was the man who had told the people that this was their land, and that nobody could move them off it, or bother them. And I suspected that Nadu had something to do with the theft of medicine from Sankabar. I said very little. Nadu was now the member of parliament for the Simien area, and the General felt that the only thing to do was to win him over. I agreed, but it stuck in my gullet.

Nadu. In Swiss House, sitting by the fire with his feet on the stone fireplace. Leaning in conspiratorial whisperings with the General, Captain Asafaw, and Yemanu.

The following day, after taking a walk to the escarpment edge, the General talked again with the Geech elders and made many promises to them. In return, he got them to promise that they would cut no more forest, and neither would they plow steep slopes. Before plowing they were to ask Mesfin and me about which land was fit. We agreed that Mesfin and I would meet with the elders in a few days, and go over the land with them.

Tag's lions chewed the heads off two chickens that some peasant brought to try to sell to us. They didn't eat the chickens, and Tag, Mesfin, and I wanted to clean them and cook them. The other Ethiopians were horrified.

Then we went down to Sankabar. The weather had been lousy, the paths muddy. We heated up my Japanese bath. John, Tag, and I bathed, but the others all declined. They used so much firewood that they had to pull their chairs way back from the fire. Abahoy frowned from the door of the kitchen. That wood would have lasted us three

317

days or more, and the stocks of dead wood in Sankabar were sorely depleted. Soon we would have to start bringing it in by donkey.

With my notebooks full of writings, quotations, promises, plans, and instructions, we returned to Debarek on July 28. The General wanted Mesfin and me to come down to take part in some meetings with local officials.

After beers in Berhanu's bar, Tag took the Land Rover and drove the big shots to look at the Lemalemo road. I chose not to go into Berhanu's bar, having quarreled once in there.

When they came back from their drive, Kassa's brother-in-law, the re-elected member of parliament, invited us all to a feast in his Debarek house. Ethiopians were always doing this. They would lay on a huge meal, then when everything was ready to eat, they would tell you that they wanted you to come. You either had to offend them badly by refusing, or chuck all plans and go and eat for two or three hours. And at these feasts their generosity was overwhelming. Nadu joined this party, and so did Captain Asafaw, and the mayor of Debarek, a man I had never met before.

We crowded into the little house, its floor freshly strewn with grasses, and took our places on benches, chairs, and low stools. Small glasses of araki were passed around. The Ethiopians took the glass, raised it, and drank to the host. The atmosphere was slightly tense, and I sensed that this was due to my attitude toward Nadu. I had not spoken to him. What the hell. He had won. For a loser to carry a grudge is unmanly. We had brought our biggest guns to bear on him and he had beaten us. I took a glass of the clear, fiery alcohol and raised it, standing.

"I drink to Agafari Nadu. Congratulations." I tossed the stuff back and said it again in English. The Ethiopians clapped and laughed, while Tag and John smiled. Nadu rose to his feet. He seemed genuinely happy. He gave a long, rambling speech which General Mabratu translated for us. Nadu said that he was a Christian, and a sincere man, and that he was sorry if he had done anything to offend me, and that anything wrong he had done was done in ignorance, and that now he hoped we could be friends and brothers again. He held out his hand to me. We shook hands. Then he turned to Tag and held out his hand. Tag grinned and shook it. The grudge was gone, I suppose.

As the eating and drinking went on, Nadu asked Tag if he would like to marry his daughter. Tag replied that he would be a troublesome son-in-law, and they all laughed. Nadu said no, no, he would be a fine son. Tag asked how old the maid was. Nadu said that his daughter was eight years old. Tag explained that it was not the custom for Americans to marry girls who were so young. Nadu said that these young marriages were good, for the girl would grow up with the young man.

Everything was very jovial, and we ate and drank an impossible amount.

I drove the Land Rover through the fog to Gondar. General Mabratu and John rode in front; the General was saying that he thought the combination of British officers and Ethiopian men was an excellent one.

"We do not want you to leave us, Nicol. Won't you reconsider your decision?"

"No, sir, I am very sorry," I said. And I was sorry too.

There were more talks in Gondar, and all kinds of plans were made. The General went around with a copy of *National Geographic*, showing pictures of national parks in Kenya, telling officials how important parks were, and for once they began to listen.

The night of our arrival in Gondar we had dinner together, and John, Tag, and I stayed in the dining room until late, listening to the General talking about the history of his country and about the cultural links with countries and tribes as far away as Nigeria. He looked tough in a roll-necked sweater, and enthusiastic, and he made us all very hopeful.

The four guards who had been on duty at the time of the robbery in Geech were brought down for an inquiry to be held at the police headquarters. At the end of it, the General gave them one month to find out who did the job and to return the equipment. Nearly everybody thought it was the guards themselves, but I was not sure. They knew who did it, but I do not think they did the actual theft. I suspected that they were afraid of the thieves, or of the man who directed the thieves. If they were unable to produce results, they were told that they would have to pay for the missing stuff. Four thousand dollars worth of it. Their basic salary was thirty-seven dollars and sixty-five cents a month. The shock on their faces was something to see.

Several years ago, when General Mabratu had been the assistant commissioner of police, General Seyoum had worked under him. Now we were assured of good cooperation with the police. We were promised a good officer and a team of men to follow up Bogale Mersha's case, and the general forest-cutting trouble in the Simien.

I had gone with General Mabratu to the new police club. Workmen were erecting a big canopy outside. A stage had been put up. General Seyoum stood on the stage and waltzed solo around it, grinning.

"It will be a nice dance. You must come. The police band is good."

"I'm sorry, but I have to return to the Simien."

"I give you permission to stay, Nicol," said General Mabratu.

"Thank you, sir, but Mesfin and I have agreed to meet with the Geech people about their farmland."

General Seyoum invited us for drinks. He said nice things about me. He said that I was fast-tempered, but I was an honorable man, and the people had begun to know and like me. Now that I had decided to go, everybody was being nice.

General Mabratu and I were driven out to the airport in a police Land Rover. The others had already gone. On the way he pointed out the spot where he had seen thousands of Italian vehicles parked at the fall of Gondar. He talked about the campaign. He ran away from home when he was a boy and joined the British Army in the fight against the Italians. He talked about the fall of Gondar, and of how, soon after the allies had taken the city, there was a fight between the South Africans and the Ethiopian patriots, who exchanged machine-gun fire in front of the post office. Trouble over looting or something.

Mesfin and I saw him off and then went back. We had only a few days in the Simien before having to come down again and go to Addis for a big wardens' conference, the first of its kind.

Running up and down the mountains in the rains was getting tedious. I liked to be in my own camp. Back there, there were always little troubles with the guards which kept life interesting.

. . . Guard Kebede reports that Guard Endeshaw has been taking bribes from the leopard-skin dealers in Zarema . . . hardly surprising. Any proof? No, none. Only hearsay. Even if we had proof, and we took him to court, he would get out of it, probably through the Dejasmatch.

Nadu is elected

. . . Guard Azezew is walking around with his rifle loaded and cocked. I have a hunch, inspect the rifle, fine him ten dollars, and take it away from him for a week. He is mortified.

. . . Three guards have acute gonorrhea and don't respond to penicillin treatment. I dose them to the gills with chloramphenicol, and to heck with their bone marrow or whatever.

. . . One mule has a skin disease and has to be isolated and treated several times a day.

. . . Dure, the muleteer, got into a fight in Debarek and knocked a guy out.

. . . Guard Chane is in jail again, this time for stealing a horse. I wished they would hang him.

I walked up to Geech in drizzle and rain, and all along the path were three kinds of orchids. There was a small white orchid with a heavy scent, and a large one, colored royal purple and flecked with white, and another shade-loving orchid which grew in damp places under the tree heather, which was a pale, waxy yellow, with strange, horned petals. White balsam grew in profusion in high bushes along the Sankabar paths, and there were thousands of red-hot pokers, violets, buttercups, scabious, and hundreds of others.

The path climbed out of the fog and drizzle at the top of the Djinn Barr ridge. I could look back on the valleys, filled with dense white cloud like cotton fluff. The sun was bright on the ridge, the clouds brilliant white, and the barley-covered slopes a deep, emerald green. The stream was full and roaring, hurling itself over its falls and boiling round its bends. The sound of the great fall, hurtling down into the abyss, was a dull, muffled roar, hidden in the clouds. The stream by our camp was so full that it was hard to get across, and it had washed away our water pipes. And at the top of the ridge a group of shepherd boys sat on the ground, making woolen hats, twisting the strands of wool against their bare legs and weaving the strands into tight, waterproof hats in patterns of white, gray, brown, and black.

On Sunday, August 3, Mesfin and I went out to the Geech farm-land and met the elders. We were supposed to go over the plots and tell them which were all right for plowing.

The first plot was fairly flat, and we said it was all right. Other slopes were very steep and should not be plowed. On some of these, only a year old, gullies had begun to spread. When we said that they should not plow these slopes, an old man with one eye and

321

a large white turban said that they would not plow them, but another old man protested in a quavering voice that he was plowing steep slopes down by the river and had no intention of stopping. Others spoke. They said they would plow all the land, regardless of slope, erosion, or anything else, until the government pushed them out.

"Mesfin, ask them if they would have enough food if they did not use all the land for barley."

They said no, they would not.

"Then why did you agree to cooperate with us, when you knew it was impossible?"

"We talked, and we decided to see what you would do."

Those with plots on flat land would not share with those who held land on slopes. Neither could they solve the problem of the re-distribution of land, and they would not attempt to tackle it. Nobody could blame them for that. Those who had flat land said they would plow the flat land. Those who had land on slopes said they would plow this land too.

Then an old man said they did not want to move off the land, and many others agreed. He said that he did not believe his people could survive on any other land.

"But if you can live on land as hard and as poor as this, you could live anywhere, and the government will provide you with new, rich land, far better than this."

The men protested. They did not, could not, believe that any land was better than Geech. They sounded like back country farmers anywhere. And there was no point in our discussing it. They would continue to plow every inch of land they had claimed, and had to do so in order to live.

I asked how long their ancestors had lived here. Some said one thousand five hundred years, and some said a thousand years. And all tried to tell me that all of the land had been farmed for that long, which was ridiculous. I asked if their people had followed Islam from the very beginnings, and they said, very emphatically, that they had.

Did they know the birthdate of the Prophet? According to my book, the Prophet was born in 570 A.D. and began his mission in 610 A.D.

The Islamic warrior Mohammed Gran overran Abyssinia in the early part of the sixteenth century. From what I read, I believed that the ancestors of the Geech people were either converts at the time of Mohammed Gran, or had come with him. The Geech people looked no different from the other peoples of the Simien, which suggested to me that they had been converted. Before the Islamic invasions, the country had been a closed pocket of Christianity, sealed from the world for a thousand years. Mohammed Gran was defeated and killed in 1543, and the Moslems went south again, leaving pockets of their faith in such areas as the Simien. Guard Mitiku once told me that the Geech people had come to the land only a few centuries before, as allies of the Christians, to fight the Felasha. The Simien was the stronghold of the Felasha, the so-called Black Jews, and even now there were several Felasha villages there. The tides of conquerors and religions had passed over the Simien several times. The highland ambas were easily defended, and the deep valleys and cliffs, and the distance and difficult paths between the various communities, had stamped their imprint on the people.

But who knows what the history of the Geech people was? Nobody seemed to have kept any records, or knew of any records, and not being a historian I could only read books, speculate, and imagine.

That day, while Mesfin and I were away from the house, Tag's lions caught and ate Tsehai's puppy. Tsehai was too hysterical to do anything about it, and the lions, being bullies, seemed to know it.

Curtains of drizzle were drifting over the highlands in the afternoons. Mesfin and I were beginning to look forward to going to Addis Ababa.

20

A DEMOCRATIC PRINCE

We were driving back from Addis Ababa after the game wardens' conference. It seemed that things were really happening with the Wildlife Conservation Department now. I was thinking about it, singing to myself and watching the roads unwinding from Kombolcha to Makale. We had passed through the green country of Shoa, and the hotter land of Wallo, and all along the way boys were cracking whips, startling me with the sound, which was like a pistol shot. It was some kind of boys' festival, in which boys compete with each other with whips, and everywhere the boys were practicing. In the town of Kombolcha, where we spent the night, it sounded as if there was a battle going on, so many boys were cracking whips, and the sound rang off the buildings and the hill at the back of the new Italian hotel.

We passed through Dessie early in the morning, when dew sparkled on the lush grass and the blue-green eucalyptus. Mesfin was quiet, but I knew he was optimistic too. The General had made many promises during the conference, and he seemed to realize that the field staff had been neglected.

Colonel Girma, of Customs, had caught an illegal dealer trying to smuggle four hundred leopard skins out of the country. Certain people in our department had tried to stall the case, through the back door of the Palace, but it was going to court. Colonel Girma was on to a bigger haul too.

But old habits die hard. During the conference, there was a shifty-looking Moslem hanging around the office, drinking tea with certain officers. He saw me coming out of the conference room, and his eyes widened. This was the illegal trader I visited with my Japanese friend, and he knew me now. He now knew all the officers in the department. Officers in the department had been tipping off the dealers, and taking a percentage on the skins, stamping them with the department stamp.

Then there was a hassle over the "honorary game wardens." A handful of these were genuinely deserving people, seriously concerned about wildlife and doing something to help it. But more than a hundred people had been issued cards, and these cards were worded almost exactly as ours. Nearly every illegal skin dealer in Addis Ababa was now an "honorary game warden," as were a host of other well-known poachers, many of whom had also been issued professional hunters' licenses, quite wrongly. Some were friends of Major Gizaw, who of course had been one of the most infamous poachers in the Empire before the Emperor elected him to the post of director, or general manager, of our department. We all knew that these honorary game wardens had been using their cards to pass game-control road blocks, and had been taking people out hunting illegally.

Of course, fiddles with allowance allotments, uniforms, license fees, and what-not were legion. The headquarters staff had been naïve enough to think that nobody, least of all the foreigners, knew anything about it. The General had been icily amused at the discomfort of certain officials as, one by one, the acts of corruption were uncovered. But we would see if it could change.

As we came into Tigre, the land and houses changed abruptly. It was dry and rocky, and cactus, thorns, and candelabra euphorbia were common. Houses were square, not round, and were built skillfully of stone instead of poles and mud. Roads were generally better, and didn't have as many cattle blocking them.

Mesfin and I decided to spend the night in Makale, the capital of Tigre, then go on the next day to Asmara. We were going to pick up some machine parts there.

The Abraha Castle Hotel in Makale is a fine place, managed by a beautiful and gracious Indian lady. The hotel is a converted castle, set in gardens on a rise overlooking the town. After a bath, a change of clothes, and a long, cool drink, I sat in the lounge reading

Punch and listening to a Joan Baez record; "The trees they do grow high and the leaves they do grow green" . . . it seemed a fitting song for an old castle.

After dinner, I was sitting at the table, talking to my hostess and a couple of other guests, when four men came in. The first man was dressed in very casual clothes. Another man carried a tool bag. The others wore suits. Everybody in the room stood and bowed. I didn't know what it was all about, but stood anyway. They went to one end of the dining room where a large fish tank had been set into a window. The window frame was broken, and the man had evidently come to fix it. People buzzed around, treating the man in casual clothes, the workman, with unusual deference.

"Who is that guy?" I asked the bearded young Ethiopian next to me.

"Don't you know? That's Ras Mengesha Seyoum."

Ras Mengesha Seyoum, the Governor General of Tigre and grandson of the Emperor Johannes.* In working clothes, scraping away at broken concrete with a cold chisel, fixing a broken window frame in a hotel.

The Indian lady explained. "His Highness is the only one in Makale who can do this sort of thing, so I rang him up and asked him to come."

The prince was famous for this eccentricity. He liked to work with his hands. Under him, many new roads and other projects were going ahead in Tigre, and while the work was going on, he often went out to drive a tractor or swing a pickaxe alongside the coolies. He was the complete opposite of everything I had thought about the Ethiopian aristocracy.

The young man with the beard was a development officer, concerned with various projects: roads, forestry, tanneries. On hearing

---

* When the British forces under General Napier invaded Ethiopia on a punitive expedition against Emperor Theodore, they were given great assistance by a certain Ras Kassa. (Names are confusing in Ethiopia; Theodore himself was once called Lij Kassa.) In return for this help, the British handed over guns, small arms, ammunition, and stores when they left in 1868. By 1872, Ras Kassa had defeated the rival lords and then rose to supreme power in the north, declaring himself to be Emperor Johannes (John). He fought the Emperor Menelik in the south and forced him to do obeisance, and he also fought the Egyptians and defeated them soundly in 1875 and 1876. He was killed in a battle against the dervishes in 1889, whereupon Menelik claimed the Empire of Abysinnia.

my job, he said he wanted to take Mesfin and me to talk to Ras Mengesha in the morning.

That night I didn't sleep well. There seemed to be hundreds of hyenas around the town, attracted no doubt by the scent of the slaughterhouse. As I lay awake, I remembered accounts of the aftermath of battles in Tigre, and I imagined hyenas and jackals on the deserted battleground, worrying the bodies of the dead. Castle at night. Rocky hills. Silent town. Howling, chuckling hyenas. It was eerie.

We went to the prince's residence in the morning. He had a modern house built onto a fine old castle, the former home of Emperor Johannes. We were ushered into a beautiful drawing room, with plush carpets, fine furniture, old weapons and pictures on the walls, and photographs of Ethiopian and European royalty here and there. Outside, on the veranda, an old priest was reading Scriptures, reciting them to himself in a monotonous mumble.

Ras Mengesha soon joined us and told us to sit down. He was very interested in us, in our work, and in the Simien. He said that seventeen years before he made a hunting trip to the Simien to capture Walia. He asked how many Walia were left now.

"About a hundred and fifty, sir," I answered.

He looked surprised. "No, there must be more than that. We saw many."

"If you went to the Simien now you would not recognize it, sir. Most of the forest has gone, and most of the Walia have either been shot or have died off. We are trying to hang on to what is left."

And thus we talked about wildlife and national parks, and the talk came round to Ras Mengesha's plans to open up the lowland region of Shire, near the Takazze River. There was a great deal of game there. Lions, leopards, gazelles, and even elephant and giraffe; at least, so they told us. He wanted us to come and look at it, and see if we agreed with his idea to make it a sanctuary.

"If we do not do something now it will be too late. We will make a road into there. We will arrange guides, vehicles, everything for your safari. We will come with you."

It sounded exciting, but I knew that time was too short for me to do it. Ah, if this had happened a year ago!

"I have some lions from Shire. Would you like to see them?" We went out into the garden, past the swimming pool in which a large frog was swimming. The lions were in large cages and were well cared for.

"There are many more. But the people kill them, you see." I said I would write that night and inform John Blower, and would press the department to do something.

"I think you must do it yourself. I have written to Major Gizaw about this, and have received no answer, so perhaps the department is not interested."

I assured him that General Mabratu would be interested, and hoped I was right.

We went back into the house. I admired the weapons on the wall. A vicious-looking scimitar. Two flintlock pistols. A great cannon of an elephant gun. They used to do a lot of elephant hunting in the old days. Not now though, for they had killed nearly all the elephant off. In the old days the warriors on their tough ponies would ride in close to the elephants, and slash with scimitars at the great beasts' legs, hamstringing them. Then they would kill them. It was a great mark of courage and manhood to kill an elephant, and I recalled how our game guards were awed when Mesfin told them he had killed twelve elephants in Tanzania. (It was part of his training, culling off overlarge herds in a park.)

I particularly admired a long-barreled, muzzle-loading rifle that looked very Arabian. Ras Mengesha said it had been given to his grandfather by the Tzar of Russia.

We said good-bye to the prince, again promising to do what we could. It was mid-August, and I would leave in two months for Japan. I knew in my heart that I could do nothing but write letters and talk, which usually achieves very little in Ethiopia.

I was taking photographs of the castle. Mesfin and the development officer were talking, leaning on the sun-heated hood of the Land Rover.

"You should not leave our country," said the bearded one. "Work here has only just started. We need people like you, people to go out and work in the country, work with the people, and be enthusiastic. We do not need people just sitting in the big city, taking high salaries and staying in offices. Do not leave yet."

I laughed. "Mesfin can take over. He knows as much as I do."

"Yes, he knows much. But he does not have the experience yet.

You would help him if you stay, just for another year. It will make a big difference."

"He is telling the truth," said Mesfin.

But the decision had been made. "Come on, let's go and have some coffee," I said, "and then we should be on our way to Asmara."

After Makale, the houses were nearly all enclosed in walled compounds. They were built of yellow stone, and had small, high windows. Once past Adigrat and into Eritrea, the roads were superb, markedly different from the roads in Shoa or Begemdir.

Guerrillas of the Eritrean Liberation Front were fairly active along this road, and I had our government papers and the pistol well hidden. Sometimes they stopped buses, or burned gasoline tankers. A couple of hundred kilometers outside Asmara we passed an army convoy. The trucks were stopped on the road, and soldiers in full battle kit were unloading stores and ammunition. An officer angrily waved me on as I slowed down.

We reached Asmara at five P.M. It is a clean, modern town. It is so like what I imagine an Italian town to be that it was hard to believe I was in Ethiopia. Many good restaurants serve excellent Italian food. The streets are clean, there are hardly any beggars, and nobody defecates in public. Our business took a few days, and that was good. It meant evenings with friends there, cool beer at sidewalk tables, seafood, pasta, and red wine.

We returned to Gondar via Axum. We stopped the car on the Tigre side of the Takazze River. The bridge was guarded by an old Italian block house, now manned by police. The big river formed the boundary between Tigre and Begemdir. Across from us was the district of Simien. The black walls and towers of the High Simien stood in a forbidding, mysterious line. The highland was dark with cloud, although we were in sunshine. Rain had fallen in the mountains, and the great river raced in a muddy flood toward the Sudan. I pointed across to the Begemdir side of the valley.

"Do you notice anything, Mesfin?"

"Simien?"

"Yes, that too. But look. On the Begemdir side there are many patches of cleared forest. They are even doing it now. On this side of the river there is no forest cutting."

"I know. They say that Ras Mengesha will punish the people very severely for cutting even a single tree. He dreams of restoring some of the old forests."

A river's width away, under the control of the Dejasmatch, the land was being raped into the desert, just like Tigre. One side of the river was trying to restore forest and the other was destroying it. I said harsh things about Begemdir and the bloody old Dejasmatch, and we drove across the bridge. The road up out of the valley, like so many in Ethiopia, zigzagged up impossible slopes, and was built by Italians.

There had been heavy rains in the Lemalemo area, causing slides of mud and rocks that blocked the road in several places. Five graders were working to keep the road clear. This was only the beginning. Practically all the trees and shrubs had been cut off, and there was nothing to hold the soil. They were even trying to plow, or cultivate by hoe. If they didn't reforest, they could easily lose the road completely. I had told Dejasmatch Araya, but he ignored it, and I had told the Highways Authority and they had said, yes, you are quite right, but did nothing to pressure the old man into controlling the peasants.

While we were away, a police team, headed by a tough lieutenant named Berhanu, had gone into the Simien to follow up the forest-cutting troubles. Together with some of our game guards, they went down and arrested Bogale Mersha. Bogale threatened them with his rifle, but in the end Guard Tedla seized him, wrestled the gun away from him, and put him under guard. They also arrested his wife, two farmer-priests, one man from Shagné village, and another from Zarema. They marched them under guard to Debarek and put them in jail there.

Later, Guards Mitiku and Tedla told me what had happened. Mitiku was a great mimic, and as he told the story, he threw out his chest, spoke in a deep voice, looking down his nose the way the old Dejasmatch did when he was angry. The Dejasmatch had been speaking to the lieutenant, even before the patrol went in.

"Do not bother this man Bogale Mersha. He is a good man, a big man, and he has not cut trees."

But the lieutenant had received his orders from General Seyoum, and he intended to follow them.

When the patrol returned, the old Dejasmatch raged at them, ordering the police to release the prisoners. But he had reckoned with the wrong man. Lieutenant Berhanu was built like a rock, and had the nature of a rock as well. Bogale shouted insults and threats from between the cracks in the rough-hewn, mud-plastered jail walls, but nobody listened to him. The prisoners would be held in jail until their trial on September 8.

Soon after I got back to Sankabar, another police and game guard patrol brought down about twenty prisoners from Amba Ras. They sat on the wet grass in front of my house. The guards said the men had been complaining, saying "Nicola is a kind man, but you are cruel." It was drizzling. We pitched tents for the prisoners and gave them grass mats to sleep on. The police would have kept them out in the rain all night. The men all seemed stunned by their arrest, for they were silent and acted as if they couldn't believe that the threats of myself and the guards had actually come about, especially since Nadu's victory.

I had brought a visitor up with me, a young man named Martin Adam from Selwyn College, Cambridge, who said he was traveling through the country as cheaply as possible. I was glad he came. He taught me the names of several plants, and a lot about various types of barley, but best of all he taught me about the parasol mushrooms which grew in great profusion in the Simien and which I had been dismissing as "toadstools." The field mushrooms—champignons —were almost over, and when Martin brought the parasol mushrooms home and ate them, recommending them to me, I found out that I had been passing up one of the most expensive delicacies that can be found on a Japanese table. It was such a pity that Sonako wasn't there to enjoy them.

The guards were all surprised that I ate these things, but Mitiku said that during the war, the old people would make wat from them, and Tedla remembered that some lowland people also ate them.

With the help of informers, I now knew for sure the names of the two big skin dealers in Zarema. They were both rich Moslems, with telephones, and they traded mainly in grain, oil seeds, cowhides, and the skins of sheep and goats. The leopard, serval, colobus monkey, and monitor lizard provided a very lucrative sideline. The skins were collected mainly in October and November, and were brought in by peasants from the lowland valleys of the Simien, and from those living in the direction of the Sudan. The skins went out to

Asmara by various means; sometimes wrapped in mats or sheep-skins and carried by a peasant, sometimes hidden in bundles of skins and hides going out by truck. Both of the dealers were Eritreans, and one of them had a relative in Asmara who had a shop that sold skins and trophies to tourists. Dejasmatch Araya's father was Eritrean. Our informers told us that the Dejasmatch frequently received bags of charcoal from these men in Zarema, and that Guard Chane, who had relatives there, and who was on good terms with the dealers, was taking bribes to keep quiet, and was serving the Governor. I was sure the old man was taking a nice cut, but of course could not prove it.

In this part of the country it was generally Moslems and Italians who handled this illegal business. It netted thousands, perhaps millions, of dollars. In Asmara the sale of wild-animal skins and the products made from them was booming. I don't want to seem rude to a very fine people, but the Italians seem very keen on this stuff.

We knew the whole story pretty well, but could not make it stand up in court, particularly in a corrupt court. Sure, we could nab the odd peasant coming in with a couple of skins, but that was no good. We wanted to hit the big dealers and the corrupt officials who shielded them.

And personally, I'd like to hit, in any sense you like, the big American, European, and Japanese fur shops, and the poncy fashion designers and painted old harridans who market the skins, and I'd like to see the old bags and tarts who buy leopard, cheetah, serval, or tiger skin coats get their arses pinched in a leopard gin trap. Mind you, I like fur myself, I don't see anything wrong with cultured mink. But enough people have gone over the practical reasons for wanting to preserve the remaining big cats, so I won't bother.

There was also a tremendous trade in live grivet monkeys. The locals were getting a dollar an animal. They were going to Asmara, and thence to laboratories in Europe. Most of this was done with no licenses, or with phony ones, issued on payment of bribes. Recently the department had been on to it, but it was going to take time. The animals were not treated well, and a large number died.

Up in Geech, Tag had a visitor. It was John Rivers, our English friend from Debarek. I went up to see them, and arrived in time for the exodus of Tag and his lions, Ruby and George. Tag too had decided to leave the Simien. He was sick of the lack of progress and the trouble with locals. He had been having trouble getting pack animals and was behind schedule. For some days he had been trying to coax the lions to follow him out, but they would only go so far, to the borders of their Geech territory, beyond which they refused to budge. The cubs were quite big now, and Tag had no cage large enough to carry them. He decided to give Ruby sleeping pills to make her more easily manageable, so that he could carry her out. John Rivers and Tag consulted on the dosage. They gave her a hell of a lot, but it didn't work.

On the last exasperating morning, Tag, John, and Guard Zeleka chased the lions all over the highland moor. In the end, Tag borrowed belts from everybody's trousers and tied Ruby's legs. He hoisted her on his shoulders and carried her a few kilometers to the top of the trail leading down to the stream. George followed part of the way, yowling, but in the end he refused to move, and Tag had to go back, catch him, truss him, and carry him too. Tag's back was all scratched, but he didn't seem to mind. Once out of their territory, the lions decided to walk, and gave no more trouble. They spent the night in Sankabar, and went on to Debarek in the morning. There Tag put them in the Land Rover, intending to drive them to Awash.

Guards Zeleka and Tedla reported early in the morning to ask for allowances before going down to testify at a preliminary hearing of Bogale Mersha's case.

It was a fine morning. After seeing the men off, I went out. The sun on the dew made it gleam like quicksilver clinging to the grass, to lady's mantle and to maiden hair. Hills of deep green rose to meet a sky of deep blue. Swallows dipping and diving. I watched the shadowed valleys gradually flood with light, and the white waterfalls come alive with moving silver. The sounds of water were very clear, and it was so quiet that I could even hear a donkey braying below the great cliff, and the far-off calls of shepherd boys. The sun felt strong and good on my skin. But by nine o'clock, cotton wool clouds formed at the escarpment rim, and by noon we were again shrouded in fog, with thunder all around us.

That night, while reading after supper, I heard a hyena whoop. Mogus leaped up, snarling and growling, and pawed at the door. I took a rifle. Recently one of our horses had been injured by a hyena.

We went after it, and it ran off toward the Amba Ras side of the Sankabar ridge. Mogus was bristling with hatred. Guard Nagur came out and called after us.

"The hyena has gone. It fears brother Mogus. He is a strong dog. Lord, please now come to my house, I have some good talla."

He showed me into the house and gave me the stone seat by the Eskimo-style oil-drum stove. The house was lit by an oil lantern. I hoped they would have electricity one day. Nagur's children were sleeping, wrapped in a gabi. His wife poured talla into an old tin can. She poured a little into the palm of her hand, sipped it, and passed the can to me. It was the thick, unfiltered stuff of the Simien known as "korafe." It had a nutty, slightly bitter flavor. It was cool, and I liked it, although it usually gave me stomach trouble.

We talked. It was surprising how much I could understand and get across even with my poor command of Amharic. Nagur was telling me about his time in Gambella, in the south. He insisted that the sun rose in the south and set in the north down there. I listened politely. Mogus growled and went outside. He had heard a rat.

"It's OK, Mogus. Come in." He came in and looked at me.

"Sit." He sat by me while I fondled his ears.

"He is not a dog," said Nagur. "He has the heart of a man." Mogus and I went home. The hyena would not come back. I felt strongly that the companionship of my dog was a precious thing, especially at night, when we sat by the fire, I reading and writing.

The next morning I got up at dawn and went out to observe Walia. Mogus wanted to come too, but he frightened the Walia off. I picked up his chain, meaning to tie him in the house until I came back. The dog jumped up and ran into the kitchen, ears back, tail between his legs. I wondered what the hell was going on, and called him. But he would not come. When I went toward him, chain in hand, he crouched and snarled, something he had never done to me before. Was it the chain? I raised it, speaking softly, and he crouched, teeth bared. Why was he afraid of the chain? He never used to be. It used to signify walks, and now whenever he was chained, I always gave him some treat, usually raw eggs and milk. I put the chain down and called him to me. He came, seemingly embarrassed by the whole business. But there was no doubt about it. While I had been away, somebody had beaten him with the chain. Who could it be? Surely not Abahoy, and certainly not Mesfin.

A democratic prince

I had been worried about my dog. I could not take him to Japan. Mesfin wanted him, but I wondered how long they would be together. Recently I had found him difficult to manage. Ever since the boys in Gondar had stoned him as a puppy he had hated Ethiopian children. He chased them, and though he never bit them, he was a big, strong, fast dog, with jaws that could crack a sheep's leg, or a child's, with no trouble. I had taught him to jump for the throat, and sometimes in practice, his charge would knock me over. But I had been a very poor master. I had left him for long periods of time. And now, this new business with the chain was nasty. He might be dangerous, he might have developed a kink in his personality. Animals and men are most dangerous when triggered by fear.

I went out in the evening, taking the dog. He roused two klipspringers and chased them, refusing to come to heel. Before, he would chase only a few yards, then come to heel. What could I do with him? I had no time to retrain him, or to correct the poor training.

The next day, Nadu came down from Amba Ras, bringing a lot of papers. He had been claiming money for the work done on the house he built at the top of the hill, the one we had taken over. The department had ordered me to pay him, and I refused, saying that he had no receipts, and that the sum he claimed was ridiculously high. However, he was now a member of parliament. The General ordered me to pay him. The receipts Nadu brought were phony. I pointed out to Nadu that the receipts were all in his own handwriting. He said the men he paid were unable to write, which was probably true. But I knew they were phony. No proof, no proof. He looked his elegant best. He was going down to Debarek. I wrote him a note, saying that I did not have the money, and that if they chose to, the department could pay him at headquarters.

Nadu went down to Debarek. He spoke with Dejasmatch Araya and visited Bogale Mersha in jail. Then he telephoned General Mabratu and asked if the General would give orders for the release of Bogale. Bogale was a good, important man, a gentleman who never harmed the forest. General Mabratu had seen the photographs and our reports. He slammed the receiver down, having told Nadu to go to hell.

Colonel Tamurat was warned by telephone to guard against attempts by Dejasmatch Araya and Nadu to spring Bogale Mersha from jail before the trial.

Tsehai was going to take the park accounts to Addis. He brought his fourteen-year-old wife Yeshe down to Debarek. It was late afternoon, and the fog had cleared from the highlands. Yeshe was cooking, and I went out to look at the steel-blue thunderclouds that surrounded us. They towered way up, classical cumulus nimbus, their tops giving way to wispy cirrus. A wash of salmon pink lay over distant purple hills, and here and there ragged skeins of rain trailed from cloud bottoms, reminding me of great jellyfish, moving slowly over a clear sea, trailing deadly tendrils. We were high, so high that hills looked like waves, or ripples in sand.

A flock of choughs tumbled and clowned, voices raucous and funny. Francolin took off from slopes, with a strong flutter followed by a long, cackling glide. White clouds stood around some rock faces like voluminous skirts.

At six P.M. a heavy hailstorm passed over us, dropping ice pellets as big as beans. I ran outside and collected handfuls, put them in a glass and poured in whiskey, not because I was thirsty or needed anything, but because the idea appealed to me. The storm passed, the hail melted, and oblique sun rays hit water droplets hanging on every twig and leaf, making them look like diamonds.

A fantastic storm was raging over Geech, and I went out to stand in the sun, watching the lightning tongues and dark backdrops of cloud and rain. Way below, swollen rivers were orange-brown with mud.

On a line outside my house, fifty stiff woolen hats hung like mute bells. I bought them from the shepherd boys.

Below, clouds clung to lowland hills, and the clouds were white, ripped and tattered at the edges. Wind-pulled shawls? Horses' manes?

I turned to Tsehai. "Look at that. Isn't it fantastic?" He laughed unnaturally, as if I had made a joke, and didn't bother to look out of the window. I went out, sat on a damp rock until it was dark, looking and thinking.

The next day was foggy and dark. The guards found three sheep which had been missing. I had bought those sheep for their New Year feast. The sheep had been neatly and cleanly killed by a jackal. Abahoy cleaned and skinned the sheep, and to his horror, I said that I intended to share the meat with Mogus.

I was painting the windows, shutters, and doors of the house a

A democratic prince

bright red. Nadu came. He had been to Addis Ababa. He had come to talk to me about Abahoy's quarrel with old man Techane and Techane's son—the one Abahoy had stabbed. Nadu wanted me to hold back Abahoy's pay and hand it to the old man. I refused. Abahoy said he would pay in November. Nadu spoke an oath and held out his hand, palm up, for Abahoy to slap it, repeat the oath, and seal the promise. Abahoy looked away, betraying the fact that he was lying. He would lie, but would never break an oath. Nadu warned him he would have to go to court. But I knew that Abahoy was thinking of going to Addis Ababa after I left.

Guard Zeleka came back. The trial was still pending, and Bogale Mersha was still in jail. Zeleka reported to me, asked for more allowances, then went up to his hut. I went up to see him, to talk about in-park patrols. He was sitting by the door, with Guard Azezew's rifle in pieces. He had taken it off the man and looked at it. The barrel was totally blocked with dirt, though the outside was polished. It was an old Italian rifle, with a long barrel. Zeleka had told Azezew to clean it but he was useless. We would fine him, and take the rifle from him for a week, but it would do no good. None of the Simien guards could ever remember or appreciate the need to keep the guts of a rifle clean. To them, only the outside was seen, by them or by others, and only the outside was important. Zeleka muttered curses and insults, and would work all day on it.

Night. Lightning playing on hills some fourteen miles away. Owls hooting.

On September 8, Mesfin went down to Gondar to get salaries. Guards Zeleka, Nagur, and I went out toward Addis Gey where people were cutting forest. On the way, we stopped and looked down on Bogale's house. Some men were plowing down there. Bogale had been tried the day before, but we had not yet heard the results. A narrow footpath led from the top down to Bogale's place, and as we passed, a peasant came panting up, carrying a small goatskin bag of grain. Zeleka asked the man if he knew Bogale, and boasted that now Bogale was going to pay for his stupidity in annoying us. The peasant smiled and said nothing.

Several hundred trees had been cut at Addis Gey. Fearing us, the people had hidden, and there were no men around, all of them having run off into the woods.

A new house frame was standing. In a rage, I told the guards to go and sit a little way away, facing the opposite direction. Then I tore down the frame, leaving it a jumbled pile of logs on the ground. My face and back ran with sweat. What could we do?

It rained like hell on the way back. The paths were slippery, the streams swollen.

A baby ground-scraper thrush was fluttering helplessly in a flooded meadow. I picked it up and carried it inside my shirt, hoping to keep it alive and raise it at home. But on the way it died in my hand. I laid the dead bird by the path, and looked up, feeling very sad, and noticed that the Maskal flowers had dusted all of the hillsides with gold.

The news of Bogale's trial had gone ahead of us. When we got back to camp we learned that he had been fined a paltry thirty dollars and released, boasting that the foreigner and his soldiers could do nothing against him, and that his enemies were going to regret all of this. The judge, a man called Sendaku, had been bribed. The fine would not even pay for the allowances of even one of the guards sent down to testify at the trial.

Zeleka spat on the ground. He said that now we could expect serious trouble from Bogale and his men. The news would travel fast, and the people would all begin cutting trees with a vengeance. They would know that the courts would do little against them, and yet also, I think, they recognized the very fact that the trial had been held as the thin edge of the conservation wedge. They would cut as much as they could, while they could.

It was Zeleka and Nagur who came to tell me. They left me trembling with fury. I pounded the punching bag for an hour before I could control myself enough to sit down and drink coffee.

Guard Tedla returned toward evening. He was stamping and gesturing with rage. I said the courthouse was a bribe house, and Tedla liked the term, kept repeating it, making gestures as if hurling something to the floor. "Truth! By God! Bribe house! Bribe house! Truth! By God!"

Night. Bats chirping, dipping. Owls hooting, winging against the deep purple sky with a silent, deep-flapping flight. A few grass rats scuttling in the walls.

I was in a depression. We had fought like hell to get Bogale Mersha to jail. And now this. I had little doubt that the Addis Gey cutting had been encouraged by the people hearing the news. This year the destruction would be the worst ever, especially after I left.

And on top of all this, I had just heard the news about Tesfae and Mamo, the drivers. They got twenty years each. Twenty years in an Ethiopian jail would be worse than hell. It was as good as a death sentence, or worse. Yet the Simien relatives of the dead man were unsatisfied. They were appealing the sentence, pressing for a hanging. They had quarreled over the blood money, and each brother had wanted to keep his share, depriving the man's wife and children. Damn and hell and shit.

The sun came out the next day, giving us a fine morning. Mogus and I went for a walk along the escarpment. We came across a herd of gelada. Mogus took off like a shot. The gelada bolted, but one female fumbled picking up her young one. I yelled at the dog and ran along the dangerous rocky slopes, trying to get there. He snapped at the baby baboon, who screamed in terror. Three big males forgot their fear and charged, driving the dog back, but he closed again to fight them. I had never seen him look so savage before. I got closer, yelling, and the dog saw me, and bolted for the giant heather woods, refusing to come back.

I went back to the house and got a rifle. I followed after him, calling him. Had he come back to me then, perhaps things would have been different. But he slunk around like a cur. Did he sense the danger in me?

Later, when I had given up and was in the house, he slunk around, then forgot himself, and began his usual game of chasing crows.

I went out and called him. He was very nervous, and all anger went out of me. He was my dog, the companion of many lonely nights, and I had left him too long alone, neglecting him by my absence. But he was in a national park, and had shown himself to be potentially dangerous. I fondled his big head and held him to my chest. He looked up at me. I got a good piece of meat and put it in front of him. Then, while he was eating it, I went around behind him and shot him in the back of the head.

His body looked so different in death. He was just a dead dog. Before, he had been a presence, a friend, a companion. And I remembered everything about him, his sighs at night, his enthusiasm for walks and rough play, his abhorrence of my harmonica playing, his soft whining in the early morning when he wanted me to get up, the way he had always gone everywhere with my young son.

I dug a grave in front of my house and laid him in it. It had been sunny, but as I was filling the grave, a cold mist came in from the cliffs, and it grew dark quickly. Just as I was pounding in the head-board, with his name burned on it with a hot iron, a storm came, the worst I had experienced in the Simien. Water roared in gullies and streams, it made new streams down all the slopes, and flooded the cobbled front of the house. The dog's dish floated outside the door in a great, rain-pocked puddle. A flood five feet deep thundered past the spring, and on the cliff path to Sankabar, landslides tore down through the trees, destroying chunks of the trail.

But the rain washed away the blood and the loose soil around the grave. It was three o'clock in the afternoon. Abahoy came to the house. He heard what I had done and began to rage at me, and I realized for the first time that he truly had been fond of the dog. I warned him, and he shut up and left the house.

. . . And I am sad, and sad, and sad, and my heart feels like a dull lump in my chest, and I go into my room, throw myself on the bed and weep like a child. In the living room, my son's photograph stared out at me with seeming reproach, and I couldn't stand it, and turned the photograph down, for a while at least. . . .

That night, Zeleka, Mitiku, and Abahoy came to the house. They said they would not leave me alone, and that all the men, as well as the wives, had been weeping. Zeleka seemed to understand, and tried to explain to Abahoy. I didn't want to talk about it. We drank katikalla, the local moonshine, and got drunk.

On the shelf, there was a Japanese children's book, a simplified version of an ancient Chinese story of a monkey called Songoku, who set out with a priest to fetch some holy Buddhist scriptures. The monkey was a wild fellow, always getting into trouble, but he was strong and had magic powers, and always helped the priest out. I read it, translating it into broken Amharic for Mitiku and the others, who were delighted.

Zeleka, Mitiku, and Abahoy loved to see pictures, especially Aba-hoy. Since he had begun working for me he had seen so many that now he was beginning to understand them. The majority of the Sim-ien people had never seen a picture, and it meant nothing to them. They would turn it upside down, admiring the color, but not seeing the shape or what the picture tried to depict. They would even turn a picture of a man upside down, looking puzzled. Pictures were scrawls on paper and could not be associated with solid, three-dimensional things, or with living creatures. Perspective in pictures was especially puzzling to them. Ethiopian paintings, those seen in the big, fine churches, were flat, with no perspective, and indeed, the greater majority of Simien people had never even seen those. We are so used to being able to teach and demonstrate with pictures, diagrams, and maps that we forget it is a learned skill. Of course, some of the Simien men, like Abahoy and Mitiku, had seen pictures and could understand what they depicted, though even they could not recognize details. These pictures in the Japanese children's book were very simple, and the three men pointed and guffawed as I told them the story.

Late at night, when they were going to leave, Abahoy stopped at the door and said he would sleep in the house, as Mogus was not here. I told him that it was all right, and Zeleka laughed, saying that I had a rifle, and could defend myself.

But in the blackness of my room, the memory of the death of my dog kept repeating itself over and over again in my mind like a looped film. Mental pictures: gunshot, body stiffening, blood from the mouth, eyes glazing, one paw twitching. I twisted and turned, pushing my face into the pillow, trying to get away from my own memory. Sleep was impossible.

And while I was wondering if I was going crazy, and while the dark room spun around me, the night quiet was shattered by the awful whoop of a hyena. The hyena was right close to the house. Never before had one dared to come so close. It knew the dog was dead. It was whooping and sniffing around, and chuckling evilly, and the Celtic part of me became afraid of the supernatural, and for a long time I lay still in the bed, unable to see in the darkness, and unable to move, sweating profusely.

Then it broke, and I leaped out of the bed, grabbing a rifle, going out into the night, stark naked, cursing. But the hyena ambled away, and I could not shoot.

The hyena went away. I returned to bed, leaning the rifle against the wall, within easy reach. And tried to sleep.

21

SIMIEN: A NATIONAL PARK

It was the Ethiopian New Year, the feast of Saint Yohannes. I slept in, not wanting to face the world. People were banging at the door, but I ignored it. Finally they went away. I tried to sleep again, but couldn't. The people came back, and the banging started once again, more insistently. Muttering angrily, I got out of bed, pulled on shorts and boots, and went to the door, ready to shout at the intruders if it wasn't something important. I wrenched the door open.

Three children stood there, holding small bunches of flowers, violets, scabious, and Maskal daisies. They handed the flowers to me and wished me happiness. All those sour morning thoughts choked in my gullet. I bent down, picked up the smallest child, a boy about five, and hugged him. I called them all into the house, found candies and biscuits, made them sit down, and mixed up powdered juice crystals. To each child I gave a picture book. The children sat stiffly, staring with wide eyes around the house, feeling a little bit afraid perhaps, but not crying or protesting. When they left they clutched candies for the other camp children, and they ran laughing up the hill, delighted especially with the old picture books.

Later, Zeleka and Kebede came down, and they too brought flowers. I invited them in and we had a cup of tea together. There was going to be a feast. I should come and eat with them. The women had been cooking all the previous day, and there were three sheep to be slaughtered, one of which I had presented to them. There would be talla, tedj, katikalla, meat, injera, and spiced bread.

Resplendent in clean slacks, shirt, and jacket, I went around the houses, taking food and drink at each. The sheep to be slaughtered were tethered to the central poles of the houses. They would have their throats cut inside the house, and the house and family would be blessed for the year. The women wore clean white shammas, and the men wore their gabis. Abahoy wore full national dress and looked like a real Amhara gentleman. Tedla's wife was magnificently pregnant. The baby was due any moment, and she said it kicked like a boy. Kebede's wife was very pretty, and she fluttered her long eye-lashes at me when she passed the drinking horn, more from kindness than from flirtation.

After the killings and the blessings, the dead sheep were carried out to be butchered. The men hung them from the branches of a tree. Thick-billed ravens alighted nearby, watching and waiting. The men were happy, arguing about which part of the sheep was best. Even Dure, the Moslem muleteer, was happy enough, and amused us all with his antics and jokes. He couldn't eat meat killed by Christians, but he had two nice chickens for his feast, and he would share the bread, injera, and coffee, and maybe he might have a sly nip of katikalla.

I had to eat four times, in four houses. They filled me with meat and drink until it was painful. Zeleka made a speech, mostly blessings and thanks to myself. It was all embarrassing in a way, especially as I felt very deeply. I had cursed and criticized these men, but in two years we had become close.

In the late afternoon, everybody came down to the house for tea. Abahoy brewed up two big camp kettles of it, and we threw in a couple of pounds of sugar.

Mitiku pointed to the bookshelves and said to another man, "The master has many books, especially with pictures of foreign lands and animals."

Zeleka took a book, querying me with a glance. I nodded.

"Here, you cold-country peasant. What is this?" He pointed to a picture of a wildebeeste.

"It is a gazelle," said one.

"No, it is a kudu," said another.

A third thought it was a buffalo. Zeleka laughed and tried to explain. The next picture was of an ostrich.

"Truly," said Abahoy, "it is that which is known in our country as 'the horse of Satan.'" I knew that to be the huge ground hornbill, fairly common in the lowlands.

"No," said Zeleka. "Would they put devil eggs on the roof of the church?" He explained what it was, where it lived. "You men should all go to the south lands and see all the wonderful animals in our country."

"Truly," said Nagur, "when I went to Gambella I saw many strange animals and learned much."

"If I am sent to the south, I will go," said one guard, "though before the master came, I would have refused. I would not leave my country before. But the master left his country to live and work with us, and he has taught us many things. Now I would even go to other lands to see things."

"Even though you go to Gambella, or Omo," said Zeleka, "you are still in Ethiopia, you still serve the same Emperor. Must we not serve the Emperor anywhere in his lands? Are we not all Ethiopians? Mr. Nicol came to live with us. Now he will leave. It is a sad thing."

They shook their heads, and were all quiet.

"The new warden is a very good man," I said. "He was a soldier. He is good and brave."

Zeleka shrugged. "But how long will he stay with us?"

"Perhaps three months." They had to be told. There was no permanent replacement. Major John Bromley, the tough ex-British Consul from Asmara, now employed as game warden for Eritrea, was going to take over the park for a short time, while they tried to find another warden. He had taken the Awash Park over when Peter Hay left. Now he was coming to the Simien. I would go down the next day and meet him in Gondar. Then we would come back, and I would sign over all the park assets to him. There would be a transition period of just over two weeks. Then it would be all over for me.

When they all left, the house was very quiet. Several pots of flowers stood on the table. I took them all out and laid them on Mogus' grave.

That night again the hyena came back, trying to dig Mogus out of the earth. I went out into the night with the rifle, but the hyena was a quick, shambling ghost in the blackness, and it was too dark to see the sights. Oh, for a 12-gauge shotgun and a charge of buckshot! All night long I waited by the window with the gun, in the dark, silent house, guarding the grave of my dog until gray light stole into the eastern sky. When it was light I drank coffee, then went out and piled the grave with big rocks. There was something evil, sinister, about that hyena.

Tag had taken the Land Rover to carry the lions to Awash, so I had to go on the bus from Debarek. A little man who called himself the assistant lawyer was in Debarek, fussing around about the release of Bogale Mersha, and telling me about the bribes that Bogale had paid to the judge and to a certain police corporal. It was all rather annoying.

The bus wasn't too crowded. A drunken Eritrean kept yelling at me in Italian, which I could not understand. I yelled back at him in Amharic, saying that I was English, and could not understand Italian. But the man kept on. An old patriarch, white-haired, white-bearded, in national dress, with a long black cloak, shouted at the drunk, telling him to speak either English or Amharic or shut his noise. He said that English and Ethiopians fought together to drive the Italians out of this land, and he had no cause to insist on using their language. Other people in the bus clapped and laughed, and I felt sorry for the Eritrean, who just presumed that all white men spoke Italian. The old patriarch sat down, hitching his cloak, revealing for an instant two treasured things attached to his belt—a Bible in a leather case and a big old .45 service revolver. I bowed to the old man who looked as fierce and proud as a hawk. He nodded, but didn't smile. A rifle-carrying villager stood up and told the old man who I was, and he turned again and asked if I was well. I replied that, with thanks to God, I was.

That day, not so many people were boarding the bus. This made the bus early, for it was the embarking and disembarking of passengers that took the most time. Not wishing to come into town ahead of schedule, the driver stopped four kilometers out of town and waited for half an hour. The passengers got out, uncomplaining, and walked up and down the road, taking the opportunity to urinate. Two years before, this sort of thing would have infuriated me. Now I didn't care.

In Gondar the next day, I phoned General Mabratu and told him about Bogale's case. He said he thought the whole affair was disgraceful, and promised to do something about it.

A driver from headquarters brought back our Land Rover from Addis Ababa. The back seats were all ripped up by the two lions.

The driver was a nice fellow. He too had been fighting in Korea, and had been wounded, and had gone to Japan for treatment. His English was quite good.

"Sir. They tell me you go to Japan."

"That's right. In the middle of October."

"Please do me a favor. I knew this girl in Yokohama." He produced a yellowed, tattered photograph of himself and a round-faced Japanese girl. He was in uniform, and looked very young and handsome.

"Please, go to her and tell her my kind wishes. She live in Yokohama." He had her address. But it was about eighteen years old. Did he really think I could find her now? And if I found her, there was a good chance that she was married, with children, and did not wish to be reminded of a love affair with a foreign soldier.

"You write to her. If she answers, I will take her a present from you. If she doesn't answer, she has moved, and I don't think I can find her. Japan has changed since you were there." He nodded, and put the photograph away. Then he took his bag and his rifle out of the car and walked toward a cheap hotel. I called after him, promising to see him in Addis Ababa, and reminding him to take the bolt out of the rifle if he didn't want trouble with the police in town.

Major John Bromley arrived with his two poodles. Mrs. Bromley would come up later, alone, from Asmara. We stayed at the Iteghie Hotel. The younger of the poodles crapped in the lounge. There was a great flurry over that. Buckets, mops, spray deodorant. Then it did it again, right in the middle of the dining room, while everybody was eating. John was pretending he couldn't see it.

We fiddled about in town. Signing over bank accounts, introductions to officials and tradesmen. John and Colonel Azziz were old friends, dating back from the time when John was British Consul near the Kenya border, and Azziz was stationed down in the district. John also knew General Seyoum very well. In fact, John and his wife knew practically every important person in the country.

When we got to Debarek, I had some trouble to handle. One of Dejasmatch Araya's servants had killed a pregnant bushbuck, and had been caught by Guard·Takalé. The old Governor was trying to threaten and cajole Takalé off the case, but Takalé dug his heels in. We had to go to see Dejasmatch Araya anyway. I asked the old man about it, saying that it was very embarrassing when one's own men did bad things, and that I knew this, and that I sympathized with him, and with his anger with his servant, who had so disgraced him, even after he had promised General Mabratu his cooperation. It took a long time for me to get all that across, but he understood, and pretended a righteous indignation with his servant, who was an ignorant man. How could this man shoot a bushbuck? Perhaps he mistook it for a baboon? He had ordered him only to shoot baboons. I nodded . . . yes, yes, sometimes our men did not understand us.

Going at it like a bull at a gate would only get the old man furious, and he would probably take his fury out on Takalé.

John Bromley had also met Dejasmatch Araya before, at some official function in Axum. They greeted each other, and I told the Dejasmatch that John was taking over from me. He shook his head, saying that I was a bad man for leaving the Simien.

Mrs. Bromley was going to drive to Debarek from Asmara in a few days' time. We got Zeleka to wait in Debarek for her, and we asked Dejasmatch Araya to keep his eye open and see that she was all right. He promised to do so, and I knew that for this sort of thing he was a man of his word. He called a servant and ordered him to bring us tedj.

On September 18 we had an easy, pleasant ride to Sankabar. John liked the house, although he had been used to far better quarters in Awash.

It was that night that Tedla's wife gave birth to the baby boy, and Tedla ran down in the early morning to tell me. Things were happening.

. . . Guard Takalé had divorced his wife in Lemalemo and was going to marry Guard Tedla's youngest daughter. She was about fourteen years old. His wife in Lemalemo was without support for herself and her two children.

. . . An expedition of botanists from the university in Addis Ababa had set up a camp in Geech. They were collecting plants all over the highland and the Djinn Barr Valley. They came and camped in Sankabar. I offered them a hot shower, and we had a couple of evenings together. They had collected over two hundred different flowers, many of which had yet to be identified. They said there must be at least ten different kinds of orchids in the park. Had time permitted them to explore the escarpment foot, they suspected that they could have found at least six hundred different plants in the Simien. It was evident that this place was just as important for botanists as it was for zoologists.

It was certainly the time for flowers. Hills were covered with Maskal daisies, and with alternative carpets of blue sage, or great fields of orange and red-hot pokers, scattered ox-eye daisies, clover, buttercups, scabious, and lots of flowers with long Latin names. Along pathways the jasmine was sweet, and there were masses of paired white balsam flowers. Around the rocks grew pennywort and violet, and a slender, long-stemmed plant that looked like a gladiolus. The giant heather was in blossom too. Its flowers were tiny white bells, and they made the dark green trees look as if they had been dipped in silver-gray paint. Like jewels, tiny blue flowers grew in the close-cropped grass. There were geraniums and pinks, and a tall yellow flower that looked to me like a hollyhock. On the south-facing slopes of the Sankabar ridge the aloes were just beginning to flower, fleshy, prickly leaves of a purple-green, with orange flowers. I had never seen so many flowers. A mixture of high mountain and forest, desert and meadow, Europe and Africa.

One of the botanists even found a willow tree growing in the Khabar Valley.

There were four members of the group, an English couple, and a Dutch couple. I asked if they had seen Walia. The topic brought out the fact that one of our guards, probably Ambaw, had told them there were at least a thousand Walia left in the park. Ambaw was Nadu's man. Although he had accompanied Dr. Nievergelt and seen for himself how few Walia there were, he still kept to Nadu's figures. This was what Nadu was telling officials, and they believed him, as Ambaw had believed him, despite the fact that Ambaw himself had seen the careful spotting and counting, the daily observations, the recognition of marked animals. I was afraid that now Nadu was going to parliament, he would be listened to by the lawmakers, and they would believe his figures. Afterward I was ranting to Mesfin about it.

"Oh, those guards," he said. "They know nothing, but they can be stubborn. You know, they sent one of the Addis guards out with a hunter and his client. One day they shot a big warthog. The guard checked it off on the list as a buffalo. The hunter saw this. He thought it was just a mistake, so he told him, 'Hey, that is not a buffalo, it's a warthog.' Then the game guard thought the hunter was trying to trick him, and he insisted. He wouldn't let them shoot a buffalo, even though they had paid a lot of money for the license. They were really mad when they got back to Addis."

It was a credible story. Some of our men could not tell aardvark from hyena, and had not a clue about lowland animals. And it was difficult to teach them, for they were so stuffed with folklore, and they could not "see" pictures.

The botanists left, and John and I were left in Sankabar, waiting for Mrs. Bromley to arrive, and going through stores, making an inventory of every item. We hauled out the tents, to dry and check them after the long damp season. The rainy season had pretty well come to a close. The park files needed a lot of explaining. I wondered how it was possible to accumulate so much paper in only two years. We had just the medicines to check over when I put down the pencil and suggested a walk up the hill. The weather was clear, the view superb, and there was a chance of seeing Walia.

We walked slowly up through the carpets of blue sage and the sweetly scented thyme. Stopping, we looked down on the house, with a faint blue feather of smoke from the kitchen chimney.

A big lammergeyer was circling around, holding something in his feet. He came round and dipped into a dive. I pointed excitedly. "Look! He's got a bone!"

The big bird dropped the bone, and it hit the rocks behind my house, bouncing about six feet. The lammergeyer landed, strutted over to the bone and pecked at it. No luck this time. He picked it up again and took off. Once in the air he transferred the bone from beak to feet with a smooth movement. He circled a couple of times, then stooped into a dive again, releasing the bone halfway. We could see it clearly. It hit the rocks. The lammergeyer landed. Holding the bone down with a big, talonned foot, he pecked away the cracked bone splinters and ate the marrow. We had been watching what many scientists had debunked as mere folk legend.

When we got to the top of the hill, I looked down and saw three klipspringers, grazing on ledges just below. Although I had seen it hundreds of times, I never grew tired of the view. It was indescribable, and now, with the rains just over, it was all green, gold, blue, and purple.

On the fifth day, while we were still in Sankabar waiting for Mrs.

Bromley, some people came to the door. Foreigners—a slim young man and an attractive girl. They greeted me by name, in the Japanese language, and introduced themselves as Pierre and Delphine. They were French. They had been traveling through the country, and having heard about the Simien and the strange Englishman living up there, they had decided to come and visit.

We had much in common. They too loved Japan, and had recently spent some time there, studying. Delphine was a professor of the Chinese language, and both could read and write Chinese characters. They spoke Japanese well, and Chinese (so they said) even better.

I invited them in for tea and food. Yes, they would stay the night. And a bath? A real Japanese-style bath? The idea so amused them that they jumped up and went out with me to gaze upon the deep stone tub. We chattered in a mixture of Japanese, English, and French.

In the afternoon, we went for a walk and picked a few flowers. On returning to the house, Delphine asked if I had a flat, shallow flower dish. There was one. And did I have any "kenzan"—the spiked weights used in flower arranging. Indeed I did. From half-packed boxes here and there I produced all that was needed to make a Japanese flower arrangement. The three of us were laughing. It was like a game. John sat in a chair by the fire, smiling. We must have seemed very juvenile to him at that time. Delphine made two classical arrangements. One was placed in a niche in the wall, against a sort of screen of bamboo that I had built into the wall especially as a backing for flower arrangements.

The talk and the flowers brought strong memories of Japan. Some excitement was mounting in me. I was going back, to my family and friends. A thousand images came to my mind.

Pierre and Delphine went up to Geech. They spent a night there and returned to Sankabar. So we had another night together.

We were sitting around the fire, talking. John had produced some very good gin and whiskey, while I was drinking katikalla.

"Is that stuff strong?" asked Pierre.

"Yes," I answered nonchalantly, and to prove a point, tossed half a glass of it into the hot fire. It exploded, and a gush of blue flame blew outward, singeing people's eyebrows and hair.

"See?" I picked up the jug and poured a nip more. "Would you like some?"

Simien: a national park

"Christ, no!"

"John, I think we have to go up to Geech tomorrow. There's not much time left. We can leave Abahoy with the house, and he will look after your wife when she arrives. I'm sorry, but I can't see any other way."

He was worried about his wife, even though he knew her to be as capable as any man in the bush, but he agreed. We would go up to Geech.

So we went up the next day, and on the way we stopped off for a picnic lunch at the promontory overlooking the Djinn Barr falls. Pierre and Delphine came with us as far as the lunch spot, to see the falls. It was a good day. Quite a lot of water was flowing, and the sun in the mist of the falls made two rainbows.

I gathered sticks, made a fireplace of stones, and lit a small fire. We had tea, coffee, baked beans, black bread, cheese, and even a pot of caviar and a bottle of red wine. I loved this place. The sound of the falls was powerful, and the abyss was awe-inspiring; to the north, windowed by the mighty towers, spires, and faces of the Geech cliffs, was a wide view of lowland hills. The deep gorge below was thick with forest. Trees on the lookout point gave cover, and thus it was a good place to spot Walia and birds.

John was impressed. He had been to the Simien before, some years ago, but this was the first time he had seen the falls from a good angle.

"If ever there is a road to Sankabar," I said, "then this would be a fine spot for the less energetic guests. It is only an hour's walk from the camp, and downhill. They could leave their cars there, walk along that beautiful path with all those flowers, or perhaps along the escarpment path. We could have mules for them if they wanted them. At the meadow we could have a little coffee shop, a nice round, thatched, stone-built place with big windows and a veranda. Then, with a bit of work on the path leading to this point, and a guard rail at the last bit, they could enjoy the falls and the whole scene. We could have some salt licks down on those ledges, so the Walia would be attracted. This must be one of the most spectacular waterfalls of any park in the world. Look at that drop."

Whenever I came to a place like this, I got carried away with enthusiasm, ideas, and plans.

After lunch, Pierre and I scrambled down a couple of hundred meters to get a better view of the lower series of falls, hidden by the sheer depth of the abyss.

We sat on a grassy ledge, by a tree that leaned out over the drop, talking. He talked about Kyoto, and the people there, and carried my thoughts back to the ancient city. When I was about fourteen years old, I had conceived a wish to visit Kyoto and see the stone garden in the temple of Ryoanji. I was twenty-two by the time the wish was realized. The garden was smaller than I had imagined, but serenity was there.

"I wonder," I said, "if it is possible to achieve the peace and tranquility in a temple in a city that one can achieve in a place like this. Kyoto is fine, and beautiful, but let's face it, it is still a city. You don't have to go too far to bump into cars and people, and smell exhaust fumes." Pierre said little. Oh, we talked of the solemn boom of the temple bells in the morning, and about the narrow and exciting back streets, and the soft accents and gentle manners of the girls.

No place of manmade beauty, or of religion, could ever give me the peace of mind that the Simien had begun to give me. I tried to give myself and others the impression that I was a drinking, fighting, cursing swashbuckler, but in truth I was a contemplative being, and Simien, especially in the past six months, had given me a chance to look out, out onto vast and distant mountains, and horizons lost in farness, and strange birds and rare animals, and the looking out had given me introspection. I had seen perhaps brief glimpses of soul. All around me were patterns of life, so vast, so minute, so wild, so ordered, but above all, so logical and perfect. Yes, yes, Kyoto and its temples were serene, beautiful, ordered . . . but nothing, nothing to compare with all this. When man tries to create beauty his works are commendable, but somewhat trifling. When he ignores evil, however, the ugliness he creates is enormous. In going back to Tokyo, I was going to throw myself into some of that ugliness.

"Do you know, Pierre," I said, "you can look down on all those hills, and you won't see a single stinking chimney, nor a tangle of poles and cables, and although those hills are full of people, there is not one electric light, no garbage dump filled with plastic. And this is what we call underdeveloped. If it wasn't for the erosion I would perhaps call it lovely. Smell the air. Taste it."

The wind carried a wisp of forming cloud and whisked it around into the abyss.

Simien: a national park

"We had better be going."

Pierre went first. He was lithe, slim, and surefooted.

I leaned back against the grass-covered ledge and closed my eyes. Thoughts of Japan made me sad and happy. My wife and children were there, and the baby was due any time now; we had family and friends, and there were so many fine sushi shops and little bars, and quiet hidden temples, and poetry in the language and souls of the people, but Tokyo was so filthy, noisy, ugly, and the Simien was so peaceful, clean, beautiful. Images blended. I could picture temples on the cliffs, and hear bells amid the thunder of the falls.

I opened my eyes. Time to go up. Ah, stretching was fine. Wine, caviar, and beans. What a mixture. I turned my face to the right, and my heart jolted, almost as if in fear. A perfect orchid grew only a foot from my face. On the way down I must nearly have trodden on it. It was perfect. A sort of yellowish green, with small, delicate, horned petals. I had never seen this one before. It must be a cliff-dwelling orchid. I looked around the ledge, but saw no more. Perhaps it was rare. Putting my hand out very slowly and gently, as if to a small wild animal, I touched the flower. Then I left it, and climbed up, stopping halfway to pee down into the abyss, for I have a secret urge to pee from high and famous places, and I was sure that one day this would be one.

Walking up the steep, familiar paths to Geech, I got a feeling that the orchid had been placed there especially for me, which was kind of silly, but I could not shake off the feeling. And neither could I put it into words, or even explain it away to myself. So I said nothing.

◇◈◇◈◇

Mesfin had bad news. The people at Geech had decided that they would no longer work for us. Lowland Moslems from Antola had been abusing and cursing the Geech men, blaming them for the trouble being caused about forest cutting and the pressure that was being put on all the villages around the Simien.

"You let the first foreigner pitch his tent on your land, and the blame lies with you. You should have driven them out then, but later you worked for them, helped them build houses. Now the

353

foreigners are well organized, and they are preparing to throw you out."

They could never see that this was a government project, and the foreigners were merely servants of the government.

The pride of the Geech people was hurt, and the bitter, angry feelings spread to the Christians in Amba Ras, who also provided many men for our labor force. The Geech men gathered, and swore that they would not work anymore for the park, for its staff, or the visitors, and neither would they sell eggs, bread, sheep, or goats to us.

At this time we had four Amba Ras men working for us as coolies. One day they came to Mesfin, asking for a guard escort to see them home. A gang of men was supposed to be waiting at the crossing of the Djinn Barr, ready with clubs to beat the workers.

When Mesfin finished reporting all this, I put my head in my hands, leaned on the table, and swore. I could see it coming. From this, the people themselves would suffer the most. Last month we paid enough in wages to keep a whole village fed for six months. The work on the park had been a great boost to the highland economy, and as it developed, it would mean much more than a few quintals of barley. But Nadu's victory and Bogale's piddling fine had given the troublesome chiefs and sheiks confidence.

Outside, I found two men, one from Amba Ras and one from Geech. I told them to take messages to the villages. If they wanted to beat our workers, first they must fight me. I issued a challenge. I offered to fight six men, with sticks. If they knocked me down I would pay a hundred dollars to each of the six men. Before the fight we would sign a paper, saying that the blame for any injury rested on nobody, but that I had issued the challenge. If I beat them, they would promise not to bother the coolies, nor threaten them or their families. The two men, one of them a guard, were shocked, but they took the challenge. I was leaving soon. The answer had to come quickly, if it came at all. I doubted very much if anyone would take it up.

In the last six months especially I had been using the oaken practice sword and the heavy fighting stick. I was fitter now than I had ever been in my life. Running, climbing, karate and stick practice in the high, pure mountain air had sharpened reflexes and toned muscles.

The locals were mostly afraid to even watch while I practiced, especially the karate kata, for they thought it was some.kind of evil magic. There was not a chance of a fight, though in a secret, evil place in my heart I wanted it to come about. The challenge could perhaps quieten the noisy, boastful ones, and give confidence to the coolies. But for how long? I was going to be only another week in the Simien.

Tsehai was back. It was he who cooked up our eggs and coffee. "Where is Yeshe?" I asked.

"She went down to Gondar and ran away from me. It is too cold for her up here, you see."

I guffawed. Tsehai smiled and Mesfin made a joke.

"Why should I care? There are many girls. I can easily find another."

He was grinning, standing with hands on hips like a washerwoman, still with a damn silly pink towel round his head. I choked and spluttered in my coffee. Everything was stupendously funny.

. . . Why should I care . . . why should I care . . . flies in the buttermilk, shoo fly shoo . . . and Bogale Mersha was farming all of the land he cleared, in open defiance of court orders, and neither the Russians nor the British were going to come to help us build the road, and Nadu was going to parliament, and I was leaving, and one mule still had trouble with a skin disease, and why the hell should I care? . . .

"Damn it, Tsehai. That is a fine philosophy. That's what makes you so fat and happy."

"Yes, and anyway, I was getting bored with her, you see. I need a new one now."

On the way up from Asmara, Mrs. Bromley had been stopped by a policeman at Dib Bahar. He had refused to let her pass, and she slept the night in the car. When the Dejasmatch heard about it, he fined the man a month's pay. Mrs. Bromley arrived while we were in Geech.

And while we were still in Geech, my two Chinese vet friends came up stiffly on mules. They said it was their last chance, and after I had gone they would not choose to come up here. We spent a day out at the escarpment edge, taking photographs, but we saw no Walia.

When the time came to say good-bye to Geech it was an odd feeling. I could not really believe that I was leaving. John and Mrs.

Bromley went on ahead, while I made one last check. The camp site had changed. When I came there had been two low-walled huts. Now there were two finished houses, and two more almost completed, and material gathered for building new guard quarters. It was not much. We would have so much more if the money had been provided, but it was so much more than before.

I went down through Geech village. This was the day that they would meet me, if they were going to take up the challenge. My friends went on ahead. I stood in the middle of the village and shouted. Nobody came out. I caught up with my friends.

On the last day, the game guards and workers held a big feast for me. They must have spent half a month's salary each on it. Lots of food, alcohol, and emotional speeches.

After the feast and the speeches there was still work to do. We caught one of the mules, and our small black stallion, tied their legs and threw them down. We held the mule down first. She had a big blood blister on her spine, and this had to be drawn. The horse had been bitten in the flank by a hyena. The mule was easy and quiet, but the stallion was fierce, and knocked Dure the muleteer out with his knee. But we got him down, and one of the Taiwan vets, Dr. Pung, cleaned out the deep wound. The stallion rolled his eyes, snorted. I wondered if he had managed to get a kick in at that damned hyena.

Most of my stuff had already been packed and sent down, so there wasn't much to do. All my old clothes I gave to Abahoy, who especially cherished a tweed jacket, a red Canadian bush shirt, and a pair of Japanese climbing boots.

The men's salaries had been late in coming, so I lent each of the men ten dollars to see them through the festival period. I didn't expect to get the money back. But that was a misjudgment, for all of the men returned the money to me the day before I left. And for them, it wasn't easy to do. Those bastards in Addis Ababa who owed me money never ever paid me back, although their salaries were far greater.

The Bromleys came down with me. They would drive me and my stuff to Gondar. The park was all signed over to John now, and I was no longer game warden of the Simien Mountain National Park.

It was a glorious morning. I went out early and saw one small female Walia below the house. Then back for breakfast.

Simien: a national park

The mules were ready to leave at about ten. I took one last walk up to the top of the hill above the house, to my favorite spot, and I looked out for one last time. There were the hills, painted with the colors of millions of flowers and the dark green swathes of remaining forest, and eagles, lammergeyers, griffon vultures, and falcons were small circling specks above and below. Down by the house everybody was waiting. I said a prayer to the wind, and asked that the park be preserved, and hoped that one day I might return. Then I picked a small bunch of yellow flowers and strode down the hill. Doing things for the last time brings a conscious awareness of every minor detail, and now I was doing many things for the last time.

I put the flowers on the stones of my dog's grave and walked away from the house which I had designed and built, and the beautiful meadow around the house that had been a great joy for two years. I could hear the spring bubbling in the cool grove of giant Saint-John's-wort and tree heather. Abahoy and all the others followed me. The Bromleys went on ahead, leaving me alone with "my" people. They were weeping, especially the women, the older guards, and Abahoy. Mitiku pushed his children forward, and they stooped to kiss my feet. But I remembered, and I caught them and raised their faces to kiss them all. I kissed all the wives, and Tedla's wife brought out the new baby, and I was too choked up to say anything. Then I walked away from the camp, and the guards and Abahoy came with me, while the women wailed loudly.

At the borders of the park I said they should go back.

"Sir," said Zeleka, "I hear speak on radio. Simien now park. Haile Selassie say Simien park. No good for you go now. Why you no wait? All come good."

So the Emperor had at last proclaimed the Simien as a park!

"Good! Good!" I said. "Now you work with Mesfin and the new man. It is your work now. I am finished."

"If you go, lord, this place is nothing for me." It was Nagur. Tears ran down his cheeks.

"No, no. You are Ethiopian. This is your land. I thank God, and I thank you, that I have seen it."

We shook hands. Abahoy urged me to send photographs, and I said I would. I mounted the horse and kicked it into a trot. The small group standing at a bend in a trail saluted, and Mitiku called out

"Go with God," and I left the Simien, with an unspeakable heaviness in my chest.

It was an easy ride down, and daydreams flitted through my mind as the horse jogged along. At the bottom of the big hill, while the horse drank, I sat on the stream bank, letting memory kiss pictures and hopes of it all. Two years.

A mass of flies had settled on freshly dropped cow dung. The flies gleamed in the sun like metallic, blue-green jewels. The dung was covered completely. They would lay eggs, and the sun would dry the surface. The maggots would hatch and move to the bottom of the drying pat. Then perhaps a thick-billed raven would come, and with a quick flick of his specially adapted bill, he would turn it over and eat most of the maggots. But some would escape and become flies. Some always escaped. God grant that some of the Walia survived too.

The barley was beginning to ripen in the sun. The fields ranged in color from pale green to gold, with patches of a wild grass, a delicate thing whose frail stems were now bearing seeds, and which added swathes of a silvery purple color to the gold, green, and yellow. There were many, many flowers in the fields, and it seemed to me then that never had these hills outside Debarek had so much color.

With their long tails like streamers, whydahs flew in wavering flight over the barley, and bishop birds flashed their scarlet wing patches, and all kinds of seed-eaters chirped and squabbled, and doves flew in flocks, gray and dusty blue, with hints of pink around the necks.

Down by the stream, a golden jackal trotted along, hunting rats maybe, showing only the top of his back and his bushy tail. I felt that now there should be an eagle to see, an eagle, in high, slow, majestic flight, above it all, making it perfect. But I could not see an eagle, and felt disappointed.

Coming down the path, heading toward the mountains, was a group of riders. Nadu and his followers. We both reined in our horses and leaned across the saddle horns to shake hands. He didn't get off his horse and neither did I. For politeness' sake he pretended sadness at my going, and said many things. Then we both rode on, he toward the Simien, and I away from it.

I got off the horse at the steepest part and led it up the hill. At the top we stopped, and I adjusted the cinch. The eucalyptus trees of Debarek were now in sight. I looked back. The clouded dome of Ras Deschan was just in view.

An augur buzzard, with belly as white as the purest snow, circled overhead, crying to his mate who was higher. The note was a gentle sound. I took off my hat, and called out to them, and thanked them for watching me, and cried that they should say good-bye once more to everything on my behalf. And they circled, their white underbellies sharp against the blue sky.

The horse was eager to go. It was a strong animal, a stallion, brown, with a white blaze on his forehead, borrowed from Tedla. Like its master, it had eyes that were fierce. I mounted, and the horse picked its way down through the deeply rutted pathways to the meadow. The others were ahead. The horse swung into a gallop, and it ran hard, its unshod hooves kicking up bits of turf, and pounding a dull rhythm on the ground. Hoof beats like drum sounds on the close green grass. Herdsmen watching scattered cattle, and watching the wildly running horse, and waving, and crying out as we passed . . . "Aaaieeee! Bravely! Bravely!"

Wind, whipping at the loose tail of a shirt. Hat clutched in one hand. Knees gripping the sweat-runneled flanks, and, looking down, small blue flowers trace lines on the fast flowing ground, and looking up, the sky is wide and blue and rimmed by hills.

A stream wanders across the meadow, and we gallop closer, closer, and an exhilaration takes me, and for the sky, the meadow, and the horse, a yell comes up from deep in the belly . . .

"Yaaaah!"

And the horse gathered itself and leaped clear over the stream.

EPILOGUE

After leaving Ethiopia in October of 1969 I heard nothing about the Simien until January of 1970, when I received a letter from John Blower.

A team from *Life* magazine had gone into the Simien and got good photographs of Walia. Other news was that the official Imperial Proclamation had been printed in the *Negarit Gazeta* on October 31: the Simien was now a national park by law, and its boundaries were those drawn up by John Blower and myself.

However, although this was encouraging, it seemed that the situation in the park was deteriorating. More land had been plowed up, more forests destroyed, and, almost daily, rifle shots were heard around the escarpment where the Walia were living. Chief Guard Zeleka had been thrown in jail on the orders of Dejasmatch Araya. Apparently the charges were phony.

Better news came in April. His Royal Highness Prince Bernhard of the Netherlands, president of the World Wildlife Fund, had visited the Simien. Along with him went the Minister of Agriculture, the Governor General of Begemdir, the Governor of Simien (Dejasmatch Araya), General Mabratu (general manager of the Wildlife Conservation Department), John Blower, two biologists (including Leslie Brown, the well-known author and biologist from Kenya), and a team from an international magazine. They were taken in by two helicopters. It must have been the biggest thing to happen in the High Simien since Theodore was crowned Emperor at the church at Derasghie. The mountain people gathered, including a mass of colorful priests in full regalia from Derasghie and from all the churches around. Agafari Nadu was there, in a new dark city suit, galloping around on his horse, showing off.

The royal party spent two days in the Simien. His Highness saw the park, the Walia, Simien fox, gelada baboons, and was impressed with it all.

Bogale Mersha, the lowland forest cutter who had given us so much trouble, was visited. The Prince had the helicopter land at his door, and then gave Bogale a lecture about not destroying forest.

Ethiopian newspapers carried stories that the Geech villagers had agreed to be resettled out of the park. They had been shown new land, and they liked it. The government had promised to assist them in the move, to compensate them, and to give them aid in food, money, and even flour mills (potentially a great source of income in the Simien, where farmers travel for miles to get their grain milled) until they were settled in their new homes.

There was a storm of comment about this, and many outsiders felt that the government could not expect the Geech people to leave their ancestral land. However, the villagers had agreed to it, and several were pleased, for the new land offered new opportunities. There was no force involved, as I had thought there would have to be.

But up until the date of writing, the move has not taken place.

In September of 1970 I got a long letter from General Mabratu, general manager of the Wildlife Conservation Department. (By this time John Blower had left and had gone to Nepal.) He had lots of encouraging news about the Simien.

Mesfin, my former assistant, had taken over the park. Several buildings had been constructed according to the plans I had left behind. These included seven new guards' quarters, two offices in Geech, two offices in Sankabar, one big store in Sankabar, and, best of all, a clinic.

Mesfin and I had pushed hard for that clinic. It had been staffed with a trained dresser* from the Health College in Gondar.

Mesfin now had a construction supervisor on his staff.

Local courts had become stricter. Thirty people had been prosecuted and punished for offenses against the park, and twenty-two of them had been jailed for three months. Now every man in the

---

* The Public Health College in Gondar trained men in three categories—health officer, sanitation officer, and dresser. The dresser is a kind of nurse, trained to treat people at a simple clinic.

Simien knew what the national park project was about. The park boundaries had been marked out by a big patrol, led by Dejasmatch Araya. Newsmen accompanied the party, which was a big one, with police, guards, and a biologist.

Dejasmatch Araya, Governor of Simien, retired. He was replaced by a younger, educated man.

The police captain at Debarek was also replaced by an energetic and efficient man.

But sadly, at the point of writing, nobody had begun to build the road into the Simien, although a survey team of the Indian Army Engineering Corps was due to arrive and begin work in October.

So that's the story of the Simien Mountain National Park to date. This book covers a period of two years, from October, 1967, to October, 1969.

The story I have written is a personal one, intended to express my own feelings and emotions about a little-known people and country. I beg indulgence for any shallowness or inaccuracy which might annoy those people, especially Ethiopians, who have a deeper understanding than I. Looking over the manuscript, I see that there is so much left unsaid, but that, I guess, is the way with most books.

My heart and hopes will ever be extended to the proud people, the incredible cliffs and mountains, the crystal air, and the unique wildlife of the Simien. Adieu.

C. W. Nicol

Tokyo, October 20, 1970

A Note on the Type

The text of this book was set in Caledonia, a Linotype face designed by W. A. Dwiggins. It belongs to the family of printing types called "modern face" by printers—a term used to mark the change in style of type letters that occurred about 1800. Caledonia borders on the general design of Scotch Modern, but is more freely drawn than that letter.

Composed and bound by The Colonial Press Inc., Clinton, Mass., and printed by Halliday Lithograph Corp., West Hanover, Mass.

Typography and binding design by Virginia Tan